VIRGINIA 1705-1786:

DEMOCRACY OR ARISTOCRACY?

# VIRGINIA
# 1705-1786:
# DEMOCRACY
# OR
# ARISTOCRACY?

by
ROBERT E. and B. KATHERINE BROWN

*Michigan State University Press*

EAST LANSING, MICHIGAN

★
★
★
★
★

# Contents

VIRGINIA 1705-1786:

DEMOCRACY OR ARISTOCRACY?

# Introduction

BEGINNING with the first decade of the twentieth century and extending through World War II, historians in general interpreted early American history in terms of class conflict involving opposing ideas of aristocracy and democracy. According to this view, aristocratic practices and institutions, imported from Europe, developed in this country through acquisition of large estates by a few wealthy men, through the use of entail and primogeniture which increased the concentration of land, through restriction of political participation to the few by religious and property qualifications for voting and office holding, and by inequitable representation which gave a preponderance of political power to the most aristocratic areas of the colonies.[1]

Given this concept of class conflict in colonial times, one would expect to find a similar interpretation applied to the American Revolution and Constitution. Carl L. Becker set the pattern for the Revolution when he claimed that this was both a contest for home rule against the British and an internal class conflict between upper and lower classes over which group should rule at home in America. Becker conceived of the Revolution as a dual movement for independence and the democratization of American society, with the latter more fundamental than the former.[2] J. Allen Smith and Charles A. Beard injected class conflict into our view of the Constitution by contending that the adoption of the Constitution was a conservative counter-revolution by the aristocratic upper classes to recapture control of the country from the democratic lower classes, who had gained this control through the Revolution.[3]

Since World War II, however, some historians have begun to question the validity of the Becker-Beard interpretation. Evidence produced by these historians seems to indicate that class differences were not as sharp as we once believed, that participation in politics was much more widespread than the old accounts indicated, and that perhaps agreement was more important than difference. The evidence suggests that widespread economic opportunity produced a society which was fundamentally middle-class rather than upper-lower-class in its orientation, and because economic opportunity produced a society of property owners, far more men participated in public decisions than we once believed.[4]

In spite of the inroads made on the old interpretation, the results of current inquiry have by no means been accepted by all historians; or if they accept it, they do not always consider it as universally applicable to all colonies. Statements have been made that what was true of Massachusetts did not necessarily, or even probably, apply to other colonies such as Virginia or New York. At one time historians believed that democracy

3

meant the acquisition of the right to vote and to be represented, and thus that the people did not acquire democracy until the time of Andrew Jackson. Now, and without defining what they mean by democracy, some historians are suggesting that even the acquisition of voting and representation does not signify a democratic society before 1776. The implication is that in spite of these so-called "democratic" rights for the lower classes, the upper classes still maintained aristocratic power by various devices.[5]

In the following chapters, and in the light of both previous and current interpretations, we have attempted an analysis of Virginia society before the American Revolution. If one defines history as the process by which mankind reached its present state of development through thought and action in the past, we can understand such important events as the American Revolution and the adoption of the Constitution only if we have an accurate understanding of the milieu from which they emerged. Long referred to as a "tight little aristocracy," a colony in which "the government, from the very first settlement to the Revolution, was aristocratic, even oligarchic," [6] as a colony and state where "democracy was as yet unborn; aristocracy was still in the saddle," [7] and as a colony where "birth into one of the ruling families was almost essential" to a political career,[8] the Old Dominion offers an excellent testing ground for old and new interpretations alike.

In a very real sense, all aspects of the society studied here might well be appraised through the concept of democracy versus aristocracy, if one considers these not merely in their political connotations but as concepts which pervade all human activity. In this work we have assumed that the democratic philosophy and its opposite, the aristocratic philosophy, may be involved not only in the voting franchise and political representation but also in such other fundamental aspects of society as economic and educational opportunity, religious freedom, and class attitudes. We therefore have presented our findings largely as a study of the extent to which Virginia was aristocratic or democratic before the American Revolution in these areas and how, if any, these practices were influenced by the war. This approach should go far in determining the extent to which internal class conflict was a factor in precipitating the Revolution in Virginia.

In developing our work, we shall attempt to make our method and meaning as explicit as possible to eliminate any chances of misunderstanding. As they are introduced, we shall try to define such loaded, and often undefined, words as democracy, aristocracy, radical, liberal, conservative, upper class, middle class, and lower class. We have also proceeded on the assumption that the historian has two tasks to perform if he would understand the past and how it contributed to the evolution of the present. He must attempt to uncover the "absolute truth" of history—that which happened and the reasons why it happened, the events and their causes and consequences which nothing can change. But even more important, the historian must ascertain what contemporaries believed to be true. Men act on the basis of their beliefs, whether true or false, with the result that mistaken beliefs may become the cause of events. So through-out our work, we have attempted to find out what the people of the time believed about their society; then, having discovered this, we have used whatever evidence we could—statistics and examples from wills, deeds, tithable lists, quitrent rolls, or voting lists—to check on the accuracy of their beliefs.

In a work of this nature, authors naturally acquire obligations for help from others, obligations sometimes too numerous to acknowledge in de-tail. Our thanks go particularly to the librarians at the Alderman Library in Charlottesville, at the Virginia State Library and the Virginia Historical Society in Richmond, at the Institute of Early American History in Williamsburg, and at the Library of Congress. We have appreciated, too, the microfilming of county records by the Utah Genealogical Society and the courtesies extended to us by various county clerks when we have checked the originals. Our thanks go especially to Mr. William H. White, Jr., and the Alumni Board of Trustees of the University of Virginia Endowment Fund for the grant of a Thomas Jefferson Fellowship, and to Mrs. Leone Buhl for excellent work in typing a difficult manuscript.

## NOTES

1. For an excellent account of both the old interpretation and more recent research, see Edmund S. Morgan, *The American Revolution: A Review of Changing Interpretations,* Service Center for Teachers of History, American Historical Association (Washington, D.C., 1958).

2. Carl Lotus Becker, *The History of Political Parties in the Province of New York, 1763-1776* (Madison, 1909), Ch. I.

3. James Allen Smith, *The Spirit of American Government* (New York, 1907); Charles A. Beard, *An Economic Interpretation of the Constitution of the United States* (New York, 1913).

4. For discussion of revisionism see Edmund S. Morgan, *The Birth of the Republic* (Chicago, 1956); Morgan, *The American Revolution;* Robert R. Palmer, *The Age of the Democratic Revolution: A Political History of Europe and America, 1760-1800* (Princeton, 1959); Bernard Bailyn, "Political Experi-ence and Enlightenment Ideas in Eighteenth-Century America," *American His-torical Review,* LXVII (Jan., 1962), pp. 339-51.

5. For a reflection of changing interpretations see Merrill M. Jensen, *The Articles of Confederation* (Madison, 1940); *The New Nation* (New York, 1950); "Democracy and the American Revolution," *Huntington Library Quar-terly,* Aug., 1957, pp. 321-41; see also T. Harry Williams, Richard N. Current, and Frank Freidel, *American History: A Survey* (New York, 1961), p. 57 for a reflection of this change in the textbook field.

6. Louis B. Wright, *The First Gentlemen of Virginia: Intellectual Qualities of the Early Ruling Class* (San Marino, Calif., 1940), pp. 2, 39. See also pp. 6, 49, 52, 57.

7. Carl Bridenbaugh, *Seat of Empire: The Political Role of Eighteenth-Cen-tury Williamsburg* (Williamsburg, 1950 [1958 ed.]), p. 75. See also pp. 7, 8, 12, 15, 17, 38, 67, 70-78.

8. Charles S. Sydnor, *Gentlemen Freeholders: Political Practices in Wash-ington's Virginia* (Chapel Hill, 1952), p. 78. Sydnor's thesis (p. 60) is that Virginia's politics combined democratic and aristocratic elements; throughout

his book, however, as his chapter headings indicate, he placed much greater stress on aristocracy than on democracy. Although Richard L. Morton in *Colonial Virginia,* 2 vols. (Chapel Hill, 1960) speaks of a "ruling aristocracy," (I, 168), in general his views are more moderate than those of Sydnor, Wright, or Bridenbaugh.

# CHAPTER I

## *Economic Democracy*

IF WE WOULD UNDERSTAND Virginia society before the American Revolution, we must first determine the extent of economic opportunity or economic democracy in the colony. Were economic conditions conducive to the formation of sharp economic class divisions, or was there economic opportunity sufficient to ameliorate class conflict? Could the poor agricultural worker, the artisan, the overseer, the apprentice, or the servant better himself economically, or was he destined to remain in a condition comparable to the propertyless proletariat of a later industrial age? The answers to these questions will not only tell us something about Virginia society before the Revolution but will also reflect much light on the nature of the American Revolution and on the formation of the later state and Federal constitutions.

One way to get at the problem of economic democracy is to see what contemporaries thought of their society. By itself, this method would be insufficient, since it is subject to the biases and whims of the observers. But as long as people are motivated by what they believe to be true, as well as by the truth itself, it is essential that we know what they believed; their observations can then be corrected, if necessary, by more objective evidence.

Foreign observers were particularly impressed with the extent of economic opportunity in this country compared with Europe, especially because of the availability of cheap land. A British official, William Eddis, claimed that many people migrated to the colonies because of the favorable opportunities. He had conversed with many intelligent planters who left England because of adverse circumstances there, and if such conditions continued, a multitude of valuable members of English society must leave and come to America, where land could be procured for a trifling consideration and where the greatest encouragement was held out to skill and application.[1] A writer in the *Gazetteer* noted that numbers were leaving England for the colonies in search of plenty. Every ship bound for America was crowded with passengers, many of them skilled mechanics.[2] In 1773, unfavorable conditions in Ireland due to heavy rents and low prices for linen caused many of the poorer people to migrate. Thomas Preston wrote that, as a result, his company's ships would not be able to carry the "numerous families & people that are going to America," and it was generally believed that this would not be the greatest year for the exodus.[3]

Economic opportunity created many problems for English ship captains, who complained that their men deserted in the colonies. As Governor Spotswood said, the sailors dispersed "through the country to better their circumstances by turning planters." [4] Virginians encouraged this desertion by harboring and entertaining the sailors, employing them in their own service, concealing them from their masters, and helping them to escape to neighboring provinces.[5] This practice continued throughout the pre-Revolutionary period.[6]

When the Revolution broke out, American leaders planned to use the opportunities open to new colonists to undermine the morale of Hessian soldiers. A committee of Congress advised Washington against exchanging Hessian prisoners: "We think their capture affords a favourable opportunity of making them acquainted with the situation and circumstances of many of their countrymen, who came here without a farthing of property, and have, by care and industry, acquired plentiful fortunes, which they have enjoyed in perfect peace and tranquility until these invaders have thought proper to disturb and destroy these possessions."[7] Apparently they convinced some Hessians. In 1786, Adam Hunter wrote that one Aggie had just married one Christopher Brown, a Hessian, who had been overseer for General Weedon the year before.[8] Two years later, Hunter reported that "Aggie & her Hessian husband" had "a fine house plantation & several Negroes in Culpepper & live on the fat of the land."[9]

Cheap land meant that even the poor could eventually become landowners and planters. One observer said that rather than work for and be subservient to others, a poor man chose to get land so he could be his own master and provide a small estate for himself and family.[10]

Cheap land also created opportunities for men who might otherwise have become tenants, or improved the bargaining power of those who did become tenants. In opposing a large grant of land to Horace Walpole and Associates, acting governor William Nelson said that Walpole would have to let out the land in small parcels at reasonable rents, "since men in this quarter of the globe where it is so easy to become absolute proprietors of lands, are not fond of farming them [rented lands]. It is a vast encouragement to the improvement and cultivation of the lands," Nelson continued, "when they can enjoy the pleasure to reflect that their posterity will receive the benefit of the labour they bestow." [11]

Economic opportunity in the form of available land meant that artisans who so desired could abandon their trades to become planters. One observer remarked that tradesmen who paid for their own passage usually desired to live on a plantation rather than follow their usual trade, because this gave them a surer maintenance. With the produce they raised, they could then buy what they needed.[12] Peter Fontaine wrote that there were "no tradesmen or artificers of any sort but what became planters in a short time." [13] Fontaine also declared that "every Virginia tradesman must be at least half a planter" and therefore could not be depended on as a trades-man.[14] And William Eddis proposed an unlikely alternative: either artisans who migrated to this country were disappointed in their expectations for success in their trade (which was certainly not true), or their natural wish to obtain a permanent establishment induced a great majority to buy land, which, comparatively speaking, he said, bore no price.[15]

Another observer's comments seem to indicate that Eddis was wrong in his diagnosis that artisans bought land because they were disappointed in their trades. This man, probably an artisan, expressed surprise that no more tradesmen had migrated to this country from England. He assured his correspondent that Virginia was one of the best countries he ever saw for all sorts of tradesmen except weavers, for carpenters and blacksmiths earned 7s. 6d. a day, and other artisans received comparable wages.[16]

Some contemporaries believed that cheap land would prevent the development of manufacturing in Virginia. Eddis said that America would require a considerable population before the inhabitants could profitably divert their attention from agriculture: to settle and cultivate land must be their first great objective. Labor was too high for use in manufacturing, he said, and he might have added that the high price of labor was directly related to cheap land.[17] Governor Francis Fauquier likewise believed that Virginians could import more cheaply than they could manufacture, which "must always be the case as long as they have plenty of land." Fauquier added the further reason that Virginians were "too indolent to engage in manufacture or work of any kind." [18]

The rapid increase of population in Virginia was further evidence of economic opportunity, according to William Gooch. The Governor said that youths married early, which, combined with the prolific temperament of the women and immigration of servants and slaves, must necessarily occasion great increases in the population. This was especially true in Virginia, he continued, where a bountiful nature furnished the con-veniences of life with less labor and anxiety than in many places of the world.[19] Later Gooch repeated his statement, noting again the ease with which a man could acquire a living.[20]

Both Gooch and Fauquier placed the blame for their failure to raise colonial troops on the opportunity for acquiring land in Virginia. Gooch could entice only fifty volunteers for the West Indian expedition in 1740, though he offered three pistoles and half a crown as a bounty. He attrib-uted his failure to the fact that white men in Virginia were "all planters, and such as have their plantations under their own management." [21] Again in 1746, the Governor could raise only one company of soldiers because recruiting officers from other colonies had enlisted all the idle men "out of a country settled only by planters." [22] And Governor Fauquier, having a similar difficulty in raising men for the army in 1759, gave as the reason that "every man in this colony has land and none but Negroes are laborers." [23]

Even the dearth of towns of any size in Virginia was attributed in part to the easy acquisition of land. Robert Beverley wrote that the "liberty of taking up land, and the ambition each man had of being lord of a vast, tho' unimprov'd territory," plus the fact that numerous rivers provided shipping at every man's door, had resulted in no settlement that could really be called a town.[24] Governor Spotswood also noted the rural character of Virginia, where men lived dispersed on their plantations, possessing all the food necessary for human life or even luxury.[25] And Andrew Burnaby, writing in 1759, had this to say about the smallness of towns: "This is owing to the cheapness of land, and the commodiousness of navigation; for every person may with ease procure a small plantation, can ship his tobacco at his own door, and live independent." When the colony became more thickly settled and land became more expensive, Burnaby believed that people would be obliged to follow trades and manufacturing. This would necessarily create towns and larger cities, but such was not likely to happen for some centuries.[26]

One of the best accounts of economic opportunity in Virginia is to be found in the letters of William Proctor, tutor for William Byrd at Westover and later a minister in Amelia County. In addition to his £20 sterling in salary, Proctor received extra pay as companion of his pupils and had his linen made and mended. He expected that Byrd would procure a parish for him worth £100 sterling a year or help him to become a husbandman on land of his own—the latter occupation, if well understood, the best employment in Virginia. In fact, Byrd suggested that Proctor become both a planter and a parson.[27]

Proctor enthusiastically urged his countrymen to take advantage of the opportunities offered by the Old Dominion. He proposed a partnership in farming in which he would procure land by patent and contribute money and management while the others contributed labor and whatever else they could. There would be deprivations at first, but in all probability success would be the reward of diligence in a few years. Later they would have greater ease and the opportunity to transmit a little freehold estate to their children. Proctor said that in Virginia "a poor man, if diligent, may in a short time (less than seven years) become able to purchase & set up upon, perhaps a mile square of land." A man with some education could open a public school at 16s. per pupil or work for a merchant at £10 sterling and accommodations. He could "have land of his own very cheap, without depending upon any or paying rents." If his friends in Scotland did not believe him, they could send observers to learn how much better were living conditions in Virginia than in Scotland for husbandmen and artificers. Men could have land at a shilling an acre, with a little down and the remainder later as they could procure it by their labor, until they had good estates and arrived by degrees at ease, as he had seen some do even since he had been in Virginia.[28]

According to historian Robert Beverley, economic opportunity was so great in Virginia that it fostered laziness among the people. They had flax, hemp, mulberry trees, fur and wood, but they bought clothing and wooden ware from England "to the eternal reproach of their laziness." He censured Virginians for "a laziness that is unpardonable. If there be any excuse for them in this matter, 'tis the exceeding plenty of good things, with which nature has blest them; for where God Almighty is so merciful as to work for people, they never work for themselves."[29]

Contemporaries, then, seemed to believe that economic opportunity existed in abundance, especially for the common man. How accurate were their analyses, and how true were their statements? Were they simply engaged in spreading favorable propaganda for some personal benefit?

Since the key to economic opportunity seems to have been virtually free land, the ease or difficulty of land acquisition becomes the first problem; for land ownership, as we shall see, had a significant bearing on class structure and political privilege.

During the eighteenth century the common man—who is our main concern—could acquire land in several ways. For certain fees, he could get a patent to land either from the King or from the proprietor if he lived in the area north of the Rappahannock River, called the Northern Neck. If he came into the country as an immigrant, he was entitled to a "head-right" or "importation right" of fifty acres. He could buy land from one of the land speculators or land jobbers who had received a large grant from the King, and of course he could buy land from others who had acquired it by whatever means. In addition, he could inherit or receive land as a gift, marry someone who owned land, or lease land for a term of years or on a life lease.

First to be noted is the fact that land belonging to the King was easily acquired. To encourage migration to Virginia, the British had adopted the policy of granting a headright of fifty acres to anyone who went to the colony. Graft had entered into the headright system, however, and in practice not only the settler but several others also received headrights. If the imported person was an indentured servant, the captain of the ship which brought him, the merchant who sold him, and the man who bought him also claimed fifty acres each.[30] Headrights were freely bought and sold in Virginia; according to Robert Beverley, the headright was no great privilege, as anyone could buy such a right for a piece of eight. Rights were as commonly sold as the land itself, he said, so that anyone who did not have a right by importation could easily purchase one.[31]

Probably because headrights were sold so freely, the British government adopted the policy of selling rights, called treasury rights, to anyone who wanted to purchase them. The common man who was not entitled to a headright could thus buy a treasury right to fifty acres for five shillings.[32] As we shall see later, this amounted to between one and two days' wages for a worker.

In general, and in spite of abuses, the land policy of the British and colonial governments tended to favor the settler on the land rather than the land speculator. Fraud in the headright system brought legislation limiting such rights to the imported person only, and authenticity of claims had to be proved in court. In addition, the government required certain improvements on the land, known as "seating" the land, which would be a matter of course for the settler but expensive for the speculator.[33] After passage of the "treasury right" law in 1710, a man simply chose a piece of vacant land, made entry with the county surveyor, then purchased as many treasury rights as he needed at 5s. 10d. current money for each fifty-acre right. The surveyor surveyed the land, lodged a plot in the Secretary's office, and the Secretary made out a patent for the usual fees. To hold his land, the patentee had to "seat" it and pay a yearly quitrent to the King of one shilling for each fifty acres.[34]

Perhaps the land laws were violated or circumvented, as other laws occasionally are, but we have some evidence that they were effective. As prominent a man as Gawin Corbin could patent 15,000 acres in 1722 at a cost of £75 in treasury rights alone and then lose the land because he failed to seat it.[35] John Price lost the 1,444 acres that he patented in Louisa in 1750 and the land went to Benjamin Brown for four headrights and £6.5.0 in treasury rights, showing that both rights were still used.[36] And George Washington, who tried to acquire land illegally in 1774, was told by the surveyor that the title would not be valid, that the surveyor would forfeit his bond, and that Washington had better follow the letter of he law strictly.[37]

We also have good evidence on the total amount that the common man paid for land under the treasury right system. In addition to rights, he paid fees to the surveyor, county clerk, colonial secretary, and governor, the latter fee—from the time of Governor Dinwiddie—a pistole if the grant was for more than 100 acres. Jefferson told of a patent for 234 acres costing £3.16.0,[38] and one John McClure acquired 140 acres in 1753 for rights and fees totalling £3.0.6.[39] The latter, as we shall see, was less than the termination pay for an indentured servant at the end of his indenture, and of course the fee would be less if a man patented under 100 acres.

The records also tell us that a great deal of land was patented in Virginia even in the period close to the Revolution and after the granting of large tracts had ceased in 1754.[40] For a period of one year from October 25, 1765, to October 25, 1766, for example, there were grants for 77,798 acres.[41]

That economic opportunity was available for the common man can be inferred from the fact that a large percentage of farmers owned relatively small acreages. We sometimes get the impression that the tidewater was an area of many large planters and few small planters, and that the reverse was true in the piedmont and frontier counties. As Tables A and B indicate, however, this was not true. The tidewater was much more heavily dominated by men with 200 acres or less than was the backcountry. Two-thirds of the tidewater planters held 200 acres or less, and nine out of ten held 500 acres or less. These figures do not include tenants, most of whom held less than 200 acres, so the dominance of the small landowner was even greater than the tables indicate. Furthermore, Prince William County

## TABLE A. LANDHOLDING IN TIDEWATER COUNTIES

| | Norfolk[42] | | Richmond[43] | | | | | | | | Lancaster[44] | | | |
|---|---|---|---|---|---|---|---|---|---|---|---|---|---|---|
| | 1771 | | Before 1744 | | 1744 | | 1751 | | 1768 | | 1750 | | 1773 | |
| Acres | No. of Men | % of Total | No. of Men | % of Total | No. of Men | % of Total | No. of Men | % of Total | No. of Men | % of Total | No. of Men | % of Total | No. of Men | % of Total |
| 0-24 | 11 | 2.2 | 0 | 0 | 1 | 0.3 | 1 | 0.5 | 1 | 0.4 | 0 | 0 | 0 | 0 |
| 25-99 | 103 | 20.5 | 37 | 20.9 | 68 | 20.8 | 31 | 16.2 | 43 | 18.3 | 53 | 21.6 | 83 | 28.7 |
| 100-200 | 214 | 42.6 | 80 | 45.2 | 166 | 50.9 | 94 | 49.2 | 98 | 41.5 | 108 | 44.0 | 126 | 43.6 |
| 201-300 | 71 | 14.2 | 19 | 10.7 | 25 | 7.9 | 21 | 11.0 | 31 | 13.1 | 33 | 13.4 | 33 | 11.4 |
| 301-400 | 32 | 6.3 | 10 | 5.6 | 18 | 5.8 | 13 | 6.8 | 21 | 8.9 | 18 | 7.3 | 13 | 4.5 |
| 401-500 | 21 | 4.1 | 10 | 5.6 | 14 | 4.2 | 8 | 4.1 | 11 | 4.6 | 12 | 4.9 | 8 | 2.7 |
| 501-600 | 8 | 1.5 | 5 | 2.8 | 7 | 2.1 | 3 | 1.5 | 5 | 2.1 | 4 | 1.6 | 6 | 2.0 |
| 601-700 | 4 | 0.7 | 3 | 1.7 | 7 | 2.1 | 3 | 1.5 | 6 | 2.5 | 1 | 0.4 | 4 | 1.3 |
| 701-800 | 6 | 1.1 | 1 | 0.5 | 2 | 0.6 | 3 | 1.5 | 1 | 0.4 | 6 | 2.4 | 1 | 0.3 |
| 801-900 | 6 | 1.1 | 3 | 1.7 | 4 | 1.2 | 1 | 0.5 | 3 | 1.2 | 2 | 0.8 | 0 | 0 |
| 901-1000 | 10 | 1.9 | 0 | 0 | 1 | 0.3 | 1 | 0.5 | 2 | 0.8 | 2 | 0.8 | 3 | 1.0 |
| 1001-1500 | 11 | 2.1 | 4 | 2.2 | 9 | 2.7 | 7 | 3.6 | 8 | 3.3 | 3 | 1.2 | 6 | 2.0 |
| 1501-2000 | 2 | 0.4 | 4 | 2.2 | 3 | 0.9 | 3 | 1.5 | 2 | 0.8 | 3 | 1.2 | 4 | 1.3 |
| over 2000 | 3 | 0.6 | 1 | 0.5 | 1 | 0.3 | 2 | 1.1 | 4 | 1.6 | 0 | 0 | 2 | 0.6 |
| Totals | 502 | 100 | 177 | 100 | 326 | 100 | 191 | 100 | 236 | 100 | 245 | 100 | 289 | 100 |

TABLE B*.   LANDHOLDING IN FRONTIER COUNTIES

| Acres | Loudoun[45] 1769 | | Halifax[46] 1755 | | Prince William[47] 1737 | | Prince William[47] 1754 | | 1773 | | Augusta[48] 1760-62 | |
|---|---|---|---|---|---|---|---|---|---|---|---|---|
| | No. of Men | % of Total | No. of Men | % of Total | No. of Men | % of Total | No. of Men | % of Total | No. of Men | % of Total | No. of Men | % of Total |
| 0-24 | 0 | 0 | 0 | 0 | 0 | 0 | 1 | 0.2 | 2 | 0.7 | 2 | .+ |
| 25-99 | 16 | 5.5 | 0 | 0 | 4 | 1.7 | 8 | 1.8 | 14 | 5.2 | 55 | 4.6 |
| 100-200 | 97 | 33.8 | 17 | 15.0 | 54 | 23.0 | 163 | 37.3 | 107 | 39.5 | 309 | 26.1 |
| 201-300 | 53 | 18.4 | 20 | 17.7 | 30 | 12.8 | 71 | 16.2 | 47 | 17.3 | 288 | 24.3 |
| 301-400 | 38 | 13.2 | 25 | 22.1 | 17 | 7.2 | 47 | 10.7 | 26 | 9.2 | 250 | 21.1 |
| 401-500 | 30 | 10.4 | 8 | 7.0 | 29 | 12.3 | 37 | 8.4 | 17 | 6.2 | 96 | 8.1 |
| 501-600 | 15 | 5.2 | 9 | 7.9 | 14 | 6.0 | 21 | 4.8 | 12 | 4.4 | 65 | 5.5 |
| 601-700 | 14 | 4.8 | 5 | 4.3 | 18 | 7.6 | 17 | 3.9 | 7 | 2.5 | 34 | 2.8 |
| 701-800 | 6 | 2.0 | 6 | 5.3 | 11 | 4.7 | 16 | 3.6 | 5 | 1.8 | 23 | 2.0 |
| 801-900 | 5 | 1.7 | 2 | 1.7 | 5 | 2.1 | 9 | 2.0 | 4 | 1.4 | 13 | 1.0 |
| 901-1000 | 2 | 0.7 | 1 | 0.8 | 6 | 2.5 | 4 | 0.9 | 3 | 1.1 | 13 | 1.0 |
| 1001-1500 | 7 | 2.4 | 6 | 5.3 | 22 | 9.4 | 23 | 5.2 | 8 | 2.9 | 19 | 1.6 |
| 1501-2000 | 1 | 0.3 | 7 | 6.2 | 10 | 4.2 | 6 | 1.3 | 8 | 2.9 | | |
| over 2000 | 3 | 1.0 | 7 | 6.2 | 14 | 6.0 | 13 | 2.9 | 11 | 4.0 | 14 | 1.1 |
| Totals | 287 | 100 | 113 | 100 | 234 | 100 | 436 | 100 | 271 | 100 | 1181 | 100 |

* These figures do not include most of the leases. For example, of 218 leases in Prince William from 1731 to 1776, 211, or 96 plus per cent, were for 400 acres or less and over 86 per cent were for 200 acres or less. Nine of the twenty deedbooks are missing, so the 218 leases should have represented about 55 per cent of the total leases.

was changing from a frontier to a tidewater county after 1759, when Fauquier County was formed out of the western part of Prince William, and certainly would be tidewater by 1773. In any event, it is evident that the small landowner was predominant even in tidewater Virginia.

The rent rolls, it should be noted, give us the minimum, but not always the maximum, acreage that a man held. For example, Frederick Fishback appears on the 1760 Prince William list as a small planter with fifty acres, but Fishback also paid quitrents on 925 acres in Culpeper County.[49]

Economic opportunity was reflected also in the growth of population throughout the colony—a confirmation of Governor Gooch's view. Spotswood once wrote that the people would not submit to a census because of their fear of a capitation tax, so total population was estimated from the tithables. Since only white males over sixteen were tithable, the white population was estimated at four times the white tithables, which meant that those under and those over sixteen were about equal. Negro population was estimated at twice the tithables because both males and females over sixteen were taxed. Gooch's figures of 30,000 Negro and 21,000 white tithables in 1730 would thus make a total population of 144,000.[50] By 1755, the population had grown to an estimated 293,472.[51] Governor Fauquier gave a figure of 340,000 in 1763. He said the increase was "very fast," amounting to more than fifteen per cent in four years.[52] And by 1774, Lord Dunmore placed the population at 500,000.[53] After the Revolution, George Chalmers said he could demonstrate that the populations of Virginia and Maryland had doubled every twenty-five years since 1700.[54]

As might well be expected, population growth after 1755 was most rapid in the frontier counties where economic opportunity in the form of cheap land was the greatest. A comparison of the growth of population from 1755 to 1773 in the three major sections of the colony—the tidewater, the lower piedmont, and the upper piedmont and frontier—demonstrates this.[55] Of the twenty-eight tidewater counties, only three lost population during this period—Gloucester 4.1 per cent, Middlesex 1.4 per cent, and Warwick 3.5 per cent. Of the remaining twenty-five, twenty-three were established prior to 1730 and gained from 3.9 per cent (King and Queen County) to 68.7 per cent (Norfolk): the other two, Fairfax and Prince William, both essentially frontier counties until well after 1755 although located partly in the tidewater, gained 152.6 and 190.7 per cent respectively. Six of the counties gained no more than ten per cent. The gain was greater in the fifteen lower piedmont counties. None lost population and the gain ranged from 8.3 in Louisa (the only county to gain less than eighteen per cent) to 196.9 (Lunenburg). And in this area too, the greatest growth came in those counties nearest the frontier—Cumberland (132.1), Lunenburg (196.9), and Prince Edward (128.2). By far the greatest gain, and no loss, was found in the fifteen upper piedmont and frontier counties, only eight of which were established by 1755. Of these eight, Orange County grew the least, 26.1 per cent; Culpeper was next with 69.7, and the rest ranged from 107.7 (Augusta) to 553.9 (Halifax).

The effect of the frontier on population growth is probably best exemplified by the history of Prince George County after 1714. In that year, the county had 1,040 tithables. Fifty-six years later, in 1770, the same area contained eleven counties (Prince George, Amelia, Bedford, Brunswick, Charlotte, Dinwiddie, Halifax, Lunenburg, Mecklenburg, Prince Edward, and Pittsylvania) and 26,412 tithables, an increase of 2,540 per cent.[56]

No account of economic opportunity in colonial Virginia would be complete without some discussion of the role of the land speculator. Sometimes we get the impression that land speculators usurped most of the good land, thus making it difficult for the common man to acquire land. The facts, however, tell an entirely different story.

Speculators sold their land, and because men could always patent land from the King, they had to sell at a price within the reach of the common man. The usual price for land sold by the holders of large grants was £3 for 100 acres, although much land sold for less than this. In the thirty-two years from 1741 to 1773, the Beverley family sold 71,541 acres in Orange and Augusta counties for a total of £3,602. This was less than one shilling an acre and amounted to an average income of £113 a year, excluding the cost of the land and quitrents. Of the 267 sales, 200 or seventy-five per cent were for 400 acres or less, and 142 were for £12 or less. During the same thirty-two years, the Borden family sold 84,666 acres for £4,328, or a little more than £135 a year. Of 296 sales, 242 or eighty-one per cent were for 400 acres or less and 194 sold for £12 or less. Other speculators, such as the Hites and Pattons, were disposing of land in the same way.[57] In 1740, five men, John Smith, Zachary Lewis, William Waller, Benjamin Waller, and Robert Green, received a grant of 100,000 acres on the James and Roanoke Rivers in Augusta County. Twenty-one years later, and before much of the land had been settled, Lewis sold his rights to William Thompson for £260 current money, or an income of about £7.14.0 a year, assuming that each partner paid £100 in treasury rights for the original grant.[58]

When land grants are described in acres, we sometimes have an erroneous notion of how large these grants were. The 71,541 acres sold by the Beverley family would have meant about 112 square miles or a tract 11.2 miles long and ten miles wide. The Borden sales of 84,666 acres would have been 132 square miles or a tract 13.2 miles long and ten miles wide. The 100,000-acre grant to the five speculators was 156 square miles or a tract thirteen miles long and twelve miles wide. These are still sizeable amounts of land, but when we consider the thousands of square miles of vacant land available at the time they do not loom as large as we are sometimes led to believe. Augusta County at the time of these grants included at least 5,000 square miles if we count only the part of Augusta now in Virginia and exclude the part in West Virginia and Kentucky.

William Byrd was still another speculator who sold land in small parcels and at a low price to small farmers. Byrd sold the following tracts in Halifax County during the years 1752-1766.[59]

| Acres | Tracts | Acres | Tracts |
|-------|--------|-------|--------|
| 0-99 | 15 | 500-599 | 13 |
| 100-199 | 32 | 600-699 | 3 |
| 200-299 | 63 | 700-799 | 8 |
| 300-399 | 32 | 800-899 | 2 |
| 400-499 | 17 | 900-999 | 3 |
| | —— | 1000-1499 | 6 |
| | 159 | 1500 or more | 2 |
| | | | —— |
| | | | 37 |

Of the 196 sales, 159 or 81.1 per cent were for less than 500 acres. Even the sales of large tracts lose their ominous connotations when we realize that Henry Hardin bought 1,000 acres from Byrd in 1762 for £7.10.0, Jacob Dye bought 1,040 acres in 1762 for £5, and Joseph Login bought 400 acres for £3.[60] The Halifax deeds show that Byrd often sold land at £1 to £2 for 100 acres, a price less than the cost of patenting land. In short, Byrd was selling land that was well east of the mountains and at a price, as we shall see, that the ordinary man could easily afford.

There is other evidence to indicate that land speculation was not as profitable as one might suspect and did not hinder acquisition of land by the common people. Governor Gooch said that former Governor Spotswood, who had been accused of land grabbing, had actually been at great expense in settling his lands. Instead of receiving benefits from this investment he had, in fact, suffered great misfortune.[61] How great will appear in Chapter V. William Nelson, long-time member of the Council and acting Governor in 1770, also denied that speculators made great fortunes out of land. Nelson regarded land speculation as such a questionable investment that he had declined to engage in it despite ample opportunities. He believed that there was little profit in it, and experience had proved him right, he said, for some Councillors who had received grants never had and never would receive a shilling of profit. Some grantees residing on the frontier had profited by surveying and selling land, but they deserved their gains. Nelson named the family of James Patton as having benefited from Patton's grant, but well they might, he said, for Patton had lost his scalp to the Indians as the price he paid for it. Speculators sold land at £3 per 100 acres, Nelson continued, which was little more than it would cost a man to patent 300-500 acres on his own.[62]

Governors Gooch and Dinwiddie believed that the poor people actually benefited by the granting of large tracts to speculators. Gooch said that speculators had to improve their lands and thus encouraged the "meaner sort" to settle. He pointed to the backwardness of settlement in Brunswick, where few large grants were made, compared with Spotsylvania where the greatest tracts had been granted.[63] Gooch made large grants with the stipulation that the promoters settle one family for every thousand acres.[64]

Dinwiddie, who had once opposed large grants, claimed later that land jobbers had been of service in promoting settlement of the backcountry. They parcelled out land to poor people from the northern colonies who could not otherwise afford to come to Virginia to patent land for themselves.[65]

If a man did not want to live where land could be patented or where speculators were selling it, he could always buy other land in any county. Every issue of the *Gazette* carried advertisements for land sales. The single issue for February 19, 1767 (P & D), had 61,872 acres listed, while the issue of March 17, 1768, had 38,859 acres. This land was in Pittsylania, Surry, Halifax, Orange, Gloucester, King William, Prince George, Bedford, Nansemond, Charles City, York, Sussex, and Amherst counties. A seller might advertise that poor people could buy any amount desired.[66] Others, such as Charles Carter's executors who offered 14,000 acres in Prince William and Fauquier counties in 1768, agreed to divide the land to suit purchasers.[67] We must remember that only a small part of the land was cultivated even in the settled areas of Virginia. Andrew Burnaby estimated that not a tenth of the land was cultivated in 1759, so there was available land everywhere.[68]

A poor man without sufficient cash could also get land with a small payment and pay out the balance on installments. William Beverley sold much land this way, usually in tracts of 200-600 acres. For example, William Nance bought 400 acres for £10 which he paid in four years.[69] In 1750, James Patton sold 2,306 acres to Joseph and Esther Crockett at £4.5.0 per hundred acres. The Crocketts made an initial payment of £31.6.5, and by August 5, 1767, owed only £5.10.0.[70] Philip Claiborne advertised 1,100 acres for sale in King William, much of the purchase price to be on credit.[71] Purchasers of Byrd's land in 1761 were to pay off the principal in ten years at five per cent interest.[72] In 1764, Samuel Kerchval of Orange County bought 100 acres from carpenter Uriah Garten for £35, then gave Garten a mortgage for £33, so the initial payment was £2.[73] Much land must have been purchased on the installment plan, for the deeds often say that the land being sold was land where the buyer lived.

A poor man who bought land on time was not only buying a place to live but also income-producing property that would help him to pay off his mortgage. In addition, the labor he put into the land increased its value so that within a few years it might be worth several times the original price. The following chart illustrates the increased value of lands in Halifax County between 1753 and 1769, and also the cheapness of land in a piedmont county well east of the mountains.[74] These examples could be multiplied thousands of times in the deeds of all the counties, and probably mean that there was a little of the land speculator in men of all classes.

The land records indicate that land east of the mountains could easily be acquired either by patent or by purchase up to the time of the

Revolution, and that the great bulk of these acquisitions were for relatively small acreages. Of 1,119 patents under Governor Spotswood, none was for more than 10,000 acres, only six were for more than 4,000 acres, and 958, or 86.6 per cent, were for less than 500 acres.[75] In the fifteen

| Name | Acreage | Date Purchased | Price | Date Sold | Price |
|------|---------|----------------|-------|-----------|-------|
| John Bates Jr. | 261 | 9-17-53 | £ 165.0.0 | 12-31-60 | £ 550 |
| John Bobbat | 160 | 1-6-64 | 20.0.0 | 9-30-65 | 37 |
| Jasper Billings | 100 | 11-19-61 | 20.0.0 | 2-19-62 | 40 |
| Richard Brown | 312 | 2-29-54 | 56.0.0 | 7-16-55 | 80 |
| Henry Chambers | 324 | 11-17-57 | 8.0.0 | 12-18-64 | 150 |
| Jacob Cox | 89 | 3-18-62 | 10.0.0 | 6-16-63 | 70 |
| John Dean | 330 | 3-21-65 | 15.0.0 | 4-1-66 | 40 |
| Samuel Davis | 183 | 7-21-63 | 15.0.0 | 3-21-65 | 75 |
| William Evans | 264 | 5-19-57 | 6.12.0 | 2-5-69 | 150 |
| Pryant Easley | 200 | 2-15-64 | 26.0.0 | 1-7-69 | 50 |
| James Hembree | 220 | 5-20-62 | 2.5.0 | 12-9-62 | 50 |
| Richard Jones | 140 | 9-18-60 | 1.15.0 | 5-17-61 | 15 |
| James Irwin | 124 | 8-21-53 | 2.4.0 | 5-15-60 | 75 |

years from 1736 to 1751, there were 748 individual land surveys in Amelia County, of which 667 were for less than 500 acres and 630 were between 100 and 499 acres.[76] In Albemarle County there were 378 separate surveys to 265 individuals in the years 1744-48. Of these, 195 individuals received only one grant.[77] In the same county there were 235 land sales from 1757 to 1760, of which 218 were for less than 500 acres.[78]

Still another factor which contributed to economic opportunity was the desire of the British and colonial governments to have people settle on the frontier and the concessions they offered to achieve this goal. Measures included the appropriation of money for guns and public buildings, exemption from taxes for ten years, and, if the settlers were foreign Protestants with their own ministers, exemption from church tithes for a number of years.[79] Finally, in 1753, the Virginia legislature urged the British government to encourage frontier settlement by giving settlers land and exempting them from payment of quitrents for ten years, and these provisions were granted with a limit of 1,000 acres for each settler.[80]

There is little doubt that people took advantage of the opportunities offered by the frontier, especially after the defeat of the French and Indians in 1763. Washington urged Governor Botetourt to grant land that had been promised to soldiers because otherwise poor men with large families, looking for land for the future, would settle on the grants promised to the soldiers.[81] Reverend John Brown of Augusta said that old frontiersmen there were "on the wing" to new frontiers for land, and Brown himself wanted land farther out on the frontier for his children.[82] William Crawford, who said he never saw so many people crowding out for land, had difficulty in keeping land that he was trying to acquire for Washington on the Ohio.[83] Washington himself had earlier urged his neighbor, John Posey, who owed him considerable money, to sell his property, pay his debts, and take what he had left out to the frontier for a new start. Washington claimed that what Posey would have after his debts were paid would enable him to buy enough land to be worth five times his present wealth in twenty years. Washington said he would advise his own brother to do this under the same circumstances.[84]

The lower classes were not the only ones who resorted to the frontier as a place of opportunity. In 1773 Thomas Glascock of Richmond County answered an advertisement by George Washington for settlers on the Ohio. Glascock wanted 500 acres where he could retire with the remains of his shattered fortune, and he asked how soon he could sell out in Richmond and move to the Ohio.[85] Glascock was the man who had ended the long political career of Landon Carter by defeating Carter for a seat in the House of Burgesses in 1768.[86]

Andrew Burnaby used extravagant language in describing opportunity on the frontier in the Shenandoah Valley in 1759. The land along the river was rich and fertile; the settlers, mostly German, gained a comfortable living by raising stock for the troops and sending butter down the river. If there was such a thing as happiness, Burnaby said, they enjoyed it. Far from the bustle of the world, they lived in the most delightful climate on the richest soil imaginable, surrounded by beautiful sylvan scenes, lofty mountains, clear streams, waterfalls, rich valleys, and majestic woods. They had few diseases, were robust, lived in perfect liberty, were ignorant of want, and had few vices. They had "what many princes would give half their dominions for, health, content, and tranquility of mind." [87]

The extent to which cheap land offered economic opportunity to the common man cannot be fully appreciated until some comparison of land prices is made with common commodity prices and wages. It would mean little for a man to be able to patent fifty acres for 5s. or to buy 100 acres from a speculator for £3 if these sums were beyond his financial competence.

Prices of wheat, with production per acre, provide an excellent basis for estimating the value of land. In 1762, wheat was 3s. 2d. per bushel in Augusta County and varied from 4s. to 6s. in the tidewater.[88] Acreage yield varied from seven bushels on poor land to thirty bushels on good land.[89] William Byrd expected to average twenty bushels on 250 acres in 1773.[90] Thus the cost of £3 for 100 acres of land from a speculator in Augusta would have equaled nineteen bushels of wheat or the yield of about one acre of fair land, and the price of patenting less than 100 acres from the government would have been about ten bushels of wheat, or the yield of half an acre.

Corn and tobacco prices and production provide another index.

William Penn asserted that a man of ordinary industry in Virginia could produce 3,000 pounds of tobacco and twenty barrels of corn a year.[91] Just before the Revolution, tobacco prices ranged from 12s. 6d. to 25s. per hundred and corn varied from 10s. to 15s. a barrel in the tidewater.[92] At this rate, the value of corn and tobacco produced yearly by this ordinary man would have been somewhere between £28 and £51 and the price of 100 acres at £3 would have been one-ninth to one-seventeenth of his yearly income. Today economists believe that a man can safely buy a home at a price of two or three times a man's annual income, and of course homes are not usually income-producing as was land in colonial times.

In terms of livestock, the £3 paid for 100 acres of land was equivalent to one good cow, half of a fair horse, or three sheep. Horse prices varied from £2.10.0 to £12, cow prices from £1.16.0 to £3.3.0, and Washington valued a slaughtered sheep at £1.3.5 for meat and wool.[93] As one observer said, "even the most indigent person has his saddle-horse, which he rides to every place, and on every occasion." [94] If a poor man could afford to own a saddle-horse, he could, if he desired, also own land. Under these circumstances, it was little wonder, as observers noted, that most men in Virginia acquired land.

Lest one get the mistaken notion that these prices were high, the following items should be noted. In 1765, the Governor of Virginia received a salary of £2,060 sterling for the year.[95] When Washington ordered a light post chariot from England for a friend in 1762, he stipulated that the price was not to exceed £100 sterling, but in 1768 he paid £315.13.6 for a fancy chariot for himself.[96] Martha Washington complained about the quality of a £20 imported suit of Brussels lace, then ordered a £40 suit for her daughter, Martha Parke Custis.[97] At the rate of £3.16.0 for a patent on 234 acres of land, the £40 suit would have been equal to the cost of 2,500 acres of land, or of 1,300 acres from a speculator at £3 for 100 acres.

On the frontier, men had the added opportunity of hunting and trapping to acquire the means of purchasing cheap land. One man in Augusta County received £21.6.6 for wolf bounties in 1759, enough to purchase 700 acres of land even from land speculators.[98] Another inhabitant of Augusta had 370 pounds of skins at 17d. a pound and two elk hides at 15s. each for a total of £27.14.2.[99] The total would have paid for 900 acres, and the two elk hides alone would have been half enough to pay for 100 acres.

Compared with the price of land, wages were such that any artisan could soon acquire an ample amount of land for himself. In 1751, Carter Burwell offered £4 a month for bricklayers.[100] A sailor could earn 45s. a month while the ship was in Virginia waters and eleven guineas for a voyage to Cadiz.[101] A tutor at Symes's Free School received £31 in rent from the school lands besides other perquisites.[102] Journeymen tailors could earn 10s. to 12s. 6d. a week (£26 to £32.6.0

a year) plus meals, drink, lodging, and washing.[103] In 1772, an advertisement claimed that a sober and industrious tradesman could earn more than £100 a year in Hampton town,[104] and Richmond town advertised that any discreet tradesmen, especially carpenters, could earn a "genteel provision" for themselves and families if they had honest industry and did not aspire to rank as gentlemen in extortion, insolence, and laziness.[105] Washington paid one carpenter £40 a year plus a house, 400 pounds of meat, twenty bushels of corn, and the privilege of keeping a garden and two cows.[106] An illiterate carpenter received £25, a house, 300 pounds of meat, and fifteen bushels of corn.[107] Turner Crump, overseer of Washington's slave carpenters, had an annual salary of £30 and a percentage of the cost of all work done. In building a barn for a neighbor, Crump made a bonus of £16.3.1 for thirty-eight days.[108] The bonus alone would have purchased more than 500 acres of land from a speculator. In 1772, Washington could not hire a "young man" to work with his carpenters for less than £30 a year, and a well-recommended carpenter, Roger Tandry, asked £50.[109] Youell Attwell, a shipcarpenter, worked for Robert Carter at £6 a month for himself, £4 for his apprentice, and £2.12.0 for his slave, while John Ferguson and his apprentice or indentured servant received £4 each per month plus board and lodging.[110] When we consider that the Byrds, Beverleys, and Bordens were selling land at an average of £3 per hundred acres or that a man could patent the King's land at 5s. for fifty acres, it is easy to see how tradesmen and artisans became landowners.

The deeds indicate that many artisans were able to pay substantial prices for property they bought. The following list represents purchases by artisans in Loudoun County in the years 1757-1766 at a time when they could have purchased land from speculators at £3 or less per 100 acres.[111]

| Acres | Price | Acres | Price | Acres | Price |
|---|---|---|---|---|---|
| 418 | £ 50 | 35 | £ 6 | 332 | £ 50 |
| 100 | 20 | 670 | 335 | 371 | 85 |
| 575 | 100 | 122 | 45 | 1,685 | 500 |
| 210 | 15 | 55 | 40 | 13 | 13 |
| 216 | 32 | 469 | 105 | 380 | 518 |
| 100 | 20 | 50 | 8 | 315 | 160 |
| 355 | 10 sterl. | 450 | 100 | 180 | 260 |
| 3 | 30 | 3 | 45 | 260 | 50 |
| 100 | 85 | 150 | 30 | 193 | 160 |
| 122 | 20 | 150 | 30 | 153 | 550 |

A detailed study of a few typical artisans will suffice to indicate the economic opportunity for such workers. Daniel Dale, shipwright, lived on a ten-acre tract containing a boatworks, owned houses in Portsmouth and Norfolk and had twenty-one slaves.[112] John Cundiff, Lancaster shoemaker, left two sons some land and six cattle; a third son received six cattle and £87.10.0; one daughter got six cattle, a slave, and £20; a second daughter was to share the remainder of his estate, and if the estate was more than £350, son John, probably already provided for, was to get a share.[113] Blacksmith Aaron Higginbotham of Albemarle County paid £100 for the 200 acres on which he lived in 1759,[114] and blacksmith James Anderson of Augusta County patented 400 acres, 200 of which he sold to his son James.[115] Richard Brown of Norfolk, joiner, bought property in Norfolk with Hudson Brown for £160 in 1759. They divided their property in 1761; then in 1768, Richard bought a house and lot for £40.17.4. On the 1771 tithable list, he possessed two servants, eight tithable slaves, and a chair. In 1772 he bought real estate valued at £358, and in 1773 he bought additional real estate for £300.[116]

These are only a few of the multitude of examples that could be cited, but they indicate clearly that anyone with any claim to a skill as a trades-man could easily earn enough to buy land. Since board, lodging, and wash-ing were usually included, the worker could save money if he so desired.

Advertisements in the newspapers indicate opportunity for workers of all sorts. Prospective employers advertised for overseers, millers, book-keepers, schoolteachers, gardeners, bricklayers, coachmen, tailors, black-smiths, cabinet-makers, oystermen, carpenters, postal clerks, well-diggers, sailors, barbers, cooks, and many others. In contrast, very few men ever advertised *for* a position. Sometimes the competition was such that one employer would lure away the employees of another. When Alexander Finnie of Williamsburg advertised for barbers and peruke-makers, John Anderson, wigmaker, placed a similar advertisement with the following addition: "N.B. Whereas my honest neighbour, that has advertis'd for two or three journeymen, has lately seduced one from my service, in a clandestine and undermining manner; which I am well persuaded, that no man but one of his principles would have done: Therefore it's to be hoped, that one of the number he has advertised for, will come into my service, in lieu of him who has been so villanously cajo'd as above, who may depend on having good encouragement." [117]

Men who could not pay the small amount necessary to acquire land, or preferred to buy a slave as some did, could always lease land in Virginia. So anxious were landowners to get tenants onto new land that they usually allowed three to six years free of rent for the tenant to get started. Typical rents were £2 to £4 a year for 100 to 150 acres, an amount to be com-pared with previous prices and wages.[118] In contrast, Washington received £45 a year for a house in Williamsburg, and editor Rind of the *Virginia Gazette* paid £60 a year.[119] Landlords often had difficulty in finding tenants, and Washington, for example, finally tried to import Palatines to settle on his land when he could find no tenants in Virginia.[120]

In addition, tenants could, and often did, sell their leases and their im-provements for a tidy profit, sometimes even before they started to pay rent. For example, Robert Wickliffe leased 100 acres for two lives from

John Brett in 1763, then sold his lease to Cuthbert Bullitt for £30 in 1765.[121] The same John Brett, in turn, paid Benjamin Tyler £60 and 2,000 pounds of tobacco a year for land that Tyler had leased from Thomas Arrington in 1755.[122] Landlord George Mason paid his tenant James Rickets £20 to break a lease for life in 1733, and Joseph Brown sold his 200-acre lease to George King for £80.[123] Thomas Lamb leased land from George William Fairfax, then sold his lease for £100 to George Dike.[124] With such profits, these tenants could then have purchased hundreds of acres of land from a speculator.

Even schoolteachers and ministers, not usually included among the opulent, found the door of opportunity open in Virginia. Joshua Fry, professor of mathematics at William and Mary College, quit his position and "retired to the back settlements in order to raise a fortune for his family." [125] In Albemarle County, schoolmaster William Forbes purchased 175 acres from Richard Woods for £25 in 1760.[126] Jonathan Boucher, schoolteacher and minister, began his career as a tutor in England at £8 a year, worked up to £30 in six years, but on coming to Virginia, in 1759, received £60 sterling plus board and room and the privilege of taking four additional students at whatever price he could get. As a minister in Caroline County in 1763, Boucher also ran a plantation and kept a school for thirty boys. At the age of thirty-two, he estimated his annual income at £250 and his net worth at £700.[127] Minister John Ormsby of Amelia patented 6,240 acres between 1738 and 1746, James Maury of Albemarle paid £250 for 686 acres in 1767, and Alexander Scott of Stafford left over 8,000 acres to his brother James, also a minister, who already possessed 2,000 acres in Prince William with a very good two-story brick house.[128]

Factors for British and Scottish firms, usually poorer men of some education, also prospered in Virginia. John Hook started in 1763 as a storekeeper at £35 a year, changed to another firm at £40 a year, and by 1767 was a partner in this company. In 1771 he bought 300 acres of land and talked of investing £1,000 in a venture capitalized at £4,500.[129] William Allason came over as a factor at £60 and stayed to become a well-to-do merchant and planter.[130]

Logically, indentured servants and apprentices would have comprised the lowest class after they finished their servitude, but the deeds, tithable lists, and quitrent rolls belie this assumption. Even for these men economic advancement was readily available, and though they are not always easy to trace in the records, the evidence indicates that servants and apprentices often acquired considerable property.

For one thing, very few former servants and apprentices remained in a community to become day laborers. There is no way of tracing their movements, but the deeds of western counties, for example, contain the names of many artisans from eastern counties who went west for land, so we can assume that many servants and apprentices went where opportunity was greatest after they had served their time. Of sixty-four artisans and apprentices in Spotsylvania whose names appear on the records and who did not vote in 1765 and 1771, fifty-six were not listed on the tax records of 1775-76. Four of the eight who remained acquired land, the record of a fifth was mutilated, and three still had no land. In addition, twenty-one former artisans or apprentices voted in 1765 and 1771, an indication that they owned land, but seventeen of these were missing by 1775-76.[131]

The Norfolk records provide convincing proof that servants, apprentices, and workers either moved elsewhere or, if they remained, acquired property in land or slaves. Of eighty-six such men on the Norfolk Borough tithable list for 1751, only nineteen remained three years later in 1754. Of these, four now paid tithes for themselves and for from one to three slaves. Alexander Ross and his son John were listed as servants or workers for one Dupree in 1751, but in 1754 Ross had two slaves.[132] By 1771, only fourteen of the original eighty-six servants and apprentices who were listed in 1751 were still in Norfolk, and of these only two still worked for someone else. Eleven of the remaining twelve owned from one to twelve slaves, three also owned land outside the Borough, and one, John Ross, owned fifty acres only. Eight of the twelve voted in either the 1768 or the 1769 election.[133]

A brief summary of additional material from the Norfolk deeds and other records will indicate the extent to which these former servants, apprentices, and laborers prospered. William Colley, who inherited only a cow at his father's death, paid £135 for 111 acres of land in 1756, sold land for £130 in 1763, and in 1764 paid £300 for 96 acres.[134] Philip Carberry bought two lots in Norfolk for £6.12.6 and £7.10.0 in 1763, then in 1764 was able to pay £200 for additional real estate.[135] John Dunn, blockmaker, bought a house and lot for £70 in 1759, had a house, lot, and four slaves when he died in 1777, and his estate claimed a loss of £657 in 1778 as a result of the burning of Norfolk.[136] On his death in 1772, James Esther left furniture, tools and shop furniture, and a half interest in a sloop.[137] Lewis Hansford, called "merchant" by 1759, bought real estate worth £350 in 1759 and a house and lot for £50 in 1762, borrowed £500 in 1766 and £100 in 1769, and in 1775 lent money to Edward Hansford, carpenter and joiner, and to John Dunn, Jr., possibly the son of the John Dunn above.[138] Nicholas Poole, silversmith, bought part of a lot in Norfolk for £15 in 1769, then died in 1772 leaving a house and lot and three slaves.[139] And so it went with the other eight, all of whom acquired substantial amounts of property.

As it was in Norfolk Borough, so also was it in Norfolk County where servants and apprentices either disappeared from the records or acquired property if they remained. Of sixty-eight in 1751, only nineteen remained in 1771, and of these only six did not have taxable property. Twelve men, including one who had no taxable property, voted in 1768 or 1769.[140] And of the six who did not have taxable property in 1771, four had owned property at one time or bought it after 1771.[141]

In summary, then, if we would have a proper perspective of the society in Virginia which fought the Revolution and adopted the Constitution, we must first understand that it was a society in which there was a great deal of economic opportunity for the common as well as the uncommon man. Cheap land was available by purchase or by patent, artisans' wages were high, and the almost universal desire to own land or other property meant that most men were independent farmers or tradesmen who worked for themselves with profit as the motive.[142] And because most men possessed property, there was a general consensus on the inherent benefits of property ownership. In succeeding chapters we shall encounter additional evidence of economic opportunity as we develop other aspects of Virginia society in the eighteenth century.

The discussion to this point poses the question of whether or not one is entitled to call economic opportunity "economic democracy." If democracy means absolute equality and economic democracy means absolute equality of economic possessions, then of course Virginia before the Revolution did not have economic democracy. But if by economic democracy we mean opportunity for all men of all classes (excluding, of course, slaves, who will be discussed later), then Virginia had a great deal of economic democracy. This did not mean that the poorest man could always become as wealthy as the richest, although this did happen occasionally, but if he was diligent, he could improve his lot a great deal in the Old Dominion.

When we view these facts in relation to possible class conflict in the colony, economic conditions do not appear conducive to sharp class differences. According to James Madison in *Federalist* No. X, men acquire different amounts and kinds of property because of inherent differences of ability, training, and desire. If we can believe this, the important consideration is that there should be the opportunity for men to better themselves to the extent of their abilities, and this appears to have been true in Virginia. If the danger of class conflict arises when men can blame the economic structure rather than their own efforts for failure to advance their position, then Virginia, with its extensive economic opportunity, was not fertile ground for class conflict.

## NOTES

1. Nov. 2, 1771, William Eddis, *Letters from America, Historical and Descriptive; Comprising Occurrences from 1769, to 1777, Inclusive* (London, 1792), pp. 109-10.

2. Reprinted in *Virginia Gazette* (Purdie & Dixon), Nov. 17, 1768. Hereafter publishers Purdie and Dixon will be referred to as P & D.

3. Thomas to William Preston, May 23, 1773, Preston Papers, Virginia Historical Society (hereafter referred to as VHS).

4. Spotswood to Lords of Trade, Aug. 18, 1710, Alexander Spotswood, *The Official Letters of Alexander Spotswood* . . . , 2 vols. in *Collections of the Virginia Historical Society*, new series (Richmond, Virginia, 1882, 1885), I, 3.

5. *Journals of the House of Burgesses of Virginia, 1695-1702*, pp. 269, 344. Hereafter these Journals will be referred to as *House Journals*.

6. *Virginia Gazette*, June 5, 1752.

7. *American Archives* . . . , ed. by Peter Force, 9 vols. (Washington, 1837-53), 5 series, III, 1459.

8. To James Hunter, Jr., June 13, 1786, R. M. T. Hunter Collection, Alderman Library, University of Virginia.

9. James Hunter, Jr., to his wife, February 1, 1788, Hunter Collection.

10. "Thoughts concerning America by Mr. Hasenclever," Shelburne Papers, on film, Colonial Williamsburg.

11. Nelson to Lords of Trade, Oct. 18, 1770, *House Journals, 1770-72*, p. xxv.

12. Observations of J. S. Sprogell, Oct. 21, 1731, British Transcripts, Public Record Office, Colonial Office 5 (Photostat, VSL), v. 1323, p. 266. Hereafter cited as PRO, CO5.

13. To Moses Fontaine, March 30, 1757, Maury Papers, Alderman Library, U. of Va.

14. To John Fontaine, June 7, 1754, *ibid.*

15. 1773, Eddis, *Letters*, pp. 142-43.

16. William Barker, Jr., to John Palmer, Dec. 16, 1758, Webb-Prentis Papers, Alderman Library, U. of Va.

17. 1773, Eddis, *Letters*, pp. 142-43.

18. Fauquier to Lords of Trade, Dec. 16, 1766, Kings' MSS (British Museum, Additional MSS); also in PRO, CO5, v. 1331, pp. 237-38.

19. Answers to queries from Lords of Trade, July 23, 1730, Gooch Papers, PRO, CO5, 324/49 (3 vols.), I, 179, VHS.

20. Answers to queries, 1749, Gooch Papers, III, 971.

21. Gooch to My Lord Duke, May 2, 1740, Gooch Papers, II, 588.

22. Gooch to ?, Aug. 26, 1746, Gooch Papers, III, 865.

23. Fauquier to Amherst, c.1759, Amherst Papers, in British Transcripts, Public Record Office: War Office 34 (Library of Congress) v. 37, Pt. I, p. [38].

24. Robert Beverley, *The History and Present State of Virginia* (1705), ed. by Louis B. Wright (Chapel Hill, 1947), pp. 57-58.

25. Spotswood to brother John Spotswood, Aug. 17, 1710, Spotswood Papers, Colonial Williamsburg.

26. Andrew Burnaby, *Travels Through the Middle Settlements in North-America in the Years 1759 and 1760* (London, 1775), p. 20.

27. William Proctor to his brother, July 1739, Amelia County Deed Book 8, pp. 156-61, Virginia State Library. Hereafter cited as VSL.

28. *Ibid.*, pp. 154-65.

29. Beverley, *History*, p. 295.

30. William Waller Hening, *The Statutes at Large; Being a Collection of all the Laws of Virginia* . . . , 13 vols. (Richmond, Va., 1809-23), III, 304-29.

31. Beverley, *History*, pp. 274, 277-78.

32. Hening, *Statutes*, III, 304-29.

33. *Ibid.*, II, 244; III, 304-09; IV, 37-42, 81-83; V, 424-28; Beverley, *History*, pp. 274, 277-78; *House Journals, 1712-26*, pp. 65, 67, 69, 72-73.

34. Method of taking up land in Virginia, 1753, PRO, CO5, v. 1327, pp. 561-64; James Blair to ?, Sept. 23, 1763, "Papers on Quitrents and Customs Confiscations," British Museum, Additional MSS. 38337, on film at Alderman Library, U. of Va.

35. Orange County Deed Book 2, p. 115, VSL. Unless otherwise stated, all county records cited such as deeds, wills, rental and tithable lists are to be found on microfilm at Virginia State Library, Richmond, Va.

36. June 1, 1750 and Nov. 26, 1756, The Morris Family Papers, Alderman Library, U. of Va.

37. Andrew Lewis to Washington, May 9, 1774, *Letters to Washington and Accompanying Papers*, ed. by Stanislaus M. Hamilton, 5 vols. (Boston and New York, 1898-1902), IV, 347-51.

38. To William Wood, July 17, 1772, *The Papers of Thomas Jefferson*, ed. by Julian Boyd, Lyman H. Butterfield, and Mina R. Bryan, vols. 1—(Princeton, 1950-  —), I, 94.

39. Receipt, May 25, 1753, Preston Papers, VHS.

40. Order in Council, July 18, 1754, PRO, CO5, v. 1328, pp. 187-88.

41. John Blair to Fauquier, May 20, 1767, Shelburne Papers.

42. Norfolk County Tithables, 1771. For a general statement on size of landholding about 1700, see Richard L. Morton, *Colonial Virginia*, 2 vols. (Chapel Hill, 1960), I, 364-65; for an opposing view of size of landholding in tidewater and piedmont, see John Fiske, *Old Virginia and Her Neighbors*, 2 vols. (Boston and New York, 1897), II, 187-88.

43. Richmond County Rentals. All lists except 1744 are probably for one parish only, and not the same parish. The above totals do not include women —18 women before 1744, 30 in 1744, 14 in 1751, and 18 in 1768—which again indicates that the 1744 rental is the only possible complete one. Only three of those who owned 25-99 acres did not live on their land in 1744—two orphans and a resident of Maryland who planned to return.

44. Lancaster County Rentals, 1750, 1773.

45. Loudoun County Rentals, 1769.

46. Halifax County Tithables, 1755.

47. Prince William County Rentals, 1737, 1754, 1773. Prince William represents a transition from a frontier to a tidewater county. Figures for 1773 were taken after Fauquier County was separated from Prince William.

48. Augusta County Rent Roll, 1760-62, Preston Papers, VSL.

49. Prince William County Rental, 1760.

50. Answers to queries, July 23, 1730, Gooch Papers, I, 179.

51. Observations on the tithables, PRO, CO5, v. 1328, p. 365; Dinwiddie to Lords of Trade, Feb. 23, 1756, *ibid.*, p. 359.

52. Answers to Queries, Jan. 30, 1763, *ibid.*, v. 1330, p. 396.

53. Report of the Earl of Dunmore, March 18, 1774, Strachey Papers, on film (Colonial Williamsburg), I, 260; PRO, CO5, v. 1352, p. 14.

54. To Charles Monroe, March 22, 1789, Aspinwall Papers, Massachusetts Historical Society *Collections*, 4 Ser., vols. 9 and 10 (Boston, 1871), X, 826.

55. "A List of Tithables in the Dominion of Virginia, 1755," PRO, CO5, v. 1328, pp. 363-64; Total Tithables, 1773, *Virginia Magazine of History and Biography*, XXVIII, 81-82; Fairfax County List of Tithables for 1749, The Papers of George Washington (Library of Congress), XVI. Hereafter cited as Washington Papers.

56. *Virginia Gazette Supplement* (P & D), June 14, 1770.

57. Abstracts of deeds from Orange County Deed Books 6-16 and Augusta County Deed Books 1-19, *passim*.

58. Augusta County Deed Book 10, pp. 78-79.

59. Halifax County Deed Books 1-6, *passim*.

60. *Ibid.*, Book 3, pp. 320, 328, 332.

61. To Lords of Trade, Nov. 6, 1728, Gooch Papers, I, 75-78.

62. Nelson to Lords of Trade, Oct. 18, 1770, *House Journals, 1770-72*, pp. xxii-xxv; Nelson to Hillsborough, Oct. 15, 1770, PRO, CO5, v. 1348, pp. 198-99.

63. To Lords of Trade, Nov. 6, 1728, Gooch Papers, I, 75-78.

64. Method of taking up land in Virginia, 1753, PRO, CO5, v. 1327, pp. 561-564.

65. To Lords of Trade, June 16, 1753, *ibid.*, pp. 530-31.

66. *Virginia Gazette*, Aug. 18, 1738.

67. *Ibid.*, May 19, 1768 (P & D); for opposing views on ease of acquiring

land in early eighteenth-century Virginia, see Wright, *The First Gentlemen of Virginia*, pp. 55-56; Hayes Baker-Crothers, *Virginia and the French and Indian War* (Chicago, 1928), p. 23; Isaac Samuel Harrell, *Loyalism in Virginia* . . . (Durham, N. C., 1926), pp. v-vi, 8-9.

68. Burnaby, *Travels*, p. 44.

69. Beverley MSS, William Beverley Account Book, Beverley Manor Accounts (VHS), p. 43 and *passim*.

70. Estate of James Patton, Aug. 5, 1767, Preston Papers.

71. *Virginia Gazette*, June 12, 1752.

72. *Ibid.*, Jan. 16, 1761.

73. Orange County Deed Book 13, p. 483.

74. Halifax County Deed Books—(Bates Jr.) Book 1, p. 49, and Book 3, p. 145; (Bobbat) Book 5, pp. 88, 529; (Billings) Book 3, p. 213, and Book 6, p. 265; (Brown) Book 1, pp. 73, 127; (Chambers) Book 1, p. 337, and Book 5, p. 395; (Cox) Book 3, p. 260 and Book 4, p. 319; (Dean) Book 5, p. 285 and Book 6, p. 149; (Davis) Book 4, p. 347 and Book 5, p. 284; (Evans) Book 1, p. 268 and Book 7, p. 348; (Easley) Book 5, p. 217 and Book 7, p. 322; (Hembree) Book 3, p. 376 and Book 5, p. 124; (Jones) Book 2, p. 204 and Book 3, p. 189; (Irwin) Book 1, p. 98 and Book 2, p. 153.

75. PRO, CO5, v. 1318, pp. 345-403.

76. Amelia County Land Surveys, 1736-51, Amelia Tithables, VSL.

77. Albemarle County Order Book, 1744-48, *passim*.

78. Albemarle County Deed Book 3, *passim*.

79. Spotswood, *Letters*, I, 143; II, 70; Hening, *Statutes*, IV, 77-79; V, 57-58, 78-80; *Virginia Gazette*, Nov. 24, 1738 and Jan. 12, 1738/9.

80. *House Journals, 1752-58*, pp. 115-16; Aug. 24, 1754, PRO, CO5, v. 1348, p. 216; *Acts of the Privy Council*, Colonial Series, ed. by W. L. Grant and James Munro, 6 Vols. (Hereford and London, 1908-12), IV, 235-38; *Virginia Gazette*, March 14, 1755.

81. Dec. 8, 1769, George Washington, *The Writings of George Washington from the Original Manuscript Sources, 1745-99*, ed. by John C. Fitzpatrick, 39 vols. (Washington, 1931-41), II, 528.

82. To his brother, Dec. 12, 1770, Preston Papers, Draper MSS 2QQ119 (Univ. of Wis.)

83. To Washington, March 15 and May 1, 1772, *Letters to Washington,* IV, 117-22.

84. To Posey, June 24, 1767, *Writings*, II, 455-60.

85. Glascock to Washington, Aug. 23, 1773, *Letters to Washington*, IV, 251.

86. Landon Carter Diary, 1776, Sabine Hall Papers, Alderman Library, U. of Va.; Richmond County Order Book 16, pp. 491-97; *House Journals*, Burgess List, 1768.

87. Burnaby, *Travels*, pp. 73-74.

88. Nov. 8, 1762, Preston Papers, VHS; Carter's Grove Account Book, 1764-86, pp. 42, 48, VHS; Philip Ludwell Lee to William Lee, April 10, 1770, July 24, 1772, Lee-Ludwell Papers, VHS.

89. Richard Henry Lee, Miscellaneous, undated, Lee-Ludwell Papers, VHS; John F. D. Smyth, *A Tour in the United States of America* . . . , 2 vols. (London, 1784), I, 58-59.

90. *Virginia Gazette* (Rind), Sept. 2, 1773.

91. Albert Cook Myers, ed., *Narratives of Early Pennsylvania, West New Jersey and Delaware, 1630-1707* (New York, 1912), p. 203.

92. Philip Ludwell Lee to William Lee, April 10, 1770 and July 24, 1772, Lee-Ludwell Papers, VHS.

93. *Virginia Gazette* (R), Dec. 1, 1768; Washington, *Writings,* I, 130, 135; *House Journals, 1752-58*, p. 380; Hening, *Statutes*, VII, 22-25; Nov. 24, 1757 and Aug. 31, 1763, Preston Papers, VHS; Washington, *Diaries*, I, 177, 314.

94. Smyth, *Tour*, I, 23.

95. Richard Corbin to Hanbury, Jan. 29, 1765, Richard Corbin Letterbook, 1758-1768, Colonial Williamsburg.

96. To Robert Cary, March 16, 1762 and June 6, 1768, *Writings*, II, 374, 488-90.

97. To Mrs. S. Sharpe, July 15, 1772, *ibid.*, III, 88.

98. April 18, 1759, Preston Papers, VHS.

99. Alexander Boyd to William Thompson, 1762, Preston Papers, VHS.

100. *Virginia Gazette*, Aug. 20, 1751.

101. *Ibid.*, Oct. 12, 1752.

102. *Ibid.*, March 5, 1752.

103. *Ibid.*, Oct. 11 and 24, 1751.

104. *Ibid.* (P & D), Sept. 17, 1772.

105. *Ibid.*, Sept. 24, 1772.

106. July 30, 1768, Washington, *Diaries*, I, 282.

107. Feb. 25, 1771, Washington Papers, XII, 56.

108. Oct. 22, 1761, Washington, *Diaries*, I, 178n.

109. James Hill to Washington, May 14, 1772, *Letters to Washington*, IV, 128-29.

110. Receipts, Sept. 27, 1773, and March 17, April 7, and July 8, 1775, Robert Carter Papers, 1772-85, VHS.

111. Loudoun County Deed Book A, pp. 3, 28, 148, 258, 363, 444, 448; Book B, pp. 8, 36, 125; Book C, pp. 15, 23, 27, 138, 362, 491, 495, 531, 635; Book D, pp. 52, 180, 215, 268, 292, 433, 448, 548; Book E, pp. 116, 197, 238.

112. Norfolk County Will Book 1, p. 183.

113. Lancaster County Will Book 20, p. 79, 1765.

114. Albemarle County Deed Book 2, p. 91.

115. Augusta County Deed Book 11, p. 789.

116. Norfolk County Deed Book 19, pp. 66, 258; Norfolk County Will Book 1, p. 176; Norfolk County Deed Book 24, p. 124; Book 26, pp. 4, 35, 119; Norfolk County tithables, 1771.

117. *Virginia Gazette*, Sept. 26, 1745.

118. For examples, see Loudoun County Deed Book B, pp. 184, 192; Book C, pp. 207, 272, 282, 484; Book D, pp. 404, 623; Richmond County Deed Book 10, p. 68.

119. April 28, 1760, Washington, *Diaries*, I, 157; Richard Henry Lee, *The Letters of Richard Henry Lee*, ed. by James C. Ballagh, 2 vols. (New York, 1911, 1914), I, 46.

120. Jerdone to Capt. Hugh Crawford, Nov. 22, 1759 and Sept. 2, 1762, Francis Jerdone Letterbook, 1756-63, Jerdone Papers, William and Mary College Library; *Virginia Gazette*, March 5, 1752, and March 3, 1753; Washington, *Writings*, III, 185-87.

121. Prince William County Deed Book Q, pp. 70, 298.

122. *Ibid.*, p. 340.

123. *Ibid.*, Book B, p. 104; Book R, p. 78. See also Book M, p. 79; Book P, pp. 34, 331.

124. Loudoun County Deed Book E, p. 127. See also Book D, p. 401, and Book E, p. 60.

125. Lewis Burwell to Lords of Trade, Aug. 21, 1751, Gooch Papers, III, 1066.

126. Albemarle County Deed Book 2, pp. 284-86.

127. Reverend Jonathan Boucher, *Reminiscences of an American Loyalist, 1738-1789 . . .*, ed. by Jonathan Bouchier (New York and Boston, 1925), pp. 14, 15, 21, 23-24, 30, 40-41, 59-60; Boucher to Washington, May 21, 1770, *Letters to Washington*, IV, 26.

128. Amelia County Land Surveys, 1736-51, Amelia County Tithables, VSL; Albemarle County Deed Book 4, p. 411; Hening, *Statutes*, VII, 630-34; *House Journals, 1761-65*, p. 121.

129. Letters of August 1, 1763, Dec. 2, 1767, and March 7, 1771, John Hook Letterbook, 1763-1772, VSL.

130. Allason Papers, VSL.

131. Spotsylvania County Deed Books, *passim*; Spotsylvania County Will Book D, pp. 528-33; Spotsylvania County Tax Accounts, 1775 and 1776.

132. Norfolk Borough Tithables, 1751, 1754.

133. *Ibid.*, 1751, 1771, VSL; Norfolk County Election Polls, 1768, 1769; Norfolk County Deed Book 24, pp. 112-15, 211-15. Only taxable slaves are listed here.

134. Norfolk County Will Book I, p. 263a; Norfolk County Deed Book 18, p. 2; Book 22, pp. 41, 43.

135. Norfolk County Deed Book 21, pp. 51, 52; Book 22, p. 36; Norfolk County Will Book 2, p. 198.

136. Norfolk County Deed Book 18, p. 184; Norfolk County Will Book 2, p. 101; *House Journals, October 1778*, pp. 57-60.

137. Norfolk County Will Book 1, p. 213.

138. Norfolk County Deed Book 19, p. 16; Book 20, p. 123; Book 23, p. 93; Book 24, p. 131; Book 27, p. 48.

139. *Ibid.*, Book 24, p. 210; Norfolk County Will Book 2, p. 14.

140. Norfolk County Tithables, 1751 and 1771; Norfolk County Deed Book 24, pp. 112-15, 211-15.

141. *Ibid.*, Book 17, pp. 120, 167; Book 18, p. 204; Book 23, pp. 155, 199; Book 24, p. 165; Book 28, p. 21; Book J., p. 72; Norfolk County Will Book I, p. 252; Book 1, pp. 34, 145.

142. For a contrasting view see Jackson T. Main, "The Distribution of Property in Post-Revolutionary Virginia," in *Mississippi Valley Historical Review*, XLI (Sept. 1954), 243-44.

CHAPTER II

# The Structure of White Society

GIVEN THE FACT of extensive economic opportunity in colonial Virginia, what type of society evolved in the Old Dominion during the eighteenth century? Did a small upper class dominate a large lower class, as has sometimes been claimed?[1] Or did Virginia follow the pattern of some of the other colonies by having a relatively small group that would fall in the upper class, a large number who would be considered in the middle class, and a small number in the lower class?

That there were differences of economic and social status in Virginia as in other colonies would not be surprising. As long as Virginia was a free and unregimented society, there would doubtless be some men who possessed more of the world's goods than others, whether acquired by their own efforts or by inheritance, and these differences in the possession of wealth would certainly cause men to divide somewhat into social groups with similar interests.

So the problem is not so much whether there were different "classes," which can be accepted as an axiom, but to determine their nature and their relation to each other. What was the relative size of the distinguishable classes, and was the social structure rigid or was there sufficient fluidity to allow much social mobility? How easy or difficult was the movement from one class to another? Was the class structure based on legal privilege or was it merely a question of some men having greater ability, wealth, or influence than others? How far apart were the extremes of the upper and lower classes? And particularly, was there antagonism between classes or were the men of a lower station attempting to emulate or join rather than to annihilate the men in the class above them?

Two contemporary travellers, Thomas Anburey and J. F. D. Smyth, viewed Virginia as a three-class society. The upper class, more respectable and numerous than in any other colony, was composed of gentlemen of the best families and fortunes, worldly men of liberal education, polished manners, carriages, and silver plate. The middle class, "a strange mixture of characters," comprised about half of the population. Hospitable, generous, and friendly, they could also be rude, ferocious, haughty, and tyrannical toward their slaves. They loved gambling and dissipation, particularly horse racing and cock fighting, combined elegant accomplishments and savage brutality, yet were often valuable and intelligent members of the community. The lower class, which usually composed

32

"the greatest part of mankind," were "fewer in Virginia, in proportion to the inhabitants, than perhaps in any other country in the world"—an interesting statement in view of previous interpretations. Yet even those of this class who were rude, illiberal, noisy, and turbulent could also be generous, kind, and hospitable, Anburey and Smyth declared. The "lower people" possessed an impertinent curiosity disagreeable and troublesome to strangers, were averse to labor and addicted to liquor, and when intoxicated were extremely savage and vindictive.[2]

A closer analysis of the interpretations by Anburey and Smyth, however, reveals many contradictions. Anburey wrote that "the spirit of equality or levelling principle was not so prevalent in Virginia, as in the other provinces; and that the different classes of people [in Virginia] supported a greater distinction [than those in other colonies]." Yet his description of the middle and lower classes does not indicate deference in any way. In fact, Smyth wrote as follows: "I have observed that throughout all the back country, indeed I had almost said throughout all America, there seems to be no such thing as any idea of subordination, or difference of ranks in life; excepting from the weaker to the stronger; and from the slaves to the whites." At the same time, Smyth noted that many of the middle class possessed fortunes "superior to some of the first rank, but their families are not so ancient, nor respectable; a circumstance here held in some estimation." [3]

Smyth had discovered that men who should have been lower class did not consider themselves as such, a fact which greatly complicates any division of people into rigid classes. On a trip to Kentucky, he had hired a young man to accompany him, and this is the account that he gave: "However, although I now call this man my servant, yet he himself would never have submitted to such an appellation, although he most readily performed every menial office, and indeed any service I could desire; yet such is the indolence, folly, and ridiculous pride of those ignorant backwoods men, that they could conceive it an indelible disgrace and infamy to be styled servants, even to his Majesty, notwithstanding they will gladly perform the lowest and most degrading services for hire." [4]

As if to complicate the problem, other men emphasized equality rather than class difference in characterizing colonial society. Edmund Randolph spoke of "the season of general equality" which prevailed in Virginia at the time of the Stamp Act.[5] And John Chalmers, a Maryland Loyalist, declared that men of fortune and family usually attained high rank in the British army, but that unfortunately genius and ability were not the monopoly of such men. They often possessed a meanness of pride, he said, "a quality ever obnoxious to the attainment of information in America where equality of manners renders such pride more odious than in any other country. . . . In America, the order of men, emigrants excepted, destined to fill armies lived too happily and equally to be charmed with the life of a soldier." [6]

Another contemporary, St. George Tucker, looked upon Virginia society as much like present-day American society—that is, a society in which the individual could do much to determine his own status. Tucker wrote to his sons that from their earliest childhood he had endeavored to inculcate in their minds "that every man is respectable in society in proportion to the talents he possesses to serve it. A blacksmith, a cobbler, a wheelwright, if honest men, are respectable characters in their proper spheres—but a man of science, a philosopher, or a legislator, as they have talents to be more eminently and extensively useful, so are they more eminently and generally respected." The world, he continued, was a circle about every man of such size as his ability made it. A good chairmaker or cabinetmaker might be well known for five miles around Petersburg, but men such as Washington, Franklin, and Rittenhouse were known all over the world. It was up to each individual, he told his sons, to decide what size his world would be.[7] Tucker, then, would emphasize talent and accomplishment rather than artificial marks of distinction.

Years after the American Revolution, Tucker criticized William Wirt, the biographer of Patrick Henry, for his interpretation of Virginia society as "aristocratic." Wirt was perhaps the first to emphasize this interpretation which has been so widely adopted by later historians. Tucker said that the upper classes rode in coaches, chariots, or on fine horses, but they never failed to lift their hats to a poor man and they generally shook hands with every man in a courtyard or churchyard. As far as Tucker could judge, "the planter who owned half a dozen Negroes, felt himself perfectly upon a level with his rich neighbor that owned an hundred." In the lower countries, he continued, there was among the free whites no dependence except that of overseers. Concluded Tucker: "My opinion of what is called the aristocracy of Virginia, at that period is, that if ever there were a race of harmless aristocrats, they presented that picture." [8]

These somewhat contradictory or opposing accounts present difficult problems for the historian. Anburey and Smyth drew no sharp lines of demarcation between lower and middle or middle and upper classes. Where does one class end and another begin? And in what class does a man put himself, since this would be a guide to his actions? If status symbols are important in human relations, as psychologists say, a man's hopes for himself or his children might well have been as important in designating his class status as were his economic possessions.

Fortunately, other records in addition to contemporary opinions give some information on class divisions, but even these do not make the distinctions as clear as one would desire.


## A:  THE UPPER CLASS

The upper class in Virginia was the one most easily identified. The term "gentleman" signified a member of this class, and whenever we find a man designated as "gentleman," we can be sure that in his own eyes, or in the eyes of someone else, he had achieved some status. The problem, then, is to ascertain with more accuracy than did Anburey and Smyth just who these "gentlemen" were.

The term "esquire" obviously denoted a "gentleman," but seems to have referred to men who held appointive office under the King. Hugh Jones said in 1724 that "except the honourable, the Council, and some commissioned in posts by His Majesty or his orders, who are nominated esquires," the only distinguishing titles of honor for Virginia gentlemen were in militia titles.[9] In the House of Burgesses, some men were designated "esquires" and some "gentlemen," a distinction that appears to have been due to office rather than wealth.[10]

While some men in Virginia believed that the term "gentleman" applied to personal characteristics or achievements, others appear to have emphasized birth and wealth. To one writer, "no man deserves the appellation *a Gentleman* until he has done something to merit it," and he branded as nonsense the common phrase among the rich, and from them adopted by the poor, that a man was born a gentleman.[11] Another writer made philosopher and gentleman synonymous: to him, a man's behavior, thoughts, and sentiments made the gentleman. The lowest mechanic with virtue was above the man of wealth and honors who lacked virtue.[12] The Reverend Jonathan Boucher said that clergymen were "often by birth, and always by education and profession, gentlemen." He urged that ministers be given salaries commensurate with their stations, for "in Vulgar reckoning, a mean condition bespeaks a mean man," [13] a statement which signifies approval of the upper class by the lower class. And the Reverend James Maury spoke of "the vulgar, both small and great," indicating that, to him, property alone did not make a "gentleman." [14]

Some people seem to have felt that a man was a "gentleman" if he considered himself so. Such was true of John Warden who had served as a tutor for Thomas Jones in 1768-69. Warden had received £10 for his passage over and £30 sterling for the year, an amount often earned by a mediocre overseer. In 1771, Jones wanted Warden to board and room at Jones' house in exchange for tutoring Jones' two sons. Warden complained that on occasion he had not been treated as a "gentleman," for the sons said they hated him, threw his poverty up to him, and considered him no better than an indentured servant. Warden agreed to accept Jones' offer only if he were treated as a gentleman, but not otherwise.[15]

Although it might have been significant in the seventeenth century, the prefix "Mr." before a man's name did not mean anything by way of social distinction in eighteenth-century Virginia. "Mr." might signify anyone of any station. Landon Carter often referred to his overseers as Mr. Edwards or Mr. Beale. In a mood of sarcasm, he even called one of his slaves "Mr. Tony." [16] John Harrower spoke of Mr. Anthony Fraser the overseer, Mr. Becks the taylor, and Mr. Brooks the carpenter.[17] Thomas Lee of Lancaster was referred to as gentleman, planter, and Mr. In the settlement of his estate, a statement was made that part of the inventory consisted of "cash due Mr. Lee from Mr. William Griggs." Mr. Griggs was an illiterate planter who signed with a mark.[18] And tutor Philip Fithian spoke of being in the garden and picking up the spade of Mr. Gregory, the gardener.[19] Perhaps "Mr." differentiated whites from blacks, but this is not certain.

Fithian, a Princeton graduate and tutor for Robert Carter, saw considerable difference between the upper classes in New Jersey and Virginia. In New Jersey, he said, a gentleman might have only 400 acres of land, associate freely with farmers and mechanics without fear of stigma, encourage ingenuity and industry, and when not actually engaged in public service, work with his domestics on his farm and eat with them at the same table. In Virginia, however, a gentleman could own £30,000 in slaves alone, and even though he was deeply in debt, consider himself as much above others as his visible property exceeded theirs. Even intellectual attainment had its price: a Princeton tutor, said Fithian, would be rated at £10,000 without question as to family or background.[20]

Sometimes, however, Fithian's entries in his diary contradicted his own account of sharp class differences in Virginia. Fithian described an evening at the Robert Carters' as follows: "We have an addition to our numerous family, one Mr, I forget his name, he is a cooper, tho', & an Irishman, & seems to be pretty smart; I sat the evening with him in Mr. Randolphs room."[21] This would not indicate such a wide chasm between gentlemen and white workers as Fithian seemed to imply.

There is no doubt that some upper-class families, such as Carter, Custis, Ludwell, and Lee, had a great deal of wealth, but differences in amount even among those gentlemen were significant. Robert "King" Carter of Corotoman, Lancaster County, possessed on his death over 1,000 slaves, 300,000 acres of land, and £10,000 sterling in money. There were forty-six "plantations," each with overseer and from two to thirty-three slaves. The home plantation had seventeen indentured servants or hired men and thirty-three slaves.[22] In 1774, Carter's grandson Robert of Nomini Hall possessed 600 slaves and 60,000 acres of land scattered throughout Virginia and Maryland. In addition, he owned a large part of the iron works at Baltimore.[23] Washington's stepson, John Parke Custis, possessed "a very large fortune" of 15,000 acres of land, 200 to 300 slaves and £8,000 to £10,000 on bond in 1773, yet all this did not produce the £1,500 to £1,600 that Custis would need to travel in Europe.[24] Philip Ludwell of Green Spring, former estate of Governor William Berkeley, had property valued at £12,482 in 1770—7,102 acres in freehold, 952 acres on lease, property in Jamestown and Williamsburg, 164 slaves, 217 cattle, 17 horses, and 190 sheep.[25] William Lee, who married a Ludwell, said that Green Spring did not yield five per cent in profit.[26] In spite of the spread of wealth, these men were all "gentlemen."

Wealth, then, in land, money, or slaves was certainly one element in distinguishing the "gentlemen" from the rest of society, and if a man lost his wealth he might also lose some of his status. Fithian visited one Mr. Camels, comptroller of the customs, to meet Camels' "neat, handsome,

genteel, & sociable" daughter. But Camels had "unfortunately been reduced to low circumstances" through trade, and said Fithian, "his family
does not now meet with so great respect, as I am told they formerly
did—." [27] The father of Mann Page almost ruined the Page family by taking up land "in order to be respected as the richest man in the country."
Page, a member of the Council, died so heavily in debt that the son had
to sell entailed lands.[28] The Page family did not lose status, but the fact
that wealth won respect rather than animosity is significant in our study
of classes.

If some men in the upper class possessed considerable wealth, others
might be "gentlemen" or "esquires" and have very little. Washington
visited Solomon Hedges, Esquire, a justice of the peace for Frederick
County, who, far from living in luxury, had neither tablecloth nor knives
to eat with at dinner.[29] Washington also loaned money to Colonel Robert
Steward "without security and without interest, having nothing but the
word of a gentleman of no estate to repay it to me again." [30] An example
of Smyth's statement that the middle class often had more wealth than
the upper class is to be found in Prince William County, where George
Eskridge, Gentleman, had an estate of £165.8.5, including five slaves,
but Daniel French, who was not a gentleman, had eleven slaves and an
estate of £344.10.7.[31] The following inventory of the estate of John
Bates, gentleman and member of the vestry of Antrium Parish, Halifax
County, tells its own story.[32] The entire estate was not worth half as much
as one of Robert Carter's better slaves.

| | |
|---|---:|
| 1 desk | £   1.5.0 |
| 1 bed & rug | 4.0.0 |
| 1 d'o | 1.15.0 |
| 1 d'o | 2.15.0 |
| 1 old leather trunk | 0.2.6 |
| 1 old chest | 0.1.3 |
| 5 old chairs | 0.10.0 |
| 6 stone plates | 0.7.6 |
| 2 dishes, 1 basin, 7 plates, 3 spoons | 0.13.6 |
| 1 tea kettle | 0.10.0 |
| 1 coffee pot, coffee mill and candlestick | 0.6.0 |
| 1 tea pot, 1 box iron & 1 heater | 0.4.6 |
| 2 pr. old cotton card, 1 pr. old c [?] | 0.2.0 |
| 1 cross cut saw, iron wedges | 1.0.0 |
| 1 pr. saddle bags, 1 cotton wheel | 0.15.6 |
| 1 flax wheel, 1 large iron pot | 1.2.6 |
| 1 small iron pot & 1 old Bible | 0.4.6 |
| 1 man's old saddle | 0.12.6 |
| 1 cow & calf & 2 yearlings | 5.15.0 |
| 1 horse | 4.0.0 |
| 1 pr. old Brokin fire tongs | 0.1.6 |
| 1 candlestick | 0.0.9 |
| 1 old negro fellow named Toby | 5.0.0 |
| 1 old negro woman named Dido | 1.0.0 |
| 1 sheep, 2 hogs | 2.8.0 |
| | £34.12.6 |

A note said a few things could not be found.

Gentlemen of the upper class might well be in debt far more than their estate was worth, so that while they appeared to be affluent, they actually had very little. Philip Grymes, Esquire, deputy receiver-general, left a debt of £18,338 to the British government for quitrents due.[33] Thomas Wright Belfield, gentleman of Richmond County, held 3,000 acres in fee simple, including his home plantation of 1,500 acres, but his debts were more than the 3,000 acres, his slaves, and his personal estate were worth.[34] Unlike some of the other Carters, Charles Carter of Cleve in King George County left an estate encumbered with over £16,000 in debts and legacies. As all the slaves would not bring sufficient money to cover the debt, the Assembly allowed the executors to sell 25,496 acres of land.[35] When the act was disallowed in England, the Assembly docked the entail on 12,305 acres of Carter's land.[36]

Undoubtedly, as Anburey and Smyth said, education was also a factor in determining whether a man was in one class or another. Richard and Elizabeth Ambler admonished their sons to take full advantage of the educational opportunities afforded them, for many children capable of learning were condemned to a life of hard labor because their parents could not give them an education. The children should therefore appreciate the fact that their parents were above the lower class and were able to give them such an education which, if not wasted, would preserve them "in the same class and rank among mankind." [37] The Amblers did not claim to be in the upper class, but only that they were not in the lower class.

Anburey and Smyth rated education as one of the chief characteristics of a gentleman, but the records do not substantiate this view entirely. The deeds and wills furnish many instances of men who signed their name with a mark yet were called "gentlemen." A few examples must suffice. Elias Edmunds, "Gent," of Lancaster signed legal papers with a mark, yet he had four plantations totaling 1,064 acres and a personal estate of £2,163, including some sixty-five slaves.[38] Richard Gilmour also called himself "gentleman" and signed with a mark, but he owned over 3,000 acres in Lancaster, 700 acres in Frederick, and a personal estate of £1,011.[39]

If Anburey and Smyth believed that the Virginia gentlemen were more numerous than in other colonies, there were others who believed that the upper class was neither very rich nor very extensive. The Reverend James Maury said there were "but very few" Virginia gentlemen who were "born to an affluent fortune" if by affluent was meant a fortune that would supply a surplus over and above a man's wants. Most men who desired to be above the common herd had to engage in some lucrative business. Such men finished their formal education at the age of fourteen or fifteen years, then were placed under some eminent man of business. But, concluded Maury, "gentlemen of this sort are frequently called to the highest posts of honor & trust in this country." [40] In short, some "gentlemen" were not very well educated and would really be in what one might easily call the upper middle class.

Distinctions in food and housing were not as sharp between "gentlemen" and others in Virginia society as one might suppose. Beverley said that gentlemen generally ate wheat bread, although some preferred corn pone. The poorer sort had little relish for wheat and did not use it, not because they could not, but because they would not bother to grow wheat as they would have to fence it.[41] In housing, gentlemen might live in handsome, commodious, and capacious homes of brick or wood, but likewise the "common planters" lived "in pretty timber houses, neater than the farm houses are generally in England." [42] There was a difference, but it was not as great as we would expect.

Perhaps there were men whose influence commanded privileges, just as there are today, but being in the upper intellectual or economic class did not automatically carry privilege with it. Robert Wormeley Carter, son of Landon Carter, was indicted by a grand jury of Richmond County "for swearing two profane oaths with in [sic] twelve months last past." [43] When Allan Howard, gentleman, built a mill on Rockfish River which entirely obstructed the passage of fish, the General Assembly ordered him to tear it down within two months or pay a fine of a thousand pounds of tobacco.[44] And the Reverend Thomas Davis of Norfolk, who voted in 1769 for winners John Wilson and Thomas Newton, still had to take the oath that he was qualified to vote.[45]

That the gentleman class was fluid and open to recruitment from below can be demonstrated by innumerable examples. Dale Carter of Lancaster, for instance, leased forty acres of land in 1734, became a deputy sheriff the same year, was inspector of tobacco by 1741, and by 1758 was a gentleman justice of the peace. In 1768, he was both sheriff and a candidate for the House of Burgesses. Carter never paid quitrents on more than 170 acres of land nor tithes on more than eight slaves, and at death in 1776 he owned four slaves worth £200 and had a total personal estate of £300.[46] William Carr of Prince William was the son of a farmer with 150 acres of land, but by 1767 he was a "Captain" and in 1773 paid quitrents on 826 acres. Called "gentleman" by 1762 and "merchant" by 1771, Carr, according to William Lee, made a capital fortune from a beginning of not more than forty shillings.[47]

Fluidity of social classes in colonial Virginia is also attested to by the fact that artisans sometimes became gentlemen. In 1760, John Redman, millwright and carpenter, took an apprentice. In fact, John, Joseph, and Solomon Redman were all millwrights and carpenters, and all took apprentices.[48] Solomon was listed for 100 acres on the rent rolls, and in 1765, John Redman had 300 acres.[49] Yet in that same year of 1765, John Redman was referred to as "gentleman," which would not seem to make the title very imposing or exclusive.[50] Silas Hart of Augusta first appeared in the deeds as a mason in 1749. By 1756 he was called "gentleman," a title that continued throughout his life. His wife's name and the absence of other Harts in the deeds is assurance that Silas Hart the mason was also Silas Hart the gentleman.[51]

Poor boys also went up the social ladder in the Old Dominion. One Pasture or Pasteur was the son of a "very honest industrious man" who lived in Williamsburg and who, "though in low circumstances, breeds up [a very?] large family with reputation." The son attended William and Mary College where he was an usher, had "learning, ingenuity, modesty, and sobriety," [52] and would certainly have been a member of the upper classes after his ministerial training. The well-known Edmund Pendleton received a rude education as apprentice for Benjamin Robinson, clerk of Caroline County Court, qualified for the Virginia bar in 1741 at the age of nineteen, and received a certificate which reads "Edmund Pendleton Gentleman." Yet this rustic ex-apprentice received the highest vote for Burgess from Caroline County from 1752 to 1775, was president of one of the Revolutionary conventions, speaker of the first House of Representatives under the Constitution of 1776, and in 1777 became a judge of the state's highest court.[53]

It has often been said that the Virginia upper class maintained its position to some extent through intermarriage. This was probably true in some instances, but as the following example shows, we would need to know about the marriages of all the sons and daughters if we would understand the upper class completely. Landon Carter was furious when his daughter Judy ran away and married without her father's consent. When Judy returned for her first visit, Carter would not receive her husband. He asked how "such a creature" could maintain a woman who had always lived well and delicately when he had only a poor pittance of an estate—a bit of land and about six slaves. Carter planned to provide for his daughter, but her husband was not to benefit.[54]

Being a "gentleman" did not mean that one's close relatives were in the same class—an element generally associated with aristocracy. William Portlock, Sr., gentleman of Norfolk Borough, left plantations to three sons and slaves to three others on his death in 1750, but none of these sons was ever referred to as "gentleman" in the available records.[55] The Reverend Robert Rose had a brother Alex who was an "overseer and joiner," but as Jonathan Boucher said, Rose, as a minister, was undoubtedly considered a "gentleman." [56]

In a class-ridden society, one would expect to find a great deal of solidarity among the upper classes, but this was not always true in Virginia. For example, there was Arthur Lee's challenge of James Mercer to a duel and Lee's failure to appear when Mercer accepted.[57] Peter Randolph and Ralph Wormeley carried a dispute over 2,000 acres of land all the way to the Privy Council at great expense to both.[58] The Carters and Grymes contested a commission bitterly,[59] and Washington was often at odds with his merchants, Carlyle and Adams, although they paid about the same amount for pews in the Alexandria church. [60] In Lancaster, Thomas

Pinckard, gentleman, county justice, sheriff, and owner of considerable land and slaves, sued Edwin Conway, gentleman and one-time burgess, for calling Pinckard a "sheep stealer." Conway denied the charge, then countered that Pinckard had used "scurrilous words" about Conway.[61] In Mecklenburg County there was a long-standing feud between burgess Matthew Marable and county justice David Christopher. Christopher was accused of breaking into Marable's store to prevent Marable's election and then releasing a man accused of wounding one of Marable's slaves.[62] And the daughter of Thomas Mann Randolph of Goochland County declared that burgess Paul Carrington of Charlotte County was a bitter enemy of the Randolph family.[63] As we shall see later, such controversies among the upper classes are particularly significant for our understanding of Virginia politics.

One important reason for the absence of solidarity among the upper classes was the conflict of interest that existed between planters and merchants. In 1773-74, the planter-merchant controversy broke into the open in the pages of the *Virginia Gazette*. The merchants' quarterly meetings at Williamsburg were looked upon by planters as inimical to their interests because of conspiracies to set prices of both colonial exports and imports. There were proposals that the planters also organize, set prices, and elect men to buy and sell for them.[64] Harry Piper, factor for Dixon and Littledale, admitted that the merchants had placed a 12s. per hundred limit on tobacco in 1774, but very few planters would sell at this price. The planters were not in a good bargaining position, however, for if they sold tobacco for cash to a merchant other than the one they usually patronized, the latter would refuse them credit.[65]

From a doctrinaire point of view, one might expect sharp class conflict between the gentlemen and other classes in Virginia, but far from being feared and hated, members of the upper class seem often to have been honored and respected by the common people. At the funeral of Colonel John Hutchings, long a burgess from Norfolk Borough, the coffin was carried by six reputable tradesmen, not by members of the upper class, and was followed by "a very great concourse of people of all ranks and degrees, who universally lamented the loss of so worthy a member of society. . . ."[66] Governor Fauquier recommended John Page, Presley Thornton, and Colonel Lewis Burwell for the Council as "men of property and much respected in this country."[67] William Byrd III, who had distinguished himself on Braddock's campaign in 1755, was "generally esteemed" for "his great abilities and personal accomplishments" even though he was "infatuated with play [gambling]" and lost most of his estate.[68] Philip Fithian also noted that "people of fortune" were the "pattern of all behavior" in Virginia,[69] and a writer in the *Gazette* declared: "Let the principal gentlemen but set the example, they will be quickly followed by the bulk of the people."[70]

If one can say that Virginia had an "upper class," one can also say with equal assurance that it was a "class" of many gradations open at all times to men of talent and ambition. Based on many factors—wealth, family, education, achievement, self-evaluation—many of its members, by European standards then or our own standards now, would be middle-class at best. There were undoubtedly some personal animosities on the part of members of the lower and middle classes toward particular members of the upper class, but the gentlemen as a group were rather to be emulated and joined than annihilated. To be on the safe side, in the following chapters we have included in the upper classes anyone with any claim to a title of distinction even though it seems quite obvious that some so included were not really "gentlemen."

## B:   THE MIDDLE CLASS

Although the title "gentleman" commonly marked the upper class, there is no such identification for the "middling sort" who, as Anburey and Smyth said, were so varied as almost to defy description. Lacking formal education but not ability, and often possessed of more property than the upper classes, they were obviously as a class not very deferential toward their "betters." If St. George Tucker was correct in saying that a man with half a dozen slaves considered himself the equal of a man with a hundred, the problem of drawing meaningful class lines becomes extremely difficult. At the upper limits, when did a man cease to be middle-class, and at the lower limits, at what point, economically and psychologically, did he pass from lower to middle-class?

Merchants were particularly difficult to classify, for while there were many men who were both merchant and gentleman there were also many merchants who were not designated gentlemen. These would undoubtedly fall in the middle class. Andrew Burnaby drew a line of distinction between the two in Williamsburg when he described the town in 1759 as having some 200 houses and not more than 1,000 people, black and white, including "ten or twelve gentlemen's families constantly residing in it, besides merchants and tradesmen." [71] Whatever the class status of merchants and tradesmen, they were certainly not gentlemen in Burnaby's reckoning. It is also of interest that he did not designate any "laborers." Merchants were referred to as "young Scotch-Men" and towns were described as "inhabited in a great measure by factors from Scotland," and these merchants were, or probably considered themselves, middle-class. [72]

The following example demonstrates both the danger of considering "merchants" as upper-class and the difficulty of designating class status. Cited as a "merchant" and creditor in a 1771 mortgage, Henry Fleming of Norfolk Borough advertised in the *Gazette* in 1772 as a "saddler." He was rated on the 1771 tithable list for one slave and one servant or apprentice and he never purchased real estate in either the borough or the county. [73] A reasonable surmise would be that Fleming was an artisan who aspired to be called "merchant."

In attempting to differentiate class lines, it is also pertinent to note that merchants often had divided economic interests, doubling as both merchants and planters. Peter Fontaine explained in 1757 that a man "could not hire a servant or slave for love or money," and unless he was willing to work at hard labor, the only solution was to buy land and slaves. For this reason, Virginia had "no merchants . . . of any sort but what became planters in a short time." [74] The deeds amply confirm this observation.

In addition to many of the merchants, most planters would have to be considered middle-class. "Planter" in colonial Virginia meant farmer and "plantation" meant only the land under cultivation. A man might farm a large or small acreage, but it would still be called a plantation and he would be designated a planter. Whenever he achieved the status of the upper class, he was usually called something other than planter, so the term in the records almost invariably meant someone below the upper class.

What proportion of the planters would be considered middle-class? We have already seen in Chapter I that most Virginians were landowners. Jones' statement that most men had land of their own, Gooch's claim that the whites were "all planters, and such as have their plantations under their own management," or that Virginia was a country "settled only by planters," Fontaine's statement that Virginians were "all of one trade viz planters," and Fauquier's declaration that "every man in this colony has land and none but Negroes are laborers," all testify to the fact that Virginia was a colony of landowners. Were these landowners middle- or lower-class? Or more precisely, did they consider themselves middle- or lower-class?

In a strict Marxian sense, most if not all independent landowning farmers would probably be considered middle rather than lower class. They were men who owned capital goods in the form of land, livestock, and farm utensils; they raised crops and livestock for profit; and they were not a propertyless proletariat dependent upon others for wages as a livelihood. Anburey and Smyth believed that many of them owned slaves, a belief verified by the records, which would certainly not make them proletariat.

Unless the agricultural area around Port Royal was unusual, a large percentage of these property-owning farmers would have to be considered in the middle class. One observer stated that the town of Port Royal itself was inhabited largely by Scotch factors "and the circumjacent country by planters, in general in middling circumstances." [75]

Andrew Burnaby noted a practice in Virginia that seems to point to a middle-class attitude, both economically and psychologically speaking. This was an aversion to labor and a desire among all classes of whites to own land and slaves. Burnaby commented in 1759 that Virginians, rather than applying themselves "to laborious occupations, occupations militating with their dispositions, and generally considered too as the inheritance and badge of slavery, will gradually retire westward, and settle upon fresh lands, which are said also to be more fertile; where, by the servitude of a

Negro or two, they may enjoy all the satisfaction of an easy and indolent independency." Burnaby also believed that this westward movement for better land and easier living would keep the coastal lands thinly populated.[76] Instead of being squeezed out by aristocrats, as has sometimes been said, it would appear that small farmers moved west to improve their lot. And one might venture the guess that men who went west to get better land and to live on the labor of a slave or two were middle- rather than lower-class in their outlook.

Many tradesmen or artisans must also be counted in the middle class, and again the question raises itself as to the exact point where such a person ceased to be of the lower class. Like the planters, they were not propertyless proletariat but mainly small entrepreneurs who owned capital goods, often land and slaves or servants in addition to a shop, and who worked for themselves with profit as their incentive.

Peter Fontaine contended, and the deeds bear out his contention, that most tradesmen or artisans acquired land and combined the occupations of craftsman and planter. Fontaine declared that "every Virginia tradesman must be at least half a planter" and therefore could not be depended upon as a tradesman.[77] Later he reiterated that the colony had "no tradesmen no artificers of any sort but what become planters in a short time." [78] Did such men consider themselves lower- or middle-class?

The deeds, wills, and other sources give us innumerable examples of shopkeepers and artisans who acquired more than sufficient property to be considered middle-class. Alexander Kerr, jeweler of Williamsburg, had store goods, furniture, a plantation of 100 acres, seven slaves, livestock, grain, and in Williamsburg a brick house, store, coachhouse, stable, office houses and a large garden fronting on Main Street.[79] Daniel Dale, shipwright of Portsmouth, had a ten-acre tract with a boatworks, houses in Portsmouth and Norfolk, considerable furniture, and twenty-one slaves.[80] Moses Chilton, illiterate shipcarpenter of Lancaster County, served as ensign in the militia in 1767 and died owning a good estate including twelve slaves.[81] And Robert Wilkinson, blacksmith, bought 150 acres for £50.15.0 from gentleman Edmund Waller, who had mortgaged the land to merchant John Semple for £60. This is an example of the lower class benefiting at the expense of the upper class, for merchant Semple lost on the transaction and of course Waller, a gentleman, lost his land.[82]

There are also numerous examples of artisans who moved up in the social as well as economic scale. Thomas Talbot went from plain shipwright in 1743 to "captain" and then to "gentleman" in 1774. Talbot first bought sixty-six acres of land in 1743 for £32.10.0, but he continued to acquire property and in 1754 he took an apprentice. By 1759, he was able to buy property in Norfolk Borough worth £1,150 and by 1771 he also had twenty-nine tithable slaves. Talbot did not receive any inheritance from his father, who died in 1755.[83] In Augusta County, Silas Hart, a mason in 1749, became a "gentleman" by 1756.[84] Evidence on artisans, such as the above, makes it dangerous to consider artisans as members of the lower class, either economically or psychologically.

Richard Blackburn of Prince William particularly demonstrates this danger. Identified as "carpenter," Blackburn purchased 130 acres for £23.8.0 in 1733, then in quick succession acquired various tracts totalling over 3,500 acres. Within fourteen months of his first purchase he was designated "gentleman." He continued to appear in the documents as gentleman or carpenter for a year or so, but eventually carried the title of a gentleman only. Blackburn was a major in 1741, the year he ran unsuccessfully for burgess. A tithable list for 1747 shows that he had two overseers and nineteen tithable slaves in Dittengen Parish, where he was now "colonel," and by 1754 he was listed on the rent rolls for 13,813 acres.[85] Blackburn's career obviously illustrates social mobility. If we had used only the records for 1733, he would have appeared merely as a carpenter. But a detailed check shows that this carpenter became a colonel, a sheriff, a candidate for the House of Burgesses, and the largest landowner on the county rent rolls.

Although there were probably some artisans who were deferential toward their "betters" in Virginia, there were others who were belligerently independent. Washington once criticized one of his millers for drinking and neglecting the mill. The miller replied that it had been an ancient custom for men to be convicted before they were executed, and he would like some of those ancient privileges. He denied neglecting the mill, and as for drinking, he had used his own money which he thought every free man had the right to convert to whatever use he thought proper. He accused Washington of passing judgment without adequate information, referred him to John Ballendine for a true account, and offered with a partner to buy the mill if Washington was still dissatisfied and would give them some time to pay.[86]

Strangely enough, most tenants must also be included in the middle rather than the lower class. For one thing, they very often owned land in addition to the land they leased. An example is Samuel Combs, farmer, who leased 150 acres for life in June, 1760, then in October, 1761, purchased 140 acres for £28.[87] Joshua Gore, who leased 300 acres in 1758, bought 1,726 acres in 1760 for £170.[88] It was also common for tenants to be slaveowners, perhaps because labor was more profitable than land. Thomas Allen, who owned 106 acres and leased 170 acres, had two slaves, and this type of example could be multiplied many times.[89]

The following evidence would indicate that we need to revise our thinking about the status of tenants, and especially that we should make sure that we have sufficient evidence before we draw conclusions. Philip Ludwell, who owned the 6,078-acre Green Spring estate near Williamsburg, was also a tenant on 952 acres of land.[90] Washington bought land from Sheriff Sampson Darrell, yet Darrell was one of Washington's tenants.[91] Thomas Jett of King George County was listed for 2,001 acres on the 1773 rental, but he also leased tracts of 150, 176, 250, 300, 150, and 168 acres.[92] Then there was William Montague of Lancaster who in 1773 rented 343 acres to Robert McTyre but in turn rented 400 acres from Lucy Smith.[93] George Heale, Lancaster gentleman, burgess, and sheriff, paid quitrents on 1,837 acres but also leased 500 additional acres in Lancaster and 122 acres in Richmond County.[94] An incautious use of the Richmond County records might make Heale appear only as a small tenant with 122 acres. In Prince William, several men, such as Jeremiah Bronough, Henry Peyton, John Bayliss, Cuthbert Bullitt, John Hooe, Hawson Hooe, William Ellzey, and James Scott were tenants but also "gentlemen." [95]

Like some of the planters, merchants, and artisans already cited, a tenant could climb up the social ladder if he was not already there. An example was James Hamilton of Loudoun County. In 1758, Hamilton leased 150 acres for three lives from planter Mahlon Janny, with the £3 rent to be waived for three years. By 1760 he purchased 421 acres from the Fairfaxes for £61, and within three months, now designated "gentleman," bought another 500 acres. From this time forward he was always called a "gentleman" as he continued to buy and sell land, and by 1765 he had also acquired the title of "Colonel." [96] Again this points up the danger of judging a man's social status or aspirations by a spot check, for in 1758 Hamilton would merely appear on the records as a poor tenant.

Nowhere in the thousands of records we have surveyed have we found evidence that any social stigma was attached to the status of tenant in colonial Virginia. The attitude toward a tenant at that time appears to have been similar to our modern attitude toward a renter. Persons today who live in rented houses or apartments, or on rented farms, are as socially acceptable as those who own their own homes or farms, although frequently they are less affluent. The same attitude apparently prevailed in Virginia two hundred years ago.

If the ownership of capital goods in the form of land, slaves, merchandise, and tools made a man a member of the middle class, then many merchants and most planters, artisans and tradesmen were probably in, or considered themselves in, the middle class. And if we can judge by the deeds and by the alacrity with which they adopted any title of distinction, they seemed to be more concerned to join the upper class than to have the upper class join them. Psychologically, the middle class might well have included many more than the approximate half of the population estimated by Anburey and Smyth.

## C: THE LOWER CLASS

In their analysis, Anburey and Smyth stated that the lower class was smaller in Virginia than in any other country, but this merely raises the question of what economic and psychological factors are to be used to determine when a man is, or believes himself to be, lower-class. In a Marxian sense, the lower class would be limited to an industrial proletariat, but since there was no such thing in agrarian colonial America, we must look elsewhere for the lower class.

A natural place to start would be with the "poor," but Virginia, like other colonies, did not have many poor people, certainly not poor compared with those of Europe. Robert Beverley claimed that the colony had few in either extreme of poor or rich: Virginia was "the best poor man's country in the world," with such fine climate and fertile soil that no one was poor enough to beg or want food, though many were lazy enough to deserve poverty. He said it took one parish nine years to find anyone to claim a £5 gift left to the poor, and then the money was given to an old woman. Accident or sickness might cause a man to need aid or to seek exemption from taxes, but few ever asked for or needed charity.[97]

Other evidence also points to the absence of a class of poor people in Virginia. Hugh Jones declared that servants, when free, could become day laborers, overseers, or tradesmen, or rent small plantations for a trifle. Because of good wages, the few poor were the aged, lame, or sick, not the able-bodied, and poor children were apprenticed to learn a trade to support themselves.[98] An example is the keeper of the poor in Portsmouth Parish, Norfolk County, who had only four people under his care in 1776, three of whom were blind and a fourth unable to use her limbs.[99] Then there was Anguish Alexander, "a poor ancient man," who was exempt from taxes but who had £75.6.11 in livestock and household goods when he died.[100] Burnaby said he traveled 1,200 miles without seeing a single person who asked for charity, a situation connected with the fact that land could be acquired so easily,[101] and both Jones and Smyth noted the absence of beggars.[102]

Like those of the classes above them, even the poor often acquired property in land and slaves. One man declared that a poor man in Virginia chose to be his own master by getting a small estate for himself and family rather than being subservient to others.[103] "Poor honest Daniel Stone," a worker for George William Fairfax, who earned £20 a year in wages, asked Fairfax to keep this money to buy him a slave, which Fairfax did.[104]

Virginia, in fact, enacted laws to prevent the development of a poor class. The law prevented a man from moving around without paying his taxes, justices of the peace could take up idle persons and bind them to service, neglected children could be bound as apprentices, and women were fined or whipped for giving birth to illegitimate children. A law that would horrify social workers today required that persons on relief wear a badge on the sleeve of their outer garment.[105]

There was no "industrial proletariat" in Virginia, and a permanent white labor class was virtually as non-existent as the poor. In 1764, Washington was interested in a mechanical tree-puller, for he said it was impossible for slaves to clear sufficient land "and labourers are not to be hired here."[106] A society established in 1773 to promote useful knowledge pointed out that "in a community where labourers are few, and those chiefly slaves, mechanical inventions will be particularly serviceable." [107] And Peter Fontaine justified slavery on the ground that a servant could not be hired "for love or money," so a man, unless he was willing to work at the hoe or ax, had to buy a slave.[108]

Among the lowest of the lower class would probably be men who thought of themselves as "laborers," but very few men referred to themselves in this fashion. Muster rolls in the Washington Papers provide striking evidence of this, and because of the recruitment practices in Virginia the muster rolls themselves were apt to be filled mostly with the lower class. As the following chart shows, less than 2.8 per cent of 681 recruits called themselves laborers, although some of the fifty-three whose occupation was not given might have been. About fifty-five per cent came from areas other than Virginia and chances are that many of these were former indentured servants. But the significant point is that so few of these men called themselves laborers.[109]

| Origin | Planters | Artisans | Laborers | Others | Occupation Not Given | Total |
|---|---|---|---|---|---|---|
| Virginia | 172 | 100 | 5 | 0 | 29 | 306 |
| Other Colonies | 20 | 21 | 0 | 1 | 3 | 45 |
| England & Wales | 51 | 91 | 3 | 1 | 5 | 151 |
| Scotland | 22 | 18 | 2 | 0 | 7 | 49 |
| Ireland | 35 | 64 | 7 | 0 | 8 | 114 |
| Other Countries | 4 | 10 | 1 | 0 | 1 | 16 |
| Totals | 304 | 304 | 18 | 2 | 53 | 681 |

It should be noted, however, that these militiamen, who comprised about as low a class among the free whites as one would find in the colony, were anything but deferential as a lower class should be. Militia drafted for one month's service left their posts at the end of the month without waiting for their relief.[110] According to Washington, they would "go and come when and where they please, without regarding time, their officers, or the safety of the inhabitants, but consulting solely their own inclinations." Because of opposition, orders had to be carried out by force, "to such a pitch has the insolence of these people arrived, by having every point hitherto submitted to them," while the militiamen, in turn, threatened "to blow out" Washington's brains. "Every mean individual has his own crude notions of things, and must undertake to direct," he declared. "If his advice is neglected, he thinks himself slighted, abased, and injured; and, to redress his wrongs will depart for his home." [111]

The army also furnishes evidence of an absence of class conflict between upper and lower classes. Calling the militia "discontented turbulent fellows" and "obstinate and perverse," Washington declared that they were "often egged on by the officers, who lead them to acts of disobedience." [112] Furthermore, deserters were encouraged by the fact that "some Gentlemen below [in the tidewater] have been so imprudent as to offer for a small consideration to defend them against any damage for deserting." [113] And Governor Dinwiddie said that magistrates and other civil officers aided deserters as well as discouraging and preventing enlistments, even though these men were for their own protection.[114]

Two items in the *Virginia Gazette* suggest that perhaps even the few who were poor did not want to be identified with the lower class. One writer pointed out the psychological importance of "name-dropping"— that people in all stations like to have it known that they know and associate with people of a higher station, a fact that contributed to imitation and extravagance.[115] Another writer maintained that the most effective way to lower a man in the world's esteem was to call him poor, for such was human nature and the practice of the world that disrespect if not contempt inevitably accompanied poverty and a mean appearance. What man would pay any regard to, or be influenced by, the poor, this writer asked? [116]

Governors Gooch and Dinwiddie, who considered tradesmen and small planters, not propertyless laborers, as the "lower" or "lowest" classes, also believed that these lower classes emulated the upper classes. In urging the burgesses to discourage gambling, swearing, and excessive drinking in their home counties, both governors declared that gambling especially had been generally practiced "among the lower class of our people." By lower or lowest classes, both men said that they meant "tradesmen and inferior planters, who in all countries are apt to follow the examples of their superiors." [117]

Tradesmen and inferior planters might well have been the lowest class among Virginia whites, but this fact merely complicates an analysis of class structure. If they were the lowest class, they were also property owners, some of land, some of slaves, and some of both. And the records seem to indicate that one of their aims in life was to accumulate more land and slaves. If the more prosperous tradesmen and planters were middle-class and the inferior tradesmen and planters lower-class, was the difference between them only the amount of property they held? If so, at what point did they cease to be lower-class and become middle-class?

St. George Tucker considered overseers to be the only dependent class of free white men in the tidewater area, but there is even some doubt about this. What would be the status of William Taylor, an overseer-blacksmith for Robert Carter, who received £269.8.10 for his share of the crops for three years (1768-1770) and £11.10.4 for twenty-five days' work as a blacksmith?[118] What about William Graves, who received £100 a year from the Burwells of Carters Grove, who bought a slave from Burwell for £70, and who had a cash balance of £232 due in 1768? [119]

A further complication in the class status of overseers is the fact that many of them owned land as well as slaves or servants. For example, the Lancaster County tithable list of 1745 shows that John Brown, Charles

Smith, and James Bush all worked for someone else but paid tithes for a servant each. Several others, whose own tithes were paid by other men, owned slaves—Thomas Gresset (two slaves), William Kelly (two slaves), Alexander Matson (three slaves), and John Parish (one slave).[120] In Amelia County, overseer Thomas Bevill had two slaves, and William Cassel, an overseer for Robert Bolling, had an overseer and six slaves of his own.[121] When Washington was trying to get possession of property that he bought from William Black, he allowed James Hill, an overseer, to buy Black's stock as well as Black's Negro miller and wife.[122] And John Billingsby, overseer for Colonel Thomas Jones for some fifteen years, left his wife a lease on 100 acres of land, eight slaves valued at £155, and a total personal estate of £223.16.6.[123] Examples of overseers who owned land or slaves or both can be found on almost any tithable list for any county, a fact which would certainly raise questions about the social status of overseers.

Furthermore, although a man might appear on the tax lists as an overseer, he was not always a poor man who had to work for other people. When Washington was looking for someone to manage the Custis estate, several overseers were recommended to him. Gentlemen Bernard Moore and Edmund Pendleton recommended Pendleton's brother John, referred to as a "young gentleman." Others recommended John Hopkins, a good judge of plantation affairs and a man with a small independent fortune of his own, or John Hill, who possessed "a pritty estate" which he improved fast. In contrast, James Hockaday was honest and industrious, but he only looked after a small plantation of his own.[124] And Richard Henry Lee planned to hire the son of Colonel Fontleroy [or Fantleroy] of Naylor's Hole as an overseer of industry, skill, and honesty.[125] In short, we would not get an accurate picture of Virginia social structure if we were to assume that a man who appears as an overseer was necessarily of the lowest class.

The class status and social aspirations of an overseer are particularly evident in John Beale, overseer for Landon Carter. Beale, who had been asking £20 a year, did so well with Carter that he actually received £50 as his yearly share. When Carter later visited his plantation and dined with Beale, he noted that his overseer lived well and that Mrs. Beale acted "the part of a fine lady" with her dress and "at least two maids besides her own girl to get the dinner & wait upon her." Carter supposed that she did this to show her respect, but he would "rather have seen the diligent industrious woman" instead of the "fine lady." [126]

An overseer's dependence on and deference toward his employer might well have been determined by his individual disposition or by other opportunities. Richard Henry Lee informed his brother William that William's overseer Edwards had resigned because he had "met with an offer that he prefers to yours." [127] Landon Carter often had trouble with his overseer John Beale, who threatened to leave Carter's employment and who, according to Carter, "like a true Beale . . . was too great to submit" to Carter's terms.[128] Carter, who discharged one overseer and had another quit as a result, accused both men of cheating him and declared that he could not see how an overseer could otherwise have acquired "the estate in land & Negroes which he has got." Carter also referred to John Northen, overseer for John Tayloe, as "a fellow of such a surly disposition that I am persuaded he would shoot his own father," [129] which hardly sounds deferential.

Although we do not have statistics to substantiate this statement, our general impression from the records is that many overseers were young men who were serving what amounted to an apprenticeship as plantation managers. Many of them were undoubtedly sons of men who owned land and slaves, and certainly many of them expected to own land and slaves of their own at some future date.

In addition to free whites, two other groups of bonded whites—apprentices and indentured servants—have often been considered among the lower classes. Since they were either learning a skilled trade or working under contract for a specified number of years at a specified wage or to pay their passage to the colony, it would be quite natural to assume that they were among the poorer people. So we shall want to know who they were, what their status in society was, how they were treated in law and in practice, and particularly their opportunities for getting ahead in the world once they had completed their term of service.

It is often difficult to tell from the records whether a man or boy was an overseer, stepson, journeyman-tradesman, apprentice, or indentured servant. The master or employer usually paid the tithes on the above categories of persons or workers without any clear distinction as to their status, and other records that might give us this information have disappeared. The tithable lists show that many a person whose tithes were paid by someone else, and who might therefore be considered an apprentice or servant, had the same name and was probably the son of some man in the community who owned both land and slaves. While we have tried to distinguish between the apprentices and servants in the following pages, such a distinction is not always possible and some of our information may well include overseers, journeymen, and stepsons.

Apprenticeships served several purposes in colonial society. They were a method by which boys or men could learn a practical trade to earn a living. Sometimes this training came after a boy had completed his formal education at the age of fourteen or fifteen years. For poor people, however, the apprenticeship might also be the means of acquiring a measure of formal education, as contracts often required the master to teach the apprentice reading, writing, and casting accounts. And orphans, as well as the poor, could be apprenticed by county officials as a method of assuring that such people would not become public charges.

In Virginia the apprentice system was apparently much more favorable to the apprentice than it was in Europe. Instead of the master receiving a fee for training the apprentice, the scarcity of labor meant that the master usually paid the apprentice. As a minimum, the apprentice was taught a trade and reading and writing if he could not read and write already, and was given freedom dues of £3.10.0 at the end of his service.[130] Individual indentures show that he often received more than this minimum. For example, laborer Samuel Steele apprenticed himself to a joiner for three years and was to receive £3 a year and training in the trade.[131] Sometimes the terms included clothing, food, lodging, laundry, some education, and at the end of service, a complete suit of clothing, a complete set of tradesmen's tools, or both.[132] Landon Carter took an apprentice for five years to learn the business of a plantation steward with the stipulation that the boy, aged fifteen, was to receive £10 a year for his last two years.[133]

While we are prone to think of apprenticeship as an institution for the lower classes, it was, in fact, an accepted part of the educational system for all classes. James Maury, in explaining that there were few rich men in Virginia and that most men had to engage in some business, said that many boys finished their formal education at the age of fourteen or fifteen, and were then placed under some eminent man of business. Yet "gentlemen of this sort" were "frequently called to the highest posts of honor & trust," he said.[134] William Lee, the son of the late Thomas Lee, gentleman of Lancaster, apprenticed himself to a carpenter.[135] The Reverend James Maury apprenticed his son to a Mr. Jackson, "a very worthy friend." [136] Samuel McCoy, who left his plantation to his son Caleb, apprenticed Caleb to his friend Samuel Happer.[137] And William Bradley, Norfolk merchant, willed that after his son had completed his education in Latin, French, and mathematics at age seventeen, he was to be bound out to some business.[138] So the fact that a man had served an apprenticeship did not necessarily mean that he was poor or lower-class.

Ample opportunity meant that an apprentice did not have to remain among the propertyless lower classes after the expiration of his service. James Baker of Norfolk, apprenticed to a shipcarpenter for three and a half years in 1760, bought fifty acres and buildings with a friend for £25 in 1765, had acquired four slaves by 1771, and bought property in Norfolk for £178 in 1772.[139] Caleb Manning of Portsmouth, apprentice blacksmith from 1765 to 1770, had an apprentice, a wife, and a house and lot worth £30 by 1772.[140] Robert Beverley claimed that apprenticed poor orphans, who tried to improve themselves, "generally get well married, and live in plenty, though they had not a farthing of paternal estate." [141] Orphan John Flowers, apprentice joiner from 1768 to 1775, had two tithable slaves by 1779 and four by 1781.[142] And James Newby, one of six children of an illiterate planter who lived on a 75-acre farm, inherited one shilling in 1742, leased land and became a voter by 1758, inherited the land where his mother lived in 1762, became deputy sheriff in 1764, lieutenant of the militia in 1767, owned 322 acres in the county in 1773 and three tithable slaves in 1775.[143]

An apprentice who had finished his term did not necessarily feel that he must show deference to his former master. Landon Carter had continual trouble with William Beale, who was bound to Carter at the age of eighteen for three years as a steward. Beale stayed as a steward after his term, but by 1775 he and Carter were in sharp conflict. Carter, who called Beale "Mr. Violent," complained of Beale's vanity and temper, and finally decided to discharge him for being obstinate and refusing "to follow any orders but his own proud inclination." Actually, the two patched up their differences, but Beale was certainly not deferential.[144]

It would also appear that indentured servants had a much better chance in this country than in Europe of improving their class status. They always received £3.10.0 in termination pay, which would have allowed them a start as a tenant on some land, and often they received much more than this. William Porteus of Culpeper, for example, was to get £20 at the end of his service.[145] John Tait wanted an indentured blacksmith for four or five years at £10 a year and keep,[146] and Robert Beverley was willing to go as high as £30 a year for a servant who was a joiner.[147] Men could and did voluntarily extend their term of service in exchange for instruction in a trade,[148] evidence that they were not too unhappy as servants, and once they had learned a trade, there were many opportunities for them.

Whatever we might think of the class aspects of indentured servitude, contemporaries were fairly well agreed that the system was beneficial to the servant himself. John Harrower, though well educated, could not get any kind of work in England, even "for the bare support of life." He said that "all places here [England] at present are entirely carried by friends and interest, and many hundreds are starving for want of employment, and many good people are begging." No one ever reported such conditions in the colonies. Down to his last shilling, Harrower had to engage as a tutor in Virginia, but once there he was happy with his condition and soon planned to send for his wife and children.[149] One man, who witnessed the sale in Virginia of a group of dirty, half-naked, and almost starved servants who had been treated no better than slaves, remarked: "I must say this if these pore divels behave wall it's as fine country as I ever was in in my life and the pepel in gernral are a very good sort of pepel and as fine climmet for halth." [150] And minister James Maury, in favoring a scheme to import servants, said it would be equally advantageous to the servants and to Virginia.[151]

Although many indentured servants moved to other areas than the one where they served their indenture and are therefore difficult to trace, we do have evidence that servants who were ambitious could prosper in Virginia. James Robb, an indentured carpenter for Robert Carter in 1733, had an indentured servant of his own by 1736. In 1739, Robb petitioned the county court to change a road running through "his plantation." In 1740, he took an apprentice and another in 1742. By 1745, Robb had three servants and three taxable slaves, and when he died in 1747 his estate included the three slaves and over £250 in personal property. The

1750 rental indicates that Robb's plantation was 130 acres, and the 1741 election poll shows that he was a voter.[152] David Currie, listed as a servant for one Mr. James on the Lancaster County tithable list for 1746, later served as Anglican minister in Lancaster for at least eighteen years, was a voter, and by 1755 had three servants, sixteen tithable slaves, and two two-wheel carriages.[153] John Frazer, who spent five years of servitude at the rope walk in Fredericksburg, became one of the owners of the establishment at the end of his servitude.[154] And one Price, an indentured servant for the company in which John Hook was involved, married the daughter of a Colonel Callaway before his indenture had expired.[155]

The career of servant James Donnellane illustrates the ample economic opportunity for indentured servants who would take advantage of it. Donnellane, a servant of Christopher Kirk in Lancaster, ran away in 1732, was gone fourteen days, and had to serve eleven months and twenty-eight days extra for his escapade. By 1737, he was apparently on his own, for he collected by court action a debt of 265 pounds of tobacco and costs against Peter Riviere, Jr.[156] In 1742 he was listed as a weaver, bought 125 acres of land for 9,000 pounds of tobacco, and imported a servant of his own.[157] He had a wife, Margaret, by 1744, at which time he sold fifty acres and a house for 3,500 pounds of tobacco and a pistole. A few days later he bought 225 acres for 14,000 pounds of tobacco.[158] On the 1745 tithables he was listed for two taxable slaves, the rental of 1748 shows that he owned 200 acres, and he voted in the 1741 election.[159] This, of course, was in the old tidewater county of Lancaster, not out on the frontier where land was cheap.

Many convict servants were quite obviously in the lower class and appeared to be determined to remain as they were. Sold for seven years instead of the usual four or five for regular servants, the convicts often caused colonists a great deal of trouble and expense.[160] They burned the homes of their masters or of officials who crossed them; they ran away, often to England, where they committed other crimes and were again transported; and one was even accused of running off with his master's wife.[161]

For those convicts who were honest and desired to work, however, Virginia certainly offered a better opportunity to rise in the world than did England. Hugh Jones, who declared that few convicts had ever lived so well as they did here, said those who desired could serve their time with ease and satisfaction to themselves and their masters. When they were free, those who wanted to make good at an occupation other than crime could work at day labor, rent a small plantation for a trifle, become overseers, or follow their trade. "The plenty of the country, and the good wages given to work-folks occasion very few poor," Jones concluded.[162] Even surveyor of the customs William Eddis, who condemned servitude bitterly, contradicted himself by saying that convicts could prosper in America if they desired. If they were honest and industrious, convicts could move to a community where they were unknown and "pursue with credit every possible method of becoming useful members of society." [163]

## D: WOMEN

Although our concern in this study is not primarily with the women of colonial Virginia, some discussion of the status of women, slight though it may be, is essential, for the status of women is often a measure of the class structure of a society.

A woman in the Old Dominion possessed both disadvantages and advantages. Unable to vote and not otherwise equal to men before the law, she could still retain possession of her own property if she desired when she married, she was assured a third of the estate when the husband died, and he could not sell his property without her consent.[164] Furthermore, many women conducted their own businesses, often those concerning other women, or managed their husbands' businesses after the husband had died. One woman, Clementina Rind, received the overwhelming vote of the House of Burgesses to succeed her deceased husband as public printer of Virginia.[165]

Then as now, women did not usually receive the same wages as men. James Galt was paid £100 a year as keeper of the hospital for the insane, but his wife got only £25 as matron.[166] Washington paid Mary Wilson, a housekeeper, 15s. a month, or £9 a year.[167] Yet if a woman had extraordinary skill at some trade, she could command a salary comparable to that of a man. Thomas Randolph was to get a male weaver to instruct weavers for Mrs. Randolph, but instead he sent her a woman. The woman was to get £30 a year if she managed the weavers and spinners, but £40 if she just wove cloth herself.[168]

Colonial attitudes toward women probably varied greatly from individual to individual. Landon Carter had little admiration for women in general. He believed that women had "nothing in the general view, but the heady contest at home. It began with poor Eve & ever since then has been so much of the devil in women." [169] On the other hand, both House and Council were willing to grant women more rights than was the Privy Council in England. In one case, the husband of Francis Greenhill had left her and never returned, and by law she could not sell her property as long as he was alive or not known to be dead. A law allowing her to dispose of her estate regardless passed the House and Council but was disallowed in England.[170]

Poems in newspapers and almanacs indicate that women's problems have not changed essentially from that day to this—but the problems were not one of class.

> Custom, alas! doth partial prove,
>   Nor gives us equal measure;
> A pain for us it is to love,
>   But is to man a pleasure.

> They plainly can their thoughts disclose,
>   Whilst ours must burn within:
> We have got tongues, and eyes, in vain
>   And truth from us is sin.
>
> Men to new joys and conquests fly,
>   And yet no hazard run:
> Poor we are left, if we deny,
>   And if we yield, undone.
>
> Then equal laws, let custom find,
>   And neither sex oppress;
> More freedom give to womankind
>   Or give to mankind less.[171]

Other records confirm the problems of womankind as expressed in this poem, but we have seen little evidence of widespread demands for equal rights.

In spite of restrictions, women could lead a full life if they so desired, as the following example illustrates. In a contest over the property of one William Spiller, an alcoholic, witnesses testified that Spiller intended to die without a will so the law would dispose of his estate, for he would have nothing to do with the slaves his wife had acquired while she lived apart from him, as they had come by "the Devil" and could go the same way. These slaves were believed to have been given her by one John Edge and one Lakehorn, with whom she had lived while separated from her husband. She had also lived with a John Walker and a Moses Jeffries. While living with Walker, she became pregnant by Jeffries; there were several fights between the two, and finally Jeffries drove Walker away. Witnesses also testified that Spiller drank as much as a gallon of rum in three days and was never sober enough to make a will. Spiller said he could not explain the influence that his wife had over him, for she could prevail on him to do whatever she wanted. Mrs. Spiller also confided in another witness that whether Spiller was drunk or sober, she could influence him in any way she pleased by hugging and kissing him. After Spiller died, Mrs. Spiller married Moses Jeffries, who had been her overseer for many years. In a society where gifts of slaves replaced mink coats, Mrs. Spiller obviously led an interesting life without hindrance from either law or custom.[172]

Judging by contemporary accounts and other records, white society in Virginia can be divided roughly into three classes—upper, middle, and lower—but the lines of demarcation between them are difficult indeed to establish. The differences were more a matter of degree than of kind. It was not a society in which some men had all the property and education and most men had none, but one in which some men had more of both items than did others. And because it was a matter of degree rather than kind, class differences were not apt to be sharp, for men aspired to join the ranks of those above them. Social mobility, apparent both to contemporary observers and in the local records, was the great mollifier of class differences.

Presumably class conflict can be effective only if people recognize that they belong to a particular class which has interests diametrically opposed to those of another class, and this situation does not appear to have prevailed in colonial Virginia. Psychologically, men whose economic possessions might have qualified them as lower class did not always identify themselves with this class in their thought and actions and the persistent tendency of the lower orders to imitate and respect those above them moderated the significance of class conflict in the colony.

## NOTES

1. Terms such as "ruling aristocracy," "ruling classes," "landed gentry," and "planter aristocracy" are frequently used to describe the leaders of eighteenth-century Virginia. See for example Louis B. Wright, *The First Gentlemen of Virginia*, pp. 2-3, 38-39, 49; Richard L. Morton, *Colonial Virginia,* I, 168; Carl Bridenbaugh, *Seat of Empire*, new ed. (New York, 1958), p. 8 and *passim*; Charles S. Sydnor, *Gentlemen Freeholders* (Chapel Hill, 1952), pp. 60, 77, 78; W. E. Woodward, *George Washington* . . . (Garden City, N.J., 1926 [1942 ed.]), pp. 21, 117-19; Clifford Dowdey, *The Great Plantation* (New York and Toronto, 1957), p. 7; John Cooke, *Virginia: A History of the People* (Boston, 1883), pp. 365-68, 378; Isaac Samuel Harrell, *Loyalism in Virginia*, p. 182; John C. Miller, *Origins of the American Revolution* (Stanford, Calif., 1943 [1959 revised reprint]), pp. 55-57; Thomas P. Abernethy, *Western Lands and the American Revolution* (New York, 1959), p. 158; H. J. Eckenrode, *The Randolphs* (Indianapolis & N. Y., 1946), p. 56, and *Separation of Church and State in Virginia* (Richmond, 1910), p. 34; John Alden, *The South in the Revolution, 1763-1789* (Baton Rouge, La., 1957), pp. 26-37; Jackson T. Main, "Sections and Politics in Virginia, 1781-1787," in *William and Mary Quarterly*, 3rd ser., XII (1955), pp. 97-98. For more modified views see John Fiske, *Old Virginia and Her Neighbors*, II, pp. 203-04; T. Harry Williams, Richard N. Current, Frank Freidel, *A History of the United States*, 2 vols. (New York, 1959), I, 72-73; Thomas Jefferson Wertenbaker, *The Planters of Colonial Virginia* (written in 1922), in *The Shaping of Colonial Virginia* (New York, 1958), pp. 159-61.
2. Thomas Anburey, *Travels through the Interior Parts of America; in a Series of Letters, By an Officer*, new ed., 2 vols. (London, 1791), II, 329-33; Smyth, *Tour*, I, 23, 41-43, 65-68, 329-30.
3. *Ibid.*
4. *Ibid.*, p. 356.
5. Edmund Randolph, History of Virginia, Section II on the Revolution, p. 1, VHS.
6. Aspinwall Papers, Massachusetts Historical Society *Collections*, 4 ser., X, 796, 798. Aug. 20, 1780.
7. St. George Tucker to his sons, June 12, 1787, St. George Tucker Papers, William and Mary College Library.
8. Quoted in Tyler, "Society in Caste Virginia," *William and Mary Quarterly*, 1st ser., XXII, 221-28 (April, 1914). See also Cooke, *Virginia*, pp. 368-369.

9. Hugh Jones, *The Present State of Virginia* . . . , ed. by Richard L. Morton (Chapel Hill, 1956), p. 93.

10. Hening, *Statutes,* VII, 76; *House Journals, passim.*

11. *Virginia Gazette* (P & D), March 30, 1769.

12. *The Virginia Almanack for the year of our Lord God 1762,* by Theophilus Wreg (Williamsburg, 1762), on film at Alderman Library, U. of Va.

13. Jonathan Boucher, *A View of the Causes and Consequences of the American Revolution* (London, 1791), p. 233.

14. To Robert Jackson, July 1762, Maury Papers.

15. John Warden to Thomas Jones, Dec. 24, 1771, Papers of the Jones Family of Northumberland County, Virginia, 1649-1889, bound in 35 vols., Library of Congress. Hereafter cited as Jones Family Papers.

16. Landon Carter Diary, March 16 and Aug. 8, 1770.

17. John Harrower Diary, Feb. 21, March 20, April 8, Oct. 12, and Oct. 21, 1775.

18. Lancaster County Deed Book 16, p. 211.

19. Philip Vickers Fithian, *Journal and Letters of Philip Vickers Fithian, 1773-1774: A Plantation Tutor of the Old Dominion,* ed. by Hunter Dickinson Farish (Williamsburg, Va., 1943), p. 99.

20. *Ibid.,* pp. 209-13.

21. *Ibid.,* p. 197.

22. Robert Carter Inventory, 1733, Carter Papers, VHS.

23. Fithian, *Journal,* pp. 106-07.

24. To Jonathan Boucher, May 30, 1768, May 13 and June 2, 1770, and to Benedict Calvert, April 3, 1773, Washington, *Writings,* III, 14-15, 131.

25. Appraisal of Philip Ludwell's Estate, 1770, and indenture Nov. 5, 1770, Lee-Ludwell Papers, VHS.

26. R. H. Lee to William Lee, July 7, 1770, *Letters of Richard Henry Lee,* I, 46-48.

27. Fithian, *Journal,* p. 101.

28. Gooch to Lords of Trade, Dec. 21, 1744, Gooch Papers, III, 791.

29. March 26, 1748, Washington, *Diaries,* I, 8.

30. To Robert Cary, July 25, 1769, Washington, *Writings,* II, 513.

31. Prince William County Deed Book C, pp. 81-83, 88-89.

32. Halifax County Deed Book 4, pp. 301-02; Book 5, p. 223; Halifax County Will Book O, p. 214. Inventory Dec. 18, 1766.

33. Account of quitrents due from the executors of Philip Grymes, Esquire, 1763, PRO, CO5, v. 1330, p. 367.

34. Hening, *Statutes,* V, 285-87.

35. *Virginia Gazette* (R), June 30, 1768.

36. Hening, *Statutes,* VIII, 436. For additional examples of gentlemen in debt, see chapter on debtors.

37. Aug. 1, 1748, Elizabeth Barbour Ambler Collection, Alderman Library, U. of Va.

38. Lancaster County Deed Book 13, pp. 54, 135, 186, 242, 253, 256, 305; Book 14, pp. 129, 135.

39. *Ibid.,* Book 19, pp. 45, 177; Book 20, pp. 239, 250-53. See also Accomack County Deeds, 1737-46, pp. 344, 390-91, 438; Orange County Deed Book 9, p. 48.

40. Maury to Robert Jackson, July 1762, Maury Papers.

41. Beverley, *History,* pp. 291-92.

42. Jones, *Present State of Virginia,* p. 74.

43. Richmond County Order Book 16, p. 445.

44. Hening, *Statutes,* VII, 423. March, 1761.

45. Norfolk County Deed Book 24, pp. 211-15.

46. Lancaster County Order Book 8, pp. 109, 112, 322; Lancaster County Will Book 15, p. 248; Book 20, pp. 100, 103; Lancaster County Deed Book

16, p. 49; Book 18, pp. 100, 130, 133-34; Lancaster County Rentals, 1748, 1750, 1773; Lancaster County Tithable List.

47. Prince William County Rentals, 1737, 1753, 1761, 1767, 1773; Prince William County Deed Books, *passim,* especially Book P, p. 194 and Book R, p. 338; William Lee Letterbook, 1783-87, pp. 118, 138, VHS.

48. Richmond County Deed Book 11, pp. 36, 429; Book 12, p. 134.

49. Richmond County Rentals, 1744, 1746, 1751, 1765.

50. Richmond County Deed Book 12, p. 621.

51. Augusta County Deed Book 2, part I, pp. 250, 278, 359; Book 5, p. 22; Book 7, pp. 341, 343; Book 10, p. 89; Book 11, p. 615; Book 13, p. 70; Book 15, p. 171; Book 16, p. 409; Book 19, pp. 208-09.

52. To Bishop of London, Sept. 20, 1735, Gooch Papers, II, 408.

53. David John Mays, *Edmund Pendleton, 1721-1803. A Biography,* 2 vols. (Cambridge, Mass., 1952), I, 24 and *passim; House Journals,* lists of Burgesses.

54. Landon Carter Diary, May 25, 1774. See also the Lee family in C. F. Lee, Jr., and J. Packard, Jr., *Record of the Descendants of Colonel Richard Lee of Virginia* (Boston, 1882).

55. Norfolk County Will Book 1, pp. 11, 31; Norfolk County Deed Book 13, pp. 154, 156, 158, 188; Norfolk County Tithables, 1771.

56. Reverend Robert Rose Diary, 1747-1751, March 16, 1748/9, Colonial Williamsburg.

57. *Virginia Gazette,* July 23, 1767.

58. Nov. 23, 1749, *Acts of the Privy Council,* IV, 94.

59. Robert Carter to Colonel Page, Feb. 11, 1728/9, Robert Carter Letter Book, Carter Papers, VHS.

60. Feb. 15, 1767, Washington, *Writings,* II, 444-53; Washington, *Diaries,* II, 95.

61. Lancaster County Deed Book 14, p. 286 and *passim.*

62. *Virginia Gazette* (R), June 29, 1769.

63. Extracts of a letter from Mrs. Harriet Huckley, May 13, 1856, Hugh Blair Grigsby Papers, VHS.

64. *Virginia Gazette* (P & D), Nov. 25, 1773; *ibid.,* (R), Nov. 25, 1773; *ibid.,* (P & D), Dec. 16, 1773 and Feb. 10, 1774.

65. To Dixon and Littledale, Aug. 9 and 31, Sept. 14, and Oct. 11, 1774, Harry Piper Letterbook, 1767-1775, Alderman Library, U. of Va.

66. *Virginia Gazette* (P & D), April 7, 1768.

67. To Lords of Trade, Dec. 6, 1760, PRO, CO5, v. 1330, p. 51.

68. Anburey, *Travels,* II, 328-29.

69. Fithian, *Journal,* p. 35.

70. *Virginia Gazette* (R), May 11, 1769.

71. Burnaby, *Travels,* pp. 33-34.

72. Fithian, *Journal,* p. 39; Boucher, *Reminiscences,* pp. 26-27.

73. Norfolk County Deed Book 25, p. 125; *Virginia Gazette* (P & D), Dec. 10, 1772; Norfolk Borough Tithables, 1771.

74. Peter to Moses Fontaine, March 30, 1757, Maury Papers.

75. Boucher, *Reminiscences,* pp. 26-27.

76. Burnaby, *Travels,* p. 150.

77. To John and Moses [Fontaine], April 15, 1754, Maury Papers.

78. To Moses Fontaine, March 30, 1757, *ibid.*

79. *Virginia Gazette,* Nov. 17, 1738.

80. Norfolk County Will Book 1, p. 183.

81. Lancaster County Deed Book 16, p. 178; Book 18, p. 75 and Orders in Book 18, p. 22; Lancaster County Will Book 20, pp. 116, 127, 157.

82. Spotsylvania County Deed Book F, p. 630.

83. Norfolk County Deed Book 13, p. 78; Book 14, p. 51; Book 15, pp. 33, 104; Book 17, p. 23; Book 18, pp. 213-14; Book 19, pp. 125, 292; Book

21, p. 139; Book 22, p. 43; Book 23, p. 156; Book 24, p. 259; Book 25, p. 269; Book 27, p. 2; Norfolk County Will Book 1, p. 1; Book 2, p. 103; Norfolk County Tithables, 1771.

84. Augusta County Deed Book 2, Pt. 1, pp. 250, 278, 359; Book 7, p. 341.

85. Prince William Deed Book B, Pt. 1, pp. 67, 70, 145, 149, 153, 332, 388, 442, 459; Book D, pp. 58, 167, 241; Book E, p. 524; Prince William County Rent Rolls, 1737, 1752, 1753, 1754, 1760; Prince William County Tithables, 1747.

86. April 3, 1775, *Letters to Washington,* V, 146-48.

87. Loudoun County Deed Book B, p. 346; Book C, p. 66.

88. *Ibid.,* Book A, pp. 229, 338. For other typical examples, see *ibid.,* Book D, pp. 461, 463; *Virginia Gazette* (R), July 8, 1773 (Thomas Allen); Norfolk County Deed Book 19, p. 82; Book 21, p. 137; Norfolk Tithables, 1771 (John Grimes).

89. *Virginia Gazette* (R), July 8, 1773. For other slaveowning tenants, see Washington, *Diaries,* II, 53, (1772); Richard Henry to William Lee, March 2, 1774, *Letters of Richard Henry Lee,* I, 103; July 27, 1774, William Cabell Diaries, 1751-1825, VSL.

90. Appraisal of Philip Ludwell's estate, Lee-Ludwell Papers.

91. Washington, *Diaries,* I, 127, 166-67n.

92. King George County Rental, 1773.

93. Lancaster County Rental, 1773.

94. Lancaster County Deed Book 12, p. 1; Book 14, pp. 169, 272; Book 16, pp. 49, 200; Richmond County Deed Book 10, p. 325.

95. Prince William County Deed Books P, Q, R, *passim;* Prince William County Rentals, 1760, 1768, 1773.

96. Loudoun County Deed Book A, pp. 59, 503; Book B, p. 11; Book C, pp. 278, 350, 512, 554, 559, 635; Book D, p. 650.

97. Beverley, *History,* p. 275.

98. Jones, *Present State of Virginia,* pp. 87-88.

99. *The Proceedings of the Convention of Delegates held at the Capitol, in the City of Williamsburg . . . May, 1776* (Richmond, 1816), p. 12.

100. Lancaster County Order Book 8, p. 313; Lancaster County Deed Book 13, pp. 321, 323-24.

101. Burnaby, *Travels,* p. 149, 1759.

102. Smyth, *Tour,* II, 190; Jones, *Present State of Virginia,* pp. 87-88.

103. "Thoughts concerning America by Mr. Hasenclever," Shelburne Papers.

104. Fairfax to Washington, March 2, 1775, *Letters to Washington,* V, 124.

105. Hening, *Statutes,* IV, 208-14; VI, 29-33; 475-78; *House Journals, 1752-58,* pp. 260, 279.

106. To Robert Cary and Company, Feb. 13, 1764, Washington, *Writings,* II, 413-14.

107. *Virginia Gazette* (P & D), July 23, 1773.

108. Peter Fontaine to Moses Fontaine, March 30, 1757, Maury Papers.

109. Muster Rolls, 1757-58, Washington Papers, VI, 710-12, 732-34, 760-61, 774-75; X, 12-13, 17-18, 22, 25, 29, 34.

110. *House Journals, 1752-58,* p. 374, April 21, 1756.

111. To Dinwiddie, Oct. 11, 1755, Oct. 10 and Nov. 9, 1756, July 11, 1757, Washington, *Writings,* I, 200-08, 479, 493-95; II, 93-94.

112. To Dinwiddie, July 11, 1757, *ibid.,* II, 93-94; to Col. John Stanwix, July 15, 1757, *ibid.,* p. 97.

113. Thomas Walker to Washington, June 30, 1756, *Letters to Washington,* I, 293; see also pp. 415, 444, 461, 465.

114. *House Journals, 1752-58,* pp. 319-20. Oct. 27, 1755.

115. *Virginia Gazette* (P & D), Jan. 12, 1769.

116. *Ibid.,* April 25, 1771.

117. *House Journals, 1752-58,* p. 100; *The Official Records of Robert Din-widdie, Lieutenant-Governor of the Colony of Virginia, 1751-1758 . . . ,* 2 vols., in *Collections of the Virginia Historical Society,* III and IV (Richmond, Va., 1883), I, 30. Hereafter cited as *Dinwiddie Papers.*

118. Receipts Jan. 9 and Nov. 30, 1771, Robert Carter Papers, 1705-1771, VHS.

119. Carter's Grove Account Book, 1764-1786, pp. 35, 68.

120. Lancaster County Tithable List, 1745.

121. Amelia County Tithables, 1742-43, 1762.

122. Washington to Black, Jan. 17, 1774, Washington, *Writings,* III, 179.

123. Will of Feb. 18, 1738, and inventory, Dec. 20, 1739, Jones Family Papers, IV.

124. *Letters to Washington,* IV, 87-89, 91-92, 95, 127. 1771.

125. To William Lee, June 28, 1773, *Letters of Richard Henry Lee,* I, 89.

126. Landon Carter Diary, Oct. 12, 1770 and Jan. 8, May 13, and Sept. 14, 1772.

127. *Letters of Richard Henry Lee,* I, 89. June 28, 1773.

128. Landon Carter Diary, Sept. 9, 1773.

129. *Virginia Gazette Supplement* (R), April 6, 1770; Landon Carter Diary, Aug. 8 and 29, and Oct. 27, 1770, Jan. 8, 1772, June 23, 1773.

130. Richmond County Deed Book 12, p. 114; William Cabell Diary, March 31, 1770.

131. Richmond County Deed Book 11, p. 72.

132. *Ibid.,* pp. 5, 18, 128, 373, 446; Book 12, p. 86.

133. Landon Carter Diary, Aug. 26, 1772.

134. Maury to Robert Jackson, July 1762, Maury Papers.

135. Lancaster County Deed Book 13, p. 66.

136. To Thornton, Walker, and Servis, Feb. 2, 1764, Maury Papers, Letterbook 1763.

137. Norfolk County Will Book 1, p. 132, March 21, 1765.

138. *Ibid.,* Book 2, p. 252, April 23, 1768.

139. Norfolk County Deed Book 19, p. 94; Book 22, p. 215; Book 25, p. 206; Norfolk County Tithables, 1771.

140. Norfolk County Deed Book 22, p. 144; Book 25, pp. 109, 230.

141. Beverley, *History,* p. 260.

142. Lancaster County Deed Book 18, p. 56; Lancaster County Tithables, 1775, 1779, 1781.

143. Lancaster County Deed Book 13, p. 265; Book 16, pp. 27-28; Book 18—orders, p. 17; Book 19, p. 204; Lancaster County Will Book 15, p. 194; Book 16, p. 181; Lancaster County Order Book 12, p. 77; Lancaster County Tithables, 1745, 1746, 1775; Lancaster County Rentals, 1773.

144. Indentured Servants, April 30, 1770, Sabine Hall Papers, Alderman Library, U. of Va.; Landon Carter Diary, July 20 and Sept. 23, 1775.

145. Orange County Deed Book 13, p. 77.

146. Tait to Archibald Crawford, June 26, 1756, Francis Jerdone Letterbook, Jerdone Papers.

147. To ?, c. 1765, Robert Beverley Letterbook.

148. Lancaster County Order Book 8, pp. 16, 34, 99.

149. John Harrower Diary, Jan. 24, 26, 31; Feb. 7; May 23, 26, 27; and June 14, 1774.

150. Barker to John Palmer, Dec. 16, 1758, Webb-Prentis Papers.

151. Maury to W (?), Aug. 13, 1765, Maury Papers, Letterbook, 1763.

152. Robert Carter Inventory, 1733, Carter Papers, VHS; Lancaster County Order Book 8, pp. 147, 231, 255, 335, 367; Lancaster County Deed Book 14, pp. 160-61, 195; Lancaster County Tithable List, 1745; Lancaster County Rental, 1750. Election poll for 1741 is in Lancaster County Deed Book 13, pp. 249-50.

153. Lancaster County Tithables, 1746 and 1775, in Lancaster County Loose Papers, VSL; Lancaster County Deed Book 16, pp. 27-28, 222-23; Book 18, pp. 42-43, 133-34, 154; Book 19, pp. 58-59, 112-13.

154. John Frazer to James Hunter, Jr., Aug. 25, 1782, Hunter Collection.

155. John Hook to David Ross, March 10, 1774, John Hook Letterbook, 1772-74, VSL.

156. Lancaster County Order Book 8, pp. 66, 184.

157. Lancaster County Deed Book 13, p. 276; Lancaster County Order Book 8, p. 357.

158. Lancaster County Deed Book 14, pp. 40, 62.

159. Lancaster County Tithables, 1745; Lancaster County Rent Roll, 1748; Lancaster County Deed Book 13, pp. 249-50.

160. Beverley, *History*, p. 287; Jones, *Present State of Virginia*, pp. 210-12; Abbot Emerson Smith, *Colonists in Bondage* (Chapel Hill, 1947), p. 110; Hening, *Statutes*, V, 24-26, 94-96, 545; *House Journals, 1752-58*, pp. 20, 53; *ibid., 1758-61*, p. 95; *Acts of the Privy Council*, V, 163-64, 362-63; *Virginia Gazette* (R), Sept. 2, 1773; to Lords of Trade, Feb. 22, 1738/9, Gooch Papers, II, 521; PRO, CO5, v. 1324/5, p. 313; Washington, *Writings*, III, 195, 197. 1774.

161. Gooch to Lords of Trade, March 26, 1729, Gooch Papers, I, 95, VHS; *Virginia Gazette*, March 17, 1737, Dec. 14, 1769 and May 21, 1772; Harry Piper to Dixon and Littledale, June 15, 1772, Harry Piper Letter Book.

162. Jones, *Present State of Virginia*, pp. 87-88.

163. Eddis, *Letters*, pp. 63-67.

164. Hening, *Statutes*, III, 371-76; Prince William County Deeds and Court Orders, *passim*.

165. *Virginia Gazette*, Oct. 13, 1738, June 20, 1745, April 4, 1751, and Feb. 19, 1767; Prince William County Deed Book R, pp. 228-30 (1770); *House Journals, 1773-76*, pp. 124-25.

166. *Ibid., 1773-76*, p. 269. 1775.

167. Washington, *Diaries*, I, 303. 1768.

168. Thomas Randolph to his wife, Nov. 16, 1776, Tucker Papers.

169. Landon Carter Diary, Aug. 12, 1772.

170. Order in Council, July 23, 1746, PRO, CO5, v. 1326, pp. 273-74.

171. *Virginia Gazette*, Oct. 22, 1736.

172. Prince William County Deed Book P, pp. 74-80. 1761.

# CHAPTER III

# The Impact of Slavery on White Society

No ACCOUNT of the social structure of Colonial Virginia, and no discussion of democracy or aristocracy in the Old Dominion, would be complete without some understanding of the impact of slavery. Slavery, of course, ruled out the possibility of democracy as far as the Negro was concerned, so this aspect of the institution need not concern us. We must, however, consider contemporary thought about slavery, the institutions and practices resulting from slavery, the number and distribution of slaves, whether there were either sectional disputes or conflicts between slaveowners and non-slaveowners, and what effects the institution of slavery had on the pattern of aristocracy or democracy in white society.

Some contemporaries justified slavery on the ground that slave life was not very difficult in most instances and that slaves in general were in better circumstances than the poor of Europe. Hugh Jones, professor at William and Mary College, claimed that while some masters were "too cruel and negligent" in the care of their slaves, others, because of the profit involved, were "obliged to keep them well, and not overwork, starve, or famish them" and provided other inducements for those who were laborious, careful, and honest. Slave work, he claimed, was "not very laborious," the hardest being "the felling of trees and the like, to which kind of slavery (if it must be so called) our woodcutters in England are exposed; only with this difference, that the Negroes eat wholesomer bread and better pork with more plenty and ease; and when they are sick, their owners interest and purse are deeply engaged in their recovery, who likewise are obliged to take all the care imaginable of the children of their slaves for their own great profit; so that the Negroes, though they work moderately, yet live plentifully, have no families to provide for, no danger of beggary, no care for the morrow." Jones believed that the greatest hardship the Negro had was that he and his posterity were "not at their own liberty or disposal, but are the property of their owners." But when freed, he explained, they generally did not know how to provide well for themselves. In spite of these favorable views on slavery, however, Jones opposed the institution, believing it more prudent and charitable to maintain and employ the poor of Britain than great numbers of Africans.[1]

Minister Jonathan Boucher and Governor William Gooch had views similar to those of Jones, both emphasizing a comparison with English or European laborers, not with the status of white Americans. Boucher said that many things respecting slaves were wrong, but the same could be said for workers in Britain and Europe. Slavery was neither the most intolerable of evils for the slave nor the most desirable situation for the owners. Boucher advocated abolition of slavery, not because it was wrong, but because Virginia and Maryland, both endowed with superior natural resources, were far behind most other colonies in development as a result of slavery.[2] Echoing Boucher's sentiments about the well-being of Negroes compared with the poor of England, Governor Gooch expressed the hope that a recent slave insurrection had taught the slaves to be content with their lot, for despite harsh treatment by some masters, most slaves lived "much better than our poor labouring Men in England."[3]

Opposed to these views, however, were those of the Reverend Andrew Burnaby, who saw little good in slavery or its influence on white society. Climate and other factors in Virginia made the people "indolent" and "much given to convivial pleasures." Their authority over their slaves rendered them vain and imperious, strangers to that elegance of sentiment so peculiarly characteristic of refined and polished nations. Ignorance, he said, resulted in prejudices, especially toward Indians and Negroes, whom Virginians "scarcely consider as of the human species." As a result, it was impossible even in case of murder of Negroes by whites to bring the whites to justice, for either the grand jury refused to indict, or the petit jury refused to convict. Not only was slavery a cause of weakness, he maintained, but the condition of the slaves was "truly pitiable; their labour excessively hard, their diet poor and scanty, their treatment cruel and oppresive [sic]: they cannot therefore but be a subject of terror to those who so inhumanly tyrannize over them."[4]

Thomas Jefferson was another Virginian who deplored the institution of slavery and its injurious impact on the whites. What Jefferson believed before the American Revolution we do not know, but we are certain that he sold or hired out his slaves when practical affairs dictated and advertised for runaway slaves just as other masters did. By 1783, however, Jefferson was convinced that slavery was evil and that its effect on the country was harmful. Calling slavery a "great political and moral evil," he declared that the relations between master and slave involved "the most boisterous passions, the most unremitting despotism on one part, and degrading submissions on the other. Our children see this and learn to imitate it. . . . Indeed I tremble for my country when I reflect that God is just: that his justice cannot sleep forever. . . ." Slavery bred laziness in the whites, to trample half of society was unjust, and, he warned, some day the tables might be turned with black ruling white.[5]

Actually, Jefferson was a mild white supremacist who wanted the slaves freed but transported out of the country. He feared that deep-rooted prejudices of whites and recollections by Negroes of ill-treatment by whites would result in convulsions if the two races were mixed. In memory, Negroes were equal to whites, he said, but they were "much inferior" in reason and "dull, tasteless, and anomalous" in imagination. Noting that great caution should be used in any conclusions about racial abilities, Jefferson advanced "as a suspicion only, that blacks . . . are inferior to the whites in the endowments both of mind and body," but he still insisted that freed slaves should be removed beyond the reach of mixture.[6]

For some men, slavery presented a sharp conflict between principles and interests, and while a few managed to abide by their principles, others found a satisfactory compromise between the two. In 1765, Arthur Lee decided to remain in England because of his "extreme aversion" both to slavery and the Negroes and his belief that the colonies must be dependent for a long time.[7] Robert Beverley also expressed "an aversion to Slavery" on his arrival from England, called slavery "contradictory to Humanity," felt shame for his country because of it, and said that if he ever left Virginia it would be for that cause alone. But within a few years Beverley married and became, as he said, tolerably happy in spite of slavery.[8] It was Peter Fontaine, however, who expressed the real conflict in those who felt scruples about the institution but still owned slaves: slavery was evil, but with the price of white labor so high, one must either have slaves or tend the hoe himself, so one had slaves.[9]

Descriptions of slave life by contemporaries reveal that comforts for slaves were few. On the eighty-six acre plantation of one David Curle of Elizabeth City County, the Negroes lived "in a Pen made of Poles and covered with Pine-Brush, and in bad weather retire to the Neighbours for Shelter." That such slave quarters were not unusual in outlying plantations is attested by the inventories of estates to be found in the deeds and wills. The home plantation was often well-stocked with the comforts of life, but as often as not there would be only tools and cattle but no furniture listed for the more remote quarters.[10]

In his travels, J. F. D. Smyth also found slave life not something to envy. As was the custom, he stopped for the night at the nearest "plantation," a cleared spot of some fifty acres cultivated by a young overseer and five or six slaves. It was a "wretched place . . . miserable indeed"— a one-room board structure with two doors and a glassless window, standing off the ground on blocks and swarming with fleas because of the hogs under it. Water was bad and half a mile away, neighbors were five miles distant on one side and eight miles on the other, and the only furniture was a thin chaff bed raised somewhat from the floor which served the overseer as chair, table, and couch. Smyth, who occupied the bed while the overseer slept on the floor with the Negroes, was kept awake half the night by the slaves who sang as they shelled corn by hand, and then "the disagreeable idea of such a parcel of nasty black devils, all snoring in the same room" with him, plus numerous mosquitoes, kept him awake the rest of the night.[11]

There was no doubt in Smyth's mind that the life of a slave left something to be desired, and if there was little deference among whites toward each other, there was certainly deference in Negro-white relationships. Slaves were all humility, he said, their greatest pleasure being to please the whites, and it was fortunate that they appeared content, for they led a hard life of severe labor, long hours of work, unkindness, meager food, and barbarity of treatment. Slaves of the rich fared worse than those of the poor because of their harsh overseers—"those unfeeling sons of barbarity"—but among either rich or poor there were very few kind masters. The slave's bed was a bench or the ground with a mere blanket and not always that. Female slaves fared the same, even when they bred, seldom losing a week's work because of childbirth. And finally, Smyth said, the slave's submission to injury or insult must be complete; he must not even try to defend himself.[12]

A similar account was given by tutor Philip Fithian even though his employer, Robert Carter, was generally considered "by far the most humane" to his slaves of anyone around. Fithian was disturbed about the meager food rations given to the slaves—a weekly allowance of only a peck of corn and one pound of meat. "Good God," asked Fithian, "are these Christians?" He was even more disturbed about slave treatment. Fithian heard the following explanation of how to assure obedience on the part of the slaves from an overseer of George Lee: "Take a Negro, strip him, tie him fast to a post; take then a sharp Curry-Comb, & curry him severely til he is well scrap'd; & call a Boy with some dry Hay, and make the Boy rub him down for several Minutes, then salt him, & unlose him. He will attend to his Business. . . ." The same overseer told how to extract a secret from a Negro. Lay on the floor a thick plank with a sharp hardwood peg on the upper side, strip the slave and suspend him from the ceiling by a cord so that "his foot may just rest on the sharpened Peg, then turn him briskly round, and you would laugh (said our informer) at the Dexterity of the Negro, while he was relieving his Feet on the sharpen'd Peg!" Fithian concluded: "I need say nothing of these seeing there is a righteous God, who will take vengeance on such Inventions!" [13]

Fithian also noted the servility, the deference, expressed in Negro-white relations. A slave of Carter's, he said, came in one evening to complain that his overseer had not given him the peck of corn a week to which he was entitled. "The humble posture in which the old Fellow placed himself before he began moved me. We were sitting in the passage, he sat himself down on the Floor clasp'd his Hands together, with his face directly to Mr *Carter*, & then began his Narration—He seem'd healthy, but very old, he was well dress'd but complained bitterly—I cannot like this thing of allowing them no meat, & only a Peck of Corn & a Pint of Salt a Week, & yet requiring of them hard & constant Service." Fithian noted that the Negroes were allowed small plots of ground on which they could grow potatoes, peas, and other food, but all such work for themselves must be done on Sunday as they were employed for their master during the week.[14]

Because he customarily allowed his feelings to spill out on paper, Landon Carter's diary furnishes an excellent account of white-slave relations. Carter believed that kindness to a Negro as reward for having done well was the surest way to spoil him. He denied rumors that his slaves were not adequately clothed for cold weather, for he said he allowed them one shirt and then forced them to buy linen and make a second shirt, using the money they received from the things they raised and sold. When a slave claimed to be sick but had no fever, Carter ordered him to go to work or expect a whipping. Irritated at his "suckling wenches" who told the overseers that Carter allowed them five hours a day for care of their children, Carter had them whipped and reduced their time for feeding their children to half an hour before they went to work, half an hour before breakfast, and half an hour before they went in at night. Negro women who tried to avoid work by claiming pregnancy met severe treatment. One pretended to be with child but "was a full 11 months before she was brot to bed [.] She has now the same pretence & thinks to pursue the same course but as I have full warning of her deceit if I live I will break her of that trick." Another one who refused to come out of her quarters ran away when Carter had a horse with traces brought to drag her out. She was caught and severely whipped, and had been a good slave ever since "only a cursed theif [sic] in making her Children milk my Cows in the night." Stealing, in Carter's eyes, was worse than running away, and when two slaves were caught killing a sheep, Carter ordered them taken up and tried. If one confessed, he said, that one would be cleared, but "one shall be hang'd to terrify the rest." [15]

Overseers, as Fithian and others noted, were often more severe toward slaves than were the masters, even though the overseers themselves were not of the upper class. After Landon Carter's account of how he handled his slaves, it is rather startling to realize that he considered overseers "too passionate" and warned one of them that if he could not be advised against barbarity he could go like the fool he was.[16] William Cabell refused to employ a certain overseer because he heard such shocking accounts of his cruelty to slaves and his baseness in other respects.[17] And one slaveowner cautioned his overseers to set a good example of industry and to care for the Negroes well, particularly the "Breeding Wenches" who were not to be forced to do anything injurious when with child.[18]

The reference to "breeding wenches" naturally raises the question of this practice in the colony and its influence on the whites. Marriage for slaves was never officially recognized. Fithian learned "that the slaves in this Colony never are married, their Lords thinking them improper Subjects for so Valuable an institution!" [19] Some owners, acting upon economic principles, bred their slaves like cattle. In the inventory of a deceased planter who owned eleven slaves, for instance, this item appeared: "Cash for Laying negro Wenches for Mr James Gordon Sen'r—£10.10.0." [20]

And one George Mercer, then in London, inquired of his brother if there were no profits yet from a slave named Ishmael. "I left some of his off-spring," he said, "and as I had taken care to procure him concubines sufficient, I expected his breed would have been ere now profitable." [21]

Although there was no legal marriage of slaves, there was often an unofficial union which sometimes led to difficulties. A Maryland debtor of George Washington owed Washington a slave, but the slave had a wife and children of whom he was very fond and often expressed the view that he would rather die than leave them. The debtor suggested that Washing-ton sell the slave to some close neighbor in Maryland to avoid trouble.[22] Landon Carter once fumed about his slave Timmy who claimed to be lame, a lameness due to very small shoes. "He could not walk nor stand but I found a way this day to make him do both and work pretty heartily. I have forbid him coming home to his wife at night and shall have him watch'd for they that cannot work for me cannot without great deceit walk 2 or 3 miles in the night." [23]

Miscegenation involving whites with Indians, Negroes, or mulattoes was prohibited by law, but of course the law was not always strictly obeyed. Peter Fontaine claimed that "many base wretches amongst us take up with Negroe women and many white women prostitute themselves to Negroe men by which means the country swarms with mulattoe bastards. . . ." If they were three generations removed from the black father or mother, Fontaine said, they could legally marry white people and actually did every day.[24] The mulatto child of a Negro mother presented no problem for it became a slave, but to discourage the union of white women and Negroes the legislature provided that the mulatto child of a white woman should be put out to servitude for thirty-one years. Eventually the term was reduced to service until the child reached legal age, the argument being that the former law was an "unreasonable severity towards such children." [25]

Instead of creating problems, the union of a white man and a Negro woman was sometimes considered merely a judicious mingling of business with pleasure. Thomas Anburey explained to a friend in England that he would be surprised to learn that the many mulattoes were due to "the planters having intercourse with their negroes." While at one Colonel Cole's, Anburey noticed "mulattoes of all tinges, from the first remove, to one almost white; there were some of them young women, who are really beautiful, being extremely well made, and with pretty delicate features; all of which, I was informed, were the colonel's own. I could not help reflecting, that if a man had an intercourse with his slaves, it was shameful in the extreme, to make his own offspring so; for these mulattoes work equally the same as those who come from Africa: to be sure, you may say, it is a pleasant method to procure slaves at a cheap rate." And Anburey added, there were twenty or thirty mulattoes of this description at Colonel Cole's, "notwithstanding he has a very agreeable and beautiful wife, by whome he has had eight children." [26] Unlike Colonel Cole, however, white men occasionally claimed slave women as their "wives" and attempted to procure the freedom of these wives and children.[27]

In the realm of religion, planters had mixed feelings about slave activities. Sometimes planters encouraged slaves to attend the master's church, but other masters feared that religion might have a deleterious effect. Ministers often talked of the number of conversions among the slaves in their congregations, while others suspected that church attendance and baptism would inspire pride and a desire for freedom among Negroes. Fithian recorded that Robert Carter and other slaveowners were not very pleased with the minister's sermon berating masters for their treatment of slaves.[28] There was also strong feeling among Church of England men that dissenters were having an alarming influence on Negroes.[29]

Naturally the slave was surrounded by numerous legal restrictions which reflected not only the status of the Negro but also the white man's fear of him. A slave who committed a capital offense was tried without jury before a county court, but, except for convict transports, whites whose crime involved loss of life or limb had to be tried by the General Court in Williamsburg before a jury from the county of the accused.[30] A slave received thirty lashes for lifting a hand against a white Christian, but an owner could kill a slave with impunity in process of correction. Slaves could not carry arms nor visit other plantations without permission, runaway slaves who refused to return after due proclamation could be killed, and if such a slave were killed or executed for a crime, the public compensated the owner. The extent of such cases can be found in the records of any meeting of the legislature. For example, there were forty-eight claims for slaves presented in the House from February 28 to March 30, 1752, and over 112 claims in the month following November 5, 1753.[31]

As the Revolution approached there was some mitigation in the severity of punishment for slaves, but a mitigation not approved by all slave owners. An act of 1769 prevented county courts from castrating a slave unless he had attempted to ravish a white woman. The act also acknowledged that sometimes the punishment for runaway slaves was disproportionate to the crime and "contrary to the principles of humanity." [32] And in 1772, an act provided that the death penalty could not be inflicted on a slave unless a majority of the court concurred.[33] "Such a court I am persuaded will never be got," wrote Landon Carter. "But I understand that public frugality occasioned this law that they might not have too many slaves to be paid for." Carter predicted that the law would not long remain.[34]

As this brief summary of legal regulations suggests, masters of slaves had little to fear from the law when disciplining their Negroes. Although generally if a slave was killed while being punished the master was not held liable, but in one unusual case an overseer was condemned to death for killing a slave. In this instance, the judges (the Council) earnestly solicited to have his life spared for they feared the overseer's execution would make slaves insolent and give them occasion to condemn their masters, a matter of dangerous consequence in Virginia, they believed, where slaves were so numerous.[35] There are records of two instances in which women, one the wife of a justice and the other the wife of a minister, had beaten slaves to death; in each case, in spite of the evidence, there was no conviction.[36]

Some of the conflict between master and slave is evident in the treatment of slaves who were jailed for serious crimes. Slaves confined during cold weather were not allowed a fire because they often tried to escape by burning the jail. They even cremated themselves rather than face the sure punishment that awaited them.[37] As a result, slaves were often frostbitten to the point of losing limbs or life itself.[38] One account told of a slave who had been whipped, had both ears and both legs cut off, and been castrated. Somehow he escaped, and on being captured he set fire to the jail and burned himself to death rather than return to his master.[39] Other slaves convicted of crimes or of running away dashed out their brains on rocks, or shot or hanged themselves.[40]

Not all slaves, of course, fared so badly as the runaways and those convicted of felonies. Some owners expressed real affection for their slaves, leaving them property and occasionally giving them their freedom. One James Wilson, who signed his will with a mark, gave nine of his slaves to relatives at the time of his death, but willed that his Negro man Afra and Nell his wife were to have the use of half his plantation for life, plus one cow and calf and ten hogs.[41] Another master freed his forty-year-old slave, a shoemaker, who probably took in outside work, for his fidelity, his honesty, and procuring for his master considerable money.[42] One doctor of Portsmouth left instructions in his will that eight of his slaves, including a mother and five of her children, were to be freed. He left it to his executors to determine whether it was best for the slaves to send them to England or Ireland, or to take out a license for freeing them in Virginia, or to send them with paper certificates of freedom to any of the other American provinces.[43] The executors did not always cooperate in such cases, however, and sometimes tried to sell the slaves.[44]

Given these facts, it would not be surprising to find that the whites lived in constant fear of reprisal by the slaves. One of the chief functions of the militia, in fact, was to guard against just such an eventuality. Governor Spotswood expressed both the fear of the whites and the purpose of the militia in the following plea for a stronger militia: "We cannot too cautiously conceal it [our weakness] from our neighbors and our slaves, nor too earnestly pray that neither the lust of dominion, nor the desire of freedom may stir those people to any attempts the latter sort (I mean our Negro's) by their dayly encrease [sic] seem to be the most dangerous; and the tryals of last *April* court may shew that we are not to depend on either their stupidity, or that babel of languages among 'em; freedom wears a cap which can without a tongue, call together all those who long to shake of [f] the fetters of slavery and as such an insurrection would surely be attended with most dreadful consequences so I think we cannot be too early in providing against it, both by putting our selves in a better posture of defense and by making a law to prevent the consultations of those Negroes." [45] Governor Gooch also said at one time that while Virginia had some 35,000 militia the men could not be sent very far away because of the slaves.[46] And with the coming of the Revolution, Landon Carter opposed the drafting of overseers because it would open the way to slave trouble—"an army if possible more bloody than those we are engaged with." [47]

Fear was constantly regenerated among slave owners by the many attempted slave insurrections throughout the eighteenth century. In 1710 in Surry County a negro insurrection was "happily Discovered when it was just upon the point of Execution" and the slave who revealed the plot was emancipated by an act of the Assembly. He was so detested by his fellow slaves, however, that he had to be moved to another section of the colony for safety.[48] Another major insurrection threat occurred in 1730 when many of the slaves in Norfolk and Princess Anne assembled on Sunday while people were in church and elected officers to command in their intended insurrection. The plot was detected, many were punished, and four ringleaders were executed. Some of the slaves claimed they had heard that the King had ordered their freedom as soon as they were Christians.[49] In 1767, a "mob of Negroes" caused alarm in Frederick County,[50] and in 1770 several people were killed in an insurrection of slaves on a plantation in Hanover County where the slaves had been treated with "too much lenity and indulgence" and had grown "extremely insolent and unruly." [51]

Such well-publicized insurrections caused restless nights for some slave-owners. At Robert Carter's Nomini Hall, Fithian told of great excitement one night when someone entered the girls' room, either to rob the house or to "commit fornication with Sukey, (a plump, sleek, likely Negro Girl about sixteen)." Carter announced at breakfast next morning that anyone caught in the house after the family was at rest would be hanged. And at a neighbor's one night, the wife of the master awakened to find several Negroes in the room, presumably to murder the master. She awakened her husband who ran for his gun, but his would-be assassins escaped. They were caught, and at the trial it developed that they had been hired to kill the master by his own brother, so they were whipped and dismissed. There is no record of what happened to the brother. Fithian said that the ill-treatment accorded slaves would almost justify them in any desperate attempt to gain "that Civility, & Plenty which tho' denied them, is here commonly bestowed on Horses!" Fithian himself now slept in fear, though his door and windows were locked.[52]

Whether from fear of the growing slave population or for economic reasons, Virginians did attempt on several occasions to prohibit the importation of additional slaves. Governor Spotswood believed in 1711 that a tax on imported slaves was due to the fact that the colony had more slaves than it could pay for at prevailing tobacco prices, but the importation of 4,200 Negroes from Guinea in 1752-53 indicates that exclusion was not too successful.[53] Because a simple diet and hard work made Negro women more fruitful than white women, Peter Fontaine feared the increase of slaves, "our intestine enemies," and hoped that Britain would one day consider the colonies as part of herself and stop the inundation of Virginia by slaves.[54] To Governor Fauquier, however, exclusion was purely an economic matter between old settlers, who bred great numbers of slaves and desired exclusion for monopolistic reasons, and a rising generation who desired slaves at cheap prices.[55]

Richard Henry Lee combined several motives in his arguments for excluding slaves—public benefit, fear, and moral principles. He looked upon importation as dangerous to both political and moral interests. Neighboring colonies that did not have slaves were more advanced than Virginia, and the reason, he said, was that "with their whites they import arts and agriculture, whilst we, with our blacks, exclude both." Slaves must necessarily be natural enemies to society and consequently dangerous, while their presence required cruel laws to subdue them. There were also moral issues involving religion, Lee continued, for Virginians who professed religion should practice its precepts, and by taxing imports of slaves, convince the world that they knew their true interests and paid a proper regard to the dictates of justice and humanity.[56]

These expressions of concern over the growing slave population naturally raise the question of the number of Negroes in Virginia and their distribution in the colony. Contemporary opinion and estimates from tax lists indicate that the slave population was sizeable. Both Peter Fontaine and Andrew Burnaby thought that Negroes were equal if not superior to whites in number.[57] Compilations from tithable lists give a total population of 84,000 whites and 60,000 blacks in 1730; 173,304 whites and 119,990 blacks in 1755; and in 1774, Lord Dunmore placed the population at 300,000 whites and 200,000 Negroes.[58]

Important as was the number of Negroes, even more significant from the standpoint of possible internal conflict was their distribution.[59] The common belief has been that the heaviest concentration of slaves was found in the tidewater, with gradual diminution westward through the piedmont to the mountains. Actually, as the map on page 73 shows so graphically, the greatest density of slaves existed in a strip of land which included both tidewater and piedmont counties, an area bounded roughly by the James and Rappahannock Rivers and extending from the ocean almost to the mountains.

Generally speaking, the proportion of slaves to whites gradually diminished in all directions from this concentrated area. To be noted especially is the startling contrast between Warwick County (64.7%) lying along the north of the James River and the tidewater counties of Isle of Wight, Nansemond, Norfolk, and Princess Anne (34% to 38%) just across the river on the south shore. These percentages indicate the danger of opposing tidewater to piedmont.

Equally significant from the standpoint of class conflict was the rate of

PERCENTAGE OF SLAVES IN TOTAL POPULATION, 1775

LESS THAN 1%
1 – 9%
10 – 19%
20 – 29%
30 – 39%
40 – 49%
50 – 59%
60 – 64.7%

HAMPSHIRE

AUGUSTA

FREDERICK

FAIRFAX

PRINCE WILLIAM

CULPEPER

STAFFORD

KING GEORGE

ORANGE

LOUISA

SPOTSYLVANIA

CAROLINE

HANOVER

GOOCHLAND

ALBEMARLE

CUMBERLAND

PRINCE EDWARD

AMELIA

CHESTERFIELD

HENRICO

NEW KENT

CHARLES CITY

JAMES CITY

KING WILLIAM

KING AND QUEEN

ESSEX

MIDDLESEX

GLOUCESTER

YORK

WARWICK

ELIZABETH CITY

PRINCE GEORGE

DINWIDDIE

SURRY

SUSSEX

ISLE OF WIGHT

SOUTHAMTON

NANSEMOND

NORFOLK

PRINCESS ANNE

BRUNSWICK

LUNENBURG

BEDFORD

HALIFAX

WESTMORELAND

NORTHUMBERLAND

RICHMOND

LANCASTER

ACCOMACK

NORTHAMTON

POTOMAC RIVER

RAPPAHANNOCK RIVER

YORK RIVER

JAMES RIVER

MARYLAND

NORTH CAROLINA

TABLE I. DISTRIBUTION OF SLAVE POPULATION IN VIRGINIA, 1750-1755

TIDEWATER

| County | 1750 | | | | | | 1755 | | | | | | 1750 to 1755 | |
|---|---|---|---|---|---|---|---|---|---|---|---|---|---|---|
| | White tithes | Est. white population | Black tithes | Est. black population | Est. total population | % slave in total | White tithes | Est. white population | Black tithes | Est. black population | Est. total population | % slave in total | Increase or decrease in whites | Increase or decrease in blacks |
| Accomack | 1520 | 6080 | 1000 | 2000 | 8080 | 24.7 | 1506 | 6024 | 1135 | 2270 | 8294 | 27.3 | − 56 | +270 |
| Caroline | | | | | | | 1208 | 4832 | 2674 | 5348 | 10180 | 52.5 | | |
| Charles City | 520 | 2080 | 1088 | 2176 | 4256 | 51.1 | 537 | 2148 | 1058 | 2116 | 4264 | 49.6 | + 68 | − 60 |
| Elizabeth City | | | | | | | 316 | 1264 | 812 | 1624 | 2888 | 56.2 | | |
| Essex | 958 | 3832 | 1662 | 3324 | 7156 | 46.4 | 889 | 3556 | 1711 | 3422 | 6978 | 49.0 | −276 | + 98 |
| Fairfax | 1140 | 4560 | 893 | 1786 | 6346 | 28.1 | 1312 | 5248 | 921 | 1842 | 7090 | 25.9 | +688 | + 56 |
| Gloucester | | | | | | | 1137 | 4548 | 3284 | 6568 | 11116 | 59.0 | | |
| Isle of Wight | 826 | 3304 | 840 | 1680 | 4984 | 33.7 | 810 | 3240 | 966 | 1932 | 5172 | 37.3 | − 64 | +252 |
| James City | 411 | 1644 | 1144 | 2288 | 3932 | 58.1 | 394 | 1576 | 1254 | 2508 | 4084 | 61.4 | − 68 | +220 |
| King George | 775 | 3100 | 980 | 1960 | 5060 | 38.7 | 720 | 2880 | 1068 | 2136 | 5016 | 42.5 | −220 | +176 |
| King & Queen | 1011 | 4044 | 2003 | 4006 | 8050 | 49.7 | 944 | 3776 | 2103 | 4206 | 7982 | 52.6 | −268 | +200 |
| King William | 761 | 3044 | 1801 | 3602 | 6646 | 54.1 | 702 | 2808 | 1834 | 3668 | 6476 | 56.6 | −236 | + 66 |
| Lancaster | 522 | 2088 | 1093 | 2186 | 4274 | 51.1 | 486 | 1944 | 1124 | 2248 | 4192 | 53.6 | −144 | + 62 |
| Middlesex | | | | | | | 371 | 1484 | 1056 | 2112 | 3596 | 58.7 | | |
| Nansemond | | | | | | | 989 | 3956 | 1264 | 2528 | 6484 | 38.9 | | |
| New Kent | | | | | | | 465 | 1860 | 1209 | 2418 | 4278 | 56.5 | | |
| Norfolk | | | | | | | 1132 | 4528 | 1408 | 2816 | 7344 | 38.3 | | |
| Northampton | 706 | 2824 | 845 | 1690 | 4514 | 37.4 | 609 | 2436 | 902 | 1804 | 4240 | 42.5 | −388 | +114 |
| Northumberland | 1052 | 4208 | 1177 | 2354 | 6562 | 35.8 | 980 | 3920 | 1434 | 2868 | 6788 | 42.2 | −288 | +514 |
| Prince George | 1326 | 5304 | 1997 | 3994 | 9298 | 42.9 | 650 | 2600 | 1138 | 2276 | 4876 | 46.6 | county div. | (Dinwiddie) |
| Prince William | 1360 | 5440 | 1255 | 2510 | 7950 | 31.5 | 1384 | 5536 | 1414 | 2828 | 8364 | 33.8 | + 96 | +318 |
| Princess Anne | 840 | 3360 | 789 | 1578 | 4938 | 31.9 | 840 | 3360 | 880 | 1760 | 5120 | 34.3 | No change | +182 |
| Richmond | 755 | 3020 | 1269 | 2538 | 5558 | 45.6 | 761 | 3044 | 1235 | 2470 | 5514 | 44.7 | + 24 | − 68 |
| Stafford | 909 | 3636 | 1044 | 2088 | 5724 | 36.4 | 889 | 3556 | 1126 | 2252 | 5808 | 38.7 | − 80 | +164 |
| Surry | | | | | | | 587 | 2348 | 1006 | 2012 | 4360 | 46.1 | | |
| Warwick | 202 | 808 | 638 | 1276 | 2084 | 61.2 | 181 | 724 | 665 | 1330 | 2054 | 64.7 | − 84 | + 54 |
| Westmoreland | | | | | | | 944 | 3776 | 1588 | 3176 | 6952 | 45.6 | | |
| York | 553 | 2212 | 1498 | 2996 | 5208 | 57.5 | 562 | 2248 | 1567 | 3134 | 5382 | 58.2 | + 36 | +138 |

## TABLE II. DISTRIBUTION OF SLAVE POPULATION IN VIRGINIA, 1750-1755

| County | 1750 | | | | | | 1755 | | | | | | 1750 to 1755 | |
|---|---|---|---|---|---|---|---|---|---|---|---|---|---|---|
| | White tithes | Est. white population | Black tithes | Est. black population | Est. total population | % slave in total | White tithes | Est. white population | Black tithes | Est. black population | Est. total population | % slave in total | Increase or decrease in whites | Increase or decrease in blacks |
| *PIEDMONT* | | | | | | | | | | | | | | |
| Albemarle | 908 | 3632 | 1047 | 2094 | 5726 | 36.5 | 1344 | 5376 | 1747 | 3494 | 8870 | 39.3 | +1744 | +1400 |
| Amelia | | | | | | | 1251 | 5004 | 1652 | 3304 | 8308 | 39.7 | | |
| Bedford (1753) | | | | | | | 354 | 1416 | 143 | 286 | 1702 | 16.8 | | |
| Brunswick | | | | | | | 1299 | 5196 | 976 | 1952 | 7148 | 27.3 | | |
| Chesterfield | 812 | 3248 | 974 | 1948 | 5196 | 37.4 | 841 | 3364 | 1198 | 2396 | 5760 | 41.5 | + 116 | + 448 |
| Culpeper | 877 | 3508 | 785 | 1570 | 5078 | 30.9 | 1221 | 4884 | 1214 | 2428 | 7312 | 33.2 | +1376 | + 858 |
| Cumberland | 661 | 2644 | 916 | 1832 | 4476 | 40.9 | 704 | 2816 | 1394 | 2788 | 5604 | 49.7 | + 172 | + 956 |
| Dinwiddie (1752) | | | | | | | 784 | 3136 | 1175 | 2350 | 5486 | 42.8 | | |
| Goochland | | | | | | | 569 | 2276 | 935 | 1870 | 4146 | 45.1 | | |
| Halifax (1752) | | | | | | | 629 | 2516 | 141 | 282 | 2798 | 10.0 | | |
| Hanover | 1236 | 4944 | 2239 | 4478 | 9422 | 47.5 | 1169 | 4676 | 2621 | 5242 | 9918 | 52.8 | − 268 | + 764 |
| Henrico | 584 | 2336 | 986 | 1972 | 4308 | 45.7 | 529 | 2116 | 898 | 1796 | 3912 | 45.9 | − 220 | − 176 |
| Louisa | | | | | | | 655 | 2620 | 1452 | 2904 | 5524 | 52.5 | | |
| Lunenburg | | | | | | | 1209 | 4836 | 903 | 1806 | 6642 | 27.1 | | |
| Orange | 474 | 1896 | 803 | 1606 | 3502 | 45.8 | 627 | 2508 | 1016 | 2032 | 4540 | 44.7 | + 612 | + 426 |
| Prince Edward (1753) | | | | | | | 416 | 1664 | 410 | 820 | 2484 | 33.0 | | |
| Southampton | 936 | 3744 | 866 | 1732 | 5476 | 31.6 | 973 | 3892 | 1036 | 2072 | 5964 | 34.7 | + 148 | + 340 |
| Spotsylvania | 636 | 2544 | 1316 | 2632 | 5176 | 50.8 | 665 | 2660 | 1468 | 2936 | 5596 | 52.4 | + 116 | + 304 |
| Sussex | | | | | | | 778 | 3112 | 1388 | 2776 | 5888 | 47.1 | | |
| *FRONTIER* | | | | | | | | | | | | | | |
| Augusta | 1670 | 6680 | | | 6680 | | 2273 | 9092 | 40 | 80 | 9172 | 0.8 | +2412 | + 80 |
| Frederick | | | | | | | 2173 | 8692 | 340 | 680 | 9372 | 7.2 | | |
| Hampshire (now W.Va.) | | | | | | | 558 | 2232 | 12 | 24 | 2256 | 1.0 | | |

growth of the number of slaves in the tidewater and piedmont (Tables I and II).[59] Except for four counties, three in the tidewater (Charles City, Fairfax and Richmond) and one in the piedmont (Orange), the percentage of slaves in the total population increased in all counties for which figures are available. In the tidewater, this increase was due in part to a growth in the slave population in all but two counties (Charles City and Richmond), but also to a decline in the white population in twelve counties. In all fairness, Fairfax County in 1755 should probably be considered piedmont except for a narrow strip of land along the Potomac. But in the piedmont, where the white population was growing faster than in the tidewater, the slave population was growing even more rapidly, the average percentage being 3.0 compared with 2.4 in the tidewater in those counties where there are figures for 1750 and 1755. In short, the institution of slavery was gaining headway at a more rapid rate in the piedmont than in the tidewater, so the issue was not one of slaveowning tidewater versus non-slaveowning piedmont. Patrick Henry's Hanover County was more than half slave by 1755, and Albemarle County, at the foot of the mountains, experienced a tremendous growth in Negroes during the five years.

We do not have figures for later increase in slave population for many of the piedmont counties, but those that we do have substantiate the generalization that the percentage of slaves to whites rose rapidly in the piedmont after 1755. A partial tithable list for Orange County in 1782 gives a figure of 78.8 per cent slave compared with 44.7 per cent in 1755. Two men had 84 and 82 taxable slaves, and others had 39, 32, 28, and 20, an indication that there were some substantial holders of slaves in this western county.[60] In Halifax County, the percentage of blacks in the total population went from ten in 1755 to 26.4 in 1771, again based on a partial list for 1771.[61] And in Amelia County, the proportion of slaves to whites went from 39.7 in 1755 to 51.2 in 1771 and to 64.8 in 1778.[62] With figures of 64.8 and 78.8 per cent of slaves in some piedmont counties, there was certainly no question of conflict between a slaveowning tidewater and a non-slaveowning piedmont.

In fact, growth in this later period was more rapid in these piedmont counties than in some tidewater areas. The ratio of slaves to whites in Norfolk County held about even from 1751 to 1771, at between 42 and 43 per cent, although figures for Norfolk Borough went from 33.6 per cent in 1751 to 38.5 in 1771.[63] Tidewater Lancaster, however, exhibited a steady and substantial growth from 46.6 in 1745 to 51.1 in 1750, 53.6 in 1755, and 64.4 in 1775,[64] but this was no greater than in some of the western counties.

Not only was there an accretion in the ratio of slaves to whites in most areas for which we have the data, but contrary to expectation there was also an equally marked augmentation in the percentage of heads of families who owned slaves. While the figures in Table III are for three areas only,[65] they provide at least the suspicion that there was a great consensus among the population in general over the desirability of slavery

TABLE III. SLAVEOWNERSHIP IN VIRGINIA

| | NORFOLK County | | NORFOLK Borough | | LANCASTER County | | AMELIA County | |
|---|---|---|---|---|---|---|---|---|
| | 1751 | 1771 | 1751 | 1771 | 1745† | 1775† | 1768* | 1778 |
| No. of tithable slaves | 835 | 1799 | 535 | 676 | 720 | 1275 | 813 | 3625 |
| Total family heads and estates | 687 | 1124 | 282 | 266 | 245 | 241 | 190 | 839 |
| No. of slaveowners | 291 | 512 | 142 | 185 | 167 | 187 | 134 | 649 |
| % of all family heads who were slaveowners | 42.3 | 45.6 | 50.3 | 69.5 | 68.1 | 77.5 | 70.5 | 77.3 |
| Slaveowners owning | | | | | | | | |
| 1 taxable slave | 100 | 203 | 48 | 60 | 37 | 38 | 25 | 117 |
| 2 taxable slaves | 88 | 93 | 25 | 43 | 30 | 28 | 17 | 116 |
| 3 taxable slaves | 29 | 53 | 21 | 19 | 32 | 21 | 22 | 75 |
| 4 taxable slaves | 26 | 40 | 11 | 12 | 20 | 20 | 14 | 72 |
| 5 taxable slaves | 22 | 28 | 11 | 11 | 15 | 12 | 10 | 56 |
| 6-10 taxable slaves | 16 | 67 | 19 | 31 | 19 | 39 | 28 | 136 |
| 11-20 taxable slaves | 10 | 24 | 5 | 7 | 11 | 19 | 17 | 61 |
| 21-30 taxable slaves | — | 5 | 2 | 1 | 3 | 7 | — | 10 |
| 31-55 taxable slaves | — | — | — | 1 | — | 2 | — | 5 |
| 56-102 taxable slaves | — | — | — | — | — | — | — | — |
| 103 taxable slaves | — | — | — | — | — | — | 1 | — |
| 113 taxable slaves | — | — | — | — | — | 1 | — | 1 |
| 164 taxable slaves | — | — | 1 | — | — | — | — | — |
| Per cent of slaveowners owning 5 or less taxable slaves | 91.0 | 81.4 | 81.6 | 78.3 | 80.2 | 63.6 | 65.6 | 67.2 |

† partial lists giving 4/5 or 5/7 of the county
* only a partial list—about 1/7 of the county

in spite of occasional protests against the institution. If the rich were accumulating slaves, so also were the poorer sort, and the deeds amply substantiate this fact.

Of equal interest is the fact that the small slaveowner was dominant in all three counties. Men who owned five or fewer slaves comprised the great bulk of the slaveowners in these counties, two of which were in the tidewater. After 1770 there were only ten men who owned more than thirty tithable slaves in all three areas, and significantly enough, six of the ten, including the largest, were in the piedmont county of Amelia.

A few figures on the value of slaves will indicate why so many men owned or desired to own slaves in the Old Dominion. William Lee told of a plantation near Williamsburg on which twenty-five working slaves produced forty hogsheads of tobacco at £10 each, 1,000 barrels of corn at 12s. 6d., 750 bushels of wheat at 5s., and thirty hundredweight of pork at 25s. The total was £1,250, or £50 per working slave.[66] Ann Kennon hired out her baker Cicero for a year at £30 clear of all deductions; if Cicero was worth £100, which was probable, the return was thirty per cent.[67] Robert Carter offered £18 a year, plus clothes and taxes, for a slave, and William Allason expected to get at least £9 a year.[68] Even the most highly skilled slave seldom brought more than £100, and most sold for much less, so these returns on investments probably suggest why men often bought slaves before they purchased land.

The importance of slaves to owners may also be seen in the comparison of slave property and total personal estate, including slaves, in inventories of the day.[69] Slaves comprised a large part of the total value of the personal estate of most Virginians, rich and poor alike. The examples given below are typical, and similar ratios may be found in any will or deed book for any county.

| Name | No. of slaves | Value of slaves | Total personal estate |
|---|---|---|---|
| Richard Long | 1 | £   45 | £   121 |
| John Hawkins | 8 | 390 | 519 |
| Henry Brock | 7 | 265 | 318 |
| John Sharp | 6 | 235 | 288 |
| John Coleman | 19 | 1,050 | 1,404 |
| George Long | 5 | 195 | 278 |
| Zachery Lewis | 78 | 2,885 | 3,780 |
| Thomas Duerson | 10 | 435 | 562 |
| Robert Briscoe | 1 | 35 | 103 |
| Thomas George | 1 | 28 | 64 |
| Henry Horne | 6 | 129 | 145 |
| John Branan | 1 | 20 | 36 |
| Robert Harper | 2 | 65 | 78 |

In summary, then, slavery was never a major source of internal conflict between whites in Virginia before the Revolution. Despite a few protests against the institution, the vast majority favored slavery both in theory and in practice, and even those who opposed slavery in principle seem to have succumbed to their interests. Slavery was profitable, it enabled a man to live with a minimum of physical labor, and the deeds, wills, and tax lists confirm the fact that most men, including former servants and apprentices, small planters, artisans, and overseers, desired to own slaves. Contrary to the generally accepted view, there was no sharp division between tidewater and piedmont over slavery, for many piedmont counties had higher percentages of slaves than did many tidewater counties, and almost all were increasing their black populations. Protection of slave property was of constant and vital concern to all classes of the white population. To the extent that Virginia was more "aristocratic" than a colony such as Massachusetts, slavery was undoubtedly the major cause. It created an aversion to labor among whites, it definitely set off the white man as the master in society, and it did create a lower class—the slaves—which could be exploited by the master race.

### NOTES

1. Jones, *Present State of Virginia,* pp. 75-76, 130-31.
2. Boucher, *Reminiscences,* pp. 97-98; *American Revolution,* pp. 38-42.
3. Gooch to Bishop of London?, May 28, 1731, Gooch Papers, I, 237, Fulham MSS, Virginia, No. 111.
4. Burnaby, *Travels,* pp. 53-55, 150-51.
5. Sept. 7, 1769, The Papers of Thomas Jefferson (Library of Congress), I, 33; *Virginia Gazette,* Sept. 14, 1769; Thomas Jefferson, "Notes on Virginia," *The Writings of Thomas Jefferson,* ed. by Paul Leicester Ford, 10 vols. (New York and London, 1892), III, 192, 266-68; William Byrd II expressed a similar view in a letter dated July 12, 1736, *Virginia Magazine of History and Biography,* XXXVI, 220-21.
6. Jefferson, "Notes on Virginia," *Writings,* III, 243-50.
7. Arthur Lee to Richard Henry Lee, March 20, 1765, Lee Papers, Alderman Library, U. of Va.
8. Robert Beverley to Edward Athawes, Esq., July 11, 1761, Robert Beverley Letter Book, p. la. See also subsequent letters for his later views.
9. Peter Fontaine, Jr., to John Fontaine, June 7, 1754, and to Moses [Fontaine], March 30, 1757, Maury Papers.
10. *House Journals, 1752-58,* pp. 359-61; evidence that such slave quarters were not unusual is to be found in Lancaster County Will Book 20, pp. 147-59, 193-94, 200-06, 213-16; Norfolk County Will and Deed Book H, p. 72; Spotsylvania County Will Book D, p. 178.
11. Smyth, *Tour,* I, 74-76.
12. *Ibid.,* pp. 39-40, 43-48.
13. Fithian, *Journal,* pp. 50-51.
14. *Ibid.,* pp. 128, 169-70; see also pp. 113-14, 121, 122, 173.
15. Landon Carter Diary, March 15, March 22, May 25, June 28, Sept. 8, 18, 20, 21, 1770; October 16, 1770; March 28, June 12, July 8, 1771; May 23, 1772; June 4, 1773; June 27, 1774; April 4, 1776; April 20, July 10, and Sept. 2, 1777.
16. *Ibid.,* April 4, 1776.
17. William Cabell Diary, Aug. 28, 1773.
18. Richard Corbin to James Semple, Jan. 1, 1759, Richard Corbin Letterbook, p. 40.

19. Fithian, *Journal,* p. 80.
20. Inventory of William Doggett, Lancaster County Will Book 20, p. 60.
21. George Mercer to James Mercer, London, Aug. 16, 1768, Mercer Papers, VHS.
22. Daniel Jenifer Adams to Washington, March 15, 1775, *Letters to Washington,* V, 138-39; see also Washington to Hector Ross, Oct. 9, 1769, Washington, *Writings,* II, 526.
23. Landon Carter Diary, Jan. 23, 1770; see also April 5, 1770 and Feb. 3, 1772.
24. *House Journals, 1702-12,* pp. 56, 148; Hening, *Statutes,* III, 453-54; VI, 356-69; Peter to Moses Fontaine, March 30, 1757, Maury Papers.
25. Hening, *Statutes,* V, 547-58; VIII, 138.
26. Anburey, *Travels,* II, 342-43. See also William Byrd, *Another Secret Diary,* p. 143, for Byrd's relations with his slaves.
27. Will of Francis Jordan, Norfolk County Will Book 2, p. 155; petition of Benjamin Bilberry, *House Journals, Oct. 1780,* pp. 20-21.
28. James Maury to Reverend ?, Oct. 10, 1759, Patrick Henry Papers, Undated MSS (Library of Congress); Reverend William Willie to ?, Aug. 30, 1749, Miscellaneous Collection, Miscellaneous MSS, Duke University (Microfilm, Colonial Williamsburg); Boucher, *Reminiscences,* pp. 57-59; *House Journals, 1712-26,* p. 134; James Blair to [Bishop of London?], July 20, 1730, Fulham MSS—Virginia, Box 1, No. 131; Fithian, *Journal,* pp. 252-53.
29. Force, *American Archives,* 5th Series, III, 1092-93. See also *Virginia Gazette,* April 3 and 10, 1752.
30. Hening, *Statutes,* III, 269-70; VI, 104-12; VIII, 137-39; Burnaby, *Travels,* pp. 46-48. For an example of the trial of a slave for murder, see Lancaster County Order Book 8, p. 159.
31. Hening, *Statutes,* III, 447-62; VI, 104-12, 359; VIII, 135-36; *House Journals, 1752-58,* pp. 8, 9, 14, 15, 16, 21, 24, 26, 32, 38, 43, 54, 58, 64, and 109ff.
32. Hening, *Statutes,* VIII, 358-61.
33. *Ibid.,* pp. 522-23.
34. Landon Carter Diary, May 6, 1772.
35. William Gooch to ?, June 29, 1729, PRO, CO5, v. 1337, pp. 105-06.
36. John Clayton's Account of the Case of Mrs. Wilson who killed her slave, Dec. 20, 1716, PRO, CO5, v. 1318, pp. 149-58; Prince William County Deed Book P, pp. 254-60 (Sept. 7 and 14, 1762).
37. *House Journals, 1773-76,* pp. 104, 189.
38. *Ibid., 1752-58,* pp. 26, 183; *ibid., 1758-61,* p. 96; *ibid., 1761-65,* p. 71; *ibid., 1766-69,* p. 91.
39. *Virginia Gazette* (P & D), Dec. 23, 1773.
40. *House Journals, 1752-58,* pp. 31, 39, 43, 239, 248.
41. Norfolk County Will Book 1, p. 55.
42. Norfolk County Deed Book 25, p. 123.
43. Norfolk County Will Book 2, p. 54; see also *House Journals, Oct. 1783,* p. 50.
44. See case of Rachel, *ibid., May 1777,* p. 57; *ibid., Oct. 1780,* p. 49.
45. *Ibid., 1702-12,* p. 240. For the resulting law restricting slave meetings, see Hening, *Statutes,* IV, 126-34.
46. Gooch to Lords of Trade, Feb. 23, 1756, PRO, CO5, v. 1328, p. 359.
47. Carter to *Virginia Gazette,* Sabine Hall Papers.
48. *House Journals, 1702/3-1712,* pp. 270, 276; Hening, *Statutes,* III, 536-37; Gov. Spotswood to Council of Trade, Dec. 15, 1710, Spotswood, *Letters,* I, 42.
49. Governor Gooch to Lords of Trade, Sept. 14, 1730, PRO, CO5, v. 1322, p. 299; *ibid.,* p. 212.

50. *House Journals, 1766-69*, p. 91.

51. *Virginia Gazette* (R), Jan. 25, 1770.

52. Fithian, *Journal*, pp. 241-43, 245, 252.

53. To Lords of Trade, March 6, 1711, Spotswood, *Letters*, I, 52-53. See also *ibid.*, p. 167; *House Journals, 1712-26*, p. 137; PRO, CO5, v. 1319, p. 243; Hening, *Statutes*, IV, 118, 182, 276-78, 317-22, 394; V, 28-31, 92-94, 110-11; Gooch Papers, I, 107; *House Journals, 1752-58*, pp. 1-51 *passim*; Dinwiddie to Lords of Trade, June 16, 1753, PRO, CO5, v. 1327, p. 532.

54. To [John and Moses Fontaine], March 2, 1756, Maury Papers.

55. To Lords of Trade, June 2, 1760, *House Journals, 1758-61*, p. 284.

56. Richard Henry Lee, ed. *Memoir of the Life of Richard Henry Lee, and his Correspondence . . .*, 2 vols. (Philadelphia, 1825), I, 17-19. See also *House Journals, 1758-61*, pp. 95-96, 112, 141, 148, 151, 211, 383; *ibid., 1766-69*, pp. 46-47, 118, 217; *ibid., 1770-72*, p. 248; Hening, *Statutes*, VII, 338-39, 363; VIII, 237-38, 330-38, 532; PRO, CO5, v. 1368, p. 223; *Acts of the Privy Council*, v, 287-88.

57. To John Fontaine, June 7, 1754, Maury Papers; Burnaby, *Travels*, pp. 150-51.

58. Answers to Queries, July 23, 1730, Gooch Papers, I, 179; A List of Tithables in the Dominion of Virginia, 1755, PRO, CO5, v. 1338, p. 364; Observations on the tithables, *ibid.*, p. 365; Dinwiddie to Lords of Trade, Feb. 23, 1756, *ibid.*, p. 359; Report of the Earl of Dunmore, March 18, 1774, Strachey Papers, I, 260; PRO, CO5, v. 1352, p. 14.

59. Materials for the map, page 73, and for Tables I and II are to be found in "A General List of Tithables Taken in 1750, as far as Returns were then Made," Chalmers Collection, New York Public Library, on film at Colonial Williamsburg; A List of Tithables in the Dominion of Virginia, 1755, PRO, CO5, v. 1338, p. 364. All total population figures here are estimated by multiplying the white tithes by four and the black tithes by two.

60. Orange County Tithables, 1782, and figures in Table II.

61. List of James Turner, Jr., Halifax County Tithables, 1771.

62. See Table II for 1755 figures; Tithable list for Nottoway Parish, Amelia County Tithables, 1771; Amelia County Tithables, 1778.

63. Norfolk Borough and County Tithables, 1751, 1771; see Table I for 1755 figures on Norfolk. All percentages are figured on total population as above.

64. Lancaster County Tithables, 1745 and 1775. These lists are partial but account for about 5/7ths and 4/5ths of the county respectively. See Table I for figures in 1750 and 1755. Percentages are figured on total population as above.

65. Norfolk Borough and County Tithables, 1751 and 1771; Lancaster County Tithables, 1745 and 1775; Amelia County Tithables, 1768 and 1778. For a lower estimate of the number of small slaveholders see Wertenbaker, preface to *The Planters of Colonial Virginia* in *The Shaping of Colonial Virginia*, p. iii.

66. William Lee to Richard Henry and Francis Lightfoot Lee, Feb. 20, 1773, Lee-Ludwell Papers, VHS.

67. Ann Kennon to Theodoric Bland, Aug. 16, 1763, Campbell Collection, Bland Papers.

68. Carter to Colonel W. Lewis, Dec. 28, 1774, Robert Carter Papers; to Wharton Ransdale, Jan. 13, 1775, William Allason Letterbook.

69. Spotsylvania County Will Book D, p. 101 (R. Long), p. 118 (Hawkins), p. 125 (Brock), p. 126 (Sharp), p. 134 (Coleman), p. 152 (G. Long), p. 178 (Lewis), p. 401 (Duerson); Lancaster County Deed Book 14, p. 193 (Briscoe), p. 196 (George), p. 249 (Horne), p. 287 (Branan), p. 311 (Harper).

CHAPTER IV

# Primogeniture, Entail, and
# Inheritance of Property

ALTHOUGH SERIOUS DOUBTS have recently been cast upon the influence
of primogeniture and entail in maintaining an aristocracy in colonial
Virginia,[1] a continuing general acceptance of past interpretations about
these feudal practices of inheritance makes some brief discussion of them
mandatory. Most historians in the past and many current ones have
considered primogeniture and entail as major bulwarks in establishing
and perpetuating large estates in the hands of aristocratic families,
especially in the tidewater. As one writer has recently phrased it, "an
exclusive ruling class" of Virginia, based primarily upon the ownership of great tracts of land, "achieved their desire to perpetuate their
families and their power" in part by the laws of primogeniture and
entail and in part by intermarriage. Estimates of the extent of entail
include statements that at least half and perhaps three-fourths of the
"seated" land in the colony was entailed, and naturally it follows that
when Thomas Jefferson abolished entail and primogeniture at the time
of the Revolution great social gains resulted for the lower classes.[2]

Our purpose in the present chapter is to examine the institutions of
primogeniture and entail in the light of these conflicting views to determine, if possible, their roles in the inheritance of property, how much
land was affected by this type of inheritance, who favored and who
opposed primogeniture and entail, and just how significant these feudal
vestiges were in the perpetuation of a colonial aristocracy.

## A:  PRIMOGENITURE

Primogeniture is so often coupled with entail by historians that the
unwary reader is apt to conclude that these were mutually dependent
terms. Such was not true, however, for primogeniture, which meant
inheritance by the eldest son, most often applied in descent of property
in which entail was not involved whatever. On the other hand, entail,
which meant that a man could not dispose of his property but had to
pass it on as stipulated by law, was not always accompanied by primogeniture. An entailed estate could descend to other children besides
the eldest son, including the daughters.

80

In Virginia in the eighteenth century the main use of primogeniture was in the settlement of intestate estates, that is, estates for which there were no wills. If a man owned real estate in fee simple, he could dispose of it during his lifetime in any way that he saw fit—with, of course, his wife's consent. But if he died without leaving a will, the law provided for the distribution of his estate, and it was here that primogeniture became operative. According to law, the real property in such instances went to the eldest living son, with the other children receiving a share of the personal property.[3]

On its face, primogeniture as used in intestate estates might well appear an unfair and aristocratic method of inheritance, but there were many factors mitigating its effectiveness. If the eldest son was a minor, the widow controlled all the property until he came of age, thus benefiting the younger children. In addition, the widow received a third of the estate, both real and personal, and had the use of the manor house until her dower was assigned. When the law of 1705 designated slaves as real property, it became necessary to pass new legislation securing to the other children their share of the slaves, cattle, and remaining personal property.[4]

Since primogeniture in intestate estates was not an upper-class device but applied to all classes equally, the easiest way to avoid its application and thus do justice to the younger children was for a man to make a will, even of the crudest sort.[5] One might well argue that primogeniture in intestacy was primarily a device for the poor, since most men of any property usually made wills. For example, the courts records of Lancaster County for ten years, 1733 to 1743, have sixty-nine recorded wills and thirty intestates, none of the latter including a socially prominent family. Eleven additional estates were appraised, but the records do not show whether they were intestates or non-residents. Among the thirty known intestates, no "gentleman" appears, but ten "gentlemen" made wills, and only three of the intestates had more than £100 in personal property—£151, £228, and £230.[6] Of 101 recorded wills in Lancaster from 1736 to 1750, only fourteen provided that the eldest son should receive all the land, but even in these wills the younger children received property of comparable value.[7]

As one might expect, most men were interested in the welfare of all their children, not just the eldest son, and thus the typical method of disposing of an estate was by relatively equal shares for all children. The will of Thomas Herbert, Sr., of Norfolk was typical. The eldest son received the home plantation, half of another 170-acre plantation, four slaves, and some household goods. But each of four younger sons also received a plantation, from two to five slaves, and household goods. The one daughter inherited a lot in town, nine slaves, £50, and some furniture, while five grandchildren were given one slave each. The remainder of the estate went to Herbert's widow; at her death this was to be divided equally among all the children.[8]

Another custom which greatly minimized the effects of primogeniture in intestate estates was the rather sensible practice of starting children in life by giving them property as they came of age or married. Among the eleven estates appraised in Lancaster but not specified as intestate was that of gentleman William Ball, whose personal estate amounted to £1,024. If he had died intestate, one might easily have jumped to the conclusion that the eldest son received all of the land and his share of the personal property, leaving the younger son or sons landless. But the deeds show that Ball had previously given his second son Richard 400 acres of land in 1736. William, the eldest son, received his mother's dower rights in land and eighteen slaves in 1747, and of course son Richard received a share of his father's £1,024 personal estate and either slaves or an equivalent in money when his mother died.[9]

The following examples, typical of those in the records, demonstrate the practice of providing for all the children even before the father died. When Nicholas Smith of Essex County died, he had already provided for sons Francis, Nicholas, and Samuel, and daughter Susanna Medley. Daughter Ruth Sarle received furniture and livestock, daughter Lucy Dunn got two slaves and two ewes, and grandson John Medley got livestock. The wife inherited the remaining real estate, but at her death it was not to go to the sons but in equal shares to daughter Lucy Dunn and granddaughters Ann Fisher and Ann Medley.[10] In Halifax County from 1752 to 1768 there were fifty-three deeds granting land to children, and of course this does not include grants made in other counties by citizens of Halifax.[11] Landon Carter, whose family might have been expected to resort to entail, boasted that he had maintained a large family, paid off the children's fortunes, and put out three sons with good estates.[12] And Peter Fontaine said that his father bought some 6,000 acres on the frontier and had about twenty slaves to divide among the five children he had by his second wife. Fontaine, an offspring of the first marriage, himself lived on a 1,000-acre tract.[13]

There were also other ways by which the effects of primogeniture in intestacy were softened in actual practice. If a man died intestate but it was known that he intended for all of his children to share in the estate, the estate was sometimes divided regardless of the law.[14] Or the eldest son might simply decide that, in all equity, his brothers ought to have shared in the inheritance and proceed to divide up the estate.[15] More common was the practice of deeding property to children with the stipulation that the deed was not to become effective until the parents died.[16] Such parents could die intestate and to all appearances bankrupt, but the court records in these instances would be extremely misleading.

Whatever the practice in England and other countries, there is no reason to believe that men in colonial America favored their eldest sons to the exclusion of their other children. Landon Carter often confided to his diary how insolent, imprudent, and worthless he considered his eldest son, Robert Wormeley, known as "Wild Bob." Carter refused to pay the considerable gambling debts of sons Robert and John, and he decided to leave them some of his estate "under guardianship or their wives and children will be ruined." [17] Augustine Washington divided his large estate among sons Lawrence, Augustine, George, Samuel, John, and Charles,[18] while Thomas Lee left land to sons Richard Henry, Francis Lightfoot, William, Arthur and Philip Ludwell. The third son received 4,000 acres, and the sons were to pay the daughters £2,000 for their share.[19]

Additional contemporary evidence, besides the material found in deeds and wills, verifies the view that primogeniture was relatively unimportant in colonial Virginia. Hugh Jones said that lands in Virginia were "divided every age among several children (not unlike gavel kind in Kent and Urchinfield) into smaller plantations."[20] According to Philip Fithian, Robert Carter was not influenced by primogeniture in determining his heirs. He planned to leave the management of his estate to the most able of his sons, not necessarily to the eldest.[21] And Governor Gooch wrote in 1734 that division of land, even including entailed land, among all the children was the common custom in Virginia.[22]

## B: ENTAIL OR FEE TAIL

If primogeniture was of little importance in colonial Virginia, the next problem is that of the significance of entail, especially in the perpetuation of an aristocracy. What was entail, how was it used, and what were its effects?

Entail was a legal method of limiting the descent of real property to a specific line of heirs in such a way as to prevent its transfer. These heirs were not limited to one sex. Estates could be entailed either to the male or female heirs of a donee's body, or equitable estates could be created, and entailed estates could be devised to sons, daughters, or both.[23] Furthermore, primogeniture was not a necessary ingredient of entail, although it often was operative.

Entail came to Virginia by way of the English common law, but by the time it arrived it had been greatly weakened. Originally created in the Statute De Donis passed in 1285, entail served to secure the position of the British aristocracy of that day. But by the fifteenth century, legally acceptable ways had been found to circumvent the power of entail. By the time the first settlers reached Jamestown, entails could readily be broken by such legal processes as fine or common recovery. It was this somewhat weakened form of entail that was introduced into the colony.[24]

To create fee simple or fee tail ownership, some written document was needed such as a will or deed,[25] and the special wording within that document designated whether the property was delivered in fee simple or fee tail. If a man willed land to his son "and his heirs forever," or neglected to state anything about "heirs," the son would hold the land in fee simple.[26] But if a man willed land to his son "and to the heirs of his body lawfully begotten forever," the son would hold the land in fee tail. Other phrases such as "heirs of his [or her] body," "lawful heirs," or "natural heirs," or any statement designating what body the heir is to come from could create an entail.[27] By its very nature personal property could not be entailed,[28] and therefore when terms of a bequest of personal property were such as would create entail in land, they meant an absolute gift in personalty. It is not uncommon to find wills which use terminology entailing cattle and sheep or other personal goods,[29] and as we shall see, in all probability the person making such a will did not realize that he was creating an entail on land if there was land to be disposed of.

The inheritances of gentleman George Heale of Lancaster County illustrate the methods of devising property by both fee simple and fee tail. In 1741, Joseph Heale devised several parcels of land "to my nephew George Heale and his heirs for ever." [30] Later this land was sold by George and described by him as land which he inherited "in fee simple" from his uncle Joseph.[31] Another uncle, however, entailed George Heale with several parcels of land and some slaves, using the words "to him Devised and to his Male heirs of his Body Lawfully Begotten for Ever," and if George died without heirs, the will stipulated other specific beneficiaries.[32] In later years, George had the entail on this land and slaves docked by an act of the Assembly.[33] We may thus assume that when we encounter wills with the above wording the land or slaves have been entailed in *taille male*.

Entail was generally created by will but occasionally by deed. As Professor C. Ray Keim has shown, the great bulk of property was passed in fee simple to heirs but the property entailed was mostly devised by will rather than by deed. He found this true in both tidewater and piedmont counties. For example, in Henrico County, in the decade following 1757 only four out of 375 deeds entailed lands. Charles City County records of 1766-74 revealed not a single deed in tail, but a few wills involved entail. The same was true in the piedmont counties of Albemarle, Culpeper, and Fauquier.[34]

Beginning in 1705, the laws of Virginia weakened the practice of entailing land by providing easier methods for breaking entails. Under English common law as it prevailed in the colony, entails could be "docked" or broken by court action, but a law of 1705 transferred this power to the Assembly, where at least part of those responsible were elected rather than appointed.[35] Then in 1734 the docking of small entailed estates was made easier and cheaper, expressly to help "poor people seised [sic] in fee tail of small and inconsiderable parcels of land, often times ignorant, or not designed to be devised in tail by their ancestors," or "poor people and their families, who, without it, must be confined to labour upon small parcels of land, when by selling them, they might be able to purchase slaves, or other lands more improveable." Entails on land valued at less than £200 sterling, provided the land was not contiguous to other entailed land, could be broken simply by a writ of *ad quod damnum* from the Secretary's office to the sheriff of the county.[36]

In practice, whatever the intent, the *ad quod damnum* law helped both rich and poor to avoid the restraints of entail. Governor Gooch believed that the law was especially designed for the poorer sort. The old law made docking of entails too expensive for the poor, forcing them to live on small parcels of land that had been long occupied and frequently divided among many children according to prevailing custom. If they could dispose of these small parcels to others living nearby, they could take up a larger quantity of fresh land and purchase slaves to their own and the country's benefit.[37] Gooch's statement, stressing benefits to the poor, also tells us that all of the children, not just the eldest son, inherited entailed land. But a member of the Secretary's office claimed that the men who used *ad quod damnum* did so "to defeat entails on land, to enable them to sell and convey the same, in fee simple." [38] And that the poor were not the only ones to benefit is attested by the following statement of Richard Henry Lee: "You know I have got the entail on my estate from my father dockt by writ of ad quod damnum." [39]

Before the Declaration of Independence, one other act contributed to the waning influence of entail. Beginning in 1762, the House became increasingly concerned over the leasing of entailed land, which could be done only for the life of the tenant-in-taille. A bill to allow leases "for three lives, or 21 years" failed to reach a third reading in the House in 1762, but a second try in 1764 finally produced a bill to allow such leases. This bill stated that large tracts of entailed land remained uncultivated because the owners did not have sufficient slaves to work the land, and tenants refused to lease the property because they believed that leases would expire with the life of the tenant-in-taille. The public would benefit by having such lands settled by industrious and laborious people. So henceforth, leases of entailed land for twenty-one years, or three lives, or for any other term were to be valid in law against heirs or claimants.[40]

The anomalous position of slaves in entailed estates also weakened entail in Virginia. Slaves were declared in 1705 to be real estate but were to retain some characteristics of personal estate in being subject to sale for debt. After much confusion over the status of slaves and unsuccessful attempts to restore them to a position of personal property, a law of 1727 declared that slaves could be annexed to the land and entailed but could also be sold to satisfy just debts. More confusion resulted from the entailing of slaves, and several attempts to change the law were blocked in England,[41] but as we shall see the selling of slaves for debt made cultivation of the land difficult and often led to the docking of entails on land. It was not until the first session of the legislature after the Declaration of Independence that the Assembly could pass a law abolishing entails on both land and slaves.[42]

Such, then, was the legal side of entail in colonial Virginia. Now the question is how entail functioned in actual practice—what forms it took, how extensively it was used, and the ease or difficulty with which entails could be broken.

One of the most striking things one encounters in delving into the records to see how entails worked out in practice is the great variety of combinations of entail and fee simple in the wills. Some testators divided their entailed lands among all their children.[43] One man entailed land to his four sons but then stipulated that the sons could sell or dispose of the land to each other, though not to outsiders, but by so doing, the testator allowed for the breaking of the entail for at least three of the four heirs.[44] Some men entailed slaves to a male heir but devised other slaves to a female heir in fee simple.[45] Others willed land to sons in fee simple but to daughters in fee tail.[46] Still another gentleman devised all his land to one nephew in fee tail but stipulated that in case of his death the property was to go to a niece and another male heir in fee simple.[47] Some testators devised personal property in language used for entails—probably from ignorance of legal forms, since personal property other than slaves could not be entailed.[48]

Entailing land equally among several heirs tended to weaken the effectiveness of entail in maintaining a family estate. Edwin Thacher, for example, held 5,800 acres of land "in fee tail general" during his lifetime. When he died in 1745, he left the land to his wife and four daughters as coheirs to whom the lands descended "in coparcenary." When the mother died, the four daughters and their husbands were "seized in coparcenary, in fee-tail" of her 1,112 acres.[49] William Colston inherited two tracts of land in fee tail which were divided between his two daughters when he died. One daughter left only a daughter to inherit this entailed land, but eventually the entail was broken and placed on some lots in Williamsburg which her husband owned.[50] If these lots were separated, the entail could then have been broken entirely by *ad quod damnum*.

It should be noted from the above evidence that females as well as males inherited entailed land. Sometimes we get the erroneous impression that entailed land descended intact and that it all went to the eldest son, but we must remember that women also inherited entailed estates and that these estates were frequently divided just as fee simple property was.

Regardless of entail, there were various ways by which the younger children inherited a just share of the father's estate. For example, John Spotswood, son of former governor Alexander Spotswood, left part of his indebted estate to son Alexander in fee tail and to son Robert in fee simple. When court action threatened confiscation of Robert's land, the

General Assembly stipulated that Robert was to receive part of his brother's entailed lands.[51] A father might also will that the son who inherited the entailed land was to get the entail docked to give land and slaves to a younger brother, or that he was to pay the younger brother a specified sum.[52] Ralph Wormeley, who inherited his father's real estate "in taille-male," had to pay his father's debts and bequests to the younger children, the latter including £800 sterling to one sister, £500 each to three others, and an obligation to support his sisters until they were of age or married and to educate his brother in England and to pay him £100 a year for fifteen years. Because of these bequests to younger children, the entail on the estate had to be broken.[53]

The extent of entail in colonial Virginia has been grossly misrepresented by those writers who have maintained that most of the seated area of Virginia was entailed. Although exact knowledge of the amount of land entailed is not possible, one has only to peruse the wills and deeds of Virginia counties, as the authors have done, to see that the great bulk of land in Virginia was held in fee simple. As the deeds and wills and a check of the *Virginia Gazette* amply testify, entail was the exception, not the rule.[54] Very little of the western land held by land speculators was entailed. The Randolph, Beverley, Borden, and Byrd families were among the largest holders of property in the west, little of which was entailed.[55] Even the Spotswood holdings, which were entailed, were eventually broken up by act of Assembly.[56]

Our own research corroborates that of Professor C. Ray Keim that most land in colonial Virginia was held in fee simple rather than in fee tail. Of 101 wills in tidewater Lancaster from 1736 to 1750, only seventeen were strictly entail, fifteen combined entail and fee simple, and sixty-nine were entirely fee simple.[57] Keim found that only fourteen out of thirty-nine wills in Westmoreland (1756-61), seven out of forty-eight in Middlesex (1759-72), nine out of seventy-seven in Fauquier (1759-76), ten out of 128 in Culpeper (1749-70), one out of fifty in Culpeper (1770-76), and five out of 133 in Albemarle (1754-76) contained provisions for entail. The total figure was forty-six out of 475 wills. Of the entails in Fauquier and Albemarle, none involved a large estate nor a family of great prominence, and in the county of Chesterfield entail was present in only seven of the wills of seventy-three well-known families.[58]

Considering the vast amount of land held in fee simple—land sold by Lord Fairfax and the other large land speculators, land being patented from the government each year, land descending through wills and changing hands through deeds—one can only conclude, with Keim, that the importance of entail in the Old Dominion has been greatly exaggerated.

Not only was much of the land in Virginia held in fee simple tenure, but even a considerable amount of the entailed land did not remain under entail. The law permitted the docking of entails, and just how many were docked would be difficult to say. We can count the number broken by act of Assembly, but in all probability those docked by writ of *ad quod damnum* were by far the more numerous, and the task of tracking them down would be virtually insuperable. The researcher is often confronted with two deeds in which a man sold property and immediately repurchased it. This was a method of fulfilling the requirements of the law for docking entails by *ad quod damnum*.[59]

Writs of *ad quod damnum* were also used as the second step in the breaking of entails that the law did not intend to be broken. An act of 1752 makes the process explicit. When an entail on a large estate was broken by an act of the Assembly, in most instances other property of equal or greater value had to be entailed in its place. This was doubtless designed to eliminate any objections that might arise in England to the docking of entails in Virginia. But nothing in this law specified that the newly entailed land had to be in a single parcel, and if the parcels were worth less than £200 sterling, the entail on them, in turn, could be broken by a writ of *ad quod damnum* over which Britain had no control.[60]

Landon Carter gives us the impression that men sometimes used this procedure to break entails. He said that when private bills for docking entails came up in the House, there arose a dispute over the insertion in one of them of a clause to prevent the lands settled in lieu from being sold thereafter by an *ad quod damnum*. The attorney general spoke "handsomely" against the necessity of a clause which Carter considered a just one, but he said it was only an argument and no question was put.[61] Carter was quite obviously in the minority on this question.

Entails on slaves could also be broken, either legally or illegally. The law of 1727 provided that slaves inherited in fee tail could be sold by the tenant to pay debts.[62] But obviously entailed slaves and their offspring would be extremely difficult to identify if the tenant chose to dispose of them. Apparently many did, for in 1769 the House adopted the policy of recording the names of the slaves entailed.[63] Their offspring would still be a problem, however, especially the offspring of slaves who died or of those on quarters away from the home plantation. How many entailed slaves were sold illegally or inadvertently we can never know.

Entails on estates too valuable to be docked by writ of *ad quod damnum* could be broken by act of the Assembly; 125 such acts were passed between 1711 and 1776. Most of these naturally involved the more prominent families, and among the reasons given were lack of slaves (25), sale of land (13), payment of debts (11), provision for younger children (10), lands worn out (9), and convenience of location (7). Many of the entails on land in the tidewater were replaced by entails on piedmont lands, but again it is impossible to say how many of these piedmont entails were such as could later be docked by writ of *ad quod damnum*.[64]

We sometimes get the erroneous impression that men wanted to live in the tidewater and were squeezed out by the large landowners, but such was not always true. It was not uncommon for entails to be broken on tidewater lands so the owner could move to the backcountry.[65] Such was true of William Booth, friend of William and Richard Henry Lee, who found himself too much circumscribed where he lived by the small amount of land he held. The Assembly had docked the entail, and Booth had been able to purchase a much larger tract in the backcountry. Richard Henry Lee wanted William Lee to pay "the accustomed fees" in England to the proper people to ensure passage of the bill there.[66]

Occasionally the Assembly stepped in and docked an entail to miti- gate the consequences when strict enforcement of the law would create an injustice. This happened, for example with the estate of Robert "King" Carter. Carter left some estate in fee tail to his son Robert, who died before his father did. According to the law, brother Charles Carter would have received the land and brother John Carter the slaves, leaving noth- ing for the widow and children of Robert, Jr. This law provided that the widow and children should get their intended share of the estate, re- gardless of the laws of entail and primogeniture.[67]

The Spotswood estate demonstrates how debts and bequests to younger children necessitated docking an entail, a process which usually inter- fered with both primogeniture and entail. How much land Alexander Spotswood acquired is not certain, but we do know that his estate included at least 55,750 acres in Orange County in 1747.[68] At his death in 1740, Spotswood had two sons, John and Robert, and two daughters.[69] Through primogeniture, eldest son John received the work- ing slaves and the land, some of the latter entailed. But son John was to pay his father's debts and also pay his brother Robert £3,000 sterling and each sister £2,000 sterling at age or marriage. By 1751, when John was of age and both sisters were married, he had to sell land to raise the £4,000 due to them. But the return from the sale of 19,759 acres still was not sufficient. When he died in 1767, the executors re- ceived permission to sell enough of the entailed land to pay off the debts of John's father, Alexander, and the Assembly allowed the executors to sell enough to raise £6,000 of the total remaining debt of £9,000.[70]

At death, John Spotswood repeated the same process followed by his father. He left a son, Alexander, and two daughters, the son to inherit all the land but to pay each daughter £2,000 at age or marriage. By 1771, Alexander was of legal age and was selling land in Orange and Cul- peper counties to settle these inheritance debts.[71] So primogeniture and entail did not mean that the eldest son always fared well and the younger children were neglected.

Two additional examples of docked entails must suffice to show how entail was weakened in Virginia before the Revolution. Mann Page of Gloucester County left sizeable estates to two sons and one daughter, but he also owed large debts in Virginia and England. His son Mann

Page, unable to pay the debts and legacies, had to have the entail on 30,787 acres docked and also had to sell slaves to make up the deficit.[72] John Armistead had to dock the entail on 1,710 acres to pay a sister and brother bequests of £600 sterling each. The sister forced the issue through a suit, and when brother John still failed to pay she had him confined in jail, with the result that he had to get the entail on another 700 acres docked in order to pay her.[73]

So easy and certain was the docking of entails by act of Assembly that a man could advertise entailed land for sale on the assurance that he could get the entail docked later. William Peachy advertised to sell his 600 acre home plantation in Richmond County. The land was entailed, he said, but his eldest son was of age and would join him in a petition to the Assembly to dock the entail, and he had no doubt of obtaining it.[74]

The ease by which entails were docked, as well as the maneuvering that sometimes took place, is also apparent from the following account. William Banks had 1,200 acres of entailed land in King and Queen County. He got the entail docked on 420 acres of this, which he sold, but entailed 394 acres and a mill in its place. Later the entail on the mill and 394 acres was docked, and slaves were put on the 780 acres remaining from the original 1,200 acres. When Tunstal Banks inherited the 780 acres and slaves, he got the entail docked on this and placed it on 1,000 acres which he had purchased in King William County.[75] Apparently entails could be docked almost at will.

Although the law required that the tenant-in-taille substitute property of equal or greater value for the estate in a docked entail, in actual practice, according to Edmund Randolph, this was often nothing but mockery. He said that although an equivalent was supposed to be settled on the issue in tail, legislatures often had no diligence and often much indifference in enforcing the law. The result was that an heir in tail had been obliged to accept, as a substitute for an ample benevolence, a possession which was an encumbrance, even though it had been attested to the Assembly as being of equal value with the entailed estate.[76] In the light of this evidence, it might also be of interest to know how many estates of more than £200 sterling value had the entail docked by *ad quod damnum*.

On rare occasions, the House of Burgesses balked at docking an entail, but the reason was usually obvious. In 1760 the British government disallowed three entail bills on technical grounds,[77] and in 1766 the first instance of refusal by the House of Burgesses was based on failure of the tenant-in-tail to give a reason for the proposed docking.[78] When the House learned that David Meade, a former burgess, did not even have title to the land in Halifax that he proposed to substitute for the entailed land, it refused to pass a docking bill, but later it passed one.[79] On another occasion the House rejected the petition of James Roscow, gentleman, even though Roscow was in jail for debt and could not be released without selling his entailed land.[80] Then there was the time when the House, annoyed by the delay of the Council in passing a docking bill, sent a curt note to the upper house demanding action only to have the bill rejected by the Council because of "the novelty and unusual terms of such a message." [81]

That the docking of entails resulted in the breakup of some large estates and some spreading of landownership is attested by what happened to the Harry Beverley estate. Beverley, who inherited 14,829 acres from his father Robert, was allowed to dock the entail on 9,980 acres of this tract in 1765 so he could buy slaves for the remaining land. But in 1766, Beverley, still in debt £1,500, docked the entail on the remainder of the 14,829 acres. He sold twenty-two tracts of land containing 7,733 acres to twenty-one different individuals, eighteen of the sales being for less than 400 acres, and eleven for 200 acres or less.[82]

It must be remembered, however, that while the docking of entails on estates such as those of Beverley and Spotswood did increase landownership somewhat, the initiative for docking came from " aristocrats" who needed more money to pay debts, not from pressure by "liberal" leaders or the lower classes. And it is erroneous to assume or imply that men had to wait for these estates to be broken to buy land, for they could patent land from the government at any time and every newspaper issue advertised thousands of acres for sale each week, acres which had not been entailed and which could be purchased on a fee simple basis.

Primogeniture and entail, then, were not of great significance in colonial Virginia. The two did not always go together. Primogeniture was important mainly in intestacies, which comprised only about one-third of all estates, and the bulk of intestate estates concerned the poorer families, not the rich. Furthermore, the effect even where it did apply was lessened by various factors, especially the common practice of giving children property when they came of age or married. Entail could only be created by specific language in a written will, thus excluding all intestate estates. And of those who wrote wills, few stipulated entail. Furthermore, such estates often included all children, both male and female, not just the eldest son, and even when the will was based on primogeniture the eldest son usually had to pay large bequests to the other children out of the income of the estate. Entail was not a means of perpetuating class distinctions in Virginia, for entailed estates were found among both rich and poor. And both rich and poor could readily break their entails and frequently did so, either by act of Assembly or by writ of *ad quod damnum*.

Since a great majority of men, especially those with the largest amounts of property, divided their estates by wills, there was no one-way process by which estates simply got larger and larger. While some estates increased, others declined, being broken down by sale, inheritance, and debt. We have already seen that Robert "King" Carter had over 300,000 acres of land, but that his grandson Robert had only 60,000 acres. A William Byrd II might add to the estate of William Byrd I, but most of this accumulation could be dissipated by William Byrd III. As some families declined in wealth and influence, others arose to take their places, only to decline at a future date. And all this was made possible because primogeniture and entail were not of great importance.

We shall see in our final chapter not only what eventually happened to primogeniture and entail but also who was responsible for what happened—and how this action reflected aristocracy or democracy in Virginia.

## NOTES

1. See Richard B. Morris, "Class Struggle and the American Revolution," *William and Mary Quarterly*, 3rd ser., XIX (Jan., 1962), 24; Elisha P. Douglass, *Rebels and Democrats* (Chapel Hill, 1955), pp. 301-03; Louis B. Wright, *The First Gentlemen of Virginia*, pp. 57, 321-22.

2. Carl Bridenbaugh, *Seat of Empire*, p. 8; Charles and Mary Beard, *The Rise of American Civilization*, I, 135, 293-94; see also John R. Alden, *The South in the Revolution*, pp. 330-31, 332, 335; Charles Sydnor, *Gentlemen Freeholders*, p. 128; Samuel Eliot Morison and Henry Steele Commager, *The Growth of the American Republic*, I, 239-40; T. Harry Williams, Richard N. Current and Frank Freidel, *American History: A Survey*, p. 95; John D. Hicks and George E. Mowry, *A Short History of American Democracy*, (Boston, 1956), p. 94; Thomas A. Bailey, *The American Pageant*, p. 127; Wesley M. Gewehr, *The Great Awakening in Virginia, 1740-1790*, p. 19; Philip Alexander Bruce, *The Virginia Plutarch*, 2 vols. (Chapel Hill, N. Carolina, 1929), I, 207-08; John Esten Cooke, *Virginia*, pp. 365, 446.

3. The most complete discussion of primogeniture and entail in Virginia is to be found in the unpublished doctoral thesis of Clarence Ray Keim, "Influence of Primogeniture and Entail in the Development of Virginia," University of Chicago, 1926. See especially Chapter I for the English background of primogeniture and entail; see also Leonard Daggett, "Wills" in *Two Centuries Growth of American Law, 1701-1901* (New York and London, 1902), p. 186; James Kent, *Commentaries on American Law*, 4 vols., 14th ed. (Boston, 1896), IV, para. 383; Hening, *Statutes*, III, 318; Richard B. Morris, "Primogeniture and Entailed Estates in America," *Columbia Law Review*, XXVII (1927), 24-51; see especially pp. 25, 31-32, 42.

4. Hening, *Statutes*, III, 371-76; IV, 283; V, 231-32, 444.

5. Many men who could not sign their names drew up wills and registered them with their marks. For example see will of Henry Stonham, Lancaster County Deed Book 12, p. 108 or will of William King, *ibid.*, p. 109.

6. Lancaster County Order Book 8, pp. 42-395.

7. Lancaster County Deed Books 13 and 14, *passim*; see especially Book 13, pp. 25, 55, 70, 86, 88, 89, 92, 111, 117, 119, 122, 127, 149, 155, 174, 179, 181, 314, 342; C. Ray Keim, "Primogeniture and Entail," pp. 63-64, 164-65.

8. Norfolk County Wills and Deeds, Book H, p. 260. Oct. 19, 1749. For other typical examples, see Albemarle County Will Book 2, p. 204; Lancaster County Deed Book 13, pp. 253-54; Book 14, pp. 29-31.

9. *Ibid.*, Book 13, pp. 23, 279, 301; Book 14, p. 144.

10. Essex County Will Book 11, p. 19. Sept. 16, 1755.

11. Halifax County Deed Books 1 through 7, *passim*; C. Ray Keim's research in Henrico and other counties shows the same conclusion; see "Primogeniture and Entail," pp. 100-06; for specific examples see Essex County Deed

Book 28, p. 8; Accomack County Deeds 1737-46, pp. 19, 40, 103, 244, 268, 318, 509; *ibid.*, 1746-57, pp. 41, 48, 72, 202, 218, 222, 245, 266, 279; Statement by Edmund Berkeley, May 6, 1757, Berkeley Papers; Norfolk County Deed Book J, p. 11; Norfolk County Will Book 2, p. 228; Halifax County Deed Book 5, pp. 288, 289, 291, 292; Book 6, p. 230; Lancaster County Deed Book 13, pp. 23, 93, 141, 229, 267, 315; Book 14, pp. 1, 18, 52, 131, 144, 181, 207.

12. Landon Carter Diary, July 19, 1770.

13. Peter Fontaine, Jr., to John Fontaine, June 7, 1754, Maury Papers.

14. Agreement by Andrew Miller, Oct. 15, 1766, Preston Papers.

15. Loudoun County Deed Book D, p. 40.

16. Essex County Deed Book 28, p. 331; Book 29, p. 126; for other examples of deeds of this type see Accomack County Deed Book, 1737-46, pp. 51, 184, 336, 493; *ibid.*, 1746-57, pp. 241, 246; *ibid.*, 1757-70, pp. 12, 19.

17. Landon Carter Diary, July 6, 1770; Sept. 15, Nov. 9 and 16, 1771; Feb. 12, 1774.

18. *Letters to Washington*, III, 392-97. April 11, 1743.

19. Will of Thomas Lee, Feb. 21, 1749/50, Lee-Ludwell Papers, Miscellaneous Letters, VHS.

20. Jones, *Present State of Virginia*, p. 93.

21. Fithian, *Journal*, pp. 111-12, 239-40.

22. Gooch to Lords of Trade, Nov. 20, 1734, Gooch Papers, II, 360.

23. *American Jurisprudence*, 49 vols. (Rochester, N. Y., 1936- —) Vol. 19, para. 46-55; C. Ray Keim, "Primogeniture and Entail," pp. 1-18.

24. In 12 Edward IV, the Taltarum's Case stretched the legal powers and after that time entail could be broken by "common recovery," a fictitious proceeding invented to give a tenant-in-tail an absolute power to dispose of his estate in fee simple. See James Ballantine, *Law Dictionary with Pronunciations*, 2nd ed. (Rochester, N. Y., 1948) for definition of "common recovery," and for discussion of history of entail see James Kent, *Commentaries on American Law*, IV, 13-15; *American Jurisprudence*, Vol. 19, para. 46-55; Keim, "Primogeniture and Entail," pp. 1-18.

25. Hening, *Statutes*, III, 517.

26. *American Jurisprudence*, Vol. 19, para. 12-28, 37-44; Leonard Daggett, "Wills," in *Two Centuries Growth of American Law*, p. 190; *The English and Empire Digest* . . . , 48 vols. (London, 1919-30), XLIV, 933 (Case 7892).

27. There are many and varied legal intricacies in the definitions of entail as it was practiced. See for example, *Words and Phrases*, 1658 to date, Permanent edition, 45 vols. (St. Paul, Minn., [1940]), Vol. 19, pp. 335-36; *American Jurisprudence*, Vol. 19, para. 46-55; *The English and Empire Digest*, XLIV, 933 (Case 7892); Kent, *Commentaries on American Law*, IV, 13-15.

28. *American Jurisprudence*, Vol. 19, para. 48.

29. Lancaster County Deed Book 13, p. 321 (will of Anguish Alexander); *ibid.*, Book 14, p. 195 (will of Charles Cleptron).

30. *Ibid.*, Book 13, p. 239.

31. *Ibid.*, Book 18, p. 16. 1763.

32. *Ibid.*, Book 13, p. 74.

33. Hening, *Statutes*, VIII, 63-65. Oct. 1764.

34. C. Ray Keim, "Primogeniture and Entail," pp. 55-105; see especially pp. 58-60, 93, and 103-05.

35. Hening, *Statutes*, III, 320.

36. *Ibid.*, IV, 399-400.

37. Gooch to Lords of Trade, Nov. 20, 1734, Gooch Papers, II, 360. For entails by the poorer people, see Norfolk County Will Book I, p. 186; Book 2, p. 148; Norfolk County Deed Book 15, p. 163; Book 18, p. 34; Book 20, pp. 235, 236.

38. Matt. Kemp in *Virginia Gazette*. June 10, 1737.

39. Richard Henry Lee to [William Lee], July 7, 1770, *Letters of Richard Henry Lee*, I, 50.

40. *House Journals, 1761-65,* pp. 138, 150, 160, 162, 247, 277, 300, 305, 308, 336; Hening, *Statutes,* VIII, 183.

41. *Ibid.,* III, 333; IV, 222-28; V, 432-43, 568; *House Journals, 1702/3-12,* pp. 250, 331; *ibid., 1712-26,* pp. 12, 18, 20; *ibid., 1761-65,* pp. 84, 141, 161, 162; *ibid., 1766-69,* p. 314; *ibid., 1770-72,* pp. 45, 61, 95, 97; Opinion of Mat. Lamb on Colonial Laws, Jan. 31, 1750/1, PRO, CO5, v. 1327, pp. 223-24; *Acts of the Privy Council,* IV, 138, Oct. 31, 1751; Fauquier to Lords of Trade, Jan. 10, 1763, PRO, CO5, v. 1330, pp. 255-58.

42. Hening, *Statutes,* IX, 226-27.

43. See for example case of Joseph Wharton, Lancaster County Deed Book 13, p. 313; *ibid.,* Book 14, p. 238; for other examples of children sharing entail, see *ibid.,* pp. 124, 212.

44. *Ibid.,* p. 124.

45. *Ibid.,* Book 13, pp. 135-36 (will of William Martin).

46. *Ibid.,* p. 109 (will of William King); p. 132 (will of Ruth Gibson).

47. *Ibid.,* pp. 74-76 (will of gentleman John Heale); for similar case, see will of John Mitchell, *ibid.,* Book 16, p. 56.

48. *Ibid.,* Book 13, p. 321; *ibid.,* Book 14, p. 195.

49. Hening, *Statutes,* VI, 314-16.

50. *Ibid.,* VII, 636-38.

51. *Ibid.,* pp. 723-30. 1759.

52. *Ibid.,* VI, 321-24.

53. *Ibid.,* V, 85-89; VII, 628-30.

54. Check page by page any of the many available deed and will books for colonial Virginia counties, VSL; Keim came to the same conclusion in his "Primogeniture and Entail," pp. 163-64, 164n.

55. For Randolph family see *ibid.,* p. 159; for Byrd family, see Charles City County records 1766-74, pp. 189, 469; Halifax County Deed Books 1752- —, *passim,* and Keim, "Primogeniture and Entail," pp. 94-95; for western holdings of Beverley and Borden families see Orange County Deed Books 6-16 and Augusta County Deed Books 1-19, *passim.*

56. Hening, *Statutes,* VII, 723-30.

57. Lancaster County Deed Books 13 and 14, *passim.*

58. Keim, "Primogenture and Entail," pp. 55-63, 98-106.

59. Hening, *Statutes,* IV, 399-400; V, 414-15; for examples see Accomack County Deeds 1737-46, pp. 206, 218; Norfolk County Deed Book 25, p. 186; Lancaster County Deed Book 19, pp. 129, 138, 140.

60. Hening, *Statutes,* IV, 225.

61. Landon Carter Diary, March 12, 1752.

62. Hening, *Statutes,* IV, 225.

63. *Ibid.,* VIII, 442.

64. Keim, "Primogeniture and Entail," pp. 108-28. Bills docking entails can be easily checked in the *House Journals* from 1711 to 1776.

65. See for example, Hening, *Statutes,* VIII, 665; *House Journals, 1773-76,* pp. 83, 131, 189.

66. Richard Henry Lee to William Lee, Aug. 4, 1772, Lee-Ludwell Papers.

67. Hening, *Statutes,* IV, 454-55.

68. Reverend Robert Rose Diary, Oct. 30, 1747.

69. Orange County Deed Book 5, p. 57; Book 7, p. 120; Book 10, p. 472.

70. Hening, *Statutes,* VII, 323-30; VIII, 27-33; Orange County Deed Book 12, *passim.*

71. *Ibid.,* Book 14, p. 140; Book 16, p. 124 and *passim.*

72. Hening, *Statutes,* V, 277-84.

73. *Ibid.,* VI, 405, 443 (1753-54). For other examples of docked entails, see *ibid.,* pp. 314, 448; VII, 157; Norfolk County Deed Book 20, p. 19; "A Case

stated as to the right of action in the Plantif," Sabine Hall Papers; *Acts of the Privy Council,* V, 126. Feb. 26, 1768.

74. *Virginia Gazette* (R), Feb. 14, 1771.

75. Hening, *Statutes,* VII, 293. 1759.

76. Randolph, History, Pt. 2, p. 74.

77. *House Journals, 1758-61,* p. 184.

78. *Ibid., 1766-69,* p. 32.

79. *Ibid.,* p. 320; *ibid., 1770-72,* pp. 11-12, 108.

80. *Ibid.,* pp. 59-60, 86.

81. *Ibid.,* pp. 55-56. The cost for docking entails after 1767 was £20 plus £2 for every £100 of value of the estate below £500 and £1 for each £100 above that amount. *Ibid., 1766-69,* p. 113.

82. Hening, *Statutes,* VIII, 166, 280; Orange County Deed Book 15, pp. 104, 106, 108, 110, 112, 114, 116, 145, 146, 147, 149, 229, 237, 266, 457, 458, 459, 461; Book 16, pp. 91, 93, 253, 255, 256.

# CHAPTER V

## *Debtors, Creditors, and Paper Money*

SINCE MANY INTERPRETATIONS of early American history have emphasized the role of debtors, creditors, and paper money as elements in the aristocratic-democratic dichotomy, we have attempted in this chapter to assess the significance of these three factors in eighteenth-century Virginia. Who were the debtors and creditors, and was there a debtor-creditor conflict of significance in the colony? If so, did it make a class pattern of small farmers and artisans against large planters and merchants, or a sectional pattern of backcountry against tidewater? Were the laws passed by a controlling aristocracy to protect upper-class creditors from the depredations of hostile lower-class debtors? And was paper money in Virginia a device by which the lower classes could to some extent repudiate their debts?

Anyone who attempts to untangle the debtor-creditor web in colonial Virginia must take many precautions. In the first place, the term "insolvent," which is often found on the quitrent rolls, meant only that a man had land in several counties and that he paid all of his quitrents to the sheriff of one county. In all the others he was listed as an "insolvent." [1] Then there is the question of when a man considered himself a debtor. If he was in prison and his creditors had taken all of his possessions, which were not sufficient to cover his debt, he undoubtedly felt himself to be a debtor. But what of the man who made an initial payment on a farm or shop, who gave a mortgage for the remaining price, and who used the farm or shop to pay off the mortgage and became an independent property-owning farmer or artisan? Did he consider the lender a benefactor or a class oppressor?

The documents themselves, while yielding a great deal of valid information, must therefore be used with care. Causes of £10 or more could be tried in the colony's highest court, the General Court at Williamsburg, and that court also handled appeals of less than £10, but since many of the General Court records have been destroyed much pertinent information is not available. Many mortgages, however, do exist; although these are our best source, they too must be used with caution. We might assume, for example, that a man such as Thomas Roberts of Norfolk was a debtor in financial difficulty when he mortgaged property to Samuel Boush, but further search would reveal that Roberts purchased the property from Boush on the same day that he signed the mortgage; he was thus merely buying property on time, not mortgaging property because of financial troubles.[2] Finally, there is the insoluble problem of men who borrowed from friends or relatives without security or mortgage, but one would be hard-pressed to show that these loans created a debtor-creditor conflict.

There is no question that Virginia planters were indebted to British merchants, but this was an imperial rather than an internal class problem, and it involved both large and small debtors of all classes.[3] There are statements from contemporaries to the effect that two-thirds of Virginia's planters were in debt to British merchants or factors, that nine-tenths of the creditors lived outside Virginia, and that British credit had settled most of the plantations in America.[4] In 1770, the accounts of John Norton and Son, English merchants doing business in Virginia, contain some two hundred names with debts ranging from £2,155 to very small amounts. The largest amounts were owed by men with prominent Virginia names: Philip W. Claiborne (£2,155), Mann Page (£2,027), John Baylor (£1,494), and Thomas Nelson, Jr. (£852). Thirty-six of the 200 accounts were for £100 or more and the total was £18,523.[5]

Some of these debts were contracted in the normal course of business and were paid, but others were the result of poor business practices and extravagant living to keep up appearances. British merchant Samuel Athawes wrote that Virginia gentlemen overvalued their incomes and lived up to their own estimates without thought of the consequences. On his return from England, Robert Beverley was determined not to follow the general practice of getting into debt, and one man hoped that his son would "only know the Evil of being in debt from the experience of others." [6] William Eddis said that Americans mistook profuseness for generosity and impaired both health and fortune by splendor of appearance and magnificence of entertainment. And Washington blamed the plight of many Virginia planters on their failure to devote their time and energy to management of their estates, for Negroes must be fed and taxes must be paid whether or not the estate produced anything.[7]

Sometimes Virginians started life encumbered with the debts of their fathers and grandfathers or debts accumulated by youthful folly. In 1770, Alexander Spotswood was still paying the debts that his father John had inherited from his grandfather Alexander, the governor, and Charles Carter left his heirs a deficit of £16,000. Mann Page confessed that while in college he had lost a large sum to John Page, some of which he still owed in 1774, and in 1770 Page owed John Norton and Son £2,027.[8]

While members of the upper classes were often heavily indebted to British merchants, debts of the middle and lower classes were usually much less imposing. Many of the sums owed to John Norton and Son were quite modest, but this was even more true of the amounts owed to a merchant in the colony. A list of accounts due to the estate of John Taylor, Norfolk merchant, showed the following: of the 391 debts, 220 were for less than £2, an amount that a common laborer could have paid in a

TABLE I.   NORFOLK COUNTY DEBTORS AND CREDITORS, 1763-1775

| CLASSES | SOCIAL STATUS | | | SIZE OF DEBT | | | | | RESIDENCE OF CREDITORS AND SECURITIES | | |
|---|---|---|---|---|---|---|---|---|---|---|---|
| | No. of debtors | No. of creditors | Securities | £0-99 | £100-299 | £300-499 | £500 & over | Size unknown | AREA | Creditors | Securities |
| **Upper class:** | | | | | | | | | | | |
| Gentlemen | 16 | 43 | 11 | — | 3 | 4 | 9 | — | Norfolk Borough | 89 | 23 |
| Merchants | 19 | 55 | 12 | 3 | 3 | 4 | 7 | 2 | Norfolk County | 31 | 3 |
| Mariners | 10 | 4 | — | 4 | 6 | — | — | — | Princess Anne | 2 | |
| Doctors | — | 4 | 2 | — | — | — | — | — | Nansemond | 1 | |
| Ministers | — | 4 | — | — | — | — | — | — | Northumberland | 1 | |
| Attorneys | — | 2 | 1 | — | — | — | — | — | Williamsburg | 1 | |
| Total upper class | 45 | 112 | 26 | 7 | 12 | 8 | 16 | 2 | Elizabeth City | | 1 |
| **Middle & lower classes:** | | | | | | | | | Pennsylvania | 1 | |
| Planters | 15 | 3 | 2 | 13 | 1 | 1 | — | — | England | 3 | |
| Artisans | 34 | 9 | 2 | 12 | 16 | 1 | 1 | — | Unknown | 6 | |
| Tavern-keepers | 3 | — | — | — | 1 | 1 | 1 | 3 | | | |
| Total middle and lower classes | 52 | 12 | 4 | 25 | 18 | 3 | 2 | 3 | Total | 135 | 27 |
| Women | 3 | — | — | 1 | 2 | — | — | — | | | |
| Orphans | — | 1 | — | — | — | — | — | — | | | |
| Unknown | 10 | 11 | — | 5 | 1 | 1 | 1 | 1 | | | |
| Total in all | 110 | 136 | 30 | 38 | 33 | 12 | 19 | 6 | | | |

TABLE II.  LANCASTER DEBTORS AND CREDITORS, 1741-1779

| CLASSES | SOCIAL STATUS | | | SIZE OF DEBT | | | | | | RESIDENCE OF CREDITORS AND SECURITIES | | |
|---|---|---|---|---|---|---|---|---|---|---|---|---|
| | Debtors | Creditors | Securities | £0-99 | £100-299 | £300-499 | £500 & over | Tobacco | Unknown | AREA | Creditors | Securities |
| **Upper class:** | | | | | | | | | | | | |
| Gentlemen | 7 | 13 | 11 | 1 | 2 | — | 1 | — | 3 | Lancaster | 32 | 14 |
| Merchants | 1 | 24 | 1 | — | — | — | 1 | — | — | Northumberland | 6 | 2 |
| Ministers | 1 | — | — | 1 | — | — | — | — | — | Westmoreland | 1 | 1 |
| Constables | 1 | — | 1 | 1 | — | — | — | — | — | Essex | 2 | 1 |
| Mariners | 3 | — | — | 3 | — | — | — | — | — | Spotsylvania | 1 | |
| Doctors | — | 1 | — | — | — | — | — | — | — | Middlesex | 1 | 1 |
| Total upper class | 13 | 38 | 13 | 6 | 2 | — | 2 | — | 3 | Richmond | 1 | |
| **Middle & lower classes:** | | | | | | | | | | Gloucester | 1 | |
| Planters | 12 | 7 | 4 | 9 | — | — | — | 2 | 1 | Norfolk | 1 | |
| Artisans | 9 | 1 | — | 2 | 3 | 1 | — | 1 | 2 | Prince William | 1 | |
| Tenants | 4 | 1 | — | 4 | — | — | — | — | — | England or Scotland | 3 | |
| Overseers | 1 | — | — | 1 | — | — | — | — | — | Total | 50 | 19 |
| Total middle and lower classes | 26 | 9 | 4 | 16 | 3 | 1 | — | 3 | 3 | | | |
| Women | — | 2 | 1 | — | — | — | — | — | — | | | |
| The Parish | — | 1 | — | — | — | — | — | — | — | | | |
| Status Unknown | 9 | 9 | 1 | 6 | 2 | — | — | — | 1 | | | |
| **Non-residents:** | | | | | | | | | | | | |
| Gentlemen | 1 | — | — | — | — | — | 1 | 1 | — | | | |
| Merchants | 2 | — | — | — | — | 1 | 1 | — | 1 | | | |
| Unknown | 1 | — | — | — | — | — | — | — | — | | | |
| Total in all | 52 | 59 | 19 | 28 | 7 | 1 | 4 | 4 | 8 | | | |

month; 359 were for less than £10; and only four were for more than £50. The largest debt on the list was £154.[9]

In the following charts we have attempted an approach to the problem of debtors and creditors through an analysis of mortgages over a period of years in counties representing different sections of the colony—tidewater, piedmont, frontier, and Northern Neck. These mortgages tell us who borrowed or lent money, what the social status of many borrowers and lenders was, the size of the debt, and where borrowers went to get their money. What we cannot always determine is whether the money was borrowed by someone who was increasing his economic status or squandering his fortune, and in most cases whether the mortgage was paid or foreclosed. We have covered the period of the 1760's in particular detail because it was a time of economic distress in Virginia.

The figures in Table I yield some conclusions that would be expected, but they also produce some unexpected results.[10] True to form, a large number of creditors came from the upper classes, but a higher percentage of debtors also came from the upper rather than the lower classes. The ranking of debtors by occupation, starting with those most heavily indebted, was artisans, merchants, gentlemen, and planters. The planters ranked last even though most contemporaries agreed that the great bulk of the people were planters. As would be expected also, the upper classes had most of the large debts and the lower classes most of the small ones, a natural consequence of the fact that borrowing usually has some relation to the amount of property one owns. Since mortgages generally represent considerably more property than the value indicated, it is significant that at least twenty-three in the middle-lower class had mortgages of more than £100, and five had mortgages of more than £300. And finally, a very heavy proportion of creditors and securities came from the local area.

With a few exceptions, Table II indicates that what was true for Norfolk County debtors and creditors was also true for those of Lancaster.[11] The upper classes, with most of the creditors, also had a high percentage of debtors, including the ones with the largest debts. But agricultural Lancaster did not have relatively as many debtors in the upper classes as did Norfolk with its town population. Two gentlemen, John Heath, factor for an English firm,[12] and John Stepto, justice and one-time sheriff, lost everything they owned.[13] Most creditors and securities lived in Lancaster County, but if a debtor went outside the county for money, he went to counties west and north of Lancaster rather than to the James River-Norfolk area. It is possible to determine the fate of twenty-five of the fifty-two mortgages—seventeen were paid off, eight were not, and of the eight, six were gentlemen, two being county justices, and two were planters. Such evidence adds greatly to the difficulty of dividing debtors and creditors by class.

Just as in Norfolk and Lancaster, the majority of the sixty-three mortgages found in Essex (Table III) were for small sums borrowed by men of the middle and lower classes, while a few upper-class gentlemen

TABLE III. ESSEX COUNTY DEBTORS AND CREDITORS, 1742-1763[14]

| CLASSES | SOCIAL STATUS | | | SIZE OF DEBT | | | | |
|---|---|---|---|---|---|---|---|---|
| | Debtors | Creditors | Securities | £0-99 | £100-299 | £300-499 | £500 & over | Unknown |
| **Upper Class:** | | | | | | | | |
| Gentlemen | 4 | 22 | 7 | — | 1 | — | 3 | — |
| Merchants | 5 | 38 | 4 | 1 | 1 | 1 | 1 | 1 |
| Mariners | — | 1 | — | — | — | — | — | — |
| Ministers | — | 1 | — | — | — | — | — | — |
| Total upper class | 9 | 62 | 11 | 1 | 2 | 1 | 4 | 1 |
| **Middle and lower classes:** | | | | | | | | |
| Planters | 35 | 4 | 4 | 21 | 11 | 1 | — | 2 |
| Artisans | 6 | 1 | — | 4 | 2 | — | — | — |
| Innholders | 1 | — | — | — | 1 | — | — | — |
| Total middle and lower classes | 42 | 5 | 4 | 25 | 14 | 1 | — | 2 |
| Women | 1 | — | — | 1 | — | — | — | — |
| Unknown status | 11 | 13 | 4 | 10 | 1 | — | — | — |
| Total in all | 63 | 80 | 19 | 37 | 17 | 2 | 4 | 3 |

RESIDENCE OF CREDITORS AND SECURITIES

| AREA | Creditors | Securities |
|---|---|---|
| Essex | 52 | 13 |
| King George | 3 | |
| King & Queen | 2 | 2 |
| Richmond | 1 | |
| Gloucester | 1 | |
| Hanover | 1 | |
| Westmoreland | 1 | |
| Williamsburg | 1 | |
| Yorktown | 1 | |
| England | 14 | |
| Unknown | 3 | |
| Total | 80 | 15 |

and merchants were the very heavy debtors. But in agricultural Essex, even more than in Lancaster, the relative number of large debtors was smaller than in Norfolk. One in particular of the latter indicates that being a substantial debtor was no liability socially or politically. Colonel Thomas Waring, Sr., gentleman, mortgaged property to two sons, a son-in-law, three gentlemen and three merchants in Virginia, and one firm in England, the total being £1,044 and 53,211 pounds of tobacco. Waring was a justice of the peace and soon became a burgess, a position held later by his son Francis.[15]

Essex resembled Norfolk and Lancaster, too, in the respect that debtors overwhelmingly went to local sources for their money, but unlike the other counties more creditors than usual resided in England and some of those mortgages involved small planters. Ten of the fourteen owed English creditors less than £100, and two between £200 and £299.[16]

Spotsylvania, like Norfolk, had a sizeable town population in Fredericksburg, and like Norfolk also this county, which stretched into the piedmont, had an unusually large number of upper-class debtors, but as in other counties, most of the debtors borrowed from local sources (Table IV). One of the largest debtors was Benjamin Grymes, county justice as early as 1748 and burgess from 1761 to 1771, who lost a suit to a Stafford County merchant for £3,103, and by 1764 had accumulated so many debts that he put his estate into the hands of trustees to manage, rent, or sell. His property consisted of 7,250 acres of land in eight tracts, houses and lots in Fredericksburg, a schooner and a sloop, one chariot, one chair, seventy horses, 150 cattle, 200 sheep, thirty breeding sows with their increase, seven wagons, fifteen carts, 100 axes, 120 hoes, household furniture, and 149 slaves. By 1771 he had 200 slaves, but they, with his other property, were sold. Grymes eventually leased Spotswood land in Orange County.[18] And John Waller, clerk of the county court for many years, became so enmeshed in debt that he not only mortgaged his 1,200-acre home plantation and slaves to a neighbor, but he also mortgaged the fees of his clerkship, his future corn and tobacco crops, and slaves that he would eventually inherit from his mother.[19]

The four piedmont and frontier counties of Orange, Loudoun, Halifax, and Augusta exhibit so many common characteristics in their debtor-creditor patterns that they can logically be discussed together (Tables V–VIII). In all these areas, a large percentage of debtors were not identified socially in the records. Except for Halifax County, a sizeable majority of all debtors of known status came from the middle-lower classes, and probably this would be true of most of those in the unknown group too, for a "gentleman" would be more apt to be designated as such than an ordinary "planter." Even more than in the previously discussed areas, and despite the fact that Loudoun and Orange had large numbers of tenants, the bulk of the debts in these four counties was for small sums, and even the large debts were fewer in number and smaller in size than those of more urban Norfolk and Spotsylvania. In Loudoun, for example, of the

TABLE IV. SPOTSYLVANIA COUNTY DEBTORS AND CREDITORS, 1754-1774[17]

| CLASSES | SOCIAL STATUS | | | SIZE OF DEBT | | | | |
|---|---|---|---|---|---|---|---|---|
| | Debtors | Creditors | Securities | £0-99 | £100-299 | £300-499 | £500 & over | Unknown |
| **Upper class:** | | | | | | | | |
| Gentlemen | 25 | 29 | 10 | 6 | 8 | 1 | 6 | 3 |
| Merchants | 2 | 58 | 1 | 1 | — | 1 | — | — |
| Attorneys | 3 | 1 | 3 | — | — | — | 3 | — |
| Ministers | — | 1 | — | — | — | — | — | — |
| Doctors | 1 | — | — | — | 1 | — | — | — |
| Military officers or mariners | 2 | — | — | — | 1 | — | — | 1 |
| Trustees of Fredericksburg | — | 2 | — | — | — | — | — | — |
| Total upper class | 33 | 91 | 14 | 7 | 10 | 2 | 9 | 4 |
| **Middle and lower classes:** | | | | | | | | |
| Planters | 2 | 1 | — | 1 | — | — | 1 | — |
| Artisans | 4 | — | — | 4 | — | — | — | — |
| Illiterates | 14 | 1 | — | 10 | 3 | — | — | 1 |
| Total middle and lower classes | 20 | 2 | — | 15 | 3 | — | 1 | 1 |
| Women | 2 | 1 | — | 1 | 1 | — | — | — |
| Unknown status | 57 | 42 | 11 | 37 | 12 | 1 | 4 | 3 |
| Non-residents | 5 | — | — | 2 | 3 | — | — | — |
| Total in all | 117 | 136 | 25 | 62 | 29 | 3 | 14 | 8 |

RESIDENCE OF CREDITORS AND SECURITIES

| AREA | Creditors | Securities |
|---|---|---|
| Spotsylvania | 88 | 21 |
| Culpeper* | 6 | |
| Richmond | 2 | |
| King & Queen | 4 | |
| Augusta | 1 | |
| Caroline* | 1 | 2 |
| Stafford* | 1 | |
| Essex | | 1 |
| Orange* | 1 | |
| King William | 2 | |
| Albemarle | 1 | |
| Hanover* | 1 | |
| Louisa* | 5 | |
| Williamsburg | 1 | 1 |
| Maryland | 2 | |
| Great Britain | 13 | |
| Unknown | 7 | |
| Total | 136 | 25 |

TABLE V.   ORANGE COUNTY DEBTORS AND CREDITORS, 1738-1772[20]

| CLASSES | SOCIAL STATUS | | | SIZE OF DEBT | | | | | |
|---|---|---|---|---|---|---|---|---|---|
| | Debtors | Creditors | Securities | £0-99 | £100-299 | £300-499 | £500 & over | Tobacco | Unknown |
| Upper Class: | | | | | | | | | |
| Gentlemen | 5 | 16 | 2 | 2 | 1 | | 1 | | 1 |
| Merchants | | 31 | | | | | | | |
| Manufacturers | | 1 | | | | | | | |
| County clerks | | 1 | | | | | | | |
| Total upper class | 5 | 49 | 2 | 2 | 1 | | 1 | | 1 |
| Middle and lower classes: | | | | | | | | | |
| Planters | 2 | | | 1 | 1 | | | | |
| Artisans | 2 | 1 | | 2 | | | | | |
| Tenants | 4 | 3 | | 3 | 1 | | | | |
| Illiterates | 9 | | | 6 | | | | 3 | |
| Total middle and lower classes: | 17 | 4 | | 12 | 2 | | | 3 | |
| Women | 1 | | | 1 | | | | | |
| Unknown status | 54 | | | 38 | 8 | 1 | 3 | 1 | 1 |
| Non-residents | 3 | 27 | 2 | 1 | | 1 | 1 | | |
| Total in all | 80 | 80 | 4 | 54 | 11 | 2 | 5 | 4 | 2 |

RESIDENCE OF CREDITORS

| AREA | Creditors |
|---|---|
| Orange | 47 |
| Spotsylvania | 14 |
| Essex | 3 |
| Richmond | 3 |
| Augusta | 1 |
| New Kent | 1 |
| Albemarle | 1 |
| Prince William | 1 |
| Stafford | 1 |
| Caroline | 1 |
| Yorktown | 1 |
| Great Britain | 6 |
| Total | 80 |

TABLE VI. HALIFAX COUNTY DEBTORS AND CREDITORS, 1765-1770[21]

| CLASSES | SOCIAL STATUS | | | SIZE OF DEBT | | | | |
| --- | --- | --- | --- | --- | --- | --- | --- | --- |
| | Debtors | Creditors | Securities | £0-99 | £100-299 | £300-499 | £500 & over | Unknown |
| Upper Class: | | | | | | | | |
| Gentlemen | 3 | 1 | 1 | 1 | 1 | — | — | 1 |
| Merchants | — | 20 | — | — | — | — | — | — |
| Surveyors | 1 | — | — | — | 1 | — | — | — |
| Total upper class | 4 | 21 | 1 | 1 | 2 | — | — | 1 |
| Middle and lower classes: | | | | | | | | |
| Planters | 3 | — | — | 3 | — | — | — | — |
| Artisans | — | 1 | — | — | — | — | — | — |
| Illiterates | 2 | — | — | 1 | 1 | — | — | — |
| Total middle and lower classes | 5 | 1 | — | 4 | 1 | — | — | — |
| Unknown status | 22 | 9 | — | 10 | 6 | 2 | 1 | 2 |
| Total in all | 31 | 31 | 1 | 15 | 9 | 2 | 1 | 3 |

RESIDENCE OF CREDITORS AND SECURITIES

| AREA | Creditors | Securities |
| --- | --- | --- |
| Halifax | 19 | 1 |
| Pittsylvania | 3 | |
| Prince Edward | 3 | |
| Chesterfield | 1 | |
| Prince George | 2 | |
| Great Britain | 1 | |
| Unknown | 1 | |
| Total | 30 | 1 |

TABLE VII.   LOUDOUN COUNTY DEBTORS AND CREDITORS, 1757–1770[22]

| CLASSES | SOCIAL STATUS | | | SIZE OF DEBT | | | | | |
|---|---|---|---|---|---|---|---|---|---|
|  | Debtors | Creditors | Securities | £0-99 | £100-299 | £300-499 | £500 & over | Tobacco | Unknown |
| **Upper class:** | | | | | | | | | |
| Gentlemen | 1 | 1 | — | — | — | — | 1 | — | — |
| Merchants | 1 | 10 | — | — | — | — | 1 | — | — |
| Attorneys | — | — | 1 | — | — | — | — | — | — |
| Total upper class | 2 | 11 | 1 | — | — | — | 2 | — | — |
| **Middle and Lower classes:** | | | | | | | | | |
| Planters | 4 | 2 | — | 1 | 1 | — | — | 1 | 1 |
| Artisans | 4 | 2 | — | 3 | 1 | — | — | — | — |
| Laborers | 1 | — | — | 1 | — | — | — | — | — |
| Total middle and lower classes | 9 | 4 | — | 5 | 2 | — | — | 1 | 1 |
| Unknown status | 16 | 12 | — | 11 | 4 | — | 2 | — | 1 |
| Total in all | 27 | 27 | 1 | 16 | 6 | 0 | 2 | 1 | 2 |

RESIDENCE OF CREDITORS AND SECURITIES

| AREA | Creditors | Securities |
|---|---|---|
| Loudoun | 15 | |
| Fairfax | 2 | 1 |
| King George | 1 | |
| Westmoreland | 1 | |
| Pennsylvania | 2 | |
| Maryland | 1 | |
| Great Britain | 2 | |
| Unknown | 3 | |
| Total | 27 | 1 |

TABLE VIII. AUGUSTA COUNTY DEBTORS AND CREDITORS, 1745-1773[23]

| CLASSES | SOCIAL STATUS | | | SIZE OF DEBT | | | | |
|---|---|---|---|---|---|---|---|---|
| | Debtors | Creditors | Securities | £0-99 | £100-299 | £300-499 | £500 & over | Unknown |
| Upper class: | | | | | | | | |
| Gentlemen | 5 | 6 | 1 | — | 3 | 1 | 1 | — |
| Merchants | — | 26 | 1 | — | 1 | 1 | 1 | — |
| Attorneys | 1 | 1 | — | — | — | 1 | — | — |
| Total upper class | 6 | 33 | 2 | — | 4 | 1 | 1 | — |
| Middle and lower classes: | | | | | | | | |
| Planters | 9 | 4 | — | 6 | 2 | — | — | — |
| Artisans | 9 | 5 | — | 9 | — | — | — | — |
| Inn or Store-keepers | 8 | — | — | 3 | 2 | 1 | — | — |
| Soldiers | 1 | 1 | — | 1 | — | — | — | — |
| Illiterates | 11 | — | — | 10 | — | — | — | 1 |
| Total middle and lower classes | 38 | 10 | — | 29 | 4 | 1 | — | 1 |
| Women | 1 | — | — | — | — | — | — | 1 |
| Unknown status | 56 | 65 | 16 | 41 | 12 | 2 | — | 1 |
| Total in all | 101 | 108 | 18 | 70 | 20 | 4 | 1 | 3 |

RESIDENCE OF CREDITORS AND SECURITIES

| AREA | Creditors | Securities |
|---|---|---|
| Augusta | 85 | 18 |
| Halifax | 1 | |
| Albemarle | 1 | |
| Botetourt | 1 | |
| Spotsylvania | 2 | |
| Gloucester | 1 | |
| Henrico | 3 | |
| Fairfax | 1 | |
| Williamsburg | 1 | |
| Pennsylvania | 1 | |
| Maryland | 1 | |
| Great Britain | 2 | |
| Unknown | 5 | |
| Total | 105 | 18 |

sixteen debts for less than £100, fourteen were for less than £50 and two for less than £25.[24] The largest known debts of Loudoun were those of merchant Fleming Patterson of Leesburg, who owed a Fairfax merchant £506 in 1769, and gentleman Craven Peyton, who owed £791 to merchants in England.[25] These debts were small compared to the thousands of pounds owed by some gentlemen in other areas. It is significant, too, that the Loudoun debtors included no known tenant, although one creditor, William Williams, was a leasee.[26] And finally, most of the creditors came from the same areas as the debtors, although Orange County had fourteen from its parent county of Spotsylvania.

In summary, then, these figures on debtors and creditors, unsatisfactory as they are, do establish the fact that caution must be used in any discussion of the debtor-creditor conflict. In all areas—tidewater, piedmont, or frontier—most debts were small sums owed to local creditors, the majority of debtors came from the middle-lower classes, but the big debtors were almost always from the upper class, as one might expect. There was definitely a higher percentage of big debtors in the more densely populated areas of Norfolk and Spotsylvania than in the frontier and heavily-tenanted areas of Orange, Loudoun, Halifax, and Augusta. Furthermore, there was little sectionalism involved, for the overwhelming majority of men borrowed where they lived, and if the big debtors went to the tidewater or to England for money, it was members of their own group who supplied it. There is, then, no more justification for the common usage of "debtor-farmer" than there is for "debtor-gentleman," "debtor-merchant," or "debtor-artisan," for the debtors were scattered among all groups.

The reader should also be reminded again that different types of debts created different pyschological attitudes on the part of the debtors. The hundreds of mortgages by small farmers and artisans who made a down payment on property, gave a mortgage for the balance, and used the property to pay off the mortgage provide a difficult problem for anyone attempting to determine debtor psychology. Were these men "debtors" or small entrepreneurs, and were they hostile or grateful to the men who advanced credit to them? And what was the class reaction of a man of the upper class whose property was taken by another man of the same class?

In addition to statistics, colonial laws tell whether the legal structure favored debtor or creditor, what legal interest rates were, and what processes debtors used to solve their problems. If debtors and creditors conducted their affairs beyond the pale of the law, it might be difficult to determine what actually occurred, but whether there was or was not a ruling upper class should be reflected in the debtor laws and treatment of debtors.

Perhaps because so many of the upper class were in debt, interest rates in the Old Dominion were fixed by law in such a way as to aid the debtor rather than the creditor. To prevent excessive usury, a law of 1730 placed legal interest at six per cent, then lowered it to five per cent in 1748 on the ground that high interest impoverished people and discouraged trade and industry. Any violator must forfeit double the amount lent, half going to the person who sued, and to prevent usurious contracts the borrower could force the lender to state under oath in a county court the amount of money lent and the terms of the contract.[27]

Again perhaps because all classes were debtors in Virginia, the debtor laws tended toward leniency, or at least the creditors thought they did. In 1705, the law stipulated that if a debtor could not pay he could offer his goods, which had to be accepted. If he delivered his whole estate and it was not sufficient, he was still to be released from jail at the end of three months upon swearing that he had no goods except a suit of no more than 50s. value. The law was not retroactive to previously contracted debts, it did not apply to debts of more than £10, and discharge from prison did not remove future liability for the debt.[28] But of course a man with less than £10 in property would probably not be averse to moving where he would not be liable.

Creditors complained about the leniency of this 1705 debtor law, but for many years the House of Burgesses refused to change it. In 1714, the House rejected a proposition to make land as well as slaves liable for the payment of debts of deceased persons after all personal estate was used. The House also rejected propositions that "goods seized by execution may be sold at an outcry," as well as a bill which would remedy "the hardships and injury often times done to creditors by the high valuation of goods tendered by debtors in discharge of their bodies when taken in execution." And again in 1715 the House rejected a committee report favoring sale of goods taken in execution or a more just valuation of such goods.[29]

A new law in 1726 probably aided the creditor in collecting his full due, but it also reduced the time that a debtor spent in jail. According to the preamble, long experience had demonstrated that the indulgence intended for debtors had been greatly abused, for dishonest debtors took advantages of defects in the law by tendering only the most worthless part of their goods. Partiality of appraisers often furthered these foul practices, so that creditors frequently chose to lose the debt rather than pay the excessive cost of appraisal. Then after enumerating specific rules concerning recovery of debt by seizure of goods, this 1726 law made new provisions for insolvent debtors. To prevent long imprisonment which could not benefit the creditor, the debtor, after twenty days in jail, could secure his release by delivering a schedule of his whole estate. The sheriff then sold the goods, except apparel and tradesmen's tools, and paid the creditors, and the debtor was released. Again these provisions did not apply to debts of more than £10 or 2,000 pounds of tobacco due to any one person. If the debtor could not pay jail fees, the county paid for the first twenty days and thereafter charged the creditor for the fees. The creditor could later recover these fees from the debtor, but the fact that the creditor had to pay the jail fees would probably discourage the practice of jailing people for small debts.[30]

During the following few years there were some minor changes in the debtor laws, some benefiting and some militating against the debtor. By 1734, Parliament had decreed that all lands in the British colonies were liable to be sold, as personal estate, for the payment of debts.[31] In the same year, a colonial law allowed a debtor a moratorium of a year to pay his debt before his goods could be sold. Governor Gooch said that this change greatly helped the debtor without injuring the creditor, since his debt was secured.[32] Then in 1736 an act stated that "evil disposed" persons had broken open most county jails and freed debtors and others, to the injury of creditors and the ruin of sheriffs, who were liable for prosecution. Henceforth sheriffs were not to be held liable unless juries could prove that they had aided the debtor to escape—a provision that certainly would not increase the vigilance of the sheriff. The act also reiterated the provision that a debtor must be released if he delivered a schedule and swore that this was all he had, and he must be released after twenty days if the creditor failed to pay his prison fees. All of these provisions were consolidated in the codification of the laws in 1748, a codification which contained the later controversial provision that executions in sterling were to be levied in current money at twenty-five per cent exchange.[33]

The British accepted the debtor law of 1748, but did not approve two other acts that dealt indirectly with debtors. One concerned exemption of debtors from arrest while attending fairs, a provision that would prevent creditors from attaching goods taken to the fair. The other, regulating suits in the General Court, prohibited original suits in that court for actions under £20 instead of £10, and forbade appeals to the General Court in actions of less than £10 instead of unlimited appeal. The British were mainly concerned because these provisions would harm British traders.[34] Acts of less than £20 would be tried by local justices of the peace instead of the Governor and Council.

Between 1748 and 1762 there were a few changes in the debtor laws but no major revision in debtor-creditor relationships. The provision for discharging debtors from county jails after twenty days was extended to cases in the General Court in 1753.[35] In 1755, at the insistence of British merchants and the British government, the fixed twenty-five per cent exchange rate on sterling debts was changed and the exchange rate was to be determined periodically by the General Court.[36] At the outbreak of the French and Indian War, a man who enlisted in the army was to be exempt from all taxes while in the service, his person was protected from all processes except criminal matters, and his estate was to be free from all executions or attachments if he owed less than £10 or 2,000 pounds of tobacco.[37] The same war brought a petition from Stafford County that debts might be paid with land, slaves, or other valuables by a reasonable valuation, or that a loan office be established to relieve the scarcity of cash and stagnation of trade and credit.[38] The Stafford petition was rejected, but in effect its request was granted when the Assembly issued paper money in 1757 and made it legal tender in all debts contracted either before or after the act was passed.[39] To prevent the secret gift of slaves to avoid payment of debt, another law of 1757 provided that gifts of slaves had to be made by deed or will.[40]

The most favorable legislation for debtors, however, was an act of 1762 in the nature of a bankruptcy act. Brought in by Richard Henry Lee and Richard Bland, this act declared that it was reasonable for a debtor to be cleared of all debts once he had surrendered his assets, except family wearing apparel and utensils of trade, to his creditors. There were heavy penalties, even death without benefit of clergy, for a debtor who absconded after declaring his assets, and anyone who aided in the escape of a debtor would be liable for his debts. To prevent the debtor from becoming wholly destitute, he was to receive a percentage of the money from the sale of his property if his goods paid off the creditors at fifty per cent or more of the debt.[41]

This bankruptcy act of 1762 met immediate opposition in England. It contained no suspending clause, thus violating the King's instructions that a governor should never sign a bill which in any way affected "the subjects of Great Britain, or their property." British officials and merchants who protested against the act declared that it favored debtors without properly safeguarding creditors, whereas, they said, in all trading countries the laws favored the creditor over the debtor.[42] The Lords of Trade, while considering the act just in principle, believed that it would be open to fraudulent practices. This was the occasion on which the statement was made that nine-tenths of the creditors of Virginia resided in England, and the British believed that the Virginia law favored colonial creditors at the expense of those in Great Britain.[43] In any event, the act was disallowed in England,[44] but by the time this had happened the Virginia Assembly had undergone a change of heart and had repealed the law on the ground that it might be "injurious to the credit of this colony, and may be of evil consequence to the trade thereof." [45]

Between 1763 and the Revolution there was only one significant change in the debtor laws, and that one was designed especially to aid the poor debtor. The former law had provided that if a debtor could not pay his prison fees the county would pay for the first twenty days, and then the cost would rest on the creditor. An act of 1772 declared that this was unreasonable and frequently occasioned the imprisonment of poor and indigent persons by their creditors. Henceforth, the creditor, not the public, must pay all prison fees for the debtor until the debtor was released. If the creditor refused or failed to give security for the fees, the debtor could be freed. Furthermore, fees for prisoners of the General Court in Williamsburg were raised from 6d. a day to 1s. 6d.[46] Creditors would certainly hesitate to imprison debtors for small debts under these circumstances.

How the debtor laws worked in practice is apparent to some extent from the following examples. A Nansemond writer in 1768 complained of the injustice done to creditors by the sale of goods at low prices. He said that he saw slaves worth £80 being sold for £20, and silver plate worth

£200 sold for £50. Over £1,000 worth of goods brought only £300. This writer also objected to the practice of taking from the creditor and giving to the widow when an estate was unable by many thousands of pounds to pay the demands against it.[47] In 1770, an executor for the indebted estate of one Mr. Kennon advertised the sale of the debtor's Negroes, but warned creditors that Kennon's neighbors might not be inclined to bid for these slaves as it was expected that part of them would be purchased for Kennon's family.[48] Then in 1773, Thomas Adams attached £10,000 to £12,000 in property to secure the debt that the London merchant firm of Perkins, Buchanan, and Brown owed to Thomas Hill. Adams said that the debtor laws in Virginia were designed for Virginia creditors, and if so, Hill would have to appeal to the King in Council. It would take eighteen months to two years for the courts to act and perhaps ten years for a final settlement.[49]

Complaints that debtor laws favored the debtor rather than the creditor found an echo in the description of debtor prisons by the contemporary, Hugh Jones. Speaking of Williamsburg, he wrote: "The whole ground around the capitol is surrounded with a neat area, encompassed with a good wall, and near it is a strong sweet prison for criminals; and on the other side of an open court another for debtors, when any are removed thither from other prisons in each county; but such prisoners are very rare, the creditors being there generally very merciful, and the laws so favorable for debtors, that some esteem them too indulgent." [50]

One of the indulgences was that of having extensive prison bounds and allowing debtors remarkable freedom within these bounds. Merchants complained that debtors built houses, ran taverns, and carried on business there, thus defying their creditors.[51] A notice in the *Virginia Gazette* confirms this. William Byrd said that a Mr. William Cole was still in prison bounds in Charles City, through the rigor of some of his creditors, and Cole had appealed to Byrd to build him a house there to spend his days. Byrd persuaded Cole, before Cole finally decided on this expedient, to give Byrd permission to attempt some accommodation with Cole's creditors.[52]

There were several expedients by which debtors could settle their obligations. If they mortgaged land, slaves, or personal estate, the final step was foreclosure and sale of the property. A common practice, especially among large debtors, was to set up a trusteeship of well-known men who would manage the debtor's estate and pay off his debts.[53] Sometimes debtor estates were sold by lottery if the debtor thought that he could obtain more by this method.[54] On other occasions the debtor simply absconded, especially when he had no property that was mortgaged. In Nansemond County, the sheriff's claim for 360 pounds of tobacco levied on John Arrington and John Stockdale was never paid, "the debtors haveing [sic] removed to *Carolina,* and left no estate in this colony to satisfy the same." The House of Burgesses philosophically ordered the notice to be recorded in the book of claims.[55]

The plight of Bernard Moore, King William County burgess and son-in-law of Governor Spotswood, demonstrates that not all debtors were small farmers and that being a heavy debtor was not a pleasant experience. Deep in debt to George and Martha Washington as well as to numerous other well-known men in the colony, Moore decided to sell his 3,500 acre home plantation, then organized a lottery, managed by a long list of important Virginians, to dispose of his real estate, slaves, and livestock valued at £18,400.[56] Moore wrote to John Norton that he hoped to settle his debts and have something left to support his numerous family, "but in a more saving way than we poor Virginians have been used to. This I don't mind," Moore continued, "as a little with comfort, is much better than much with the trouble I have gone threw [sic] for some years past."[57]

A mere listing of a few of the outstanding debtors in Virginia might well indicate why the colony's debtor laws did not necessarily favor the creditor over the debtor. By 1758, the estate of William Byrd III was in the hands of trustees, there were fears that the estate would not produce even enough to pay the interest on the debt, and also fears that his estate, if sold, would fall far short of his obligations.[58] Byrd held many mortgages from small farmers and artisans for land they purchased, but he also had a few mortgages of his own to worry about. George Washington suddenly discovered in 1764 that he owed Robert Cary and Company of England some £1,811, but he immediately took measures to reduce this.[59] Richard Henry Lee, possessed of five children in 1772 and "another far advanced on the stocks, with a teaming [sic] little Wife," was in serious financial trouble.[60] James Mercer, William Clinch, Benjamin Harrison, Charles Carter, Robert Burwell, and Mann Page all had money problems. Even Governor Dunmore was a debtor when the left the country,[61] and Commissary Robinson of the Church of England owed Richard Corbin £1,200 and total debts of £4,000.[62]

By far the largest debtor in eighteenth-century Virginia, but one who belongs in an individual category, was John Robinson. Robinson was speaker of the House of Burgesses and treasurer of the colony from 1738 to 1766.[63] There can be no doubt that he was one of the most popular politicians of his day, and during most of his political career he was considered among the richest men in the colony, and one of the largest creditors. But at his death it was learned that he had been using public money to save many of his debtor friends from financial ruin, that he had not taken securities for much of the money lent, and that he owed the colony more than £100,000. This produced a shock from which the colony did not recover for some time, and much of Robinson's estate was eventually wiped out.[64] Robinson was the heaviest debtor the colony ever had, but because of his use of public funds his plight was not comparable to that of the ordinary debtor.

Borrowing within the family circle seems to have been a common occurrence in colonial Virginia. Mothers borrowed from sons, brothers from brothers, and sons and daughters from their parents and in-laws.

The will books and the mortgages are especially rich in information on family debts. John Phripp of Norfolk Borough, for example, willed his son Matthew Phripp and son-in-law Stephen Wright the debts they owed him on his books.[65] The will of Moses Fontaine indicated that his brother John had borrowed £100 sterling in 1758 and paid it back in 1763.[66] One Thomas Butt willed his mother the £20 she owed him.[67] Many Spotsylvania mortgages involved men of the same surname,[68] and this was true of the mortgages of any county.

One must remember that most debtors, large and small, were actually solvent, that they had adequate property to secure their debts, and if they were debtors they were also property owners. To think otherwise would be to attribute to creditors a generosity that most did not have. Given the practices of lenders, one might suspect that many small debtors were in the position of Henry Butt of Norfolk County, who borrowed £27 and gave a mortgage on twenty-five acres where he lived as security. But shortly afterwards he sold the twenty-five acres for £300.[69] Among the wealthier debtors, Gawin Corbin of Westmoreland died in debt but was able to pay off his creditors with money from his crops and sale of some of his land and slaves.[70] Doubtless Governor Dunmore was correct when he said that "many of the principal people are much involved [in debts]," [71] but this did not mean that everyone who owed money was insolvent or thought of himself as a debtor.

Closely associated with debtors and creditors in the minds of many historians is the problem of colonial paper money. The usual interpretation has been that colonial debtors were enabled, through the device of depreciating paper money, to pay off good debts with bad money. Such a contradictory interpretation poses the question of why aristocratically-controlled colonial governments, presumably functioning in the interests of upper-class creditors, passed cheap-money bills which allowed their debtors to defraud them. So the task here is to find out what the role of paper money actually was.

Unlike other colonies such as Massachusetts, where paper money became a burning issue early in the eighteenth century, Virginia did not experience the conflicts over currency that brought turmoil elsewhere. It was not that Virginia escaped the pressures of imperialism which led other colonies to issue bills of credit backed by the taxing power of the Assembly. Virginia had a particular type of paper money which did not require legislative support.

Beginning in 1713, the Old Dominion used a form of paper money called "tobacco notes." In that year the General Assembly provided for public tobacco warehouses where inspectors would certify the quality of tobacco for export. In particular, these inspectors were to eliminate "trash" or inferior tobacco which, in the eyes of some men, inflicted much damage on the market. But the tobacco inspectors also performed a second function. They issued receipts certifying that a given amount and quality of tobacco had been deposited in the warehouse, and these receipts, or "tobacco notes," passed as currency. The value of many items—fees, salaries, wages, rents, and even the price of land—was stated in pounds of tobacco, so that tobacco notes found a ready acceptance in the colony.[72]

Tobacco was used in ordinary business activities as a substitute for coin as late as the Revolution. One of the British officers who had been captured and was retained in Virginia described the process clearly. Tobacco was lodged in warehouses, examined, and confirmed as in proper state for exportation by inspectors, he said. These inspectors "give the planter a receipt for such a quantity, and these receipts pass current as cash: Thus any one depositing tobacco in these warehouses, and obtaining a receipt, may go to Williamsburg, or any other city in the province, and purchase any kind of commodities, paying with receipts, which circulate through a multitude of hands before they come to the merchant who purchases the tobacco for exportation; thus this valuable commodity is equally Bank stock, and current coin; and the inhabitants, in describing the prices of their different purchases instead of saying 'I gave so many pounds for such an article;' [said] 'I gave so many hogsheads of tobacco.' "[73]

Eventually Virginia also had paper money, but when it came, it came because of necessary financing during the French and Indian War, not as a lower-class device to defraud upper-class creditors. When it became a creditor-debtor issue, the conflict was between British creditors and colonial debtors, the latter, as we have seen, upper as well as lower-class. Paper money, then, was primarily an imperial rather than an internal class problem in Virginia, and since we expect to devote a later volume to the British-Virginia controversy, we shall give it only cursory treatment here.

That paper money was not a class problem is best demonstrated by the circumstances surrounding its first issue, if we can believe Landon Carter. The House had passed a bill to raise £20,000 for defense. Carter, certainly not a member of the lower classes, proposed that the money be raised by printing treasury bills that would be paid off later by a tax on tobacco. Carter said that he received little support for this proposal because of the "great aversion to paper money" and because "popular prejudice prevailed." [74]

The main aspect of Virginia paper money that might give the appearance of raising class issues was the fact that it was to be lawful tender in the payment of everything but quitrents to the King.[75] But this loses its class connotations when we consider that the act creating it was passed by both House and Council, and no one has yet suggested that the members of these two bodies were of the lower classes.

The scarcity of hard money, perhaps aggravated by the depreciation of paper bills, brought a demand for a public land bank or loan office, but even this was hardly lower-class. The proposal for a public bank of £40-50,000 was made by Burgess Lunsford Lomax, representative with Edmund Pendleton from Caroline County, one of the upper tidewater counties.[76] By 1756 there were numerous petitions from various counties asking that something be done to alleviate the cash crisis, and the House appointed a committee to write a bill for establishing a loan office.[77]

The first bills of credit bore five per cent interest, but it was not long before Virginia had bills that were not interest-bearing. Again the class or sectional issue has a revealing aspect. Albemarle, a western frontier county, proposed that no more than £40,000 in paper be issued and that henceforth paper money should not bear interest. This follows our accepted idea of what a frontier county should do except for the limitations placed on the amount to be issued. But the county also petitioned that the land tax be abolished and an equal poll tax be levied on each tithable.[78] The advocacy by a frontier county of an equal poll tax instead of a property tax seems strange indeed until we remember that the average landholding in such a county was much larger than in the tidewater counties. Since much of a poll tax would be borne by the large slaveowners, the issue appeared to be what kind of property was to pay the bulk of the taxes, land or slaves.

There is something of a contradiction in the fact that the first paper money bills carried five per cent interest and yet were legal tender. One might expect the creditor class to approve of the interest but not the legal tender provisions and that debtors would do just the reverse. The answer probably lies in the fact that the legislature used both devices to prevent depreciation, and certainly the interest was designed for this purpose.[79] If there was another motive for the legal tender clause, it probably had some connection with debts owed by Virginians to British merchants.

That debts to Britain might have been a factor would seem apparent from the remarks of Richard Corbin, whose sympathies for British interests eventually brought him the position of deputy receiver-general. Corbin was among the few who opposed a paper money bill in 1758, mainly because of his concern for the bonds, protested bills of exchange, and other debts owed to British merchants. Corbin said that he would not have objected if the legal tender clause had excluded debts contracted before the law was passed and had provided for creditors. But if these were his sentiments, Corbin declared, "the majority the far greatest number have other views and other sentiments." [80]

After the French and Indian War ended and the need for colonial aid was over, the British did take action to suppress paper money; this action brought a rift between the House and Council. At the instigation of the Lords of Trade, Parliament passed an act to prevent legal tender clauses in future emissions of colonial paper money or the extensions of legal tender in paper money already in circulation.[81] In accordance with this act, Governor Fauquier issued a proclamation to call in £212,000 in paper money, but of course there was no money in the treasury to redeem this paper.[82] To provide the requisite money, the House proposed that Virginia borrow £240,000 sterling from British merchants, with £100,000 to be used to redeem paper money and the other £140,000 to be kept as collateral for colonial bank notes that would be lent on security at five per cent interest. But the Council refused to sanction either this plan or another proposal by the House, although it did agree to send the plan with an address to the King.[83]

The controversy over paper money after the French and Indian War was neither a class nor a sectional matter unless one assumes that the Council was upper-class and the House lower-class, or that the Council represented the tidewater and the House the backcountry. This was an imperial problem in which the appointed Council was now siding with the British. When such a man as Robert Beverley maintained that paper money had been absolutely necessary during the war, that the threat of an act of Parliament to end paper money was tyranny, and that the economic situation in Virginia was the result of British merchants who lived on the very vitals of the colonists, there is little room for a class or sectional interpretation of paper money in Virginia.[84]

There is no doubt that British restrictions on paper money contributed to the financial debacle involving John Robinson. As colonial treasurer, Robinson was supposed to retire and burn certain bills of credit when their time of circulation expired and when they came into the treasury. But many important Virginians were in financial difficulty, and Robinson, desirous of helping them, apparently re-issued these bills in the form of loans without taking proper security. When these irregularities were discovered following the death of Robinson on May 10, 1766, the colony was in dire financial straits indeed.[85] Obviously paper money in this episode was no device of the lower classes to defraud the upper classes.

The plan for a public loan office at first glance gives the appearance of sectionalism, but in reality is a little difficult to interpret. Thomas Lewis of Augusta County wrote of seeing a scheme in the newspaper for setting up a loan office in 1766. The plan, which he attributed to Colonel Bland, he considered rational and was almost sorry that something like it was not adopted. Lewis wished success to Colonel Bland's party and expressed regret that the uplanders by their absence gave so much strength to the adverse party.[86] This gives the appearance of a tidewater-upland split, but it would also make Richard Bland of tidewater Prince George the leader of the upland party.

That paper money was not primarily a class or sectional issue is also attested by other evidence. The House continued to propose bills of credit either issued as a land bank in which borrowers gave land as security or backed by money borrowed from England, but the Council opposed and the Lords of Trade refused to recommend any such plan to the King.[87] The House also instructed its agent in England to work for repeal of the act of Parliament which restrained future emissions of paper money.[88] But merchants who had strenuously opposed paper money because it hurt their trade with Great Britain were only too glad to have paper money when it benefited them. At the time of the disastrous James River flood in 1771, on the solicitation of the merchants, the Assembly voted £30,000 in bills of credit to aid flood victims, most of whom were merchants who had lost tobacco.[89] Richard Bland pointed out the inconsistency of the merchants in opposing paper money to be used for defense but praising the legislature for compensating them in paper money for their loss of tobacco. Bland philosophized that such would be the conduct of men who put their private interest above the public good.[90]

One final piece of evidence must suffice to demonstrate that paper money in Virginia was an imperial rather than a class or sectional issue. Robert Carter Nicholas, colonial treasurer after the death of John Robinson, representative from tidewater James City County which contained the capitol, Williamsburg, and a strong defender of the Church of England, used five columns in the *Virginia Gazette* to defend the Assembly's actions in advocating paper money. Nicholas said that he and a great majority of the Assembly were opposed to paper money in principle, but pressing necessity forced the colony to use it. An act prohibiting paper money would cause great distress, he declared, while a moderate quantity, properly backed and protected from forgery, would be of great benefit to the colony. Paper money had resulted from demands of the late war, he continued, and though the great amount and the Robinson affair had caused trouble, the colony had reduced its paper money from £539,692 to £54,391.[91] Nicholas later continued his defense of the Assembly and paper money from the attacks of opponents.[92]

The problems of debtors, creditors, and paper money in colonial Virginia are difficult at best, and ones which the historian should approach with great circumspection. Doctrinaire patterns simply do not fit. The creditors were not all upper-class merchants and large planters in the tidewater, and the debtors were not all lower-class artisans and small planters from the backcountry. The evidence does not show any class conflict in the debtor problem. The largest debtors as well as most of the creditors were from the upper classes. Some of the large debtors borrowed from England or from British merchants and factors in the colony, from other American provinces, or from other Virginia counties, but the great majority of debtors, especially small ones, borrowed from local creditors, usually from their own counties and often from members of their own families.

Neither is there evidence of a debtor-creditor sectional conflict. The areas with two of the largest towns, Fredericksburg and Norfolk, had the greatest number of large debtors, while the more strictly agricultural areas, especially the frontier counties, including those where tenantry was common, had very few heavily in debt. Because of the tobacco economy and the system of British mercantilism, many planters apparently took credit for their crops from England, but just how extensive this was is difficult to ascertain with certainty. In public laws the debtor had sympathetic treatment despite Britain's constant alertness to protect British merchants.

Paper money was also not a class or sectional issue. It was imperial, it originated in the need for finances during the French and Indian War, and its opponents were largely men who traded with Great Britain or who, like Richard Corbin, had British ties or benefited by collections of quitrents in sterling rather than paper money.

## NOTES

1. James Blair to [?], Sept. 23, 1763, "Papers on Quit Rents and Customs Confiscations," British Museum, Additional MSS 38337.
2. Norfolk County Deed Book 25, pp. 186, 188; see also *ibid.*, Book 24, p. 160; Book 28, p. 106; Book 29, p. 42; Norfolk County Will Book 2, p. 187.
3. Because a recent article indicates work in progress on planter debts to British merchants, we shall touch on this facet of the debtor-creditor problem only briefly and in relation to the internal situation, for planter-British troubles were imperial rather than class or internal. See the excellent article by Emory G. Evans, "Planter Indebtedness and the Coming of the Revolution in Virginia," *William and Mary Quarterly,* Ser. 3, XIX (Oct., 1962).
4. "Copy of Remarks on the Trade and Government of Virginia, printed in London in 1728," Miscellaneous MSS, Mass. Hist. Soc.; PRO, CO5, v. 1368, p. 149; *Acts of the Privy Council,* IV, 563-65, July 20, 1763; "The Respondent's Case, . . ." in John Lidderdale and John Harmer of Bristol, Merchants . . . vs. John Chiswell of Virginia, Esq., British Museum, Additional MSS, 36217ff., pp. 199-205. The problem of British debts due to the colonists in this period has never adequately been explored but there is some evidence indicating that the flow of debt was not always from the colonists to the British. The Virginia Council stated that " 'the factors are as often in the planter's debt, as the planter is in theirs . . .' " (see quotation in Morton, *Colonial Virginia,* II, 509), and in our study of individual debtors, we have found some evidence supporting this view. See for example, Lancaster County merchants John Heath and David Galloway, Lancaster Deed Book 18, pp. 96-97; Book 19, pp. 40, 83.
5. "List of Foreign Debtors to John Norton and Son, 31st July, 1770," John Norton Papers, Colonial Williamsburg.
6. Samuel Athawes to William Dangerfield, March 10, 1768, in Calendar of Virginia State Papers and Other Manuscripts, 1652-1781, ed. by William P. Palmer (Richmond, 1875), I, 259-60; Robert Beverley to Mr. John Bland, Virginia, Nov. 16, 1761, Robert Beverley Letter Book; Richard Corbin to Dinwiddie, July 10, 1761, in Richard Corbin Letters, p. 79.
7. Eddis, *Letters,* p. 112, Dec. 24, 1771; Washington to Edward Montague, April 5, 1775, *Writings,* III, 285.
8. Hening, *Statutes,* VII, 323-30, 445-52; VIII, 214-15; Letter of Mann Page, Jr., to "Tucker," Feb. 15, 1774, Tucker Papers.
9. Norfolk County Wills and Deed Book H, pp. 141-45. See also the affidavit of George Whiteside in the estate of Maurice Griffith, Dec. 19, 1783, Personal Papers, Miscellaneous, Library of Congress, and debtors of James Concanen of London, Richmond County Deed Book 12, p. 327.
10. All of the debtors were from Norfolk County or Borough. There were 108 mortgages involving 93 individual debtors and 75 individual creditors. These figures show each mortgage as a separate document even though one individual may have been involved in several mortgages. Norfolk County Deed Book 20, pp. 265, 293; Book 21, pp. 115, 119, 162, 170, 190-91, 219, 235; Book 22, pp. 29, 35, 37, 38, 44, 59, 61, 62, 85, 114, 128, 130, 154, 168, 172, 173, 174, 182, 189-90, 219, 229, 233; Book 23, pp. 15, 19, 26, 35, 47, 54, 69, 73, 88, 92, 93, 111, 112, 114, 142, 148, 184, 188, 200, 209; Book 24, pp. 7, 12, 18, 34, 36, 37, 41, 52, 68, 72, 75, 86, 89, 90, 93, 125, 129, 130,

131, 136, 168, 173, 174, 178, 179, 207, 209, 219, 224, 249, 255, 266; Book 25, pp. 16, 38, 55, 63, 66, 77, 97, 98-99, 107, 115, 125, 128, 144, 151, 168, 174, 188, 194, 201, 207, 220, 233, 243, 246, 249, 253, 255, 268, 269; Book 26, pp. 27, 29, 63, 72, 98-100, 113, 114, 117, 133, 138, 139, 142, 161, 166, 171, 173, 182, 189, 192, 201, 210, 215, 226, 235, 251; Book 27, pp. 26, 48, 52; Book 28, pp. 17, 19, 30, 31, 78, 138, 178. In addition to these mortgages, thousands of deeds which had been abstracted and alphabetized were combed to determine the social status of the individual debtors and creditors. See Norfolk County Deed Books 13-29 and Book J, *passim*, also Norfolk County Will Books, Norfolk Borough and County Tithable Lists, and Norfolk County Elections Polls for 1768 and 1769 in Deed Book 24, pp. 112-15 and 211-15. Space prohibits giving individual citations on social status.

11. There were 52 mortgages recorded in Lancaster in this period. Lancaster County Deed Book 13, pp. 274, 343; Book 14, pp. 36, 107, 108, 133, 134, 160, 248, 252, 270, 316; Lancaster County Will Book 15, pp. 92, 118, 168-69, 184-86, 194, 210, 235, 256, 262, 314; Lancaster County Deed Book 16, pp. 54, 62, 149, 169, 206, 211, 256; Book 17, pp. 1, 32, 34, 35; Book 18, pp. 11, 20, 28, 31, 56, 96-98; Book 19, pp. 4, 9, 13, 14, 30, 48, 69-71, 91, 99, 100, 108, 240. Additional information on social status of individual debtors and creditors can be found in the deeds and wills in above volumes, plus elections polls and tithable lists.

12. *Ibid.*, Book 18, pp. 96-98; Book 19, pp. 9, 30, 40, 83, 125; Lancaster County Order Book 12, p. 19.

13. *Ibid.*, Book 8, p. 360; Lancaster County Deed Book 14, pp. 108, 270; Lancaster County Will Book 15, pp. 184-86, 202, 207, 223.

14. Essex County Deed Book 23, pp. 203, 214, 279, 282, 288; Book 24, pp. 65, 101, 119, 229; Book 25, pp. 155, 203, 231, 286, 288; Book 26, pp. 1, 25, 97, 104, 142, 169, 179, 182, 250, 264, 288, 296, 300, 303, 309, 315, 358, 361, 374, 402, 414, 418, 435; Book 27, pp. 8, 13, 36, 40, 54, 142, 144, 167, 263, 273, 329; Book 28, pp. 38, 157, 184, 316; Book 29, pp. 85, 133, 153, 154, 162, 167, 205, 222, 223, 224, 225, 242, 248. For additional social information on individuals, see above deed books, *passim*.

15. *Ibid.*, Book 23, pp. 203, 214, 217. For election polls, see *ibid.*, Book 25, pp. 301-07 (1752); Book 27, pp. 248-52 (1755); Book 28, pp. 95-99 (1758); Book 29, pp. 1-7 (1761); Book 30, pp. 235-42 (1765), 243-48 (1768).

16. *Ibid.*, Book 23, p. 203ff. For other English creditors, see *ibid.*, p. 288; Book 25, p. 231; Book 26, p. 25; Book 27, pp. 142, 144; Book 28, pp. 38, 157; Book 29, pp. 153, 154, 222, 223, 224, 225.

17. Spotsylvania County Deed Book E, pp. 85, 121, 180, 188, 192, 207, 254, 286, 299, 319, 356, 377, 381, 443, 497, 500, 501, 502; Book F, pp. 114, 183, 234, 235, 254, 255, 281, 307, 342, 365, 401, 482, 504, 514, 529, 535, 570, 579, 582, 589, 590, 600, 605, 627, 630, 640, 643, 651, 656, 658, 663, 669, 677, 681, 682, 708, 711, 714, 718; Book G, pp. 11, 13, 14, 18, 19, 20, 29, 60, 61, 65, 88, 121, 129, 148, 149, 153, 195, 205, 213, 224, 237, 240, 249, 279, 314, 321, 325, 342, 397, 418, 440, 448, 450, 454, 527; Book H, pp. 36, 37, 80, 81, 120, 141, 163, 170, 229, 295, 306, 308, 311, 312, 354, 380, 397, 404, 406, 417, 435, 442, 444, 447, 460, 466, 472, 505, 518, 520, 548; Spotsylvania County Will Book D, pp. 146, 371. For additional social material, see deeds and wills in the above books. One of these 116 mortgages contained two debtors, hence the total of 117 debtors. There were 89 individuals who mortgaged their property in the 116 mortgages and 82 individuals who were creditors. Asterisks indicate counties bordering on Spotsylvania. Orange and Culpeper are on the west and Louisa on the south and west of Spotsylvania. Only one creditor was from Williamsburg and this was a relative. See Spotsylvania County Deed Book E, p. 85, mortgage of gentleman Edmund Waller to gentleman William Waller, for security on debt due to Benjamin Waller, Esq. of Williamsburg.

18. *House Journals, 1742-49*, pp. 261, 292-93; *ibid., 1761-65*, pp. 3-4, 181-82, 221-22; Spotsylvania County Will Book D, pp. 362, 528-33; Orange County Deed Book 12, p. 308; Book 13, pp. 73, 107; Book 15, p. 3; Book 16, p. 321; Spotsylvania County Deed Book E, pp. 285, 286, 526; Book G, p. 14; Book H, p. 127; *Virginia Gazette* (R), Dec. 1, 1768; Dec. 7, 1769; June 9, 1774; *ibid.*, (P & D), May 23, 1771; Sept. 26, 1771; Oct. 3, 1771; Nov. 4, 1773; *Letters to Washington*, III, 363, Sept. 1769.

19. Spotsylvania County Will Book D, p. 1; Spotsylvania County Deed Book F, pp. 255, 656, 669, 708, 711, 714, 718; Book G, pp. 20, 121, 195, 237, 397, 450, 454; Book H, pp. 505, 518; *Virginia Gazette* (P & D), Feb. 22, 1774. One of Waller's creditors was William Wood, his deputy clerk, but Wood was also a debtor and finally lost his property in 1774; see Spotsylvania County Deed Book H. pp. 80, 229; *Virginia Gazette* (R), June 9, 1774.

20. Orange County Deed Book 2, pp. 359, 445; Book 3, pp. 46, 47, 65; Book 4, pp. 346, 414; Book 6, pp. 20, 270, 324; Book 7, pp. 74, 76, 144, 184, 347; Book 8, pp. 56, 215; Book 9, p. 163; Book 10, pp. 320, 324, 333, 505, 528; Book 11, pp. 24, 179; Book 12, pp. 31, 69, 73, 137, 145, 175, 208, 252, 267, 272, 297, 348, 419, 500; Book 13, pp. 71, 73, 107, 257, 348, 416, 423, 432, 443, 447, 450, 461, 468, 473, 483, 489, 498, 500, 513; Book 14, pp. 1, 24, 56, 59, 70, 91, 251, 271, 273, 278, 281, 329, 459; Book 15, pp. 29, 280, 361, 384, 410, 510; Book 16, pp. 51, 53, 55, 80, 113. The occupation of the illiterates is unknown; two of the four tenants also signed with a mark. Two of the mortgages involved father-son combinations and three creditors held one mortgage, thus making 80 debtors and 80 creditors in the 78 mortgages. Most debtors contracted only one mortgage, but one man had three and a few men had two; 57 individuals or companies were creditors in the 78 mortgages, the largest creditor being Andrew Shepherd and Company with eleven mortgages.

21. Halifax County Deed Book 6, pp. 6, 179, 182, 191, 233, 260, 347, 366, 385, 389, 421, 428, 441, 454, 458; Book 7, pp. 52, 72, 78, 109, 110, 162, 176, 240, 255, 357, 397, 425, 436, 481, 509. In one mortgage there were two debtors and in another mortgage, two creditors, making a total of thirty-one debtors and thirty-one creditors or securities in the thirty mortgages. Most debtors had only one mortgage but one creditor—Thomas Yuille, James Murdock and Company—had ten of the thirty mortgages.

22. For the 27 mortgages see Loudoun County Deed Book A, pp. 37, 57, 114; Book B, p. 73; Book C, pp. 504, 685; Book D, pp. 100, 130, 147, 220, 330, 425, 706; Book E, pp. 10, 83, 150, 284, 347; Book F, pp. 19, 136, 273, 296; Book G, pp. 36, 93, 99, 187, 219. For social status see above deed books, *passim*.

23. In Augusta, there were dual debtors in three mortgages and several mortgages had more than one creditor, thus making the total of 101 debtors and 108 creditors in the 98 mortgages. The great bulk of creditors held only one mortgage but some merchants and others held several. For mortgages see Augusta County Deed Book 2, Part 2, p. 718; Book 5, p. 445; Book 8, pp. 108, 109, 373; Book 9, pp. 385, 449; Book 10, pp. 72, 368, 405; Book 11, pp. 40, 183, 217, 226, 227, 232, 336, 546, 564, 824, 831, 905; Book 12, pp. 202, 483-84; Book 13, pp. 8, 69, 71, 85, 86, 168, 215, 239, 289, 307, 336, 356, 366, 367, 497, 513; Book 14, pp. 21, 102, 112, 113, 115, 244, 295, 303, 307, 326, 464, 488, 533; Book 15, pp. 109, 143, 247, 282, 283, 291, 310, 338, 423, 481, 482, 487; Book 16, pp. 24, 41, 190, 266, 271, 275, 277, 509, 530; Book 17, pp. 8, 9, 101, 175, 221, 330, 438; Book 18, pp. 71, 175, 179, 243, 411, 426, 445, 509, 522; Book 19, pp. 37, 146, 246, 268, 329, 331, 384, 465, 481, 486. Mortgages in Augusta frequently were in the form of leases. Examples of the 500-year-lease mortgage can be found in Augusta County Deed Book 8, p. 373; Book 11, p. 831; Book 13, pp. 69, 71; Book 14, p. 464; Book 16, p. 190.

24. See leases in Orange County Deed Books, *passim;* Loudoun County

Deed Books A-G, *passim.* For contrasting view of debtors and creditors in the Northern Neck area, see Jackson T. Main, "Sections and Politics in Virginia, 1781-1787," in *William and Mary Quarterly,* 3rd Ser., XII (1955), pp. 109-110.

25. Loudoun County Deed Book G, p. 219; Book E, p. 10.

26. Compare Loudoun leases and mortgages with those of Norfolk and Spotsylvania; for William Williams see *ibid.,* Book C, p. 504; Book D, p. 626.

27. Hening, *Statutes,* IV, 294-96; V, 101-04.

28. *Ibid.,* III, 385-89.

29. *House Journals, 1712-26,* pp. 84, 92, 93, 115.

30. Hening, *Statutes,* IV, 151-67.

31. *Ibid.,* p. 452.

32. Gooch to Lords of Trade, Nov. 20, 1734, Gooch Papers, II, 360; PRO, CO5, v. 1323/5, p. 299.

33. Hening, *Statutes,* IV, 487-92; V, 537-40.

34. *Acts of the Privy Council,* IV, 135, 138, 139.

35. Hening, *Statutes,* VI, 342-44.

36. *House Journals, 1752-58,* pp. 232, 248, 258, 269, 274, 277, 278, 280; Hening, *Statutes,* VI, 478-85; *Acts of the Privy Council,* IV, 390-92.

37. Hening, *Statutes,* VI, 521-30.

38. *House Journals, 1752-58,* p. 428.

39. *Acts of the Privy Council,* IV, 390-93.

40. Hening, *Statutes,* VII, 118-20.

41. *House Journals, 1761-65,* pp. 105, 118, 140, 148, 151; Hening, *Statutes,* VII, 549-63.

42. Matthew Lamb to Lords of Trade, May 17, 1763, PRO, CO5, v. 1330, pp. 305-07. For merchant petitions, *ibid.,* pp. 309, 313, 323.

43. Lords of Trade to King, July 6, 1763, PRO, CO5, v. 1368, p. 149.

44. *Acts of the Privy Council,* IV, 563-65.

45. *House Journals, 1761-65,* pp. 181, 184, 194; Hening, *Statutes,* VII, 643.

46. *Ibid.,* VIII, 527-28.

47. *Virginia Gazette* (R), Oct. 6, 1768.

48. *Ibid.* (P & D), Nov. 8, 1770.

49. Dec. 2, 1773, Adams Papers, VHS.

50. Jones, *Present State of Virginia,* p. 69.

51. Petition of merchants trading in or to Virginia, Nov. 2, 1764, *House Journals, 1761-65,* pp. 233-35.

52. *Virginia Gazette* (P & D), Feb. 7, 1771.

53. See for example notice of sale of estate of Bernard Moore in *ibid.,* Nov. 8, 1770. See also Nov. 10, 1768, Nov. 8, 1770, and Oct. 3, 1771 for Charles Carter and Aug. 26, 1773 (R) for John Semple.

54. *Ibid.* (P & D), May 19, 1768 and Sept. 21, 1769.

55. *House Journals, 1770-72,* p. 198.

56. *Letters to Washington,* III, 287-89, 291-92.

57. July 25, 1770, Norton Papers.

58. Richard Corbin to Edmund Jennings, April 26, 1758; to Hanbury, Oct. 8, 1759; to Robert Dinwiddie, Oct. 8, 1760 and Dec. 15, 1761, Richard Corbin Letterbook; *Virginia Gazette* (P & D), Dec. 13, 1770.

59. To Robert Cary, May 1 and Aug. 10, 1764, Washington, *Writings,* II, 414-16.

60. Lee to James Steptoe, July 4, 1772, and Oct. 23, 1772; *Letters of Richard Henry Lee,* I, 68, 78, 332n.; Lee to [Dr. Wm. Shippen, Jr.], May 8, 1758 and John R. Tucker to Richard Henry Lee, March 9, 1758, Lee Papers, U. of Va.

61. For James Mercer, see George Washington to James Mercer, July 19, 1773 and March 28, 1774; to Wm. Trent, Aug. 4, 1775; to Edward Montague, April 5, 1775, Washington, *Writings,* III, 146-47, 196-98, 285, 401; George Mason to Washington, Dec. 31, 1773, *Letters to Washington,* IV, 286-88, *Vir-*

*ginia Gazette*, Feb. 19, 1767. For Wm. Clinch, see *House Journals, 1752-58*, pp. 346, 351, 353, 436-37. For Benjamin Harrison, see Hening, *Statutes*, III, 537-38. For Charles Carter, see letter to Capel & Hanbury, June 30, 1764 and letter to Robert Dinwiddie, Aug. 11, 1764 in Richard Corbin Letterbook, pp. 149, 155; Landon Carter to Thomas Martin, Sept. 24, 1766, Carter Papers, Folder 3, William and Mary College Library; *Virginia Gazette* (R), Oct. 25, 1769. For Robert Burwell, see Robert Burwell to Thomas Adams, May 26, 1771, Adams Papers, VHS. For Mann Page, see *Virginia Gazette,* March 12, 1767; Corbin to Mann Page, August 31, 1768, Richard Corbin Letterbook; Mann Page, Jr., to "Tucker," Feb. 15, 1774, Tucker Papers. For Governor Dunmore, see Robert Prentis to Robert Carter, March 25, 1783, Carter Keith Papers, File 2, VHS.

62. Corbin to Graham Frank, Aug. 3, and Dec. 7, 1768, Richard Corbin Letterbook; for other ministers in debt see Reverend William McKay, Richmond County Deed Book 12, p. 546, Jan. 5, 1764; William Allason to Reverend James Thompson, Feb. 1, 1774, Allason Letterbook, p. 273; debt of Reverend William Davis to William Byrd discussed in *Virginia Gazette* (P & D), Aug. 10, 1769.

63. Hening, *Statutes*, V, 64-65; *Letters to Washington*, I, 178n.

64. *House Journals, 1776-69*, pp. xv-xvi, 65-67, 70, 155-56; David J. Mays, *Edmund Pendleton, 1721-1803: A Biography*, 2 vols. (Cambridge, Mass., 1952), I, 358-75 (Appendix II); Fauquier to Shelburne, Dec. 18, 1766, PRO, CO5, v. 1345, pp. 125-27; Corbin to Graham Frank, Aug. 3, 1768, Richard Corbin Letterbook.

65. Norfolk County Will Book 2, p. 83.

66. Extracts of the will of Moses Fontaine, Oct. 13, 1763, Maury Papers, U. of Va.

67. Norfolk County Will Book, 1, p. 193. For additional cases see *ibid.,* pp. 127 (William Hodges), 211 (Edward Archer); Book 2, pp. 164 (Richard Jolliff), 181 (Augustus Lane), 303 (James Wilson); James Maury to Col. Peter Fontaine, Dec. 13, 1764, Maury Papers, Letterbook, 1763; Adam Hunter to James Hunter, Jr., Jan. 6, 1774, Hunter Collection; Lancaster County Will Book 20, p. 129 (Thomas Griffin); *ibid.,* p. 156 (Walter James); *Ibid.,* p. 176 (William Sanders); Richmond County Deed Book 12, p. 814 (Tarpley); Spotsylvania County Will Book D, pp. 104 (Robert Jackson), 285 (Richard Tutt).

68. Spotsylvania County Deed Book E, pp. 85 (Waller), 254 (Bradburn), 501 (Woodroof); Book F, pp. 514 (Robinson), 669 (Waller), 682 (Johnston); Book G, pp. 224 (Winslow), 249 (Johnston).

69. Norfolk County Deed Book 27, pp. 99, 102; see also the case of John Pickens of Augusta in *Virginia Gazette*, March 12, 1752; Capt. Henry McCabe to George Washington, March 31, 1775, *Letters to Washington*, V, 145.

70. Hening, *Statutes*, VII, 458-61.

71. Dunmore to Dartmouth, Dec. 24, 1774, Washington, *Writings*, III, 249n.

72. Spotswood to Lords of Trade, Dec. 29, 1713, Spotswood, *Letters,* II, 48-50; Hening, *Statutes*, IV, 247-71.

73. Anburey, *Travels*, II, 314.

74. Landon Carter Diary, Aug. 22, 1754.

75. Hening, *Statutes*, VI, 467.

76. *Virginia Gazette*, May 9, 1755.

77. *House Journals, 1752-58*, pp. 339-40.

78. *Ibid.,* pp. 427-28.

79. Hening, *Statutes*, VII, 81-84.

80. Corbin to James Buchanan, April 26, 1758, Richard Corbin Letterbook; Hening, *Statutes*, VII, 166-68.

81. "Extract of a Representation . . . 9 Feby 1764," Shelburne Papers; *Acts*

*of the Privy Council,* IV, 623-31, March 9, 1764; Fauquier to Lords of Trade, Nov. 16, 1764, PRO, CO5, v. 1331, p. 155.

82. Corbin to Hanbury, May 31, 1765, Richard Corbin Letterbook.

83. *House Journals, 1761-65,* pp. 350-51, 353, 356; *ibid., 1766-69,* pp. 115-116, 125-29; Corbin to Robert Cary, Aug. 1, 1765, Richard Corbin Letterbook.

84. Beverley to John Bland, May 5, 1763, Robert Beverley Letterbook (Colonial Williamsburg).

85. The best account of the Robinson story, which is still incomplete, is to be found in Mays, *Pendleton,* I, 144-47, 174-75.

86. Thomas Lewis to William Preston?, Dec. 16, 1766, Preston Papers.

87. *House Journals, 1766-69,* pp. 125-29; PRO, CO5, v. 1332, p. 39; Lords of Trade to King, June 10, 1768, *ibid.,* v. 1345, pp. 13-14.

88. Richard Corbin to John Roberts, May 15, 1767, Richard Corbin Letterbook.

89. Hening, *Statutes,* VIII, 501-02.

90. Bland to Thomas Adams, Aug. 1, 1771, Adams Papers, VHS.

91. *Virginia Gazette* (R), July 29, 1773.

92. *Ibid.,* Sept. 16 and 30, 1773.

# CHAPTER VI

# *The Voting Franchise*

A SOCIETY IS JUDGED by the number and kind of people who are permitted to participate in the political processes, and one method of determining whether Virginia was democratic or aristocratic is to discover who had political rights in the Old Dominion. If democracy means government by the many and aristocracy means government by the few, we must ascertain whether the few or the many could vote. Perhaps the right to vote does not in itself guarantee democracy, but a society that denied the vote to its members would certainly not qualify as democratic.

What, if any, were the legal restrictions on voting in Virginia? Did they permit participation by a large segment of the population, or did they restrict participation to a small aristocratic group? Our problem in this chapter will be to find the legal basis for politics, then in later chapters we shall see how the legal basis worked in actual practice.

By 1705, when the first comprehensive election law was passed, several precedents had been established which were to be incorporated into the 1705 law. In March of 1654/5, the law stated that anyone elected to the House of Burgesses must be a person "of known integrity and of good conversation and of the age of one & twenty years." Voting was restricted to "all housekeepers whether freeholders, lease holders, or otherwise tenants," but the word "housekeeper" was to mean only one member of a family. A year later the Assembly had a change of heart, conceiving it "something hard and unagreeable to reason that any person shall pay equal taxes and yet have no vote in elections," so it repealed that part of the election law which excluded any freeman from the vote. In other words, a man did not have to be a householder, and more than one man in a family could vote, provided, of course, they were freemen. The only restriction was "that they fairly give their vote by subscription and not in a tumultuous way." The following year, March, 1657/8, a law stated that "all persons inhabitting in this colony that are freemen to have their votes in the election of burgesses." And in 1661/2, every freeman was compelled to vote for burgesses on penalty of a fine of 200 pounds of tobacco.[1]

In 1670, however, the colony returned to the "stake in society" philosophy for designating qualified voters. According to the law of that year, the reason for the change seems to have been that indentured servants who became freemen after serving their time had "little interest in the country" and used their new-found political rights more often to cause riots at elections than to elect qualified burgesses. Furthermore, the laws of England gave a voice in elections "only to such as by their estates real or personal have interest enough to tie them to the endeavor of the public good." So henceforth only freeholders and housekeepers who were subject to public levies could vote.[2]

During the Bacon uprising there was a return to voting by freemen, but this interlude was of short duration. The Assembly of 1676 returned voting privileges to freemen on an equal basis with freeholders and housekeepers. When Governor William Berkeley returned, however, he brought with him an instruction "that the members of the assembly be elected only by freeholders, as being more agreeable to the custom of England." This time the "stake" was a freehold, not a household.[3]

Two other significant additions or modifications were made in the voting laws before 1705. In 1684 the House resolved that it was "the undoubted right of every person who holds lands, tenements or hereditaments for his own life, for the life of his wife or for the life of any other person or persons to vote in election of Burgesses for the county where such lands, tenements, etc. do lie." This meant that tenants with life leases were to be considered the same as freeholders, and it also meant plural voting, as a man could give his vote in any county where he owned or leased land, or where he was a tenant by virtue of an entail. A second modification in 1699 gave the vote to Quakers who were otherwise qualified, but freeholders who were women, minors under twenty-one years of age, or recusant convicts were denied the franchise.[4]

By the time the laws were revised in 1705, some of the voting qualifications were fairly well established. A voter must be a freeholder, a male adult of twenty-one years or older, and not a recusant convict. Quakers could make declarations instead of taking oaths as required by law, so voting was not restricted to members of the Church of England. A qualified voter was compelled to vote in every county where he owned sufficient property. The size of freehold was not specified, so any real estate would suffice. Robert Beverley described the voting qualifications as follows: "The freeholders are the only electors, and where-ever they have a free-hold, (if they be not women, or under age) they have a vote in the election." [5]

Of particular importance in our later discussion of tenant voting is the definition of a freeholder contained in this 1705 law: "That every person who hath an estate real for his own life, or the life of another, or any estate of any greater dignity, shall be accounted a freeholder, within the meaning of this act." A tenant often leased land for three or four lives— his own, his wife's, and a son or two. In short, a tenant who had a lease on real property for life or lives was equally a freeholder and voter with the man who owned land, and, as we have already noted in Chapter I and II and shall see later, most Virginia tenants had leases for life or lives.

Of significance also in the election law of 1705 were suggested provisions which were not adopted. A draft of a bill in that year would have required voters to possess twenty-five acres with a house and plantation or 100 acres of unsettled land; these provisions were eventually included in 1736. There was also the proposal that a burgess must be a freeholder and a resident of the county where he was elected.[6] One might expect that an aristocratic House of Burgesses would adopt the more restrictive freehold requirements but reject the residence requirement, since aristocrats might hope to be elected from counties other than the ones where they lived.

Another law in 1705 defined slaves as real estate, but a man who owned slaves only was not considered a freeholder under the election law. No matter how many slaves a man owned, he was not a voter unless he held land.[7] Under the law it was possible, but not probable, that a man could own a hundred slaves worth thousands of pounds and not be a voter, while the man who had half an acre of land worth a few shillings could vote. But a man who owned one or more slaves and yet did not have the right to vote was a non-voter by choice, for the price of a slave was enough to purchase considerable land.

In 1705 there was also an effort to provide for the incorporation of towns, the establishment of town governments, and the representation of these towns in the assembly. When a town's population reached sixty families, the adult "freeholders and housekeepers" could elect one burgess. The act was apparently disallowed in England, probably because it was an invasion of the King's prerogative of incorporating towns.[8] As a result, local town government never became important in Virginia except in Norfolk and Williamsburg, which were incorporated as boroughs by the King. The county system continued as the significant unit of government in the Old Dominion, but not because a "planter aristocracy" would not permit local town government.

Was this 1705 election law, then, aristocratic or democratic? According to Governor Spotswood, it was extremely liberal, conferring the right to vote and to be elected burgess on any man who possessed as little as half an acre of land. He said that men just out of servitude who could but purchase half an acre of land had an equal vote with men of the best estates in the country. On another occasion the Governor declared that "half an acre of land here makes a man as sufficient a voter, and as lawful a burgess as he that is possess'd of 10,000 acres & 100 Negroes." And half an acre, he said, was "of small value in this country."[9]

Spotswood attempted without success to get a more stringent law both for voting and office holding, and it should be noted that his chief opposition came from the "aristocratic" council. Concerned with the growing influence of transported convicts and indentured servants in Virginia elections, and spurred on by an order from the Lords of Trade, the Governor advocated a law that would raise the qualifications of both those who voted and those who held office. He proposed such a measure in the Council, but a majority would not agree. He then thought to get such an act passed by the House, but he said that the ruling family in the Council, which he did not identify, was at odds with policies of the Lords of Trade for some years past and had obstructed any measures that might have restricted either electors or the elected.[10] Obviously the "aristocrats" did not greatly fear the political power of the "lower classes," or perhaps they were afraid that they might antagonize the lower class if they attempted to restrict the franchise.

The first significant modification of the 1705 election law came in 1723 with the disfranchisement of free Negroes, mulattoes, and Indians. When this law was objected to in England on the ground that any freeman who was qualified should be a voter, Governor Gooch explained the reason for excluding these three groups. He said that there was a threatened slave insurrection in 1723 and that free Negroes and mulattoes were suspected of being involved, as they would always favor the slaves. The insolence of free Negroes led the Assembly to pass a law to punish slaves and also to fix a perpetual brand upon free Negroes and mulattoes by excluding them from the great privilege of freemen. It was also said that the law was passed to make free Negroes aware of a distinction between their offspring and the offspring of Englishmen, with whom they were never to be accounted equal. Gooch approved this philosophy. The law might seem severe to anyone not acquainted with Negroes, he said, but a freed slave had such pride that upon acquiring his freedom he looked upon himself as being as good a man as his neighbors, especially if he was descended from a white father or mother. Most of the latter were offspring of imported servants and convicts, and it would be well to preserve a decent distinction between them and their betters until time and education had extinguished their origin and altered their morals. In any event, the Governor concluded, there were so few free Negroes and mulattoes qualified to vote that taking notice of them was not worthwhile.[11]

The importance of tenants as voters is evident from disputed elections in King George and York counties in 1736. The episodes also demonstrate how little was needed to vote and that the "upper classes" were not always interested in restricting the electorate. William Robinson accused Charles Carter and John Mercer of leasing half-acre tracts for life to prospective voters "either on, or some few days before the day of the said election, in consideration for their voting for the said Charles Carter." Francis Heyward, sheriff of York County, was also accused of creating voters through life leases of small parcels of worthless land. Heyward confessed to a House committee investigating the charges "that some small time before the last *York* election, he . . . did execute nineteen leases for life to so many several persons, to make them freeholders, in order to entitle them to vote at that election. . . . That the consideration of each lease was two shillings only, and no rent." The sheriff said that he did not exact promises from the newly-created freeholders, but he admitted that he would not have given them leases if he had not thought that they would vote for his candidates.[12]

The disputed elections of 1736 demonstrate three important facts about the franchise. First, a lease for life of any small tract of land, if the lease was legitimate, was sufficient to qualify a voter. Second, aristocrats, far from restricting the electorate, were willing to create voters if it would help them to win elections. And third, elections were obviously not cut-and-dried affairs in which aristocrats elected other aristocrats to the House, for some candidates must have felt that the election was sufficiently in doubt so that they welcomed any kind of votes to win.

These fraudulent leases to create voters brought an increase in the franchise requirements in a new election law passed in 1736. The House incorporated the proposals made but not passed in 1705: to be a voter a freeholder must henceforth have at least twenty-five acres with a house and plantation or 100 acres of unimproved land. The 100 acres did not have to be all in one county, but the owner had to vote in the county where the largest part lay. Furthermore, to stop conveyances of land just before elections, the law provided that a man must possess his freehold for one year before the election unless the land came to him legally by descent, marriage, marriage settlement, or devise. Tenants with leases for life were freeholders. Quakers could vote, qualified voters were required to vote (a provision never enforced), but they had to vote only in the county where they were resident, and a man could vote in more than one county (plural voting) if he owned sufficient land there. Indentured servants and apprentices were not specifically excluded. Other restrictions imposed in 1705 and 1727, such as age, race, sex, and the exclusion of recusant convicts, continued in the new law.[13] Although there were attempts later to change it, the election law of 1736 remained in force until the Revolution.

In spite of the higher voting qualifications, Governor William Gooch obviously did not consider the franchise law of 1736 very restrictive. He called the freehold requirement "indeed too inconsiderable a qualification." But as the former law gave the vote to the possessor of "any kind of freehold," and all previous attempts "to exclude the mobb of the populace, and to establish the qualifications of the electors had proved vain," it was better to have the amount fixed. The new law was especially beneficial because it voided "all collusive conveyances to create voters," the device used by some "aristocrats" to win elections. With this beginning, Gooch hoped for further regulations that would remove from the House such members as had little to recommend them to the people except the art of stirring up discontent among the lower classes.[14]

One feature of the 1736 election law, a feature that has been neglected and deserves special notice, was the franchise requirement for town voters. To encourage trade, the General Assembly had passed laws in 1691 and 1705 by which it could set aside certain tracts of land and designate them as unincorporated towns. These towns were under the county governments except for a board of trustees who could dispose of town lots and enforce building requirements. Eventually there were some eighty-five or more towns—some, such as Fredericksburg, Portsmouth, Richmond, Dumfries, Alexandria, Yorktown and others, flourishing embryos. The election law of 1736 took note of these towns by making a special franchise requirement for them. Men who lived in such towns were voters if they possessed a freehold of a house and part of a lot in the town.[15] This meant that any town artisan who owned a house of any kind or leased a house for life was a qualified voter.

There were three exceptions to the 1736 franchise requirements for town voters in Virginia—James City or Jamestown, Williamsburg, and Norfolk—each of which was allowed to send one burgess. A mistake in the law permitted voters in James City to qualify without having houses on their lots as was required of voters in other towns.[16] Williamsburg (1723) and Norfolk (1738) were boroughs incorporated by charter from the King. Both had borough governments—mayor, recorder, aldermen, and common council. Voters for burgess had to have a lot with a house of the size determined by the legislature when the town was laid out. A man was also a voter if he had an estate of £50 current money, which of course might include real estate that did not conform to the regulations. But even more important, a man was a voter if he had served a five-year apprenticeship to a trade in the town and, after his service, was actually a housekeeper and inhabitant. Norfolk, however, definitely excluded servants from the vote until their time of service had expired.[17] This meant that artisans or tradesmen did not need any property to vote in these two towns if they had served their apprenticeships there.

Disputes over the exact meaning of the corporation charters led the Assembly to pass acts in 1742 and 1752 to explain the charters in detail and to settle doubts about voting qualifications. In addition to the above requirements, these laws made the following explanations: where there were joint tenants, only one could vote; a voter must have resided in the town twelve months before the election; indentured servants could not vote merely because they were inhabitants or residents, but the act does not say whether a servant or apprentice could vote if he owned sufficient property in the town; no one was entitled to vote simply because he had served five years unless he had actually served as an apprentice to some trade in the borough and had obtained a certificate to this effect from the Court of Hustings in the borough; and properly qualified Quakers could vote. The explanatory act for Norfolk was disallowed in England as an infringement on the King's prerogative of granting charters, but its provisions probably continued to be the rule for determining qualified voters.[18]

Closely contested elections brought disputes over the exact meaning of the franchise laws, and these in turn give us some notion of exactly how voters were determined in practice. A few examples must suffice here.

Few, if any, were excluded from voting in Virginia because of religious beliefs. The laws did not mention religion except for the exclusion of recusant convicts and the provision that Quakers could make an affirmation. Presbyterians voted, for many of the forty-one Presbyterians who signed a statement to the Essex County court in 1758 voted in the county.[19] Catholics who were not "recusant convicts" were also legal voters. George Brent, gentleman and Roman Catholic from Prince William County, voted in 1741 and for all we know in every election thereafter. But in a disputed election in 1761, Brent's right to vote was challenged by the losing candidate, Henry Peyton, gentleman, on the ground that Brent was a Roman Catholic. Both the Committee on Elections and the House itself ruled that Brent had a good right to vote, for even though he was a Catholic he was not a "recusant convict."[20] This is the only instance that we have found in which the right of a Catholic to vote was questioned.

We can never determine how many men of Negro ancestry voted in Virginia, but if their ancestry was known they were denied the franchise. Nehemiah Nichols of Elizabeth City County was reputedly the son of a white man and a mulatto woman. His grandmother was a white woman as was his wife, so his son Joseph was only about an eighth Negro. But both Nehemiah and Joseph Nichols were disqualified as voters in the election of 1756 because of race.[21]

Tenants, of course, were legal voters provided they had a lease for life on sufficient acreage to meet the legal requirements. William Davie voted in Prince William with a lease for two lives on fifty acres of land, but in 1761 George Harper, who held 660 acres, was denied the ballot on the ground that he held this land "only as tenant, at will of William Fitzhugh, Esq."[22] In other words, the permanency of a fifty-acre lease for life was considered more valuable in qualifying a voter than was a tenuous lease at will, even though the latter was for 660 acres.

A son of a tenant whose father had leased land for three lives and had included the son's name on the lease became a voter after his father's death. In 1738 one John Metcalfe of Prince William leased 150 acres for three lives—his own, his wife's, and his son John's. The elder Metcalfe did not vote in 1741, the year for which we have a poll list, although he was entitled to do so. When he died intestate in 1751, his wife and son continued to live on the leased land and paid the quitrents. Of course the son inherited the lease; and when he voted in 1761 and his right to vote was challenged, both the Committee on Elections and the House ruled that he had a perfect right to vote on the basis of the lease.[23]

The Metcalfe and Harper incidents also show that the quitrent rolls do not give us the qualified voters in a county. The statement was made in this disputed election that Metcalfe and his mother had always paid their quitrents, but the name of Metcalfe is not on the rentals from 1751 to 1761. Metcalfe undoubtedly paid his quitrents to his landlord, whose name would be on the rent rolls, but anyone examining these quitrent rolls would conclude that there was no voter in Prince William by the name of Metcalfe. George Harper, on the other hand, appears on the rent rolls from 1752 to 1760, yet his vote was invalidated.[24]

Town dwellers actually needed very little property to be qualified voters. John Dalton, tailor, leased a lot for three lives in Fredericksburg in 1768, owned no other property according to the deeds and wills, yet voted in 1771; so a lease for life in town qualified an artisan.[25] Another town voter built a house on a lot promised but never actually given to him by his brother, then built a "lean-to" extending onto the adjoining lot, which he did own. On his own lot also was "a little house 6 feet by 4 feet, not framed, but posted in the ground, having rafters on one side only, and covered in, but the boards on the side of it are mostly torn off, and it is in ruinous condition," as was also the "lean-to." But the House ruled that this man was a legal voter. Also ruled a legal voter was a man who purchased a "house" ten feet by eight feet in size and moved it onto his lot on the Saturday before the election "on purpose (as he acknowledged) to qualify him to vote at that election." After the election the "house" was used as a stable and the people who sold it said they expected it to be returned so they could use it as a smoke house. The voter himself was quoted as saying in public that this whole affair "was done under a sham," yet he was declared a qualified voter. Incidentally, both men voted for losing candidates.[26]

Land had to be legally transferred, however, before a man could qualify as a voter. One Samuel Dewberry made a verbal gift of 145 acres to his son, but the House would not accept this as a voting qualification. But the House reversed the Committee on Elections and accepted the vote of Signe Parish even though Parish had agreed to convey six of his twenty-five acres to his brother Edward for £40 and Edward had lived on the six acres for two years. The transaction had never been legalized by a deed, so Signe Parish was still considered the owner of twenty-five acres, and that qualified him as a voter. At the same time, the House disqualified Burr Calvert because Calvert had only ninety-three acres without a house or improvement, and the law called for 100 acres of unimproved land.[27]

A minister's glebe was ruled as a legal voting qualification, but even though a minister might be considered a member of the upper classes, his right to vote could be challenged. Thomas Warrington, rector of Elizabeth City Parish, had a glebe of 100 acres and buildings, but he would not take the oath required of challenged voters because he was not sure that he was legally qualified. Both the Committee on Elections and the House accepted his vote as legal.[28]

The incongruity of a law which gave the vote to one man with a part of a lot in town and a shack placed on the lot just before the election yet denied the vote to a man with ninety-three acres of land brought an attempt by the House to amend the election laws in 1762. In the new law, the hundred-acre requirement for unimproved land was reduced to fifty acres, but both the twenty-five acres of improved land and the part of a lot in town had to include a house at least twelve feet square. Although a house twelve feet square is only the size of a moderate bed-room, the legislators must have felt that it was large enough to preclude moving for election purposes. Convict transports were also denied the vote until their term of conviction had expired. Unfortunately, this law provided that an Assembly must be called at least once every three years and that no Assembly could last more than seven years, with the result that the entire law was disallowed in England as an encroachment on the King's prerogative.[29]

Although the statement has been made that the reduction from 100 to fifty acres was done to increase the ease of plural voting for the upper classes, neither evidence nor logic supports such an interpretation. The wills show that men of the upper classes seldom owned only an isolated fifty acres in a distant county. When they owned land in other counties, it was usually an amount sufficient for slave quarters under overseers so as to make it economically profitable. A more probable interpretation would be that the legislature was attempting to equalize the requirements for small farmers and town artisans, for the 1761 elections had demonstrated that town voters could vote with virtually nothing. The small landowner, particularly a young man just beginning to acquire land, was much more apt to benefit by this law than was the "aristocrat."

Again in 1769-70 the Assembly attempted to liberalize the election laws, and again without success. Except for one item, this law was exactly like the law of 1762 that was disallowed. Previously a man must have possessed his property for one year before the election to qualify, but this qualification was now reduced to six months.[30] The fate of this law was perhaps forecast by instructions to Governor Dunmore early in 1771 not to consent to any Virginia law that would enlarge or diminish the Assembly, ascertain its duration, or fix or alter the qualifications of the electors.[31] In England, the Lords of Trade deferred action on the election bill until they got an explanation of the law from Lord Dunmore.[32] As the law had a suspending clause, it could not become effective until approved in England, and approval never came.

When in our final chapter we consider the social implications of the Revolution on Virginia society, we must remember that both House and Council had been willing to lower voting qualifications before the Revolution but that this liberalization was blocked by the British government. Otherwise we are apt to think that the Revolution brought with it more internal social change than actually occurred.

That there was no great popular animosity against the voting qualifications in Virginia is attested by the fact that the old voting qualifications were kept for the election of delegates to the revolutionary conventions. In July, 1775, the Richmond Convention decreed that voters for convention delegates were to be the same as those who had previously been qualified to vote for burgesses.[33] Evidently the right to vote was not one of the revolutionary grievances.

Such were the franchise requirements in Virginia before the Revolution. Based on a "stake in society" philosophy of government, they nevertheless did not require much of a stake and were certainly not very exclusive. Freeholders with twenty-five acres of improved land or 100 acres of wild land, owners of a "house" and part of a lot in a town, and owners of £50 of estate or men who had served a five-year apprenticeship in Williamsburg or Norfolk could all qualify. In a colony where men could buy land from the government at 5s. for fifty acres or from speculators at £3 or less per 100 acres, the property requirements for voting imposed in Virginia were not very formidable. Just how formidable they were will appear in more detail in the following chapter.

## NOTES

1. Hening, *Statutes*, I, 403, 412, 475; II, 82.
2. *Ibid.*, p. 280.
3. *Ibid.*, pp. 356-57, 425.
4. *Ibid.*, III, 26, 172-75. For a different interpretation of tenant voting see Jackson T. Main, "Sections and Politics in Virginia," *William and Mary Quarterly*, 3rd Ser., XII, 97-98; Sydnor, *Gentlemen Freeholders*, p. 31.
5. Hening, *Statutes*, pp. 236-46; Beverley, *History*, pp. 241-42.
6. Draft of a bill for the election of Burgesses, 1705, Lee-Ludwell Papers.
7. Hening, *Statutes*, III, 334.
8. *Ibid.*, p. 414.
9. To Lords of Trade, Oct. 15, 1712, Spotswood, *Letters,* II, 1-2; Spotswood's answers to charges by the Assembly, March 25, 1719, PRO, CO5, v. 1318, pp. 576-79; to Secretary Stanhope, July 15, 1715, Spotswood, *Letters*, II, 124.
10. Spotswood's answer to charges by the Assembly, March 25, 1719, PRO, CO5, v. 1318, pp. 576-79.
11. Hening, *Statutes*, IV, 133-34; Richard West to Lords of Trade, Jan. 16, 1723/4, PRO, CO5, v. 1323, pp. 283-86; A. Popple to Gooch, Dec. 18, 1735, Gooch Papers, II, 422; Gooch to Popple, May 18, 1736, *ibid.*, p. 424.
12. *House Journals, 1727-40*, pp. 251, 256, 263-64, 276-77, 282-83.
13. Hening, *Statutes*, IV, 475-78.
14. To Lords of Trade, Dec. 5, 1736, PRO, CO5, v. 1324, pp. 61-62; also in Gooch Papers, II, 445.
15. Hening, *Statutes,* III, 53-69; 404-15; IV, 475-78.
16. *House Journals, 1752-58*, p. 41; Landon Carter Diary, March 9 and 10, 1752.
17. Hening, *Statutes*, V, 204-07; VI, 261-65.
18. *Ibid.*, V, 204-07; VI, 261-65; *Acts of the Privy Council*, IV, 256-57 (June 21, 1754).
19. Essex County Deed Book 27, pp. 248-52; Book 29, p. 94.
20. *House Journals, 1761-65*, pp. 126-30.
21. *Ibid., 1752-58*, pp. 339, 342, 348, 359-61.
22. Prince William County Deed Book B, Pt. 1, p. 392; election of 1741, Book E, p. 524; *House Journals, 1761-65*, pp. 126-30.
23. Prince William County Deed Book D, p. 29; *House Journals, 1761-65*, pp. 126-30.
24. Prince William County Rentals, 1752, 1753, 1754, 1760, 1761, VSL.
25. Spotsylvania County Deed Book G, p. 210; Spotsylvania County Will Book D, pp. 528-33.
26. *House Journals, 1761-65*, pp. 87-90.
27. *Ibid.*, 88-90, 126-30.
28. *Ibid.*, pp. 88-90.
29. Hening, *Statutes*, VII, 517-30; Robert Carter to Landon Carter, Jan. 1, 1764, Sabine Hall Papers; *House Journals, 1770-72*, p. 57, indicates that the

laws of 1705 (4 Anne) and 1736 (10 George II) were still in force in 1770. Some later writers mistakenly assumed that this law became effective; see for example Carl Bridenbaugh, *Seat of Empire*, p. 15; Julius F. Prufer, "The Franchise in Virginia From Jefferson Through the Convention of 1829," in *William and Mary Quarterly*, 2 ser., VII (Oct., 1927), 255-70; Elmer I. Miller, *The Legislature of the Province of Virginia; its Internal Development* (New York, 1907), p. 63.

30. Hening, *Statutes*, VIII, 305-17; *House Journals, 1770-72*, p. 57.

31. Royal Instructions to Lord Dunmore, Feb. 7, 1771, Chalmers Collection.

32. *Journal of the Commissioners for Trade and Plantations from April, 1704, to May, 1782, Preserved in the Public Records Office*, 13 vols. (London, 1920-37), XIII, 344-46.

33. Ordinance for regulating elections, July, 1775, Virginia Convention, 1775, Miscellaneous MSS, VSL; *The Proceedings of the Convention of Delegates for the Counties and Corporations in the Colony of Virginia, held at Richmond Town in the County of Henrico, on Monday the 17th of July 1775* (Richmond, 1816), p. 46; Robert Wormeley Carter to Landon Carter, July 29, 1775, Sabine Hall Papers.

# CHAPTER VII

## *The Virginia Electorate*

EVIDENCE on franchise requirements, added to extensive economic opportunity, points to a wide electorate in the Old Dominion. Just how wide will appear in the following pages, and this should go a long way toward a determination of whether the electorate was democratic or aristocratic; that is, whether it included the many or was limited to the few. Historians have differed considerably on this point, yet it is one which must be settled before we can say what type of political structure existed in colonial Virginia.[1]

Once again an exposition of assumptions and methods becomes of some importance to the reader. In our consideration of the electorate, we do not use the misleading term "percentage of the population," for about forty per cent of the Virginia population were slaves, about sixty per cent of the whites were children, half the adults were women, and some of the whites were indentured servants and apprentices. Naturally it was undemocratic to exclude slaves, servants, women, and children; but since such exclusions were made in all the colonies, the problem is reduced to the extent to which *free adult white men* were excluded from political action. In our search, we could use only a very few counties, for few had the necessary combination of deeds, leases, wills, court records, militia lists, tithable lists, quitrent rolls, and election polls. Where the proper combination did exist, we have abstracted and alphabetized these records, but because of space limitations we have made mass citations in many instances.

If contemporaries were accurate in their appraisal, the franchise laws did not exclude many adult white men. Governor Spotswood spoke as though virtually every free white man was a voter. He lamented that "the mob of this country" carried elections because recently freed servants with half an acre of land had "an equal vote with the man of the best estate in the country." Elections "where the votes and humours of the lowest mob do at present decide who shall be representatives in Assembly" and where the "bulk" of the electors consisted of "the meaner sort of people" were hardly evidence of a controlling aristocracy or a ruling class.[2] The Governor's use of the terms the "meaner sort," the "lowest mob," the "vulgar people," the "common people," and the "lowest class of the people" to characterize the voters clearly indicates that he considered the electorate as virtually all-inclusive.[3]

Governors Gooch and Dinwiddie gave comparable accounts of the

136

electorate after passage of the more restrictive election law of 1736. Gooch, who favored this law and vainly hoped that it would lead to effective restrictions later, declared that the "better sort" seldom carried a Virginia election.[4] And twenty years after the new election law was adopted, Dinwiddie remarked that "most of the people are freeholders, in course have votes for choosing assembly men, on which they strenuously insist on their privileges."[5] Men might not always vote or vote wisely, but there is no hint here of a disfranchised mass of men.

Another way to get at the electorate is to see whether or not the "poor" could vote, and here the records seem to indicate that they could. In Lancaster County, Thomas Chitwood, illiterate planter exempted from taxes as "an ancient poor man" in 1740, voted for two losing candidates in 1741. The inventory of his estate shortly after the election revealed a slave worth £10, four cattle, one horse, six pigs, and some furniture and farm utensils. The total of £25.15.11 would make it appear unlikely that Chitwood was a voter, but he was.[6] Richard Cundiff, illiterate planter who owned fifty acres, voted from 1741 on, was exempted from taxes in 1767, yet voted until his death in 1781.[7] Hugh Kelley, illiterate cooper exempted in 1738 as an "ancient poor man," sold fifty acres of land and a house in 1743, had an estate of £48.19.6 including a slave in 1758, and voted for a winner and a loser in 1741 and for two losers in 1748.[8] Ellmore George had only £13.18.4 when he died, but he too was a voter.[9] "Poor" voters are to be found in every county, yet it should be noted how many of these men owned a slave or part of a slave.

Small farmers who were not officially designated as "poor," yet who sometimes possessed less than the "poor" in worldly goods, were also qualified voters. James Mohon, who voted for two winners in 1768, for two losers in 1769, and for two winners in 1774, owned a fifty-acre plantation, a Negro girl worth £30, and a total personal estate of £41.[10] William Chilton, another independent small farmer who was even less affluent, voted in 1741 for two winners and in 1748 for a winner and a loser.[11] When he died the next year, his worldly goods aside from his land were as follows:

| | | | |
|---|---|---|---|
| iron pot | £0. 2.0 | 1 safe | £0.12.0 |
| narrow axe & tongs | 0. 2.6 | 1 rum hhd. | 0. 3.6 |
| some lumber | 0. 0.6 | 1 bed etc. | 1.10.0 |
| 1 chest | 0. 5.0 | 1 pr. button cards | 0. 1.6 |
| 2 hogs | 0. 8.6 | some pewter | 0. 8.0 |
| 1 bull | 1. 0.0 | man's saddle & bridle | 0. 7.0 |
| half a Negro | 7.10.0 | 1 mare | 6. 0.0 |
| fishing line | 0. 0.6 | 4 bottles | 0. 1.0 |
| 1 yearling | 0. 8.0 | looking glass | 0. 4.0 |
| 1 box | 0. 1.0 | 1 case & razor | 0. 1.6 |
| 1 sword | 0. 2.6 | 1 powder flask shares | |
| 4 chairs | 0. 6.0 | & candlestick | 0. 2.0 |
| 1 spinning wheel | 0. 8.0 | | £20. 5.0 |

5 sheep, a canoe, 1 suit clothes and gun (apparently not appraised)

Such examples of small farmers who were qualified voters could be multiplied almost without end from the records of any of the counties.

Being an insolvent debtor was no bar to the franchise, a fact causing one to suspect any use of the term "disfranchised debtors." The Essex County court in 1762 delivered to the sheriff a list of debtor prisoners, none of whom could furnish bail; their debts were £15, £39, £60, and £475.[12] Two of the three small debtors, Thomas Haile (£60) and John Cooper (£15), voted in several elections, Haile voting for a winner and loser in 1748 and two losers in 1752. If Haile lost his property because of his debt, he quickly regained the right to vote by leasing fifty acres for life in 1762.[13] Cooper, illiterate as well as indebted, voted for both winners in 1761 and 1765, and for a winner and loser in 1768, 1769, and 1771.[14]

Artisans outside Norfolk and Williamsburg also acquired sufficient property to vote.[15] Thomas Blanton, Fredericksburg carpenter and joiner, was typical. Blanton first bought a house and lot for £40, sold back half of the lot for £36 to the former owner, merchant Roger Dixon, later sold the remainder for £128, and bought 100 acres for £40. In 1765 he voted for both winners and in 1771 for a loser and a winner.[16] If artisans could not buy land, or lost what they had bought, they could acquire the right to vote by leasing land. Shoemakers Henry Drake and Daniel Carter of Richmond County leased and divided ninety-seven acres in 1767, and both voted in 1769.[17] William Hudson, illiterate Spotsylvania blacksmith, mortgaged and apparently lost 110 acres, but quickly regained the franchise by leasing 190 acres of Spotswood land.[18]

Even though an artisan did not appear on the quitrent rolls, and seemed on the tithable lists to be a servant or apprentice, he might still be a voter. Robert Steele, Norfolk staymaker, worked for a tailor named John Richardson, who had a slave and four servants or apprentices and who paid Steele's tithes. The story is further complicated by the fact that Steele also owned a slave and that his employer, Richardson, lived in Steele's house. In 1768, Steele did not vote, but employer Richardson voted only for one candidate, a loser. In the hotly contested and disputed election of 1769, both Richardson and Steele voted for Brickall, who lost, and for John Wilson, one of the winners.[19] Since Steele owned property in the Borough, he would not be on the quitrent roll, and if we judged him solely by the tithable list, we might mistakenly assume that he was a member of the servant-apprentice class and hence not qualified to vote.

A story in the *Virginia Gazette* in 1769 tells us not only that artisans were voters but also that wives were influential and that candidates cultivated the favor of the artisan. It seems that two candidates were soliciting the vote of Suds the barber, whose wife had prevented his pledging his vote for either. Each candidate patronized the barber and tipped him generously, leaving him still perplexed about his vote, but the first candidate resolved the issue by returning for a second shave and a second generous tip. On election day, Suds voted for this candidate—"as his wife and interest dictated," according to the storyteller. When upbraided by the disappointed candidate, who reminded Suds of his patronage, Suds replied that "the other gentleman was shaved twice."[20] A story such as this would have been pointless in a society where barbers were denied the franchise. And there is also the subtle hint that women were much more important in elections than their legal disfranchisement would lead one to believe.

In addition to artisans, there are many examples of apprentices who quickly acquired the right to vote, so that this group did not necessarily long remain among the disfranchised. The following examples were taken from Essex County where we have numerous election polls.

TABLE A.   APPRENTICE VOTING IN ESSEX COUNTY[21]

| Apprentice | Indented | Term | Voted |
|---|---|---|---|
| Abner Cox | 8/21/53 | until 21 yrs. old | 1761 |
| John Fogg, orphan | 2/18/52 | 6 years | 1758 |
| William Gillam, 17 yrs. | 1/20/56 | until 21 yrs. old | 1761 |
| Benj. Jones | 1/12/52 | until 21 yrs. old | 1755 |
| Rich. Philips, orphan | 11/16/56 | until 21 yrs. old | 1765 |
| Rich. St. John | 4/15/55 | until 21 yrs. old | 1758 |

Apprentices in Norfolk and Williamsburg could vote merely by having served an apprenticeship, but elsewhere, as in Essex, they had to possess the requisite property. Judging by the shortness of time between the end of their service and their first vote, it did not take them long to acquire the necessary property.

Although we might naturally think of overseers as disfranchised, such was not necessarily true. Some overseers were boys too young to vote, but others who were of age acquired property and the right to vote. For example, the Prince William tithable list of 1747 identifies three overseers, Robert Foster, Robert Key, and Thomas Stone. Stone voted as early as 1741, and if he was an overseer under Thomas Davis, the same employer he had later, the two voted for different candidates. On the rent roll of 1760, Foster was listed as having 150 acres but paying on 400 acres, Key did not appear, and Thomas Stone had 225 acres, but all three voted in 1761.[22] We do not know whether or not these men were still overseers, but we do know that all three acquired the right to vote and that two of the three owned land.

The records of other counties as well yield evidence that overseers became qualified voters. In 1745, John Clutton's tithe was paid in Lancaster by one Rogers, and in 1746 it was paid by one Ball, an indictation that Clutton was probably an overseer rather than an apprentice or servant. He voted in 1765, 1768, 1771 and 1774, failed to vote in 1769, and usually voted for Charles Carter, the county's biggest slaveowner. In 1773, Clutton paid for ninety-two acres on the rent roll, in 1775 he was overseer for Rawleigh Downman, and in 1779 he had a tithable slave.[23] In Amelia County, fifteen of the thirty-eight men identifiable as overseers soon disappeared from the records, but at least twenty-one of the remaining twenty-three acquired land, slaves, or both, twelve of the twenty-one voted, and the others could have done so.[24]

Still another way to arrive at the character of the Virginia electorate will be found in Tables B, C, D, and E. By abstracting the deeds of a county and by using other available records, a high percentage of the voters can be identified as to social status. Three counties—Accomack, Lancaster and Essex—had the needed combination of records covering an adequate period of time. All three were old tidewater counties, probably representative since they were similar, and more heavily populated with upper classes than were most of the piedmont and frontier counties. To be safe, we have included in the upper class anyone with any title of distinction—esquires, gentlemen, merchants, doctors, ministers, militia officers, constables, justices of the peace, lawyers, surveyors, school teachers, and mariners—although obviously many merchants, constables, and militia officers so included were not strictly upper-class.

What these charts show is that the middle and lower classes among the electorate outnumbered the upper class overwhelmingly, even in these tidewater counties. "Probable planters" were those whose status was not specifically designated but who bought acreage that would appear to place them as planters. They could have been artisans, but they were probably not gentlemen—for gentlemen were usually identified. Even the illiterates outnumbered the upper class by two or three to one. Plural voting was obviously of little significance in these counties, for even among out-of-county voters the gentlemen were outnumbered, and the gentlemen never voted as a bloc. If Virginia had a ruling class of aristocrats, they were not aristocrats because of privilege but because they could win the votes of enough men outside their class to get themselves elected.

Table E also substantiates the view that most of the voters were in the middle and lower classes. More than ninety per cent of the freeholders owned less than 500 acres of land, more than eighty per cent owned 300 acres or less, and more than two-thirds owned 200 acres or less.

Since the poor, the small farmers, artisans, tenants, overseers, and former servants and apprentices were voters, it would seem safe to say that a high percentage of the free white men were qualified to vote. There is no absolutely accurate way of telling how many men were enfranchised, but there are ways of estimating which confirm the suggestion that few were disfranchised.

One such method is to estimate the number of qualified voters in 1763 by comparing tithable lists available for some counties for 1750, 1755, and 1773 with lists of freeholders in forty-one of sixty-two counties compiled from the quitrent rolls by James Blair in 1763. Freeholders on the quitrent rolls would not include tenants whose quitrents were paid

TABLE B. SOCIAL STATUS OF ACCOMACK VOTERS[25]

| Year of Election | 1738 | 1740 | 1742 | 1744 | 1748 | 1758 |
|---|---|---|---|---|---|---|
| Total number who voted | 459 | 448 | 482 | 386 | 556 | 561 |
| Number identified economically or socially | 234 | 233 | 215 | 208 | 317 | 259 |
| Percentage identified | 50.9 | 52.0 | 43.7 | 53.8 | 57.0 | 46.1 |
| Upper class: Gentlemen (includes one tenant) | 20 | 17 | 25 | 20 | 25 | 16 |
| Merchants | 2 | 2 | 3 | 1 | 2 | 1 |
| Others | 2 | 1 | 1 | 3 | 2 | 1 |
| Total upper class | 24 | 20 | 29 | 24 | 29 | 18 |
| Middle & lower classes: Planters (including tenants) | 113 | 116 | 120 | 101 | 140 | 103 |
| Probable planters | 83 | 81 | 90 | 68 | 122 | 113 |
| Artisans or tradesmen | 10 | 9 | 16 | 12 | 22 | 18 |
| Total middle & lower classes | 206 | 206 | 226 | 181 | 284 | 234 |
| Out-of-county voters: Upper class | 3 | 2 | 6 | 3 | 4 | 3 |
| Middle-lower classes | 1 | 5 | 6 | | | 4 |
| Total identified out-of-county voters | 4 | 7 | 12 | 3 | 4 | 7 |
| Out-of-county voters with status not designated | 3 | 1 | 7 | 2 | 4 | 4 |
| Voters known to be illiterate | 66 | 62 | 67 | 56 | 67 | 38 |
| %illiterates in voters with identified status | 27.8 | 22.3 | 31.1 | 26.9 | 24.6 | 14.6 |
| % gentlemen & merchants in identified voters | 9.2 | 8.1 | 13.0 | 10.0 | 8.5 | 6.5 |
| Non-voters with known adequate property: Upper class | 2 | 8 | 6 | 14 | 10 | 1 |
| Middle-lower classes | 7 | 25 | 19 | 32 | 12 | 5 |
| Status not designated | 7 | 8 | 9 | 25 | 8 | 11 |
| Total qualified non-voters | 16 | 41 | 34 | 71 | 30 | 17 |
| Illiterate qualified non-voters | 5 | 10 | 5 | 11 | 6 | – |

TABLE E.   LANDHOLDING OF LANCASTER VOTERS, 1748-1774[28]

| Acres owned | % 1748 | % 1752 | % 1771 | % 1774 |
|---|---|---|---|---|
| 100 or less | 39.5 | 39.7 | 42.3 | 37.5 |
| 200 or less | 67.9 | 67.9 | 69.3 | 69.9 |
| 300 or less | 80.2 | 82.4 | 80.2 | 82.0 |
| over 500 | 5.5 | 5.7 | 9.4 | 6.6 |

by the landlord, town voters whose lots were not on the rent rolls, men who took out surveys for land and thus became voters but did not patent the land to avoid payment of quitrents, foreign Protestants exempted from quitrents, nor artisans in Norfolk and Williamsburg who had served apprenticeships there. But despite this, the counties where the percentage was ninety or more were scattered through all areas. In the tidewater, Essex, Middlesex, New Kent, Southampton, Sussex, and Warwick counties had ninety per cent or more. The same was true for piedmont Albemarle, Amelia, Chesterfield, Cumberland, Goochland, Hanover, Henrico, Louisa, Lunenburg, and frontier Augusta. Actually there should have been little difference between these counties and their neighbors.[29]

The average for all counties for which there are figures was 85.7 per cent; but as the following evidence demonstrates, figures for some counties were obviously too low. Piedmont-frontier Halifax is a good example. Using the tithable list and Blair's list of freeholders, one arrives at an estimate of 773 white males in 1763; since Blair gave 480 as the number of freeholders, the percentage of voters among the adult men would be sixty-two. Fortunately, we have two Halifax election polls, one for November 28, 1764, in which 500 men voted, and one for July 17, 1765, with 758 voters. Since some men voted in one but not both elections, we can count 931 different men who voted in the two elections. There is also a Halifax tithable list for February 1765; by comparing it with the 1755 list, we can estimate about 950 adult men in the county, of which 931, or ninety-eight per cent, voted.[30]

There is also ample evidence that a list of freeholders taken from rent rolls such as Blair's would include only a minimum of the qualified voters. In Prince William, only thirty-seven of the many tenant leases even stipulated that the tenants were to pay the quitrents, but only four of these—John Murray, William Lynn, Anthony Searle, Jr., and John Summers—appear on the rent rolls and they paid for land that they owned, not their leased land.[31] Tenants John Metcalfe of Prince William and James Brewer and Thomas Connolly of Richmond all voted but were not on the rent rolls. The same was true of Nathaniel Overall, Richard Tristoe, and Cornelius Kincheloe, who owned land and voted. Town voters William Tompkins and Thomas Chapman of Dumfries were not listed on the rentals, of course, and Daniel Paul, William Suter, William Brown, John Simpson, and William Taylor, listed as Prince William servants or apprentices in 1747, all voted in 1761. Others, such as John

Hendren, Abraham Gibson, John Northcut, John Oldham, and Robert
Bland paid single tithes on the tithable lists for 1747, did not pay any
quitrents in 1760, yet voted in 1761.[82]

The extent to which both the voting lists and the quitrent rolls give
too low an estimate of the qualified voters is best demonstrated in a
county where the two were taken at about the same time (Table F). The
results are almost startling. Of the 194 men who voted in Prince William,
a county with many tenants, only eighty-five, or 43.8 per cent, were on
the rent roll for 1760. The other 109 who voted were tenants, town
dwellers, or men who owned land but had avoided the rent rolls. Con-
versely, only eighty-five of the 274 men on the rent roll actually voted.
There was a great deal of indifference among those 274 and this indifference was in no way related to the amount of land a man owned. Finally,
men with 500 acres or less comprised about seventy-five per cent of those
on the rent rolls; if we add to these the 109 men who actually voted but
were not on the rent rolls and who probably were in the middle-lower
class, the preponderance of that class over the upper class was overwhelming.

TABLE F.  LANDHOLDING OF VOTERS AND NON-VOTERS IN
PRINCE WILLIAM, 1761[33]

| | |
|---|---|
| Total number of voters, 1761 | 194 |
| Voters on rent roll, 1760 | 85 |
| Voters not on rent roll, 1760 | 109 |
| Non-voters on rent roll, 1760 | 189 |

Acreages held by voters and non-voters

| Acres | 25-99 | 100-150 | 151-200 | 201-300 | 301-400 | 401-500 | 501-1000 | Over 1000 | Acreage not given | Total |
|---|---|---|---|---|---|---|---|---|---|---|
| Voters | 4 | 23 | 10 | 13 | 7 | 5 | 18 | 4 | 1 | 85 |
| Non-voters | 10 | 49 | 26 | 31 | 20 | 10 | 23 | 18 | 2 | 189 |

If slaveowners either were voters or could have sold their slaves to
buy land and become voters, a high percentage of the heads of families
in some areas were qualified voters. In Norfolk Borough 69.5 per cent
of the family heads owned slaves in 1771, and we know that many non-
slaveowners and ex-apprentices also voted there. An Amelia County
tithable list shows 77.5 per cent as slaveowners in 1782, and if even half
of the non-slaveowners could vote, as they actually did in 1761, the
percentage would be about ninety.[34]

The tithable lists also reveal that most of the servants, overseers, and
apprentices who remained in a community acquired property and became
voters. Of fifty-four such in Lancaster who remained from 1745 to 1775,
forty either voted or had sufficient land to do so, seven of the remaining
fourteen owned slaves or other property, and only seven do not appear
as property owners, but even they could have been tenants, could have

inherited property, or could have married women with property. In Norfolk Borough, only fourteen of eighty-eight such men in 1751 remained in 1771; eleven of the fourteen had acquired slaves, and eight voted in the elections of 1768 or 1769.[35] Of the four who did not vote, Daniel Barrand had an apprentice and three slaves and was a partner in the merchant company of Balfour and Barrand.[36] James Esther, blockmaker and tradesman of "credit and reputation in Norfolk," had an apprentice and two slaves, died late in 1771, and left household furniture, shop equipment, and a half interest in a sloop.[37] Nicholas Poole, silversmith, left his wife and children a house and lot and three slaves in 1772,[38] and Thomas Williamson had one slave in 1771.[39] In Norfolk County, only nineteen of the servant-apprentice group of 1751 remained in 1771; of these nineteen, twelve voted in 1768 and at least fifteen or sixteen became qualified voters.[40]

It is impossible to track down all the artisans and apprentices who left one area for another, but many of them acquired property and became voters. The deeds contain innumerable examples of men who were listed as artisans from other counties. Typical was the case of David Chevis, Norfolk mariner, who did not appear on any extant Norfolk records, but who bought a house and lot in Fredericksburg in 1764 for £25 and thus became a qualified voter. By 1773, Chevis had sold his Fredericksburg property for £40 and resided in Caroline County.[41]

In areas where tenantry was common, a very high percentage of tenants were qualified voters by virtue of having leases for life. Of the 216 leases in Loudoun County after that county was divided off from Fairfax in 1757, all were for more than twenty-five acres, 95.9 per cent were for 100 acres or more, 91.2 per cent were for life or lives, only eight or 3.7 per cent were for a term of years, and of the eleven (five per cent) with unspecified terms, several must have been for life as the tenants sold them for £10, £115, £115, £100, £100, £28, and £150 respectively.[42] At least ninety-five per cent of these Loudoun tenants were qualified voters. Of 218 leases in Prince William from 1730 to 1776, 201 or ninety-two per cent were for life or lives, seven or 3.2 per cent were for ninety-nine years, five were for twenty-one years or more, and the terms of three were not given. One of the two leases for less than twenty-one years was held by the Reverend James Scott, one of the largest landowners in the county.[43] But again it is evident that the overwhelming majority of tenants were qualified to vote.

We cannot be sure that the lease for twenty-one years or more, unless it was obviously greater than an ordinary life, actually qualified the tenant, but we do know that the twenty-one-year lease was often equated with three lives. A lease of Thomas Stanton to Guy Mook of Orange County reads "3 lives or 21 years," [44] and in 1752 John Mercer advertised that he had 30,000 acres in Fairfax and Prince William counties to lease for three lives or twenty-one years.[45] Furthermore, the law of 1764 allowing for leases of entailed land uses the phrase "for twenty-one years or three lives." [46] That ninety-nine-year leases were considered as greater than life is attested by one which reads "ninety-nine years and his life included." [47] If these leases of twenty-one years or more qualified their holders for the vote, the percentage of enfranchised tenants in counties such as Loudoun and Prince William would be just that much higher than our figures indicate.

As the example of the Reverend James Scott of Prince William suggests, many of the tenants who held leases for less than life were actually qualified voters. In Norfolk County from 1752 to 1769 there were thirty-seven leases—seven for life, eight for twenty-one years or more, and twenty-two for less than twenty-one years. [48] Of the thirty-two men involved in the thirty leases for less than life, nine voted and one was a candidate in the elections of 1768 and 1769, [49] twenty-three including the above ten had or acquired sufficient property to vote, [50] one died, [51] five either died or left the county, [52] and only three failed to acquire sufficient property as far as the records tell us. [53]

In addition to life leases, many tenants also became qualified voters by purchasing land of their own. The Loudoun tenants who sold their leases for as much as £150 could have purchased hundreds of acres from speculators, and at least thirty-one leases were sold at prices ranging from £6 to £150. [54] For example, Solomon Hoge leased 150 acres for three lives from Bryan Fairfax in May, 1761, bought 200 acres for £50 in August, 1762, sold his lease to John Jones for £115 in 1764, sold fifteen of his 200 acres for £20 in 1769, and sold the remaining 185 acres for £250 in 1770. [55]

Although most men were qualified voters and theoretically the law required that they vote, in practice they did not always exercise their political rights. Sometimes a high percentage voted; at other times the percentage was low. Of the 146 names on a road list for Richmond County, 119 or eighty-two per cent actually voted at one time or another. [56] Thirty-nine out of fifty-seven male heads of families (68.3 per cent) on a census list for one part of the county voted. [57] In Henrico County in 1750 there were 584 white tithables, which makes an estimated 438 adult white men, of which 255 actually voted in the election of January, 1751/2—a percentage of 58.2. [58] In two Accomack elections, just about fifty per cent of the adult men voted—555 in 1748 out of an estimated 1,140 adult white men in 1750, and 561 in 1758 out of an estimated 1,120 adult white men in 1755. [59] In Spotsylvania, 742 men bought or sold sufficient land between 1751 and 1772 to qualify for the franchise, but only 248 of them (33.4 per cent) voted in the elections of 1765 and 1771. [60] In the tidewater county of Essex, those who voted varied from a low of forty-one per cent in 1752 to sixty-three per cent in 1768-69, although this latter figure would be higher if the white population continued to decline as it did from 1750 to 1755 (Table G). These figures, of course, do not include those men who qualified through wills, marriages, leases, and patents, and therefore are a minimum.

TABLE G.   PERCENTAGE OF MEN WHO VOTED, ESSEX
COUNTY[61]

| Election Year | No. who voted | Estimated white tithables* | Estimated white adult males | Percentage of adult men who voted |
|---|---|---|---|---|
| 1748 | 377 | 958 | 717 | 52.5 |
| 1752 | 318 | 958 | 717 | 44.3 |
| 1755 | 356 | 889 | 666 | 53.4 |
| 1758 | 356 | 889 | 666 | 53.4 |
| 1761 | 374 | 889 | 666 | 56.1 |
| 1768-69 | 421 | 889 | 666 | 63.2 |

* White tithables in Table G were taken from the tithable lists of 1750 (958 white tithables) and 1755 (889 white tithables). Since the white population declined in these five years, the estimates of white tithables for 1758, 1761, and 1768-69 probably were less than the 889 figure that we have used and would make the percentages correspondingly higher.

Although a large number of men acquired the vote by patenting government land, many so qualified did not exercise the right. During the fifteen years from 1736 to 1751, there were some 742 individual surveys in Amelia County for some 435 different men, and only sixteen of these, or 3.67 per cent, were for less than 100 acres. If the grantees improved their land, all were qualified to vote, and if they did not, more than ninety-six per cent were qualified. Yet in 1761, only sixty-six or 15.4 per cent and in 1768 only eighty-one or 18.6 per cent of these men appear on the election polls. Furthermore, there was no class pattern of voting apparent, for the same percentage (twenty-five per cent) of those who received grants of 25-99 and 900-999 acres voted.[62] And finally, these figures suggest that perhaps then as now the real problem was not who could vote but why those qualified neglected to do so.

If possession of the right to vote by most men is democratic rather than aristocratic, Virginia must be considered democratic as far as the electorate was concerned. Most adult white men either had or soon acquired enough property to meet the voting requirements. About the only available evidence to the contrary is a famous statement made by Jefferson in 1782 which we shall discuss in the final chapter. Absence of positive evidence may not be convincing, but in a colony where every known grievance found its way to the legislature by way of petitions, grievances about the franchise are conspicuous by their absence. If there is evidence to the contrary, it should be forthcoming, but until it is, we must interpret this aspect of pre-Revolutionary Virginia history as democratic rather than aristocratic.

### NOTES

1. Wright, *First Gentleman of Virginia*, p. 65; Jackson T. Main, "Sections and Politics in Virginia, 1781-1787" in *William and Mary Quarterly*, 3rd Ser., XII (1955), pp. 97-98, 109-110; Beard, *The Rise of American Civilization*, I,

110; Julian A. C. Chandler, *The History of the Suffrage in Virginia* (Baltimore, 1901), p. 15. Charles Sydnor in *Gentlemen Freeholders* appeared to present conflicting accounts on this issue. He concluded on pp. 31-32 that only one-third to one-half of the adult men could qualify for the franchise, yet on p. 30 he maintained that land was cheap and only a one-room log cabin was needed on it to qualify a man as a voter and on p. 37 that most farmers, small and great, were enfranchised. Other writers who point to Virginia as having a higher percentage of voters than Massachusetts, which they have assumed to be very undemocratic, include Lyon G. Tyler, "The Leadership of Virginia in the War of the Revolution," in *William and Mary Quarterly*, 1 ser., XVIII (Jan. 1910), 150; Tyler, "Aristocracy in Massachusetts and Virginia," in *ibid.*, XXVI (April, 1918), 277-78; Marcia B. Bready, "A Cavalier in Virginia . . . ," *ibid.*, XVIII (Oct., 1909), 120; Carl Bridenbaugh, *Seat of Empire*, p. 15; Elmer I. Miller, *The Legislature of the Province of Virginia*, p. 64n. Many of these writers stress the power of the aristocracy in Virginia in spite of the wider franchise. For a late version of this view see Thad W. Tate, "The Coming of the Revolution in Virginia: Britain's Challenge to Virginia's Ruling Class, 1763-1776," in *William and Mary Quarterly*, 3 ser., XIX (July, 1962), 342.

2. Spotswood to Lords of Trade, Oct. 15, 1712, Dec. 29, 1713, and Oct. 24, 1715, Spotswood, *Letters*, II, 1-2, 48-50, 133-35.

3. *Ibid.*, p. 124.

4. Gooch to Lords of Trade, Feb. 22, 1738/9, Gooch Papers, II, 529.

5. To Lords of Trade, Feb. 23, 1756, PRO, CO5, v. 1328, p. 360.

6. Lancaster County Order Book 8, pp. 277, 331; Lancaster County Deed Book 13, pp. 175, 247, 249-50, 269.

7. *Ibid.*, Book 17, p. 20; Book 18—Orders, p. 8; Lancaster County Will Book 20, p. 196; Lancaster County Rentals 1750 and 1773. For elections, see footnote 26 below.

8. Lancaster County Order Book 8, p. 205; Lancaster County Deed Book 13, p. 136; Book 14, p. 8; Book 16, pp. 2, 9.

9. Lancaster County Order Book 8, pp. 209, 285, 359; Lancaster County Deed Book 14, pp. 200-01 (election poll, 1748), 244; Lancaster County Rentals 1748 and 1750. For other examples of Lancaster "poor men" see Neil Johnson: Lancaster County Order Book 12, p. 193; Lancaster County Deed Book 18, p. 115. William Galloway: Lancaster County Will Book 15, pp. 87, 287, 309; Lancaster County Deed Book 16, p. 225; Book 18—Orders, p. 6; Lancaster County Rental, 1773. Thomas Percifull: Lancaster County Will Book 15, pp. 292, 315; Lancaster County Order Book 12, p. 194; Lancaster County Rentals, 1750 and 1773.

10. Lancaster County Will Book 20, pp. 57, 78, 80; Lancaster County Rentals, 1773; for elections see Lancaster County Deed Book 18, pp. 133-34 (1768), 154 (1769); Book 19, pp. 112-13 (1774).

11. *Ibid.*, Book 14, p. 257; for elections, Book 13, pp. 249-50; Book 14, pp. 200-01. For other examples, see Norfolk County Will Book 1, p. 34; Norfolk County Deed Book 26, p. 88; Book 29, p. 112; Norfolk County Tithables 1771; election polls, Norfolk County Deed Book 24, pp. 112-15, 211-15.

12. Essex County Deed Book 29, p. 113.

13. *Ibid.*, Book 25, p. 155; Book 26, p. 1; for polls see Book 24, pp. 275-80 and Book 25, pp. 301-07.

14. *Ibid.*, Book 30, p. 30; for polls, see Book 29, pp. 1-7; Book 30, pp. 235-42, 243-48, 318-24, 496-502.

15. For typical examples of artisan-voters in Loudoun County, see Loudoun County Deed Book A, pp. 3, 28, 87, 88, 148, 178, 258, 363, 444, 448; Book B, pp. 8, 36, 125; Book C, pp. 15, 23, 27, 93, 138, 143, 146, 255, 362, 454, 491, 495, 514, 529, 531, 567, 635; Book D, pp. 1, 40, 43, 52, 93, 106, 123, 180, 215, 268, 293, 294, 300, 433, 448, 548; Book E, pp. 116, 197, 201, 214, 238. Between July, 1757, and Sept., 1766, twenty-three artisans engaged in

fifty-five real estate transactions, many of them involving several hundred acres of land valued at several hundred pounds.

16. Spotsylvania County Deed Book E, p. 468; Book F, p. 71; Book G, p. 401; Book H, p. 428; Spotsylvania County Will Book D, pp. 19, 251, 287, 300, 528-33.

17. Richmond County Deed Book 13, p. 31; Book 16, pp. 491-97; Book 17, pp. 249-56.

18. Spotsylvania County Deed Book F, p. 254; Book H, p. 347; Spotsylvania County Will Book D, p. 434.

19. Norfolk Borough Tithables, 1771, VSL; *Virginia Gazette* (P & D), May 4, 1769 and *ibid.* (R), Oct. 11, 1770; Norfolk County Deed Book 24, pp. 112-15, 211-15.

20. *Virginia Gazette* (P & D), May 19, 1769.

21. Cox, Essex County Deed Book 26, p. 292; Fogg, *ibid.*, p. 34; Gillam, Book 27, p. 186; Jones, Book 25, p. 318; Philips, Book 27, p. 241; St. John, *ibid.*, p. 100. For references to election polls, see footnote 28 below.

22. Prince William County Tithables, 1747; Prince William County Deed Book E, p. 524ff.; Book P, pp. 68-73; Prince William County Rental, 1760.

23. Lancaster County Deeds and Wills, Book 15, pp. 88, 92; Book 18, pp. 42-43, 133-34, 154; Book 19, pp. 58-59, 112-13; Lancaster County Tithables, 1745, 1746, 1775, 1779; Lancaster County Rental, 1773.

24. Amelia County Tithables, 1768; *Tyler's Quarterly Historical and Genealogical Magazine,* 33 vols. (Richmond, Virginia, 1919-52), XXXIII, 54-69.

25. The information in this table has been compiled by abstracting all of the deeds and other pertinent material in Accomack County Deeds 1737-46, 1746-57, and 1757-70. These figures are all minimum. Election polls will be found as follows: polls for 1738-44 at the end of Book 1737-46; poll for 1748 in Book 1746-57, pp. 130-43; poll for 1758 in Book 1757-70, pp. 52-56. Space prohibits separate citations for every individual involved in the study of this and other counties presented here, and since the upper classes were usually identified, probably most of those who were not identified would fall in the middle and lower classes.

26. The data in Table C have been compiled by a page-by-page abstracting of the Lancaster County Deed and Will Books No. 13 through 20 (1736-1783); Lancaster County Order Books; Lancaster County Tithable Lists for 1745, 1746, 1775, 1776, 1777, 1779, 1781; Lancaster County Quitrent Rolls, 1748, 1750, 1773; Lancaster Soldiers in Washington Papers, X, 33. Specific election polls are as follows: 1741, Deed Book 13, pp. 249-50; 1748, Book 14, pp. 200-01; 1752, Lancaster County Loose Papers, VSL; 1754, *ibid.,* and Will Book 15, p. 167; July 1758, Deed Book 16, pp. 27-28; Nov., 1758, Lancaster County Loose Papers, VSL, and Deed Book 16, p. 49; 1761, *ibid.,* pp. 222-23; 1765, Lancaster County Loose Papers, VSL, and Deed Book 18, pp. 42-43; 1768, Lancaster County Loose Papers, VSL, and Deed Book 18, pp. 133-34; 1769, Book 18, p. 154; 1771, Book 19, pp. 58-59; 1774, Book 19, pp. 112-13.

27. Essex County Deed Books 23-31, *passim,* for social status. Election polls are as follows: 1748, Essex County Deed Book 24, pp. 275-80; 1752, Book 25, pp. 301-07; 1755, Book 27, pp. 248-52; 1758, Book 28, pp. 95-99; 1761, Book 29, pp. 1-7; 1765, Book 30, pp. 235-42; 1768, *ibid.,* pp. 243-48; 1769, *ibid.,* pp. 318-24; 1770, *ibid.,* p. 385; 1771, *ibid.,* pp. 496-502; 1777, Book 31, pp. 398-402; 1778, *ibid.,* pp. 405-06.

28. Data from same sources as Table C.

29. Figures for Norfolk 1750 from Norfolk Borough and County Tithables, VSL; for other 1750 tithables see "A General List of Tithables taken in 1750, as far as the returns were then made," Chalmers Collection; "A List of Tithables in the Dominion of Virginia, 1755," PRO, CO5, v. 1328, pp. 363-65 (a notation says that the white tithables are males 18 years old and up, but this would be very unusual as they were customarily rated from 16 years up, see

Hening, *Statutes,* III, 258-61; IV, 40-44; Answers to Queries by Lords of Trade, PRO, CO5, v. 1330, p. 396, Jan. 30, 1763; from 1780 to 1787 a tax was put upon free males twenty-one years or older but tithables were still sixteen years and up in county and parish levies—see Hening, *Statutes,* X, 244, 504-05; XI, 67, 290-91; XII, 247, 431); Total tithables, 1773, *Virginia Magazine of History and Biography,* XXVIII, 81-82; Freeholders, 1763, Letter of James Blair to ?, Sept. 23, 1763, "Papers on Quitrents and Customs Confiscations," British Museum, Add. MSS. 38337.

30. Halifax County Deed Book 3, pp. 389-401; Halifax County Pleas [Court Orders] 5, p. 27; List of James Turner, Jr., Halifax County Tithables, 1771.

31. Survey of leases in Prince William County Deed Books, *passim,* especially Book Q, pp. 122, 601, 639; Book R, p. 116; Prince William County Rentals, 1752, 1753, 1754, 1760, 1761, 1767, 1773, VSL.

32. Richmond County Deed Book 10, p. 358; Book 12, p. 74; election polls in Richmond County Order Book 13, pp. 38-40; Book 14, pp. 264-68; Richmond County Rentals, VSL; *House Journals, 1761-65,* pp. 126-30; Prince William County Rentals, 1752, 1753, 1754, 1760, 1761; Prince William County Tithables, 1747; Deed Book P, pp. 68-73 for election poll, 1761.

33. *Ibid.,* for election poll; Prince William County Rental, 1760, 1761. For a similar situation compare Spotsylvania election poll of 1771 in Spotsylvania County Will Book D, pp. 528-33 with Spotsylvania County Tax Accounts for 1775 and 1776. Here 139 (48 per cent) of the 288 voters appear on the tax accounts and 149 (52 per cent) do not.

34. Norfolk Borough and County Tithables, 1751 and 1771; Amelia County Tithables, 1782, and Amelia County election poll, 1761, in Amelia County Tithables.

35. Lancaster County Tithables, 1745 and 1775; Lancaster County Deed and Will Books, 13 through 20. For Lancaster election polls see above note 26; Norfolk Borough Tithables, 1751 and 1771; election polls in Norfolk County Deed Book 24, pp. 112-15, 211-15.

36. *Virginia Gazette* (R), Oct. 18, 1770.

37. *Ibid.* (P & D), Oct. 17, 1771; Norfolk County Will Book 1, p. 213.

38. Norfolk County Deed Book 24, p. 210; Norfolk County Will Book 2, p. 14.

39. Norfolk Borough Tithables, 1771.

40. Norfolk County Tithables, 1751 and 1771; Norfolk County Deed Book 23, p. 199; Book 24, p. 165; Norfolk County Will Book 1, p. 34.

41. Spotsylvania County Deed Book F, p. 447; Book H, p. 509.

42. Abstracts of all leases, Loudoun County Deed Books A through G. Space prohibits listing individual citations. For sale of leases, see *ibid.,* Book D, pp. 145, 362, 401; Book E, pp. 60, 127, 187, 302; Book F, p. 7.

43. Abstracts of all leases in Prince William County Deed Books A, B, D, E, I, L, M, P, Q, R, T. Books C, F, G, H, J, K, N, O, and S are missing. Space prohibits listing individual citations.

44. Orange County Deed Book 1, p. 216.

45. *Virginia Gazette,* March 5, 1752, and March 3, 1753.

46. Hening, *Statutes,* VIII, 183.

47. Prince William Deed Book R, p. 351.

48. Norfolk County Deed Book 15, p. 83; Book 17, pp. 28, 50, 159, 194, 227, 276; Book 18, pp. 13, 149; Book 19, pp. 93, 166, 198, 231, 242; Book 21, pp. 86, 137, 138, 141, 194; Book 22, pp. 5, 15, 74, 112; Book 23, pp. 51, 123, 145; Book 24, pp. 81, 97, 102, 197, 226, 260; Book 25, p. 59.

49. Election polls, *ibid.,* Book 24, pp. 112-15, 211-15.

50. Alex Bruce, *ibid.,* Book 17, p. 105 and Book 18, p. 202; John Brickell, Book 23, pp. 8, 116; Thomas Best, Book 17, p. 215 and Book 26, p. 265; William and John Brown, merchants, voted 1769; Paul Loyal, voted 1769; Maximilian Calvert, voted 1768 and 1769; Andrew Duche, Book 15, pp. 54, 96;

Solomon Deans, 2 slaves, 1771, Norfolk County Tithables, 1771; John Gardner voted 1768 and 1769; John Grimes, voted 1768 and 1769; John Guy, voted 1768 and 1769; John Hunter, Norfolk County Deed Book 20, p. 23; Richard Inkson, Book 13, p. 190 and Book 14, p. 43; Norfolk County Will Book H, p. 75; James Murphree, Norfolk County Deed Book 17, p. 55 and eight slaves (1771), Norfolk County Tithables, 1771; Richard Powell voted 1768 and 1769; John Runsburg, 2 slaves (1771), left friend Frederick Bracegirdle £2,000, Norfolk County Will Book 2, p. 22; William Smith, gent., voted 1768 and 1769; John Sikes, *ibid.*, Book 1, p. 25; James Vicker, Norfolk County Deed Book 20, p. 212 and Book 22, p. 72; John Wigglay, Book 19, p. 232 and Book 21, p. 94; William Wallace, 1 slave, 75 acres (1771), Norfolk County Tithables, 1771; Norfolk County Deed Book 22, p. 123; Edward Whitehurst, voted 1768.

51. James Buntin, 1761, Norfolk County Will Book 1, p. 63.

52. Richard Berry, Jesse Brown, Noah Frost, James Henderson, Joshua Tucker.

53. Reubin Culpepper, Levi Sikes, Thomas Powell.

54. Loudoun County Deed Books A—F, *passim*.

55. *Ibid.*, Book C, pp. 51, 358; Book D, p. 362; Book G, pp. 202, 260. For other examples see Joseph Gardner, Book C, pp. 324, 664; James Hamilton, Book A, pp. 59, 503; Book B, pp. 11, 278, 350, 512, 554, 559, 635, 650; John Norton, Book E, p. 305; Book F, pp. 9, 58; William Trammel, Book C, pp. 386, 660; Book D, pp. 587, 589; Book E, pp. 220, 352; Book F, p. 96.

56. Road List, Richmond County Deed Book 13, pp. 286-88; election polls, 1741 in Richmond County Account Book 1, pp. 175-76; 1748 in Richmond County Order Book 12, pp. 123-26; 1752 in *ibid.*, pp. 353-55; 1755 in Book 13, pp. 338-40; 1758 in Book 14, pp. 264-68; 1761 in *ibid.*, pp. 381-85; 1769 in Book 16, pp. 491-97; 1771 in Book 17, pp. 249-56.

57. A List of the Inhabitants of the Fork of the Totuskey, 1775, Sabine Hall Papers.

58. Henrico County Deeds and Wills, 1750-67, pp. 102-06; "A general list of tithables taken in 1750 . . . ," Chalmers Collection.

59. *Ibid.*, "A List of Tithables . . . 1755," PRO, CO5, v. 1328, p. 363; polls in Accomack County Deed Book 1746-57, pp. 130-43; Book 1757-70, No. 3, pt. I, pp. 52-56. Dr. Lucille Griffith, in a paper before the Mississippi Valley Historical Association in Minneapolis in 1958, stated that 48.8 per cent of all men over twenty-one years of age actually voted.

60. Page-by-page survey of Spotsylvania County Deed Books E, F, G, H; polls in Book F, pp. 739-41; Spotsylvania County Will Book D, pp. 528-33.

61. Tithables from "A General List of Tithables taken in 1750 . . . ," Chalmers Collection; "A List of Tithables . . . 1755," PRO, CO5, v. 1328, p. 363; *Virginia Magazine of History and Biography*, XXVIII, 81-82. Polls are as follows: 1748, Essex County Deed Book 24, pp. 275-80; 1752, Book 25, pp. 301-07; 1755, Book 27, pp. 248-52; 1758, Book 28, pp. 95-99; 1761, Book 29, pp. 1-7; 1768-69, Book 30, pp. 243-48, 318-24.

62. Amelia County Land Survey, 1736-51, VSL; Amelia election poll, 1761, in Amelia County Tithables; election poll, 1768, in *Tyler's Quarterly*, XXXIII, 54-69.

# CHAPTER VIII

# Election Practices in Eighteenth-Century Virginia

ASSUMING that most free adult white men could vote—and that assumption is justified until better evidence than that presented in Chapter VII is forthcoming—there still might not have been democracy in Virginia. While the right to vote is basic, it does not in itself guarantee democracy. There are several questions to be answered, therefore, before we can determine whether Virginia was democratic or aristocratic.

One important problem involves the way elections were conducted, and especially whether elections were manipulated in such a way that the upper classes and not the people reaped the political harvests. So the machinery of politics becomes vital—how elections were called, how they were conducted, and whether sheriffs, other officials, or "aristocrats" determined the outcome by practices designed to influence the choice of candidates by the common people.

Fundamental to the workings of Virginia politics, of course, was the legal machinery for political action in the colony—machinery that changed very little during the eighteenth century. Beverley explained in 1705 how the election system worked. Election writs, issued from the Secretary's office under the seal of the colony and the test of the governor, were sent to sheriffs of the counties at least forty days before the election. The writ and the day of election were then publicized at every church and chapel in the county for two Sundays successively. A plurality of voters decided the election, but if any candidate was dissatisfied he could require each voter to declare upon oath whether he had enough property to vote and could demand a copy of the poll from the sheriff. Whenever a candidate or other persons believed the election illegal, they could protest by petition to the House of Burgesses. The House reviewed the affair and in case of corruption or illegal practices ordered a new election. If a tie vote resulted, the sheriff cast the deciding vote.[1] Corruption and the treating of voters to influence their votes were of constant concern to the House throughout the century. Although there were a few minor changes from time to time—such as more specific elaboration of details of the election machinery—there was no basic change of this procedure even after the Revolution when the laws were revised in 1785.[2]

There was no set time for elections, because the British carefully prohibited any colonial regulation on this matter. New elections were held whenever the Governor saw fit, and one might erroneously infer from this that few were held. As anyone can see from a glance at the *Journals* of the House of Burgesses, elections were as frequent as in modern days and sometimes more so. The *Journals* show that there were general elections in 1752, 1756, 1758, 1761, 1765, 1769 (May), 1769 (Nov.), 1771, and 1774—nine elections in twenty-two years—besides the many by-elections as incumbent burgesses died or resigned to accept offices such as sheriff, coroner, and others.[3]

Nor was there any dearth of candidates. The people usually had five or more persons from whom to choose at any major election—as the existing election polls clearly indicate. Generally two or three favorites received most of the votes, but the fact remains that there was an ample selection for the voters.[4]

In a period when men traveled by horseback, the weather might well have been an important factor in elections, but contemporary accounts reveal that only occasionally was the weather severe enough to be significant in Virginia politics. Records of that period picture the climate much as it is today—mild in winter with an occasional cold spell.[5] Very few elections were held during the coldest weeks, but even when an election was held in bad weather, it did not deter those who really wanted to vote. In a disputed Prince George election of 1752, for example, nearly eighty voters, most of them living thirty or more miles from the courthouse, came to the election even though the ground was "covered with snow, and the weather excessive cold."[6] But ordinarily the weather had little effect on travel in Virginia.

And finally, there is some question about the importance of plural voting in Virginia elections, since a man could vote in any county where he owned adequate property. In practice, however, as previously noted, plural voting was of virtually no significance. In a contested election in Fauquier County in 1769, one candidate claimed that he could have summoned seventy freeholders from adjacent counties to vote for him; he accused the former sheriff of having deliberately set the day of election to coincide with the Stafford County election. After investigating, the House Committee on Elections concluded that absentee voters from all counties except Stafford could have attended, that there were only about twenty men in Stafford who could vote in Fauquier and that some of these would not have voted for the protesting candidate. The Committee did, however, censure the former sheriff for choosing the same election day as that of Stafford County. But if all seventy of the out-of-county voters had voted for the protesting candidate, he would still have lost the election.[7]

From 1699 to the Revolution, persistent efforts were made to eliminate corruption in elections of burgesses. The act of 1699 provided that if, before an election, any candidate directly or indirectly gave or allowed to any qualified voter any money, meat, drink, or provision, or made any present, gift, reward, promise, engagement, or obligation to allow any money, meat, drink, provision, present, reward, or entertainment to procure votes, that candidate should be disqualified to sit as a burgess.[8] Later this law was interpreted to mean that a candidate was to be restricted in his treating after the election writ was issued.[9] He could do what he pleased before the writ or after the election, however. Treating of and pressure on voters continued to be a problem in spite of these regulations. As a result of various unsavory practices in 1736, a fine of £10 was imposed on tobacco inspectors for undue influence over the voters.[10] The election law of 1762, which was disallowed, prohibited treating or any attempt to influence voters by a candidate or his representative after the dissolution of the Assembly or after a vacancy occurred —a more stringent rule than the 1705 act.[11] But in spite of all attempts at regulation, as we shall see, treating and influencing of voters continued.

Open elections at which the voters registered their preferences by voice vote or by signing the polls of their favorite candidates naturally raise a question of aristocratic influence, but there is in the records no hint of dissatisfaction with this procedure. No petition was sent to the General Assembly demanding a secret ballot, and no mention of widespread concern appeared in the newspapers. Apparently the people were satisfied with their mode of voting or there would have been some evidence of discontent. Custom and habit, aided by active opposition of the British government to any use of a secret ballot in the colonies,[12] probably contributed to general acceptance of open elections; but even more fundamental was the fact, as we shall see in Chapter IX, that the voters were extremely independent in their choice of candidates. Except for those held just before the Revolution, when candidates often received unanimous approval,[13] most elections for which there are records were conducted by written poll, especially if a close contest was expected.

Far from being aristocratic affairs where gentlemen drank tea, flicked lace handkerchiefs, and influenced the votes of the common people, Virginia elections were sometimes drunken brawls where violence was the handmaid of the ballot. In Orange County, 1742, there was a riot when the poll opened, so that the sheriff had to station a deputy sheriff and another man at the doors with drawn swords to get an orderly election. At one time two men threw out the deputy sheriff bodily and tried to break his sword. Toward evening, the other guard at the door left his post and immediately the people swarmed into the courthouse "in a drunken riotous manner." One man jumped upon the clerk's table, danced among the papers, and stopped the election. The House of Burgesses ordered a new election and called the rioters to appear before the House to answer for their conduct.[14]

That elections were not cut and dried events, where aristocrats had already determined the outcome before the election is attested by an account of an Augusta County election in 1755. One side claimed that the sheriff, James Lockhart, had been partial to some of the candidates.

When the people crowded into the courthouse, the sheriff struck several of them with his staff and threatened to push it down their throats if they did not stay back. His accusers said he also refused the votes of free-holders if they intended to vote for the wrong candidate. On his part, the sheriff claimed that the opposition was at fault. Two of them had offered to wager that their candidates, Preston (a large land speculator) and Alexander, would win. When informed that the election was going against them, one of them threatened to win one way or another, even if it meant stopping the election. So they entered the courthouse, scuffled with the sheriff, put out the candles, and started a riot which ended the election. The sheriff was thrown onto a table, which broke under him, the clerks fled, and one opponent of the sheriff called out, "Lads, stand by me. I'll pay the fine, cost what it will. You know I am able." In this dispute, the sheriff won, the rioters had to pay costs, and John Wilson and Gabriel Jones, not Preston and Alexander, were elected.[15] Most elections were not as violent as these, but unruly ones were not uncommon; in fact, it was rare indeed when the House did not have to investigate at least one county election when polls were taken.

There can be no question that candidates attempted to win votes by treating the voters and that such tactics caused difficulties for the candidate both at the election and sometimes later. If friends treated for the candidate and he could prove that he was not responsible, he could avoid expulsion from the House, but men who were elected were sometimes expelled for illegal treating.[16] Occasionally candidates "distributed too much strong liquor among the people" who became "so tumultuous and riotous" that the sheriff could not take the poll.[17] Washington spent over £39 for entertaining the voters at one of his elections.[18]

On the surface, treating might well be considered an aristocratic device to influence voters unduly, but there is some question as to whether the impetus for this practice came from the candidates or the voters. All candidates, whether they won or lost, apparently felt that they had to indulge in the practice. The account of one man who "declared he was ready to vote for anyone who would give him a dram" would seem to indicate that the voters put some pressure on the candidate to treat, for someone furnished the dram.[19] Candidate John Page complained of "the expense of electioneering," the implication being that he was forced to do this regardless of desire.[20] Then there was candidate Matthew Marrable of Lunenburg who entertained a large number of voters on the day before election—using seven sheep and thirty gallons of rum—and although all of them promised to vote for him, "only one of them was as good as his word." [21]

Often the issue at an election was not whether men were qualified to vote but how to prevent the opponent's supporters from getting to the election or from voting after they arrived. Henry Peyton, the defeated candidate in a 1761 Prince William election, conveyed his friends over a flooded river and then tried to buy and wreck the boat so opposing voters could not cross.[22] A bridge across the river at Fredericksburg was demolished just three days before the election, and when asked why, a workman replied, "To laugh at the Rappahanock [sic] electors" who had to cross from Fredericksburg.[23] And in Norfolk, the losing candidate, John Brickall (or Brickell) accused winner Thomas Newton of preventing several freeholders from voting for Brickall "by offering money, and actually giving other things to them not to vote for him." Also, several of Newton's friends, "in a tumultuous and riotous manner," hindered Brickall's friends from entering the courthouse to vote. In a subsequent election, however, Newton won again.[24]

John Page's use of the term "electioneering" serves as a reminder that candidates often went to great lengths in making campaign promises that would win voter support, a practice which should not have been necessary in an aristocratic society. James Littlepage, gentleman of Hanover, opposed gentleman Nathaniel West Dandridge by using the tobacco inspection law as an issue. Going to the "lower meeting house of the Dissenters" to ask whether they would "submit to the damned tobacco law," Littlepage declared that if they would elect him, he would be "hanged or burnt" if he did not get repeal of obnoxious parts of the law. Although he openly repudiated his campaign promises on election day, probably to head off objections by the House of Burgesses, several people later testified that his promises had influenced their vote in his favor.[25] This account, incidentally, is excellent evidence that others besides members of the established Church of England were voters. In Lunenburg, candidate Matthew Marrable solicited support by promising a division of the county, and although he was disqualified by the House for this, he was re-elected in a new election.[26] In fact, so anxious were candidates to please the voters that at least one of them signed a bond for a considerable amount of money as a guarantee that he would carry out his campaign promises. The House disqualified members who were known to have made campaign promises, as illustrated above, but "aristocrats" such as Landon Carter and other burgesses not only believed that constituents had a right to exact promises from candidates but could also demand bond for the faithful execution of the promise.[27] Would that the practice still prevailed.

The House consistently concerned itself about obtaining fair play in elections. It did not countenance illegal election methods even when the offender was an incumbent burgess. Perhaps this was a question of self-defense, since in a democratic society the same illegal methods might be used against as well as for any burgess. In a Berkeley County election in 1775, the following incident occurred. Colonel Adam Stephen, delegate in the previous convention and commander of the county militia, had given notice of an election of delegates to represent the county in the next convention, but the notice was not generally known. In addition, Stephen had ordered a general muster on the same day as the election, then after militia exercises had marched the militia to the courthouse to vote—additional evidence that the militia *could* vote. The election was declared irregular, but later Stephen won in the regular election.[28]

On another occasion, the House inflicted severe punishment on a winning candidate who was also both a tobacco inspector and a county justice. In the disputed Prince William County election of 1736, Thomas Osborne was accused of serving liquor after the election writ was issued and also of using his position as inspector to force people to vote for him. The House resolved that Osborne "was guilty of very enormous misdemeanors in that office, in breach of his oath, and the duty of his said office." By unanimous vote, the House ruled that Osborne could not be seated during the present Assembly, and that the Governor be asked to remove Osborne from his position as county justice and all other offices in the government.[29] This dispute undoubtedly had great influence on the new election law of 1736 which contained curbs on the influence of tobacco inspectors.

Although we tend to think that the powerful standing committees in the House of Burgesses, dominated by the leading men, controlled Virginia politics, the records tell a different story. Final authority rested with the full membership of the House, and as the disputed Elizabeth City election of 1761 indicates, the House did not hesitate to reverse decisions of its committees. In the election, George Wythe was first in the poll, with William Wager defeating James Wallace by two votes. The Committee of Elections ruled out some votes, admitted others, and reversed the outcome of the election by declaring Wallace the winner. But the House refused to accept the Committee's decision on three votes and ended by reversing the Committee's final decision and declaring Wager the winner.[30] Instances in which the full House over-ruled the Committee's recommendations in contested elections were quite common.

When we turn to the influence of social status in elections, we find extensive evidence in the records of colonial Virginia that just being an "aristocrat" was not enough to get a man elected to the House of Burgesses. To give just one of many possible examples, William Tayloe, gentleman of Lancaster County, never could get elected to office in spite of his family name and wealth. By 1736, Tayloe was a county sheriff and by 1740 a Lancaster justice. Not poor, he paid rents on 800 acres, and when he died he had forty-six slaves, forty-nine cattle, thirty-three sheep and fifty-seven hogs plus furniture and farm equipment. In the 1741 election in which all seven candidates were upper-class, Tayloe, now a captain in the militia, ran for burgess, getting only fourth place with forty-six votes to the winners' 116 and seventy-nine. By 1752 he was a colonel and tried again for burgess, this time tying for third place. In December 1755 he received only a token vote from one person, but in July 1758 he ran for office in earnest and again ran third—only seventy-eight votes to the winners' 182 and 163. One might attribute Tayloe's lack of political success to the fact that he was a Presbyterian, except that the religious controversy was not yet an issue in Lancaster in 1741 and being a Presbyterian did not prevent the election of Richard Mitchell, a political favorite for many years.[31]

Furthermore, being an "aristocrat" did not assure continued success in politics, as the career of George Heale of Lancaster County demonstrates. As early as 1736, Heale was designated "gentleman," and throughout the next thirty years he accumulated property and offices. A county justice, Heale was a burgess candidate for the first time in 1755 but was a poor second in the race: twenty-one votes to the winner's eighty-four votes. Six weeks later, in December 1755, a regular election was held and Heale was again a losing candidate—third in the race with sixty-eight votes to ninety-three and 123 for the winners. By 1758, Heale had become sheriff and in the regular election in July of that year he received only one vote. But later in the year, at a by-election in November 1758, Heale was chosen burgess by a substantial majority of 109 to thirty-six for his opponent. At the next regular election, however, he lost his seat in the House. In May 1761, he polled a close third: 108 votes to his opponents' 126 and 161.[32] As far as we can tell, he never ran again; but as these figures show, being a gentleman, a justice, and a sheriff was not adequate assurance of continued political success.

Neither did sons of aristocrats automatically succeed their fathers in the House or win elections from other counties because of their fathers' influence. If they were successful, their success sometimes required several attempts. Landon Carter, son of Robert "King" Carter, ran a poor fourth in the Richmond election of 1735, and it took him seventeen years and several tries before he became a burgess.[33] Although Carter's son Robert Wormeley became a burgess from Richmond County, another son, Landon, Jr., received only twenty votes and ran a very bad fourth in a Prince William election in 1761.[34] Young Landon Carter, Jr., was never successful as a politician. Hampton Wade, son of Burgess Robert Wade of Halifax County, was defeated by a close vote for his father's place in the by-election of 1764, and the following year, as one of nine candidates, Wade came out fourth.[35] He was never able to win a seat in the House before the Revolution, either in Halifax or any other county. Colonel John Spotswood, another son with a famous father, could not use his family influence for much success in politics.[36] And even members of the Lee family sometimes found themselves in difficulties at the election polls.[37]

On occasion a son succeeded his father in the House, but once on his own he could not always maintain his position. Clement Reade, Sr., served as burgess with William Byrd from Lunenburg County, was appointed surveyor, returned to the House of Burgesses, and died in office. His son Clement Reade, Jr., was elected to succeed him, but the son lasted only until the next election.[38] The father's reputation probably helped to get the son elected, but only his own ability could keep him in office.

More important, an "aristocrat" who displeased the people could be quickly and easily disposed of. Landon Carter confided to his diary how the Carters were defeated in Richmond County, and how his son Robert

Wormeley went down to defeat in 1776. Landon said he could well remember when he himself "was turned out of the H.B.," because he did not familiarize himself "among the people." Two elections later his son Robert Wormeley went "amongst-them" and carried his election. Colonel Tayloe also said that his son-in-law, Francis Lightfoot Lee, was elected the same way and that young Carter and Lee would never be turned out. But what had happened? Young Carter had "kissed the arses of the people and very servilely accommodated himself to others," yet he was "shamefully turned out." Lee had been honored by being sent to the Continental Congress, and Colonel Tayloe had done everything a gentleman could do, but Lee had also been defeated. That, mused Carter, was the nature of popularity, an adulteress of the first order. Worst of all was the ingratitude displayed in the election as "even relations as well as tenants" all voted the wrong way. Carter was told that one curly-headed fellow would certainly come to vote for the old burgesses, but Carter did not believe this. When the man came, he voted for one of the old burgesses, then nullified his vote by voting for the opposing candidate.[39] There was certainly no doubt in Carter's mind that the people, not the "aristocrats," controlled the elections.

The defeat of Landon Carter years earlier in 1742 tells a great deal about Virginia elections, the role of the "aristocracy," and the efforts of the aristocrats to win votes. In 1735, Carter had run a poor fourth in the election won by John Woodbridge and William Fantleroy, both large landowners.[40] By 1742, Carter had improved his political fortunes to the extent of challenging the election of Fantleroy. The investigation by the House committee revealed that on the morning of election day one William Jordan, "an open abettor" of Fantleroy, met some freeholders who were friends of Fantleroy at the Rappahannock public bridge on the main road to the courthouse. Jordan had two gallons of rum with which he treated the freeholders. By the time they reached the courthouse several were "merry with liquor." One Thomas Lewis, who owned no land according to the rent rolls, voted for Carter, but William Lewis, an ordinary keeper, who owned 409 acres, stood at the bar asking the freeholders for whom they would vote; and before they could reply he would answer, "Fantleroy and Woodbridge." Some contradicted him but some did not. After the election one Hall came to beg Carter not to prosecute him, "declaring, that Mr. Fantleroy's friends had made him drunk, and persuaded him to vote for Mr. Fantleroy against Mr. Carter, tho' he had no vote"—evidence that there were some disfranchised men. William Jordan confessed that he had given the freeholders strong liquor and would do so again to prevent the election of Carter. The Committee on Elections exonerated Fantleroy, but resolved that Jordan had invaded the freedom of elections and that therefore Fantleroy was not duly elected. But the House reversed the Committee and seated Fantleroy. Ten years went by before Landon Carter finally won his first election.[41]

All aspects of the election processes in Virginia are apparent in George Washington's initial entrance into politics in 1755. Then a colonel in the Virginia regiment, he asked his brother to "fish at Colo. Fairfax's intentions" to make sure that he would have a chance to win if he ran for office, and also asked his brother to see whether certain important men would support him. If Fairfax ran, or if the others refused their backing, Washington intended to drop his political plans.[42] Fairfax ran in a close election that saw John West first with 232 votes, Fairfax second with 222, and William Ellzey a close third with 220. In the heated contest, Washington was knocked down by an opponent of Fairfax, whom Washington supported, and talk of a duel was averted by Washington's apology.[43] But even a Fairfax had a difficult time in Fairfax County.

A few days after the Fairfax election, and without publicizing the fact, Washington suddenly decided to run in Frederick County and was badly defeated even though he was a Washington and leader of the colony's army against the French. Colonel Adam Stephen felt that he could have enhanced Washington's chances because he claimed to have great influence in the county, but Washington had not confided in him. In the election, Hugh West received 271 votes, Thomas Swearingen 270, and Washington only 40.[44]

When Washington was finally elected in 1758, there was no doubt that the outcome rested with the common people rather than with the aristocrats. John Kirkpatrick urged him to be at the election in person as "the promises of the vulgar" were too precarious for building hopes. James Wood inquired into "the opinions of the people," found Washington's prestige still high in spite of efforts to convince him to the contrary, but warned him there was "no relying on the promises of the common herd, the promise is too oft forgot when the back is turned." Robert Rutherford wrote that Washington's friends were pushing with great ardor, "even down to Will the Hatter and his oyly spouse" who showed the greatest spirit in the cause.[45]

Other supporters were not so optimistic, however, and again it was fear of what the common people would do that caused the pessimism. Charles Smith declared that Washington's pretended friends now seemed doubtful and would not promise to vote for him, and he feared that if he took Washington's poll at the election it might alienate some of the weaker freeholders "whose votes goe as far as those of men of sense." He also warned Washington that his own brother-in-law, Fielding Lewis, had been defeated in Spotsylvania by Colonel Walker and Zachrey Lewis "by a vulgar majority." And Gabriel Jones believed that Washington's own people (tenants) and his friends had changed their sentiments and now raised doubts about matters that had seemed so clear with them before. Washington's Potomac people, he feared, would not be steadfast as they now talked of the old burgesses. George Fairfax would be there to assist, but Washington could also help his cause if he removed some complaints about the army. A wind storm and the harvest would keep many freeholders from the election, Jones continued, but Washington stood well with the Quakers.[46]

In spite of the doubts, Washington won easily, getting 307 votes to 240 for Thomas Bryan Martin, while the former burgesses, Hugh West and Thomas Swearingen, got 199 and forty-five respectively. Since the people had elected West and Swearingen in the previous election, a great many must have changed their minds. Following the poll, Washington spent £39 for entertaining the voters and was politician enough to desire that those who voted against him be included. Washington said that the best way to show his appreciation to the people in general for electing him was to make their interests his own, as they really were, and do everything he could for the country. His friend Rutherford attributed success to Washington's punctual discharge of every trust, his humane and equitable treatment of each individual, his ardent zeal for the common cause, and his influence in both the county and the House. Washington was undoubtedly aided also by the fact that the old burgesses were implicated in scandals from which they did not satisfactorily clear themselves.[47]

The story of Washington's early political experiences illustrates many truisms of politics, truisms that are still accepted today. Men seeking office felt the need for backing by influential men; elections were often extremely close even for "aristocrats" such as the Fairfaxes; elections could be pretty rough affairs, as Washington discovered; Quakers, not just Church of England adherents, were voters; a candidate was at the mercy of the common people, his own tenants among them, who appeared to be extremely independent; the vote of a poor man was as important as the vote of a rich one; and a successful candidate concerned himself with the interests of the people, not merely those of a class.

Not all of the upper classes entered politics; some did not even vote regularly, and when they did vote, they were not always on the side of winning candidates. Rawleigh Downman, gentleman and esquire of Lancaster, first voted for a winner and a loser in 1748, did not vote again for twenty years, then in 1768 and 1769 joined the overwhelming majority in voting for two winners. Downman voted only four times from 1748 to 1774, yet he was one of the wealthiest men in Lancaster.[48] James Gordon of the same county, merchant, gentleman, and probably second only to Charles Carter in wealth, voted consistently, sometimes for winners and sometimes for losers, but never ran for office and was never a justice or a sheriff.[49]

Contrary to general opinion, county sheriffs did not always have deciding influence at elections and did not always throw the influence they had on the side of winning candidates. In 1736, for instance, Speaker John Randolph of York County charged that Sheriff Francis Heyward had leased half-acre tracts of land to tenants who were expected to vote for his candidate, and Heyward was reprimanded by the House and forced to pay costs. In Halifax County where there had been several disputed elections, the sheriff in 1769 was known to favor the two challenging candidates, Walter and Isaac Coles, rather than incumbents John Lewis and Nathaniel Terry. To aid the Coles, the sheriff planned to open the polls early, for many of the supporters of Lewis and Terry lived at a distance of twenty or thirty miles. The sheriff could not influence the vote of his own relatives, and the election had to be called off when a riot ensued. Both incidents indicate that the sheriff's role in elections could be very complex and does not lend itself to easy generalization.[50]

The hotly-contested Halifax elections of 1768 and 1769 provide significant figures for establishing voting patterns in this county (Table A).

TABLE A.  VOTING PATTERNS IN HALIFAX COUNTY,
1768-69[51]

| *Candidates* | *No. of Votes Received* |
|---|---|
| 1. Nathaniel Terry and John Lewis, 1769 ................. | 104 |
| 2. Walter Coles and Isaac Coles, 1769 .................... | 105 |
| 3. Nathaniel Terry and Walter Coles, 1769 ............... | 64 |
| 4. Nathaniel Terry and Isaac Coles, 1769 .................. | 15 |
| 5. Walter Coles and John Lewis, 1769 .................... | 14 |
| 6. Isaac Coles and John Lewis, 1769 ..................... | 9 |
| 7. Nathaniel Terry only ................................. | 7 |
| 8. Walter Coles only .................................... | 8 |
| 9. John Lewis only ...................................... | 6 |
| 10. Isaac Coles only ..................................... | 1 |
| 11. Number who voted in both 1768 and 1769 ............... | 214 |
| 12. Number who voted 1768 but not 1769 .................. | 231 |
| 13. Number who voted 1769 but not 1768 .................. | 100 |
| 14. Voted Terry and Lewis in 1768, did not vote 1769 ........ | 106 |
| 15. Voted Terry and Lewis, 1769, did not vote 1768 .......... | 30 |
| 16. Voted Terry and Lewis, 1768 and 1769 ................. | 57 |
| 17. Voted Terry only 1768, did not vote 1769 .............. | 24 |
| 18. Voted for Terry 1768, someone else 1769 .............. | 14 |
| 19. Voted for Terry, 1769, someone else 1768 ............. | 44 |
| 20. Voted for Walter Coles, 1768, did not vote 1769 .......... | 68 |
| 21. Voted for Walter Coles, 1769, did not vote 1768 .......... | 49 |
| 22. Voted for Walter Coles, 1768, someone else 1769 ......... | 9 |
| 23. Voted for Walter Coles, 1769, someone else 1768 ........ | 21 |
| 24. Individual votes:  Walter Coles        191 | |
|                       Nathaniel Terry      190 | |
|                       John Lewis           133 | |
|                       Isaac Coles          130 | |

Two factions mustered almost equal numbers of men who voted for both candidates in each faction (lines 1 and 2), but 102 men split their votes (lines 3 to 6), and twenty-two voted for one candidate only (lines 7-10). Sixty-four men (line 3) voted for the eventual winners, Terry and Walter Coles, one from each faction, and it was the independent voters who determined the outcome. This independence is demonstrated by the fact that while 214 men voted in both elections, 331 missed one or the other (lines 11-13), that only fifty-seven out of 545 supported incumbents Terry and Lewis in both elections (line 16), and that many men changed preferences between elections. In the final outcome, winner Nathaniel Terry had to pay costs for his violence against Sheriff Hoskins, but he was also successful in demanding that the House clear his name of accusations made by his fellow burgess, Walter Coles.[52] And the issue in the election was obviously not a question of class, for Walter Coles had also been a former burgess.

The influence of family ties on voting in colonial Virginia seemed to be no more important than it is today. Any number of illustrations could be provided of a split vote within a family. In Norfolk County, for instance, Thomas Halstead, Sr., voted for candidates Wilson and Veale in 1768 but his son voted for Wilson and Newton in the same election. The following year the father voted for Wilson and Brickall while the son chose Wilson and Newton again.[53] If we can assume that men with the same family name in the county were related, less than half of those who voted in the four elections in Halifax between 1764 and 1769 supported their kinsmen. Of fifty-eight such voters in the four elections, only twenty-six voted for candidates with the same family name. Success of candidates in this respect varied greatly. Two Bookers voted in 1764 and both voted for Edward Booker, and eight of the eleven Wades voted for Hampton Wade. In 1765, however, eight Wades voted, but only four for Hampton, while six who voted in 1764 failed to do so in 1765. In 1765, three Tunstalls, four Greens, and three Campbells voted, but none voted for their namesakes and only one Watkins out of six voted for George Watkins. In 1768, all four voting Terrys supported winner Nathaniel Terry, but none of the four voting Lewises voted for winner John Lewis.[54]

The independence shown by Halifax voters was typical of any election in any county, where men of all classes not only differed over the choice of candidates but also changed their minds between elections. Examples in Table B illustrate these generalizations on the part of both upper and middle-lower classes in Norfolk, 1768-69. In Richmond County, twelve of nineteen grand jurors voted in 1755; all voted for Landon Carter and John Woodbridge in an election which was virtually uncontested. But in 1758, when Carter was almost defeated, six of the twelve voted for him, four voted against, and the two who did not vote were against him the next election of 1761.[56] In 1770, when the candidates were Francis Lightfoot Lee and Robert Wormeley Carter, only five of fifteen grand jurors voted for both Carter and Lee, and these did not include the two largest landowners on the jury.[57]

Among candidates, it was considered an honor not only to win but to receive the highest number of votes in an election, for this marked a man's popularity with the people and placed him first on the listing of burgesses. When John Randolph was listed ahead of Henry Blagrave before the election returns were in and on the excuse that "Mr. Randolph was a man of the greatest dignity," Blagrave protested vigorously. Blagrave said he did not know what Randolph's dignity was, but neither Randolph nor anyone else on his behalf was entitled by law or custom to crown Randolph with the honor due to Blagrave. Blagrave insisted that

TABLE B. INDEPENDENT VOTING, NORFOLK COUNTY,
1768-1769[55]

| Voter's Name | Choice 1768 | Choice 1769 |
|---|---|---|
| Gentlemen: | | |
| George Abyvon | Newton & Veale | Wilson & Newton |
| Maximilian Calvert | Newton & Veale | Wilson & Newton |
| William Orange | Brickall & Veale | Wilson & Brickall |
| Col. George Veale | Veale & Lockhart | Wilson & Newton |
| Artisans and Planters: | | |
| Isaac Luke, carpenter | Newton & Veale | Wilson & Brickall |
| John Ashley, shipwright | Newton & Veale | Wilson & Newton |
| John Perkins, illiterate planter | Wilson & Brickall | Newton & Brickall |
| John Talbot, carpenter | Brickall & Veale | Newton & Tucker |
| John Vandevort, illiterate blacksmith | Veale & Lockhart | Newton & Brickall |

Winning candidates in both elections—Wilson and Newton.

this preference had been given to him freely and lawfully by his constituents, 260 votes to 210 for Randolph, when it lay in their choice who would receive this honor.[58]

As is true today, and despite a compulsory voting law, voters frequently showed considerable apathy but turned out when the issues warranted. In Accomack County, where the population was fairly stable, 482 voted in 1742, 386 in 1744, but 555 in 1748.[59] A survey of voting records for vestrymen in Antrium Parish, Halifax, shows that of the twelve, five did not vote in 1764 or 1765, and nine abstained in 1768 and 1769.[60] Sometimes the candidates themselves voted, as did Colonel George Veale (Table B) who voted for himself in 1768, but often candidates did not vote.

Any suspicion that open elections led to early voting by the upper classes to influence the vote of the lower classes must be substantiated with evidence, not just generalizations, as Table C indicates. The figures make a significant pattern, but it is almost diametrically the opposite of what might be expected. Included were the votes of those identified as the leading men of Lancaster County—justices, sheriffs, ministers, physicians, burgesses, vestrymen, and other gentlemen. When there were real contests, as in 1741, 1748, and 1774, these men of the upper class either spread their votes as in 1748, or actually voted late in the poll, as in 1741 and 1774. Only where there was little contest, as in 1765, 1768, 1769, and 1771, did these leaders vote predominantly in the early part of the poll. In the close elections, perhaps these men were waiting until the end of the poll to cast a decisive vote, or they held off to do a little political bargaining, or they wanted to be sure of being on the winning side. Whatever the reason, their voting behavior was not what we might expect.

Comparable studies of upper-class voting in other counties show similar results. In the hotly-contested Norfolk elections of 1768 and 1769, a

TABLE C. TIME OF UPPER-CLASS VOTING IN LANCASTER[61]

| Date of Election | Candidates and their Votes | Very early* | Early | Middle | Late | Very late | Total |
|---|---|---|---|---|---|---|---|
| 1741 | Conway (116) | 1 | — | — | — | 4 | 5 |
| | Mitchell (79) | — | — | 2 | — | 2 | 4 |
| | Stepto (56) | 1 | — | 1 | — | — | 2 |
| | Joseph Ball (40) | 1 | — | 1 | — | 2 | 4 |
| | Major Ball (32) | — | — | — | — | 5 | 5 |
| | William Ball (31) | 1 | — | — | — | 1 | 2 |
| Total | | 4 | — | 4 | — | 14 | 22 |
| 1748 | Chinn (115) | 3 | 2 | — | 4 | 2 | 11 |
| | Conway (106) | 5 | 1 | — | 3 | 2 | 11 |
| | Pinckard (73) | 1 | — | 2 | 1 | — | 4 |
| | Mitchell (70) | 2 | 1 | — | — | 2 | 5 |
| | Stepto (30) | 2 | — | 1 | — | — | 3 |
| Total | | 13 | 4 | 3 | 8 | 6 | 34 |
| 1765 | Mitchell (168) | 9 | 5 | — | — | 5 | 19 |
| | Carter (145) | 10 | 4 | — | 1 | 4 | 19 |
| | R. Ball (22) | — | — | — | — | — | — |
| Total | | 19 | 9 | — | 1 | 9 | 38 |
| 1768 | James Ball (155) | 9 | 5 | 5 | 2 | 2 | 23 |
| | Carter (145) | 9 | 4 | 3 | 2 | 2 | 20 |
| | Richard Ball (65) | 1 | 1 | 1 | — | — | 3 |
| Total | | 19 | 10 | 9 | 4 | 4 | 46 |
| 1769 | Mitchell (154) | 11 | 2 | 1 | 1 | 4 | 19 |
| | Carter (139) | 10 | 3 | 1 | 2 | 5 | 21 |
| | R. Ball (29) | — | — | — | — | — | — |
| Total | | 21 | 5 | 2 | 3 | 9 | 40 |
| 1771 | Mitchell (161) | 9 | 7 | 3 | 1 | 2 | 22 |
| | Carter (135) | 8 | 6 | 4 | — | 3 | 21 |
| | Ball (31) | — | — | — | 1 | — | 1 |
| Total | | 17 | 13 | 7 | 2 | 5 | 44 |
| 1774 | Selden (151) | 2 | 1 | 3 | 1 | 1 | 8 |
| | Carter (138) | 2 | — | 2 | 1 | 10 | 15 |
| | Ball (115) | 1 | 2 | 2 | — | 4 | 9 |
| Total | | 5 | 3 | 7 | 2 | 15 | 32 |

* Since a voter's name was listed on the poll at the time he gave his vote, it is possible to arrive at his approximate voting time relative to other voters. Therefore, these categories were arrived at by dividing the total vote of each candidate into thirds—early, middle, late—and then subdividing the "early" and "late" voters again for greater accuracy.

great majority of this group voted late or very late. In 1768, only two gentlemen cast ballots among the first twenty-five voters—one a minister who voted for two losers and the other a losing candidate who voted for himself and another loser. In 1769, no gentleman voted among the first forty-five voters, there were only two among the first one hundred, and twenty-three of the twenty-eight who voted for a winning candidate did so after more than 300 men had already voted.[62] Upper-class voting in Halifax, Accomack, Amelia, and Essex counties was similar to that of Lancaster and Norfolk.[63]

If election practices in Virginia permitted the domination of a ruling upper class, such a conclusion must be arrived at through records other than the ones we have seen. The people had ample warning of impending elections, weather was insignificant, plural voting was unimportant, and there was little overt opposition to open elections. Far from being decorous, aristocratic affairs, elections were a mingling of all classes and even sometimes drunken riots where candidates were anything but friendly rivals. Candidates wooed voters by treating and were very conscious of the political power of the lower classes, but voters gained through treating were not always faithful to their promises. Not all aristocrats could get elected to office or stay elected once they gained political success, and sons seldom succeeded fathers as elected burgesses.

Naturally men used whatever tactics they could to win elections; but if Virginia had been an aristocratically-controlled society, there would have been no need to cultivate the votes of the lower classes. If candidates sought the support of well-known men who could influence other voters, this was no more than politicians in this country do today. Judging by the heated elections, the people obviously did not believe that the choice of candidates was between Tweedledee and Tweedledum. Right or wrong, they believed there was a significant difference between the candidates regardless of their wealth, just as the supporters of Hoover, Roosevelt, Nixon, or Kennedy do today.

## NOTES

1. Beverley, *History*, pp. 241-42; Hening, *Statutes*, II, 82; III, 172-75, 236-46; IV, 475-78; VIII, 305-17; *An Exact Abridgment of All the Public Acts of Assembly, of Virginia, In Force and Use* . . . (Williamsburg, 1737), pp. 12-14; *The Acts of Assembly, Now in Force, in the Colony of Virginia* . . . (Williamsburg, 1752), p. 142; *ibid.*, 1769 ed., pp. 102-03. Hereafter the last three references will be cited as *Virginia Laws, 1737*, etc.

2. Hening, *Statutes*, XII, 120-29.

3. *House Journals, passim*.

4. For example see the elections of Accomack County, Deed Book 1737-46, end of book; *ibid.*, 1746-57, pp. 130-43, 367-70; *ibid.*, 1757-70, pp. 52-56.

5. For contemporary descriptions of Virginia weather, see Answers to Queries of Lords of Trade, July 23, 1730, Gooch Papers, I, 179, VHS; Burnaby, *Travels*, p. 149; William Cabell Memorandum Book, VHS, March 6, 1775, Feb. 22, 1779; Harry Piper to Dixon and Littledale, Feb. 28, 1772 and Jan. 8, 1773, Harry Piper Letter Book; Washington to Burwell Bassett, Feb. 15, 1773,

Washington, *Writings,* III, 115; Washington, *Diaries,* II, 52-54 and *passim; Virginia Gazette,* Feb. 4, 1736/7; *ibid.* (P & D), Feb. 28, March 7, and June 6, 1771; Feb. 6, 1772.

6. *House Journals, 1752-58,* p. 50.

7. *Ibid., 1766-69,* pp. 290-91.

8. Hening, *Statutes,* III, 173.

9. *Ibid.,* pp. 236-45.

10. *House Journals, 1727-40,* p. 279.

11. Hening, *Statutes,* VII, 517-30.

12. *Acts of the Privy Council,* IV, 217-18. Feb. 28, 1754.

13. For example, in Prince George election, *Virginia Gazette* (P & D), July 14, 1774.

14. *House Journals, 1742-49,* p. 50.

15. *Ibid., 1752-58,* pp. 347-48, 381, 383, 447. Sydnor, *Gentlemen Freeholders,* p. 15ff. gives a different account of this election. For reports of other riotous elections see especially *House Journals, 1727-1740,* pp. 250, 256, 265, 274; *ibid., 1742-49,* pp. 334-35; *ibid., 1766-69,* pp. 197, 231.

16. For laws on treating see Hening, *Statutes,* III, 173, 243-45; *House Journals, 1752-58,* pp. 456-57. See also Sydnor, *Gentlemen Freeholders.*

17. *House Journals, 1727-1740,* pp. 256, 265. See also pp. 250, 274, 370; *ibid., 1742-49,* p. 50; *ibid., 1752-58,* pp. 49-50, 61-62, 343, 344, 359-61, 456; *ibid., 1758-61,* pp. 83-84; *ibid., 1770-72,* p. 254; Landon Carter Diary, March 21, 1752.

18. Washington, *Writings,* II, 241-42 and n.; Washington Papers, VIII, 189; *Letters to Washington,* II, 398-400.

19. *House Journals, 1761-65,* pp. 269-72.

20. Page to John Norton, May 27, 1769, Norton Papers.

21. *House Journals, 1758-61,* pp. 83-84.

22. *Ibid., 1761-65,* p. 17 ff.

23. *Ibid., 1742-49,* pp. 292-93.

24. *Ibid., 1766-69,* p. 197. Norfolk County Deed Book 24, pp. 112-15, 211-215.

25. *House Journals, 1761-65,* pp. 269-72.

26. *Ibid., 1758-61,* pp. 83-84.

27. Landon Carter Diary, March 31, 1752.

28. Committee Report, July 27, 1775, Virginia Convention 1775, Misc. MSS., VSL.

29. *House Journals, 1727-40,* pp. 264-65; for still another example see *ibid., 1742-49,* pp. vii, 51-52 (Amelia County election of 1742).

30. *Ibid., 1761-65,* pp. 88-90, 94-96.

31. Lancaster County Loose Papers, 1752, VSL; Lancaster County Deed Book 13, pp. 6, 174; Book 16, pp. 27-28 (1758), 222-23 (1761); Book 17, p. 6; Book 18, p. 169; Book 20, p. 2; Lancaster County Will Book 15, pp. 155, 232-33 (Dec., 1755); Lancaster Tithable List, 1745; Lancaster County Rentals, 1748 and 1750. Mitchell, a Presbyterian, was second in the election of 1761 and first in 1765, 1769, and 1771.

32. Lancaster County Deed Book 13, pp. 24, 74, 239, 282, 284; Book 14, pp. 88, 169, 190, 237, 271; Book 16, pp. 27-28, 49, 79, 200, 222-23; Book 18, pp. 16, 29, 84, 109, 163; Book 19, pp. 18, 80; Lancaster County Tithable Lists 1745, 1746, 1775; Lancaster County Rentals, 1750, 1773; Lancaster County Order Book 12, p. 1; election of 1758 in Lancaster County Deed Book 16, p. 49 and Lancaster County Loose Papers; Lancaster County Will Book 15, pp. 224, 231-33.

33. Richmond County election poll, 1735, VSL.

34. Prince William County Deed Book P, pp. 68-73.

35. *House Journals, 1758-61,* Burgess list, 1758; *ibid., 1761-65,* Burgess list, 1761; Halifax County Deed Book 2, p. 271; Book 3, pp. 389-92, 391-401.

36. *William and Mary Quarterly*, 1st Ser., X, 281; *House Journals*, Burgess lists 1756 and 1758.

37. William Lee to Richard Henry Lee, Feb. 16 and April 2, 1772, Lee-Ludwell Papers, VHS.

38. *House Journals*, Burgess lists, 1752, 1758, 1761, and 1766.

39. Landon Carter Diary, April 1, 1776.

40. Richmond Election Poll 1735, VSL; Richmond Rentals, 1744.

41. *House Journals, 1742-47*, pp. 34-35; *ibid., 1752-58*, pp. vii-viii.

42. To John Augustine Washington, May 28, 1755, Washington, *Writings*, I, 130-31.

43. Sydnor, *Gentlemen Freeholders*, pp. 24-25; Douglas S. Freeman, *George Washington*, 2 vols. (New York, 1948), II, 146.

44. Dec. 23, 1755, *Letters to Washington*, I, 158; Washington Papers, X, 59-60.

45. *Letters to Washington*, II, 345-56, 349, 374.

46. *Ibid.*, pp. 343-44, 372-74. For a view that Washington's election was the work of an aristocracy, see Sydnor, *Gentlemen Freeholders*, pp. 67-69.

47. Washington, *Writings*, II, 241-42 and n.; *Letters to Washington*, II, 206, 398-400; July 26, 1758, Washington Papers, VIII, 116, 173, 189.

48. Lancaster County Order Book 12, p. 256; Lancaster County Deed Book 18, p. 159; Book 19, p. 110; Lancaster County Will Book 20, pp. 188, 200-06; Lancaster County Tithable Lists of 1745, 1746, 1775 and Lancaster County Rentals 1748, 1750, 1773; for Lancaster County election polls 1741-1774 see note 26, Chp. VII above; survey of members of the House of Burgesses from 1752 to 1781, *House Journals, passim*.

49. Lancaster County Deed Book 13, pp. 312, 329; Book 14, pp. 1, 118, 156, 215, 216, 243, 264, 295; Book 16, pp. 51, 121; Book 17, p. 6; Book 18, pp. 4, 105, 108-09; Book 19, pp. 101, 194, 242, 261, 262; Book 21, pp. 28-29; Lancaster County Will Book 15, pp. 155, 192, 282, 283, 295; Lancaster County Rentals 1748, 1750, 1773; Lancaster County Tithable Lists 1745, 1746, 1775. For Lancaster election polls of 1748, 1752, 1754, 1755 (Dec.), 1758, 1761, 1765, see footnote 26. Ch. VII above.

50. *House Journals, 1727-40*, pp. 276-77, 282-83, 286; *ibid., 1761-65*, pp. 288, 290, 326; *ibid., 1766-69*, pp. 231-32, 242-45.

51. Halifax County Deed Book 3, pp. 401-11.

52. *House Journals, 1766-69*, pp. 246, 351-52; *ibid., 1770-72*, pp. 21-28.

53. Norfolk County Deed Book 24, pp. 112-15 (1768), 211-15 (1769). For other similar instances see Benjamin Hodges Sr. and Jr., William Nicholson Sr. and Jr., and William Owens Sr. and Jr., in the above elections.

54. Halifax County Deed Book 3, pp. 389-411.

55. Norfolk County Deed Book 24, pp. 112-15, 211-15; for another example of independence see the votes of Henry and Robert Headley and others in Richmond County elections of 1755, 1758, 1769, 1771 in Richmond County Order Book 13, pp. 338-40; Book 14, pp. 264-68; Book 16, pp. 491-97; Book 17, pp. 249-56.

56. Jury in *ibid.*, Book 14, p. 376; election polls in Book 13, pp. 338-40; Book 14, pp. 264-68, 381-85; acreages in Richmond County Rentals 1746, 1751 and 1765, VSL.

57. Jury in Richmond County Order Book 17, p. 189; election polls in Book 16, pp. 491-97; acreages from Richmond County Rental, 1768, VSL.

58. *Virginia Gazette* (R), Feb. 2, 1769.

59. Accomack County Deed Book 1737-46, at the end of book; *ibid.*, 1746-1757, pp. 130-43; *ibid.*, 1757-70, No. 3, Pt. I, pp. 52-56.

60. Halifax County Deed Book 5, p. 223; Book 3, pp. 389-411.

61. For upper-class community leaders in 1741 and 1748 see Lancaster County Order Book 8, pp. 112, 249, 250, 255, 278, 325, 329, 359, 360; Lancaster County Deed Book 13, pp. 2, 3, 243, 248, 249, 334; Book 14, pp. 97,

110, 165; Book 16, pp. 54, 103, 244; Lancaster County Will Book 15, pp. 99, 107, 165, 244; Lancaster County Rental 1750; for elections see Lancaster County Deed Book 13, pp. 249-50; Book 14, pp. 200-01. For community leaders in 1765-71 see Lancaster County Order Book 12, pp. 1, 10, 13, 17, 45, 74, 79, 256; Lancaster County Will Book 15, p. 191; Lancaster County Deed Book 16, p. 222; Book 17, pp. 6, 11, 30, 35; Book 18, pp. 26, 42-43, 73, 78, 79, 104, 105; Book 18—Orders, pp. 15, 17, 78; Book 19, pp. 16, 20, 21, 29, 46, 58, 112, 157, 164, 177, 183, 195; Lancaster County Will Book 20, pp. 144, 147; Lancaster County Deed Book 21, pp. 28-29; Lancaster County Rental 1773; for election polls see Lancaster County Deed Book 18, pp. 42-43, 133-34, 154; Book 19, pp. 58-59, and Lancaster County Loose Papers, VSL.

62. Norfolk leaders studied were George Abyvon, William Atchinson, Max. Calvert, Joseph Calvert, Lewis Hansford, Neil Jameson, Paul Loyall, Thomas Newton, William Orange, Capt. John Phripp, Humphrey Roberts, Neil Snodgrass, Andrew Sprowle, Richard Templeman, all merchant-gentlemen; Edward Archer, Cornelius Calvert, Capt. John Calvert, merchants; Samuel Boush, Jr., Matthew Godfrey, Sr., John Hutchings, Jr., Joseph Hutchings, George Veale, Thomas Veale, gentlemen; William Chisholm, mariner-merchant; William R. Curle, lawyer; Dr. Archibald Campbell; Dr. James Taylor; Reverend Thomas Davis; Reverend Charles Smith; Colonel Anthony Walke; John Willoughby, Esquire; Samuel Happer and William Happer, Jr., vestrymen. Not all gentlemen could be included in this survey because some had the same names as other men in the community and their votes could not be separated. For social data on above leaders see Norfolk County Deed Books, *passim*; election polls are found in Norfolk County Deed Book 24, pp. 112-15, 211-15.

63. For leaders see Halifax County Deed Books, *passim*; election polls are found in Book 3, pp. 392-401, 407-11; for Accomack County leaders see Accomack County Deed Book 1737-46, pp. 1-531; Book 1746-57, pp. 1-373; election polls of 1738, 1740, 1742, 1744 at end of Book 1737-46; poll for 1748 in Book 1746-57, pp. 130-43; poll of 1758 in Book 1757-70, No. 3, Pt. 1, pp. 52-56; for Amelia County material see Amelia election poll, 1761, and Amelia County Tithable List, 1762; for Essex leaders see Essex County Deed Books, *passim*; for election polls see Book 24, pp. 275-80 (1748); Book 25, pp. 301-07 (1752); Book 27, pp. 248-52 (1755); Book 28, pp. 95-99 (1758); Book 29, pp. 1-7 (1761); Book 30, pp. 235-42 (1765), 243-48 (1768), 318-24 (1769), 385 (1770), 496-502 (1771); Book 31, pp. 398-402 (1777), 405-06 (1778).

# CHAPTER IX

# *How the Electorate Voted*

"Must I again be subject to the humours of a fickle croud? Must I again resign my reason, and be nought but what each voter pleases? Must I cajole, fawn, and wheedle for a place that brings so little profit?"[1]

"Like lords and squires in the mother country, slaveowning barons took the lead in politics as they did in social affairs. At elections held in the open air in country towns they easily cowed all but the bravest freeholding farmers and named their own men for public office. If a schism among them threatened their dominion, they united again with a swiftness that took the breath of the opposition."[2]

THE ABOVE QUOTATIONS present contradictory interpretations of Virginia elections and pose the major problem to be considered in this chapter. One or the other of these two accounts must be wrong. Either the candidate subjected himself to the humors of a fickle crowd, resigned his own reason to please each voter, and cajoled, fawned, and wheedled for political preferment, or his upper-class supporters cowed all but the bravest freeholders and named their men to public office. We have already seen enough evidence in Chapter VIII to suspect that the first account is much more accurate than the second. Fortunately we have election polls, deeds, wills, laws, quitrent rolls, and other evidence so that we can discover the economic status of a large part of the voters and can determine exactly how they voted and who controlled the elections. This shall be our task in the present chapter.

The material in the following election charts entailed tedious compilation from the sources, and this could be done only in those counties where the needed combination of records still exists. Involved was the alphabetizing of election polls, quitrent rolls, and tithable lists, and the abstracting and alphabetizing of all deeds, wills, leases, and court orders for periods of many years. This information was then transferred to individual name cards and used for compiling the tables. Probable planters, as stated earlier, were men who were not designated as planters but who bought plantations that would appear to place them in this class. The upper classes—the "aristocracy"—include anyone with any kind of distinguishing title, although many so designated were probably not really members of this group. Lancaster, an old tidewater county which

TABLE 1. LANCASTER COUNTY ELECTION POLL OF NOVEMBER 18, 1741

Total Voters—202  
Number of Candidates—7

| Candidates | Upper Class | | | Middle-Lower Class | | | | Undesignated | Sign with a Mark | Slaveholding Voters (if Known) |
|---|---|---|---|---|---|---|---|---|---|---|
| | Gentlemen & Merchts. | Others | Total | Planters & Probable Planters | Artisans | Tenants & Servants | Total | | | |
| Conway & Mitchell | 1 | 1 | 2 | 8 | 1 | — | 9 | — | 4 | 3 |
| Conway & Stepto | 5 | 2 | 7 | 33 | 5 | 3 | 41 | 5 | 11 | 34 |
| Conway & Tayloe | — | 2 | 2 | 23 | 6 | 2 | 31 | — | 10 | 19 |
| Conway & J. Ball | — | 1 | 1 | — | — | — | — | 1 | — | 1 |
| Conway & Maj. Ball | 4 | 1 | 5 | 3 | 2 | — | 5 | 2 | 2 | 9 |
| Conway & Wm. Ball | 1 | — | 1 | 4 | — | — | 4 | — | — | 4 |
| Mitchell & Stepto | 1 | — | 1 | 1 | — | — | 1 | — | — | 2 |
| Mitchell & Tayloe | 1 | — | 1 | 3 | — | — | 3 | — | 2 | 3 |
| Mitchell & J. Ball | 4 | — | 4 | 18 | 3 | 2 | 23 | 2 | 7 | 16 |
| Mitchell & Maj. Ball | — | — | — | 8 | 2 | 1 | 11 | — | 2 | 6 |
| Mitchell & Wm. Ball | 2 | — | 2 | 10 | 4 | — | 14 | — | 2 | 9 |
| Stepto & Tayloe | — | 1 | 1 | 2 | — | — | 2 | — | 1 | 3 |
| Stepto & Jos. Ball | — | — | — | 1 | — | — | 1 | — | — | 1 |
| Stepto & Maj Ball | — | — | — | 1 | — | — | 1 | — | — | — |
| Stepto & Wm. Ball | — | — | — | 1 | — | — | 1 | — | 1 | 1 |
| Tayloe & Jos. Ball. | — | — | — | 3 | — | — | 3 | — | — | 1 |
| Tayloe & Maj. Ball | — | — | — | 1 | — | — | 1 | — | 2 | 2 |
| Tayloe & Wm. Ball | — | — | — | — | — | — | — | — | — | — |
| Jos. Ball & Maj. Ball | 2 | — | 2 | 1 | 2 | — | 3 | 1 | 2 | 2 |
| Jos. Ball & Wm. Ball | 1 | — | 1 | 2 | — | — | 2 | — | — | 3 |
| Maj. Ball & Wm. Ball | — | — | — | — | 1 | — | 1 | — | — | 2 |
| Mitchell only | — | — | — | 1 | — | — | 1 | — | — | — |
| W. Ball only | — | — | — | — | — | — | — | 1 | — | 1 |
| Tayloe only | 1 | — | 1 | 1 | — | — | 1 | — | — | — |
| Totals | 23 | 8 | 31 | 125 | 26 | 8 | 159 | 12 | 46 | 122 |

INDIVIDUAL CANDIDATES, LANCASTER COUNTY, NOVEMBER 18, 1741

| Candidate | Upper Class | Middle-Lower Class | Undesignated | Total Vote |
|---|---|---|---|---|
| Col. Conway | 18 | 90 | 8 | 116 |
| Mr. Mitchell | 10 | 62 | 7 | 79 |
| Capt. Wm. Stepto | 9 | 47 | — | 56 |
| Capt. Wm. Tayloe | 5 | 41 | — | 46 |
| Jos. Ball, Esq. | 8 | 28 | 4 | 40 |
| Major Ball | 7 | 22 | 3 | 32 |
| Col. Wm. Ball | 4 | 26 | 1 | 31 |

CANDIDATES BY ORDER OF CLASS PREFERENCE
(Winners in Italics)

Upper Class:  1. *Conway* 2. *Mitchell* 3. Stepto 4. Jos. Ball 5. Major Ball 6. William Tayloe 7. Col. Wm. Ball

Middle-Lower Class:  1. *Conway* 2. *Mitchell* 3. Stepto 4. Tayloe 5. Jos. Ball 6. Col. Wm. Ball 7. Major Ball

TABLE 2.   LANCASTER COUNTY ELECTION POLL OF MAY 23, 1748

Total Voters—201

Number of Candidates—5

| Candidates | Upper Class | | | Middle-Lower Class | | | | Undesig-nated | Sign with a Mark | Slaveholding voters (if known) |
|---|---|---|---|---|---|---|---|---|---|---|
| | Gentlemen & Merchts. | Others | Total | Planters & Probable Planters | Artisans | Tenants & Servants | Total | | | |
| Chinn & Conway | 9 | 2 | 11 | 21 | 1 | — | 22 | 2 | 4 | 28 |
| Chinn & Pinckard | 2 | 1 | 3 | 16 | 1 | — | 17 | — | 5 | 13 |
| Chinn & Mitchell | 7 | 3 | 10 | 33 | 10 | 3 | 46 | 3 | 10 | 38 |
| Chinn & Stepto | — | 1 | — | — | — | — | — | — | — | — |
| Conway & Pinckard | 3 | 1 | 4 | 29 | 4 | 2 | 35 | 2 | 9 | 28 |
| Conway & Mitchell | 1 | — | 1 | 4 | — | — | 4 | — | 3 | 5 |
| Conway & Stepto | 5 | 3 | 8 | 10 | 1 | 1 | 12 | 2 | 6 | 12 |
| Pinckard & Mitchell | 1 | — | 1 | 2 | — | 1 | 3 | — | 1 | 4 |
| Pinckard & Stepto | — | — | — | 5 | 2 | — | 7 | — | 2 | 6 |
| Mitchell & Stepto | — | — | — | 1 | — | — | 1 | — | — | — |
| Chinn only | 1 | — | 1 | 1 | — | — | 1 | 1 | — | — |
| Conway only | 1 | — | 1 | 1 | 1 | — | 2 | — | — | — |
| Mitchell only | — | — | — | — | — | — | — | — | — | — |
| Pinckard only | — | — | — | 1 | — | — | 1 | — | — | — |
| TOTALS | 30 | 10 | 40 | 124 | 20 | 7 | 151 | 10 | 40 | 134 |

INDIVIDUAL CANDIDATES, LANCASTER COUNTY, MAY 23, 1748

| Candidate | Upper Class | Middle-Lower Class | Undesignated | Total Vote |
|---|---|---|---|---|
| Mr. Joseph Chinn | 24 | 86 | 6 | 116 |
| Maj. Peter Conway | 25 | 75 | 6 | 106 |
| Mr. Thomas Pinckard | 8 | 63 | 2 | 73 |
| Mr. Robert Mitchell | 13 | 54 | 3 | 70 |
| Capt. Wm. Stepto | 8 | 20 | 2 | 30 |

CANDIDATES BY ORDER OF CLASS PREFERENCE

(Winners in Italics)

Upper Class:  1. *Peter Conway* 2. *Joseph Chinn* 3. Robert Mitchell 4. & 5. Pinckard and Stepto (equal votes)

Middle-Lower Class:  1. *Joseph Chinn* 2. *Peter Conway* 3. Thomas Pinckard 4. Robert Mitchell 5. Wm. Stepto

TABLE 3.  LANCASTER COUNTY ELECTION POLL OF JANUARY 28, 1752

Total Voters—182    Number of Candidates—5

| Candidates | Upper Class | | | Middle-Lower Class | | | | | Sign with a Mark | Slaveholding Voters (if Known) |
|---|---|---|---|---|---|---|---|---|---|---|
| | Gentlemen & Merchts | Others | Total | Probable Planters & Planters | Artisans | Tenants & Servants | Total | Undesignated | | |
| Conway & Chinn | 5 | — | 5 | 12 | 2 | — | 14 | 1 | 3 | 14 |
| Conway & Tayloe | 6 | 6 | 12 | 50 | 6 | 2 | 58 | 3 | 13 | 48 |
| Conway & Ball | 3 | — | 3 | 3 | 2 | — | 5 | — | — | 7 |
| Conway & Dymer | — | — | — | — | — | — | — | — | — | — |
| Chinn & Tayloe | — | — | — | 4 | 3 | — | 7 | — | 3 | 4 |
| Chinn & Ball | 13 | 4 | 17 | 42 | 6 | 2 | 50 | 3 | 7 | 44 |
| Chinn & Dymer | — | — | — | 1 | — | — | 1 | — | — | 1 |
| Tayloe & Ball | 1 | 1 | 2 | — | — | — | — | 1 | — | 1 |
| Dymer only | — | — | — | — | — | — | — | — | — | — |
| TOTALS | 28 | 11 | 39 | 112 | 19 | 4 | 135 | 8 | 26 | 119 |

INDIVIDUAL CANDIDATES

| Candidate | Upper Class | Middle-Lower Class | Undesignated | Total Vote |
|---|---|---|---|---|
| Col. Edwin Conway | 20 | 77 | 4 | 101 |
| Mr. Joseph Chinn | 22 | 72 | 4 | 98 |
| Col. Wm. Tayloe | 14 | 65 | 3 | 82 |
| Col. James Ball | 22 | 55 | 3 | 80 |
| William Dymer | — | 1 | 1 | 2 |

CANDIDATES BY ORDER OF CLASS PREFERENCE
(Winners in Italics)

Upper Class:  1. & 2. *Chinn* and Ball (equal votes) 3. *Conway* 4. Tayloe
Middle-Lower Class:  1. *Conway* 2. *Chinn* 3. Tayloe 4. Ball 5. Dymer

TABLE 4. LANCASTER COUNTY ELECTION POLL OF MARCH 23, 1754 (A BY-ELECTION)

Total Voters—154    Number of Candidates—3

| Candidates | Upper Class | | | Middle-Lower Class | | | | Undesignated | Sign with a Mark | Slaveholding Voters (if Known) |
|---|---|---|---|---|---|---|---|---|---|---|
| | Gentlemen & Merchts | Others | Total | Probable Planters & Planters | Artisans | Tenants & Servants | Total | | | |
| James Ball | 18 | 7 | 25 | 67 | 11 | 2 | 80 | 4 | 14 | 79 |
| William Ball | 3 | 1 | 4 | 31 | 5 | — | 36 | 2 | 11 | 22 |
| William Dymer | — | — | — | 3 | — | — | 3 | — | — | 3 |
| TOTALS | 21 | 8 | 29 | 101 | 16 | 2 | 119 | 6 | 25 | 104 |

INDIVIDUAL CANDIDATES

| Candidate | Upper Class | Middle-Lower Class | Undesignated | Total Vote |
|---|---|---|---|---|
| Col. James Ball | 25 | 80 | 4 | 109 |
| Col. William Ball | 4 | 36 | 2 | 42 |
| Capt. William Dymer | — | 3 | — | 3 |

CANDIDATES BY ORDER OF CLASS PREFERENCE
(Winner in Italics)

Upper Class:   1. *James Ball*  2. William Ball

Middle-Lower Class:   1. *James Ball*  2. William Ball  3. William Dymer

TABLE 5.   LANCASTER COUNTY ELECTION POLL OF NOVEMBER 10, 1755 (A BY-ELECTION)

Total Voters—114    Number of Candidates—3

| Candidates | Upper Class | | | Middle-Lower Class | | | | Undesignated | Sign with a Mark | Slaveholding Voters (if Known) |
|---|---|---|---|---|---|---|---|---|---|---|
| | Gentlemen & Merchts | Others | Total | Probable Planters & Planters | Artisans | Tenants & Servants | Total | | | |
| William Ball | 5 | 4 | 9 | 58 | 10 | 3 | 71 | 4 | 15 | 56 |
| George Heale | 3 | 1 | 4 | 17 | — | — | 17 | — | 1 | 15 |
| Richard Selden | 2 | 1 | 3 | 3 | 2 | — | 5 | 1 | 1 | 6 |
| TOTALS | 10 | 6 | 16 | 78 | 12 | 3 | 93 | 5 | 17 | 77 |

INDIVIDUAL CANDIDATES

| Candidate | Upper Class | Middle-Lower Class | Undesignated | Total Vote |
|---|---|---|---|---|
| Col. William Ball | 9 | 71 | 4 | 84 |
| Mr. George Heale | 4 | 17 | — | 21 |
| Maj. Richard Selden | 3 | 5 | 1 | 9 |

CANDIDATES BY ORDER OF CLASS PREFERENCE
(Winner in Italics)

Upper Class:   1. *Wm. Ball*  2. George Heale  3. Richard Selden
Middle-Lower Class:   1. *Wm. Ball*  2. George Heale  3. Richard Selden

TABLE 6.   LANCASTER COUNTY ELECTION POLL OF DECEMBER 23, 1755

Total Voters—143   Number of Candidates—5

| Candidates | Upper Class | | | Middle-Lower Class | | | | Undesignated | Sign with a Mark | Slaveholding voters (if Known) |
|---|---|---|---|---|---|---|---|---|---|---|
| | Gentlemen & Merchts | Others | Total | Planters & Probable Planters | Artisans | Tenants & Servants | Total | | | |
| Ball & Selden | 6 | 7 | 13 | 56 | 7 | 1 | 64 | 2 | 12 | 57 |
| Ball & Heale | 5 | 3 | 8 | 27 | 6 | 1 | 34 | 1 | 9 | 28 |
| Selden & Heale | 4 | 1 | 5 | 9 | 1 | — | 10 | 1 | 2 | 11 |
| Heale & Tayloe | 1 | — | 1 | — | — | — | — | — | — | 1 |
| Heale & Sparks | — | — | — | 1 | — | — | 1 | — | — | 1 |
| Ball only | — | — | — | 1 | — | — | 1 | — | — | — |
| Heale only | 1 | — | 1 | 1 | — | — | 1 | — | — | — |
| TOTALS | 17 | 11 | 28 | 95 | 14 | 2 | 111 | 4 | 23 | 98 |

INDIVIDUAL CANDIDATES

| Candidate | Upper Class | Middle-Lower Class | Undesignated | Total Vote |
|---|---|---|---|---|
| Col. William Ball | 21 | 99 | 3 | 123 |
| Major Richard Selden | 18 | 74 | 3 | 95 |
| Mr. George Heale | 15 | 46 | 2 | 63 |
| Col. William Tayloe | 1 | — | — | 1 |
| Samuel Sparks | — | 1 | — | 1 |

CANDIDATES BY ORDER OF CLASS PREFERENCE
(Winners in Italics)

Upper Class:   1. *Ball* 2. *Selden* 3. Heale 4. Tayloe
Middle-Lower Class:   1. *Ball* 2. *Selden* 3. Heale 4. Sparks

TABLE 7.  LANCASTER COUNTY ELECTION POLL OF JULY 18, 1758

Total Voters—218   Number of Candidates—7

| Candidates | Upper Class | | | Middle-Lower Class | | | | Undesignated | Sign with a Mark | Slaveholding Voters (if Known) |
|---|---|---|---|---|---|---|---|---|---|---|
| | Gentlemen & Merchts | Others | Total | Planters & Probable Planters | Artisans | Tenants & Servants | Total | | | |
| Wm. Ball & Carter | 25 | 7 | 32 | 78 | 11 | 3 | 92 | 8 | 17 | 94 |
| Wm. Ball & Tayloe | — | 2 | 2 | 16 | 4 | — | 20 | 5 | 10 | 11 |
| Carter & Tayloe | 6 | 5 | 11 | 31 | 6 | — | 37 | — | 10 | 37 |
| Wm. Ball & Chichester | — | 1 | 1 | 1 | — | — | 1 | — | — | 1 |
| Wm. Ball & Bailey | — | — | — | 1 | — | — | 1 | — | 1 | 2 |
| J. Ball & Heale | — | — | — | — | — | — | — | 1 | — | — |
| Carter only | 1 | — | 1 | 1 | — | — | 1 | — | — | — |
| Wm. Ball only | — | — | — | 1 | 1 | — | 2 | — | — | — |
| Tayloe only | — | — | — | 2 | — | — | 2 | 1 | — | — |
| TOTALS | 32 | 15 | 47 | 131 | 22 | 3 | 156 | 15 | 38 | 145 |

INDIVIDUAL CANDIDATES, LANCASTER COUNTY, JULY 18, 1758

| Candidate | Upper Class | Middle-Lower Class | Undesignated | Total Vote |
|---|---|---|---|---|
| Mr. Charles Carter | 44 | 130 | 8 | 182 |
| Col. William Ball | 35 | 116 | 13 | 164 |
| Col. William Tayloe | 13 | 59 | 6 | 78 |
| John Bailey | 1 | 1 | — | 2 |
| Richard Chichester | — | 1 | — | 1 |
| James Ball | — | — | 1 | 1 |
| George Heale | — | — | 1 | 1 |

CANDIDATES BY ORDER OF CLASS PREFERENCE
(Winners in Italics)

Upper Class:  1. *Carter* 2. *Wm. Ball* 3. Tayloe 4. Bailey

Middle-Lower Class:  1. *Carter* 2. *Wm. Ball* 3. Tayloe 4. & 5. Bailey and Chichester (equal votes)

TABLE 8.   LANCASTER COUNTY ELECTION POLL OF NOVEMBER 30, 1758 (A BY-ELECTION)

Total Voters—146    Number of Candidates—2

| Candidates | Upper Class | | | Middle-Lower Class | | | | Undesig-nated | Sign with a Mark | Slaveholding Voters (if Known) |
|---|---|---|---|---|---|---|---|---|---|---|
| | Gentlemen & Merchts | Others | Total | Planters & Probable Planters | Artisans | Tenants & Servants | Total | | | |
| George Heale | 13 | 6 | 19 | 70 | 10 | 4 | 84 | 7 | 20 | 74 |
| Solomon Ewell | 1 | 3 | 4 | 26 | 4 | — | 30 | 2 | 7 | 14 |
| TOTALS | 14 | 9 | 23 | 96 | 14 | 4 | 114 | 9 | 27 | 88 |

INDIVIDUAL CANDIDATES

| Candidate | Upper Class | Middle-Lower Class | Undesignated | Total Vote |
|---|---|---|---|---|
| George Heale | 19 | 84 | 7 | 110 |
| Capt. Solomon Ewell | 4 | 30 | 2 | 36 |

CANDIDATES BY ORDER OF CLASS PREFERENCE
(Winner in Italics)

Upper Class:   1. *George Heale*   2. Solomon Ewell

Middle-Lower Class:   1. *George Heale*   2. Solomon Ewell

TABLE 9. LANCASTER COUNTY ELECTION POLL OF MAY 11, 1761

Total Voters—202   Number of Candidates—5

| Candidates | Upper Class | | | Middle-Lower Class | | | | Undesig-nated | Sign with a Mark | Slaveholding Voters (if Known) |
|---|---|---|---|---|---|---|---|---|---|---|
| | Gentlemen & Merchts | Others | Total | Planters & Probable Planters | Artisans | Tenants & Servants | Total | | | |
| Carter & Mitchell | 8 | 6 | 14 | 56 | 6 | — | 62 | 9 | 13 | 55 |
| Carter & Heale | 15 | 4 | 19 | 39 | 8 | — | 47 | 5 | 13 | 52 |
| Mitchell & Heale | 3 | — | 3 | 28 | 3 | 2 | 33 | 1 | 7 | 18 |
| Carter & Dymer | 1 | — | 1 | 2 | — | — | 2 | — | 1 | 2 |
| Carter & Tayloe | — | — | — | 1 | 1 | — | 1 | — | — | — |
| Mitchel & Dymer | — | 1 | 1 | 1 | 1 | — | 2 | — | — | 2 |
| Carter only | — | — | — | 2 | — | — | 2 | — | — | — |
| TOTALS | 27 | 11 | 38 | 128 | 19 | 2 | 149 | 15 | 34 | 129 |

INDIVIDUAL CANDIDATES

| Candidate | Upper Class | Middle-Lower Class | Undesignated | Total Vote |
|---|---|---|---|---|
| Charles Carter, Esq. | 35 | 114 | 14 | 163 |
| Mr. Richard Mitchell | 17 | 97 | 10 | 124 |
| Mr. George Heale | 22 | 80 | 6 | 108 |
| Capt. Wm. Dymer | 1 | 4 | — | 5 |
| Col. Wm. Tayloe | — | 1 | — | 1 |

CANDIDATES BY ORDER OF CLASS PREFERENCE

(Winners in Italics)

Upper Class:   1. *Carter* 2. *Heale* 3. *Mitchell* 4. Dymer

Middle-Lower Class:   1. *Carter* 2. *Mitchell* 3. *Heale* 4. Dymer 5. Tayloe

TABLE 10. LANCASTER COUNTY ELECTION POLL OF JULY 17, 1765

Total Voters—172   Number of Candidates—4

| Candidates | Upper Class | | | Middle-Lower Class | | | | Undesignated | Sign with a Mark | Slaveholding Voters (if Known) |
|---|---|---|---|---|---|---|---|---|---|---|
| | Gentlemen & Merchts | Others | Total | Planters & Probable Planters | Artisans | Tenants & Servants | Total | | | |
| Carter & Mitchell | 26 | 6 | 32 | 93 | 11 | 3 | 107 | 7 | 22 | 103 |
| Carter and Ball | — | — | — | 16 | 1 | 1 | 18 | 2 | 5 | 6 |
| Mitchell & Ball | — | — | — | 1 | 1 | — | 1 | 1 | — | 1 |
| Carter & Edwards | — | — | — | 1 | — | — | 1 | — | — | — |
| Mitchell only | — | — | — | 1 | — | — | 1 | — | — | — |
| Carter only | — | — | — | 2 | — | — | 2 | — | 1 | 2 |
| Ball only | — | — | — | — | — | — | — | — | — | — |
| TOTALS | 26 | 6 | 32 | 113 | 13 | 4 | 130 | 10 | 28 | 112 |

INDIVIDUAL CANDIDATES

CANDIDATES BY ORDER OF CLASS PREFERENCE
(Winners in Italics)

| Candidate | Upper Class | Middle-Lower Class | Undesignated | Total Vote |
|---|---|---|---|---|
| Mr. Richard Mitchell | 32 | 126 | 10 | 168 |
| Charles Carter, Esq. | 32 | 109 | 7 | 148 |
| Mr. Richard Ball | — | 20 | 2 | 22 |
| Mr. Richard Edwards | — | 1 | — | 1 |

Upper Class:   1. & 2. *Mitchell* and *Carter* (equal votes)
Middle-Lower Class:   1. *Mitchell* 2. *Carter* 3. Ball 4. Edwards

TABLE 11. LANCASTER COUNTY ELECTION POLL OF DECEMBER 2, 1768

Total Voters—191    Number of Candidates—6

| Candidates | Upper Class | | | Middle-Lower Class | | | | Undesignated | Sign with a Mark | Slaveholding Voters (if Known) |
|---|---|---|---|---|---|---|---|---|---|---|
| | Gentlemen & Merchts | Others | Total | Planters & Probable Planters | Artisans | Tenants & Servants | Total | | | |
| J. Ball & C. Carter | 25 | 10 | 35 | 69 | 5 | 1 | 75 | 3 | 15 | 94 |
| J. Ball & R. Ball | 5 | 2 | 7 | 19 | 4 | 1 | 23 | 6 | 6 | 18 |
| C. Carter & R. Ball | — | — | — | 19 | 1 | 1 | 21 | 5 | 8 | 12 |
| J. Ball & Dale Carter | — | — | — | 1 | — | — | 1 | — | — | — |
| C. Carter & Dymer | — | — | — | — | 1 | — | 1 | 1 | — | — |
| Edwards only | — | — | — | — | — | 1 | 1 | 1 | — | — |
| J. Ball only | — | — | — | 3 | — | 1 | 4 | — | — | — |
| C. Carter only | — | — | — | 4 | 1 | — | 5 | 2 | — | — |
| R. Ball only | — | — | — | — | — | — | 1 | — | — | — |
| TOTALS | 30 | 12 | 42 | 115 | 12 | 4 | 131 | 18 | 29 | 124 |

INDIVIDUAL CANDIDATES

| Candidate | Upper Class | Middle-Lower Class | Undesignated | Total Vote |
|---|---|---|---|---|
| Col. James Ball | 42 | 103 | 10 | 155 |
| Mr. Charles Carter | 35 | 102 | 8 | 145 |
| Mr. Richard Ball | 7 | 45 | 13 | 65 |
| Mr. Richard Edwards | — | 1 | — | 1 |
| Capt. Dymer | — | 1 | — | 1 |
| Dale Carter | — | 1 | — | 1 |

CANDIDATES BY ORDER OF CLASS PREFERENCE
(Winners in Italics)

Upper Class: 1. *J. Ball* 2. *C. Carter* 3. R. Ball

Middle-Lower Class: 1. *J. Ball* 2. *C. Carter* 3. R. Ball 4. Edwards, Dymer and D. Carter (equal votes)

TABLE 12.   LANCASTER COUNTY ELECTION POLL OF SEPTEMBER 7, 1769

Total Voters—167   Number of Candidates—3

| Candidates | Upper Class | | | Middle-Lower Class | | | | Undesig-nated | Sign with a Mark | Slaveholding Vote (if Known) |
|---|---|---|---|---|---|---|---|---|---|---|
| | Gentlemen & Merchts | Others | Total | Planters & Probable Planters | Artisans | Tenants & Servants | Total | | | |
| Mitchell & Carter | 25 | 7 | 32 | 82 | 7 | 3 | 92 | 4 | 17 | 100 |
| Mitchell & Ball | — | 1 | 1 | 12 | 4 | 1 | 17 | 3 | 3 | 10 |
| Carter & Ball | 3 | — | 3 | 6 | — | — | 6 | — | 3 | 5 |
| Carter only | — | — | — | 2 | 2 | — | 4 | — | — | — |
| Mitchell only | — | — | — | 2 | — | — | 2 | 1 | — | — |
| Ball only | — | — | — | 2 | — | — | 2 | — | — | — |
| TOTALS | 28 | 8 | 36 | 106 | 13 | 4 | 123 | 8 | 23 | 115 |

INDIVIDUAL CANDIDATES

| Candidate | Upper Class | Middle-Lower Class | Undesignated | Total Vote |
|---|---|---|---|---|
| Richard Mitchell | 33 | 113 | 8 | 154 |
| Charles Carter | 35 | 100 | 4 | 139 |
| Richard Ball | 1 | 25 | 3 | 29 |

CANDIDATES BY ORDER OF CLASS PREFERENCE
(Winners in Italics)

Upper Class:   1. *Carter*  2. *Mitchell*  3. Ball
Middle-Lower Class:   1. *Mitchell*  2. *Carter*  3. Ball

TABLE 13.   LANCASTER COUNTY ELECTION POLL OF NOVEMBER 25, 1771

Total Voters—166   Number of Candidates—3

| Candidates | Upper Class | | | Middle-Lower Class | | | | Undesignated | Sign with a Mark | Slaveholding Voters (if Known) |
| --- | --- | --- | --- | --- | --- | --- | --- | --- | --- | --- |
| | Gentlemen & Merchts | Others | Total | Planters & Probable Planters | Artisans | Tenants & Servants | Total | | | |
| Mitchell & Carter | 27 | 8 | 35 | 81 | 5 | 2 | 88 | 7 | 13 | 100 |
| Mitchell & Ball | 1 | 1 | 2 | 17 | 3 | 1 | 21 | 4 | 4 | 10 |
| Carter & Ball | — | — | | 2 | 1 | — | 3 | 1 | 1 | 2 |
| Carter only | 1 | — | 1 | — | — | — | — | — | — | — |
| Mitchell only [R. Ball's Vote] | 1 | — | 1 | 3 | — | — | 3 | — | — | — |
| TOTALS | 30 | 9 | 39 | 103 | 9 | 3 | 115 | 12 | 18 | 112 |

INDIVIDUAL CANDIDATES

| Candidate | Upper Class | Middle-Lower Class | Undesignated | Total Vote |
| --- | --- | --- | --- | --- |
| Richard Mitchell | 38 | 112 | 11 | 161 |
| Charles Carter | 36 | 91 | 8 | 135 |
| Richard Ball | 2 | 24 | 5 | 31 |

CANDIDATES BY ORDER OF CLASS PREFERENCE

(Winners in Italics)

Upper Class:   1. *Mitchell*  2. *Carter*  3. Ball

Middle-Lower Class:   1. *Mitchell*  2. *Carter*  3. Ball

TABLE 14.  LANCASTER COUNTY ELECTION POLL OF JULY 26, 1774

Total Voters—212   Number of Candidates—3

| Candidates | Upper Class | | | Middle-Lower Classes | | | | Undesignated | Sign with a Mark | Slaveholding Voters (if Known) |
|---|---|---|---|---|---|---|---|---|---|---|
| | Gentlemen & Merchants | Others | Total | Probable Planters & Planters | Artisans | Tenants & Servants | Total | | | |
| Selden & Carter | 6 | 3 | 9 | 62 | 6 | — | 68 | 6 | 12 | 69 |
| Selden & Ball | 8 | 1 | 9 | 44 | 7 | 1 | 52 | 7 | 8 | 41 |
| Carter & Ball | 11 | 1 | 12 | 21 | 3 | 3 | 27 | 2 | 2 | 36 |
| Carter only | 7 | 2 | 9 | 5 | — | — | 5 | — | — | — |
| Ball only | — | — | — | 5 | — | 1 | 6 | — | — | — |
| TOTALS | 32 | 7 | 39 | 137 | 16 | 5 | 158 | 15 | 22 | 146 |

INDIVIDUAL CANDIDATES

| Candidate | Upper Class | Middle-Lower Class | Undesignated | Total Vote |
|---|---|---|---|---|
| James Selden | 18 | 120 | 13 | 151 |
| Charles Carter | 30 | 100 | 8 | 138 |
| Burgess Ball | 21 | 85 | 9 | 115 |

CANDIDATES BY ORDER OF CLASS PREFERENCE
(Winners in Italics)

Upper Class:   1. *Carter*  2. *Ball*  3. Selden
Middle-Lower Class:   1. *Selden*  2. *Carter*  3. Ball

should show aristocractic control if it existed, has the best combination of records; for this reason we have examined this county in depth.[3]

The most significant generalization from these fourteen Lancaster elections is the fact that in every election the middle-lower classes carried the day. Actually the two groups chose the same candidates in the same order of preference in nine elections (Tables 1, 4, 5, 6, 7, 8, 10, 11, 13). In two elections (Tables 2 and 12) the two classes preferred the same candidates but not in the same order, and here the middle-lower class preference prevailed. And in three elections (Tables 3, 9, 14) the upper class supported a loser but the middle-lower class carried its candidates. This was particularly true in the pre-Revolutionary election of 1774, when the upper class gave third place to the man who received the most votes.

A second important generalization is that all classes, including illiterates and slaveowners, tended to scatter their votes instead of voting with any apparent degree of class solidarity. In this respect, the upper class was more unified than was the middle-lower class, although even the upper class, as in 1741, 1752, and 1774, spread itself to a great extent. The result of this independent voting was that very often the two men who received the most votes in combination—for example Conway and Stepto (41) in 1741—were not the two who were elected (Conway and Mitchell). Only one election, Conway and Tayloe against Chinn and Ball in 1752, exhibits definite factionalism, but again the independent voters decided the outcome by electing one man from each faction, if such it was—Conway and Chinn. Furthermore, both classes split their vote, an indication that the issues were not determined by class.

It is not always clear what factional disputes were about, but apparently personalities were sometimes involved. In 1750 Edwin Conway, second in the Lancaster election of 1748, was at odds with Thomas Pinckard, who had run third. Both were county justices, and Pinckard eventually became county sheriff in 1753. Pinckard was suing Conway, then a member of the House, for Conway's having called him a "Sheep Stealer." Conway said it never appeared to him that Pinckard was a sheep stealer, but he was provoked because Pinckard had spoken "Scurrilous words" about him. Conway was most willing to make a public apology in the *Virginia Gazette,* some indication that he was not sure of winning the suit even though he was a burgess.[4]

These Lancaster election charts also demonstrate that men of prominent names and high positions in their counties often ran for office without success, held office for only a short while even after they were elected, or ran for a long time before winning an election. William Tayloe was fourth in 1741, and although the family name was prominent in the colony and he was a colonel, he was still a poor fourth in the election of 1758. George Heale, after three unsuccessful attempts, won a by-election in 1758 but was ousted at the next election when he ran a close third. Some members of the well-known Ball family could get elected, often after numerous attempts, but Richard Ball was never able to do so, much as he tried.

To be noted also in Lancaster is the fact that the people always had several candidates from which to choose, much as we do in our primary elections today. In the eleven major elections for two burgesses, there were fifty-three candidates or an average of nearly five per election. In the three by-elections for one burgess, there were eight candidates or an average of nearly three. As the Revolution approached, the number of candidates decreased, with only three for each of the last three elections. The sharpening of imperial issues apparently resulted in more unanimity of opinion among the people as to their choice of men to represent them.

Another way to determine the extent of democracy and the influence of the aristocracy in colonial Virginia is to compare voters according to their property and the candidates for whom they voted. Table 15, based on partial quitrent rolls for 1748 and 1750 and the election poll of 1748, indicates no discernible pattern of class voting. The most popular combinations of candidates, Chinn and Mitchell (59) and Conway and Pinckard (41), received votes from almost all acreage categories, but these were not the winning combination. The winners, Chinn and Conway, received support from all groups both together and in combination with other candidates.

Striking also in Table 15 is the fact that the small planters in Lancaster, an old tidewater county and therefore presumably "aristocratic," constituted the bulk of the voters. Of the 162 voters in 1748 who appear on the rent rolls, sixty-four (39.5 per cent) held 100 acres or less, 110 (67.9 per cent) held 200 acres or less, 130 (80.2 per cent) had 300 acres or less, and only nine (5.5 per cent) had over 500 acres. It is true that the two largest landowners, Baldwin M. Smith, gentleman from Northumberland with 1,516 acres, and Captain James Gordon, merchant with 1,094 acres, voted for winners Chinn and Conway, but so also did six men with 100 acres or less.

Even more than Table 15, Tables 16 confirms the generalization that the small planters dominated the voting and could have carried their candidates by huge majorities had they voted as a class instead of dividing their vote. More than two-thirds of the voters, not counting the unknown ones, had 200 acres or less, and 82.4 per cent owned 300 acres or less. This 1752 election appeared to be a factional fight between Conway and Tayloe on one hand and Chinn and Ball on the other, with one from each faction, Conway and Chinn, emerging as winners. The four men who had over 1,000 acres did not vote for both winners, and there is no doubt that those with 300 acres or less could have elected whomever they pleased.

Similar studies for Lancaster elections of 1771 and 1774 yield almost exactly the same results as those obtained from Tables 15 and 16 and therefore have not been included. In 1771, 80.2 per cent, and in 1774, eighty-two per cent of the voters, had 300 acres or less, and these small

TABLE 15. ANALYSIS OF LANCASTER PROPERTY & VOTING, 1748-50[5]

| Voters' Choice of Candidates* | Voters' Property Unknown | Voters with 25-99 Acres | 100 Acres | 101-200 Acres | 201-300 Acres | 301-400 Acres | 401-500 Acres | 501-999 Acres | Over 1000 | Total |
|---|---|---|---|---|---|---|---|---|---|---|
| *Chinn & Conway* | 6 | 1 | 5 | 10 | 5 | 2 | 2 | 1 | 2 | 34 |
| *Chinn & Pinckard* | 2 | 5 | 3 | 5 | 2 | — | 2 | 1 | — | 20 |
| *Chinn & Mitchell* | 9 | 12 | 9 | 13 | 4 | 6 | 5 | 1 | — | 59 |
| *Chinn & Stepto* | — | — | — | — | — | — | — | — | — | — |
| *Conway & Pinckard* | 12 | 11 | 3 | 9 | 3 | 1 | 1 | 1 | — | 41 |
| *Conway & Mitchell* | 1 | 3 | 1 | — | — | — | — | — | — | 5 |
| *Conway & Stepto* | 5 | 2 | 2 | 6 | 5 | — | 1 | 1 | — | 22 |
| *Pinckard & Mitchell* | 1 | — | 1 | 1 | 1 | 1 | — | — | — | 4 |
| *Pinckard & Stepto* | — | 3 | 2 | — | — | — | — | — | — | 7 |
| *Mitchell & Stepto* | 1 | — | 1 | — | — | — | — | — | — | 1 |
| *Chinn only* | 1 | — | — | 1 | — | — | 1 | 1 | — | 2 |
| *Conway only* | 1 | — | — | — | — | — | 1 | 1 | — | 4 |
| *Mitchell only* | — | — | — | — | — | — | — | — | — | 1 |
| *Pinckard only* | 1 | — | — | — | — | — | — | — | — | 1 |
| TOTAL VOTERS | 39 | 37 | 27 | 46 | 20 | 10 | 13 | 7 | 2 | 201 |
| *Individual Candidates* | | | | | | | | | | |
| *Chinn* | 18 | 18 | 17 | 28 | 11 | 8 | 9 | 4 | 2 | 115 |
| *P. Conway* | 25 | 17 | 11 | 26 | 13 | 3 | 5 | 4 | 2 | 106 |
| Tho. Pinckard | 16 | 19 | 9 | 16 | 6 | 2 | 3 | 2 | — | 73 |
| Mitchell | 11 | 15 | 12 | 14 | 4 | 7 | 6 | 1 | — | 70 |
| Stepto | 5 | 5 | 5 | 7 | 6 | — | 1 | 1 | — | 30 |

* Winners in Italics

TABLE 16.   ANALYSIS OF LANCASTER PROPERTY & VOTING, 1750-52[6]

| Voters' Choice of Candidates* | Voters' Property Unknown | Voters with 25-99 Acres | 100 Acres | 101-200 Acres | 201-300 Acres | 301-400 Acres | 401-500 Acres | 501-999 Acres | Over 1000 | Total |
|---|---|---|---|---|---|---|---|---|---|---|
| Conway & Chinn | 7 | 4 | 2 | 3 | 1 | 1 | 1 | 1 | — | 20 |
| Conway & Tayloe | 23 | 10 | 7 | 19 | 10 | 1 | 2 | — | 1 | 73 |
| Conway & Ball | 3 | 1 | 1 | 1 | — | — | — | 2 | — | 8 |
| Conway & Dymer | — | — | — | — | — | — | — | — | — | — |
| Chinn & Tayloe | — | 3 | 1 | 1 | 2 | — | — | — | — | 7 |
| Chinn & Ball | 16 | 11 | 12 | 11 | 6 | 5 | 6 | — | 3 | 70 |
| Chinn & Dymer | — | — | — | 1 | — | — | — | — | — | 1 |
| Tayloe & Ball | 1 | — | — | 1 | — | — | — | — | — | 2 |
| Dymer only | 1 | — | — | — | — | — | — | — | — | 1 |
| TOTAL VOTERS | 51 | 29 | 23 | 37 | 19 | 7 | 9 | 3 | 4 | 182 |
| *Individual Candidates* | | | | | | | | | | |
| E. Conway | 33 | 15 | 10 | 23 | 11 | 2 | 3 | 3 | 1 | 101 |
| Chinn | 23 | 18 | 15 | 16 | 9 | 6 | 7 | 1 | 3 | 98 |
| Tayloe | 24 | 13 | 8 | 21 | 12 | 1 | 2 | — | 1 | 82 |
| Ball | 20 | 12 | 13 | 13 | 6 | 5 | 6 | 2 | 3 | 80 |
| Dymer | 1 | — | — | 1 | — | — | — | — | — | 2 |

* Winners in Italics

planters could have elected anyone they chose, for only thirteen men in 1771 and fifteen in 1774 had over 500 acres. Men from all acreage categories voted for all candidates, especially in 1774 when Charles Carter, richest man in the county, faced a stiff fight against a newcomer, Burgess Ball. Small planters divided their votes among the three candidates, but they could easily have elected Ball had they so desired, and if twelve of them had changed their votes from Carter to Ball, the latter would have been elected.[7]

Since another tidewater county, Essex, had so many excellent election polls, and since the social status of a large number of the voters could be identified, we tabulated twelve elections from 1748 to 1778, using social status rather than acreage as a basis for our categories. But since all twelve charts are almost identical in their results, we have included only two.

These Essex County elections again demonstrate that in this tidewater county, as in Lancaster, the middle and lower classes dominated the elections and could pick candidates at will whenever they were united in their opinions. If the unidentified voters were mainly of the middle and lower classes, as they undoubtedly were, the middle and lower classes always elected the candidates favored by a majority of their numbers. But as the election of 1748 shows, this group could heavily favor one candidate—in this case William Beverley—and then divide the remainder of their votes fairly evenly among three other candidates. The upper class, on the other hand, did not always support winning candidates. They did in 1748, but in 1765 their votes, heavily favoring John Lee and Robert Beverley, could not win for Beverley, and if all of them had voted against John Lee, he would still have won.

An examination of the candidates in Essex County indicates the wide choice open to the electorate. Nine different men were elected in the twenty-three years from 1748 to 1771 in the nine full elections and one by-election (nineteen burgess seats were at stake in the ten elections). At these ten elections there were also fifty-eight candidates who received votes, an average of 5.8 per election, including one with ten candidates, one with nine, two with seven, and one with six. In three elections, 1748, 1755, and 1758, four candidates received over a hundred votes, and in six elections, three received more than a hundred, an indication that the people always had a choice and used it.

As these Essex elections demonstrate, candidates with the same family name as well as other individuals could sometimes get elected and sometimes not. For example, William Beverley, Esquire, received the highest vote from both upper and lower classes in 1748, while Robert Beverley could never get elected even though the gentlemen favored him in 1765. Francis Smith held office from 1752 to 1758 but Meriwether Smith ran without success in 1768, 1769, 1770, and 1771. Thomas Roane, Esquire, received token votes in 1765 and again in 1777, but William Roane won in 1768, 1769, 1770, and 1771. On the other hand, Colonel Thomas

TABLE 17.   ESSEX COUNTY VOTERS BY SOCIAL STATUS, 1748 AND 1765[8]

| Candidates | Total Vote | Upper Class | | | | Middle-Lower Classes | | | | | | | Status Uncertain | Unidentified |
|---|---|---|---|---|---|---|---|---|---|---|---|---|---|---|
| | | Gentlemen | Merchants | Others | Total Upper Class | Planters | Signed with Marks, Except Artisans & Tenants | Artisans | Tenants | Planters or Artisans | "Mr." | Total Middle-Lower Classes | | |
| **1748 Election:** | | | | | | | | | | | | | | |
| Wm. Beverley, Esq. | 271 | 27 | 4 | 1 | 32 | 45 | 39 | 11 | 2 | 5 | 5 | 107 | 9 | 123 |
| Maj. Wm. Daingerfield | 173 | 16 | 2 | 1 | 19 | 29 | 12 | 14 | 1 | 3 | 1 | 60 | 5 | 89 |
| Maj. Francis Smith | 148 | 5 | 1 | 0 | 6 | 24 | 28 | 5 | 0 | 3 | 2 | 62 | 6 | 74 |
| Capt. Benj. Winslow | 113 | 4 | 1 | 0 | 5 | 23 | 20 | 7 | 1 | 1 | 2 | 54 | 3 | 51 |
| John Corbin, Esq. | 46 | 5 | 0 | 0 | 5 | 5 | 4 | 3 | 0 | 0 | 0 | 12 | 1 | 28 |
| **1765 Election:** | | | | | | | | | | | | | | |
| John Lee | 300 | 24 | 4 | 3 | 31 | 44 | 42 | 20 | 1 | 5 | 4 | 116 | 6 | 147 |
| Francis Waring | 283 | 11 | 1 | 1 | 13 | 48 | 49 | 23 | 2 | 4 | 6 | 132 | 5 | 133 |
| Robert Beverley, Esq. | 138 | 22 | 4 | 4 | 30 | 17 | 14 | 14 | 1 | 3 | 2 | 51 | 1 | 56 |
| Wm. Daingerfield, Esq. | 15 | 1 | 1 | 0 | 2 | 2 | 2 | 1 | 1 | 0 | 0 | 6 | 0 | 7 |
| John Upshaw, Esq. | 2 | 1 | 0 | 0 | 1 | 0 | 0 | 0 | 0 | 0 | 0 | 1 | 0 | 0 |
| Thomas Roane, Esq. | 2 | 1 | 0 | 0 | 1 | 1 | 0 | 0 | 0 | 0 | 0 | 1 | 0 | 0 |

Waring was elected in 1752 and was followed by Colonel Francis Waring; and James Edmondson, who won in 1769 and 1771, was followed by John Edmondson in 1777 and 1778. Men such as Benjamin Winslow, John Corbin, Esquire, John Livingston, James Garnett, William Garnett, and others were never able to win.

These Essex elections should cause a great deal of skepticism about a "ruling aristocracy" or any suggested "hereditary" succession to office in the Old Dominion. With the middle and lower classes so greatly outnumbering the upper classes, a candidate, as contemporaries said, had to win popular support to be successful. Perhaps this is what Landon Carter meant when he said that his son Robert Wormeley Carter had to "kiss the arses" of the people to win. There is no evidence that a younger son or relative could succeed to office unless the voters approved of his qualifications, and we have no way of knowing how many younger sons aspired to the position of burgess but did not even make the attempt.

An analysis (Table 18) of another tidewater county, Norfolk, merely footnotes what is already clearly evident in Virginia elections: the middle-lower classes could win elections with votes to spare, but they and the upper class spread their votes about the same way. In the interests of space, we have not included the vote on minor candidates or single votes, but these did not affect the final result. The upper classes and the slave-owners reversed the first and second choices of the middle-lower classes, but both picked the ultimate winners. A number of merchants and a lesser number of artisans from Norfolk Borough had voted in county elections, but of course the Borough also elected a separate delegate of its own. That animosity between town and country was not great is attested by the fact that both county winners were from Norfolk Borough.

The 1768 Norfolk election resulted in a bitter dispute between Thomas Newton and John Brickall, with Brickall accusing Newton of illegal election practices, but the legislature was dissolved by the Governor before the dispute could be settled, and a new election in 1769 gave the voters a second opportunity. The results were the same (Table 19) except that George Veale dropped out as a major candidate, the planters favored Brickall somewhat over Newton, and the middle-lower class as a whole gave Brickall a one-vote margin. So Newton's victory came from the upper class because the planters split their vote evenly. Artisans did not follow the planter pattern, however, and Newton was again the winner by thirty-four votes. But there was no doubt that the middle-lower classes could have selected Brickall had they united behind him.

These two Norfolk election polls, when compared with an extant 1771 tithable list, prove again that men did not vote according to class or the number of acres they owned, for candidates received votes from men in various acreage categories, and men with small holdings voted for various candidates. Equally significant are the facts that fifty-three men in 1768 and forty-nine in 1769 voted but are not on the tithable list, that sixty-seven in 1768 and sixty-six in 1769 lived in Norfolk Borough and voted

TABLE 18. NORFOLK COUNTY ELECTION BY SOCIAL CLASSES, 1768[9]

Total Voters—588 (County, 511; Borough, 77). Seven Names not Legible. Number of Candidates—8

| Vote on Leading Candidates | Upper Class | | | | Middle-Lower Classes | | | | | | Undesignated | Total | Signed with Mark | Slave-owners |
|---|---|---|---|---|---|---|---|---|---|---|---|---|---|---|
| | Gentlemen and Merchants | | Others (Co.) | Total | Planters | | Artisans | | Tenants | Total | | | | |
| | Co. | Bor. | | | Co. | Bor. | Co. | Bor. | | | | | | |
| Wilson & Newton | 5 | 16 | 7 | 28 | 74 | | 21 | 9 | 0 | 104 | 7 | 139 | 25 | 81 |
| Wilson & Brickall | 6 | 12 | 2 | 20 | 127 | | 19 | 0 | 2 | 148 | 9 | 177 | 28 | 91 |
| Wilson & Veale | 1 | 1 | 0 | 2 | 3 | | 1 | 0 | 0 | 4 | 0 | 6 | 0 | 4 |
| Newton & Brickall | 2 | 3 | 0 | 5 | 7 | | 2 | 1 | 0 | 10 | 3 | 18 | 2 | 11 |
| Newton & Veale | 6 | 8 | 3 | 17 | 49 | | 46 | 11 | 1 | 107 | 9 | 133 | 14 | 84 |
| Brickall & Veale | 5 | 4 | 3 | 12 | 38 | | 13 | 0 | 0 | 51 | 7 | 70 | 5 | 35 |
| Totals | 25 | 44 | 15 | 84 | 298 | | 102 | 21 | 3 | 424 | 35 | 543 | 74 | 306 |

| Individual Candidates | Upper Class | | | Middle-Lower Classes | | | Undesignated | | | Total Vote | |
|---|---|---|---|---|---|---|---|---|---|---|---|
| | Co. | Bor. | Total | Co. | Bor. | Total | Co. | Bor. | Total | Bor. | Total |
| John Wilson | 21 | 29 | 50 | 250 | 9 | 259 | 14 | 3 | 17 | 41 | 326 |
| Thomas Newton, Jr. | 24 | 29 | 53 | 206 | 23 | 229 | 12 | 7 | 19 | 59 | 301 |
| John Brickall | 18 | 19 | 37 | 220 | 1 | 221 | 22 | 0 | 22 | 20 | 280 |
| George Veale | 19 | 14 | 33 | 161 | 11 | 172 | 15 | 4 | 19 | 29 | 224 |

Minor Candidates: Joseph Lockhart (11), Joseph Calvert (1), Matthew Phripps (2), John Taylor (1)

Candidates by Order of Class Preference, Winners Italicized:

Upper Class: 1. *Newton* 2. *Wilson* 3. Brickall 4. Veale

Middle-lower class: 1. *Wilson* 2. *Newton* 3. Brickall 4. Veale

Percentage Who Were Upper Class: 16.3.   Percentage Who Were Middle-Lower Class: 83.7.

## TABLE 19.  NORFOLK COUNTY ELECTION BY SOCIAL CLASSES, 1769[10]

Total voters—576 (County, 504; Borough, 72)    Number of Candidates—8

| Vote on Leading Candidates | Upper Class | | | | Middle-Lower Classes | | | | | | Undesignated | Total | Signed with Mark | Slaveowners |
|---|---|---|---|---|---|---|---|---|---|---|---|---|---|---|
| | Gentlemen & Merchant Co. | Bor. | Others | Total | Planters | Artisans Co. | Bor. | Tenants Co. | Bor. | Total | | | | |
| Wilson & Newton | 17 | 27 | 6 | 50 | 109 | 53 | | 22 | 0 | 184 | 25 | 259 | 30 | 171 |
| Wilson & Brickall | 7 | 14 | 6 | 27 | 150 | 22 | | 2 | 1 | 175 | 11 | 213 | 27 | 97 |
| Newton & Brickall | 3 | 2 | 3 | 8 | 34 | 15 | | 0 | 0 | 49 | 3 | 60 | 10 | 37 |
| Totals | 27 | 43 | 15 | 85 | 293 | 90 | | 24 | 1 | 408 | 39 | 532 | 67 | 305 |

| Individual candidates | Upper Class Co. | Bor. | Total | Middle-Lower Classes Co. | Bor. | Total | Undesignated Co. | Bor. | Total | Total Vote Co. | Bor. | Total | Slave-owners |
|---|---|---|---|---|---|---|---|---|---|---|---|---|---|
| John Wilson | 37 | 41 | 78 | 344 | 24 | 368 | 32 | 4 | 36 | 413 | 69 | 482 | 272 |
| Thomas Newton, Jr. | 29 | 29 | 58 | 217 | 22 | 239 | 29 | 4 | 33 | 275 | 55 | 330 | 209 |
| John Brickall | 19 | 16 | 35 | 238 | 2 | 240 | 12 | 9 | 21 | 269 | 27 | 296 | 146 |

Minor Candidates: Joseph Lockhart (20), Thomas Creech (1), George Veale (1), Robert Tucker (1), Joseph Hutchings (1)

Choice by Class:*
  Upper Class:  1. *Wilson*  2. *Newton*  3. Brickall
  Middle-Lower Classes:  1. *Wilson*  2. Newton  3. Brickall

Candidates by Order of Specific Group Preferences:
  Gentlemen-Merchants:  *Wilson* (66)   *Newton* (49)   Brickall (26)
  Planters:  *Wilson* (263)   Brickall (194)   *Newton* (145)
  Artisans:  *Wilson* (104)   *Newton* (93)   Brickall (44)

*Winners in Italics

but had no land in the county, that only ten borough voters in each year had land in the county, and that fifty-two voters in 1768 and fifty-three in 1769 lived in the county but had no land as far as the records reveal.[11] Voters who lived in Portsmouth would have voted in the county elections, of course, but these figures point out the danger of assuming that the tax lists show all the qualified voters.

Norfolk was the only county with anything resembling an urban population (Norfolk Borough had about 3,000 whites and Negroes according to the 1771 tithable list), but even here the artisans and small farmers dominated the elections. In addition to the many voters who apparently had no land, some two-thirds of those who owned land in the county had less than 200 acres, and over ninety per cent had less than 500 acres. In borough elections, men who owned houses and lots or who had served an apprenticeship were qualified, but some of these could not vote legally in county elections.

Of some interest also in our understanding of Virginia elections is the type of men who ran for burgess in Norfolk County. John Wilson was probably a Norfolk Borough shoemaker and merchant with some eleven servants or apprentices and four tithable slaves, although there was another John Wilson with two servants or overseers, thirteen tithable slaves, 970 acres of land, and two riding chairs, who might have been the candidate.[12] Thomas Newton, Jr., gentleman and merchant of Norfolk Borough, had only two tithable slaves and no land on the 1771 list, but his father, Thomas, Sr., had a servant or overseer, sixteen tithable slaves, and 1,466 acres. He owned a company which paid tithes in the county on two servants or overseers and eleven slaves, and both father and son were very active in real estate dealings in the area.[13] John Brickall, gentleman and lawyer, came to the colony from North Carolina about 1762. He lived in the county and had a moderate amount of property—seven tithable slaves and 450 acres.[14] George Veale, a wealthy gentleman living in or near Portsmouth, had the largest number of tithables of any individual in the county—one servant or overseer and twenty-nine tithable slaves compared with thirty-one slaves owned by a company in Norfolk. He was a burgess from 1756 until he became sheriff in 1761 and his brother Thomas was burgess from 1761 to 1765, but George Veale could not win another term in the House although he tried.[15]

Perhaps even more important for an understanding of political practices of colonial Virginians is the story of defeated candidate Joseph Lockhart, one of the several minor candidates in both elections. Receiving eleven votes in 1768 and twenty in 1769, Lockhart was never listed as a gentleman, he bought 100 acres of land in 1768 and 367 acres in 1770 after the elections, and a few weeks before his death in 1770 he sold 100 acres, the deed for which he signed with a mark. Shortly after his death his widow sold 189 acres and was listed on the 1771 tithable list for 476 acres and no slaves, so Lockhart must have had about 300 acres when he ran in the 1768 election. Yet this small planter, who belonged to the same class as the bulk of the voters, received very little support from small planters and artisans. Even James Lockhart, who had one slave and 200 acres, did not vote for Joseph.[16]

For variation, since the composite vote was similar to those of other tidewater counties, we have attempted to compare (Table 20) the known

TABLE 20. COMPARISON OF UPPER AND LOWEST CLASS VOTES IN ACCOMACK COUNTY[17]*

| Candidates | Total Vote | Upper Class | Lowest Class | Candidates | Total Vote | Upper Class | Lowest Class |
|---|---|---|---|---|---|---|---|
| 1738 Election: | | | | 1744 Election: | | | |
| E. Scarburgh | 182 | 2 | 39 | Parramore | 252 | 13 | 45 |
| Douglas | 172 | 17 | 19 | E. Scarburgh | 77 | 3 | 14 |
| Snead | 91 | 3 | 13 | T. T. Taylor | 39 | 4 | 5 |
| 1740 Election: | | | | 1748 Election: | | | |
| H. Scarburgh | 259 | 8 | 37 | Parramore | 302 | 16 | 47 |
| Douglas | 188 | 10 | 33 | Allen | 246 | 12 | 52 |
| 1742 Election: | | | | Douglas | 213 | 17 | 29 |
| | | | | Pitts | 98 | 2 | 11 |
| Douglas | 246 | 24 | 39 | E. Scarburgh | 82 | 6 | 16 |
| Parramore | 233 | 4 | 39 | 1758 Election: | | | |
| | | | | Parramore | 272 | 11 | 29 |
| | | | | Allen | 246 | 11 | 25 |
| | | | | Justice | 183 | 5 | 20 |
| | | | | Corbin | 140 | 2 | 17 |

*Winners in Italics

upper-class voters (gentlemen, merchants, ministers, attorneys, mariners, and schoolmasters) in Accomack County with those voters who appeared to be of the lowest class and therefore the most likely to be influenced by the upper class (illiterate planters, artisans, tenants). But even this comparison yields the same results as the others. The lower class always voted for a winner or split its vote evenly as in 1742, while the upper class preferred losers in 1738, 1740, and 1748. The upper class backed Douglas in four elections, but he won only once, when the lowest class split its vote, and a switch of seven lowest-class votes would have defeated him. Upper-class influence on lowest-class voting is certainly not apparent in these voting figures for tidewater Accomack. The lowest class spread its vote, as independent non-class-conscious voters might be expected to do, and some of these elections were extremely close and bitterly fought, both before and after the poll was taken.

Election charts for tidewater Richmond (Tables 21, 22, 23) are significant chiefly because they reflect the political fortunes of Landon Carter, son of Robert "King" Carter. Although there were many election polls in Richmond, they were all similar in outcome to those of other counties; we have therefore included only these three. The general pattern

TABLE 21.  RICHMOND COUNTY ELECTION, 1735, BY PROPERTY HOLDINGS[18]

| Candidates* | Voters Not on Rent Rolls | Voters on Rent Rolls & Acreages | | | | | | |
|---|---|---|---|---|---|---|---|---|
| | | 25-99 Acres | 100-200 Acres | 201-300 Acres | 301-400 Acres | 401-500 Acres | Over 500 | Totals |
| *Woodbridge & Fantleroy* | 23 | 16 | 23 | 8 | 4 | 3 | 14 | 91 |
| *Woodbridge & Hornby* | 29 | 20 | 29 | 4 | 1 | — | 3 | 86 |
| *Woodbridge & Carter* | 4 | 3 | 2 | 1 | 1 | 2 | 2 | 15 |
| *Woodbridge & Barnes* | — | — | 1 | — | — | — | — | 1 |
| *Fantleroy & Hornby* | 3 | — | 3 | — | 1 | — | 1 | 8 |
| *Fantleroy & Carter* | 10 | 3 | 6 | 1 | — | 1 | 2 | 23 |
| *Fantleroy & Barnes* | 7 | 1 | 7 | 3 | — | 1 | — | 19 |
| Hornby & Carter | 4 | 2 | 2 | 2 | — | — | 1 | 11 |
| Hornby & Barnes | 4 | 3 | 5 | — | — | — | — | 12 |
| Carter & Barnes | 4 | 1 | 1 | — | — | — | 2 | 6 |
| *Woodbridge only* | 1 | 2 | 1 | — | — | 1 | 1 | 6 |
| *Fantleroy only* | 7 | 1 | 10 | — | — | — | — | 18 |
| Hornby only | 15 | 2 | 7 | — | — | — | 1 | 25 |
| Carter only | 5 | 1 | 2 | 2 | — | 1 | 1 | 12 |
| Barnes only | — | — | 1 | — | — | — | — | 1 |
| TOTALS | 116 | 55 | 100 | 21 | 7 | 9 | 26 | 334 |
| Capt. John Woodbridge | 57 | 41 | 56 | 13 | 5 | 6 | 21 | 199 |
| William Fantleroy, Gent. | 50 | 21 | 49 | 11 | 6 | 5 | 17 | 159 |
| Daniel Hornby, Gent. | 55 | 27 | 46 | 7 | 1 | 1 | 5 | 142 |
| Landon Carter | 27 | 10 | 13 | 6 | 1 | 4 | 6 | 67 |
| Richard Barnes | 15 | 5 | 15 | 2 | 1 | 1 | — | 39 |
| TOTALS | 204 | 104 | 179 | 39 | 14 | 17 | 49 | 606 |

* Winners in Italics

TABLE 22. RICHMOND COUNTY ELECTION, 1755, BY PROPERTY HOLDINGS[19]

| Candidates | Voters Not on Rent Rolls | Voters on Rent Rolls & Acreages | | | | | | Totals |
|---|---|---|---|---|---|---|---|---|
| | | 25-99 Acres | 100-200 Acres | 201-300 Acres | 301-400 Acres | 401-500 Acres | Over 500 | |
| Carter & Woodbridge | 27 | 24 | 55 | 16 | 7 | 3 | 17 | 149 |
| Carter & Mitchell | 9 | 6 | 16 | 4 | 1 | — | 2 | 38 |
| Woodbridge & Mitchell | 5 | 1 | 7 | — | — | — | 2 | 15 |
| Carter only | — | — | 2 | — | — | — | 1 | 3 |
| Woodbridge only | 3 | 2 | — | 1 | 2 | — | — | 8 |
| Mitchell only | 1 | — | 1 | — | — | — | — | 2 |
| TOTALS | 45 | 33 | 81 | 21 | 10 | 3 | 22 | 215 |
| Landon Carter | 36 | 30 | 73 | 20 | 8 | 3 | 20 | 190 |
| John Woodbridge | 35 | 27 | 62 | 17 | 9 | 3 | 19 | 172 |
| Robert Mitchell | 15 | 7 | 24 | 4 | 1 | — | 4 | 55 |
| TOTALS | 86 | 64 | 159 | 41 | 18 | 6 | 43 | 417 |

TABLE 23. RICHMOND COUNTY ELECTION, 1761, BY PROPERTY HOLDINGS[20]

| Candidates | Voters Not on Rent Rolls | Voters on Rent Rolls & Acreages | | | | | | Totals |
|---|---|---|---|---|---|---|---|---|
| | | 25-99 Acres | 100-200 Acres | 201-300 Acres | 301-400 Acres | 401-500 Acres | Over 500 | |
| Carter & Woodbridge | 28 | 9 | 26 | 10 | 6 | 1 | 10 | 90 |
| Carter & Smith | 2 | 6 | 2 | 2 | — | 1 | — | 13 |
| Woodbridge & Smith | 29 | 21 | 38 | 9 | 5 | 2 | 4 | 108 |
| Carter only | 7 | 5 | 2 | 4 | 4 | 3 | 5 | 30 |
| Woodbridge only | — | — | 7 | — | — | — | — | 7 |
| Smith only | 1 | 1 | — | — | — | — | — | 2 |
| TOTALS | 67 | 42 | 75 | 25 | 15 | 7 | 19 | 250 |
| Mr. John Woodbridge | 55 | 29 | 75 | 19 | 10 | 3 | 14 | 205 |
| Col. Landon Carter | 37 | 20 | 30 | 16 | 9 | 6 | 15 | 133 |
| Col. John Smith | 30 | 28 | 42 | 11 | 5 | 3 | 4 | 123 |
| TOTALS | 122 | 77 | 147 | 46 | 24 | 12 | 33 | 461 |

was a familiar one—a large number of voters who were not on the rent rolls and were probably tenants, the bulk of the voters having less than 300 acres, more than ninety per cent having under 500 acres or not being listed, the scattering of votes of all acreage classes among different candidates, the closeness of two of the three elections where the change of a few votes would have spelled the difference between defeat and victory, the large number of men who voted for a winner and a loser or losers, and especially the number of voters (62 in 1735, 39 in 1761) who voted for one candidate only.

Landon Carter's role in these elections tells us a great deal about the difficulty in politics experienced by this son of a very wealthy and influential man. In 1735, Carter ran a poor fourth, he did not get the support of the bulk of the largest landowners, and he did not win until 1752. By 1755, all groups were fairly agreed on Carter and Woodbridge, with Carter polling the highest vote. There were 149 men who voted for two winners, unusually high, and only fifty-three who voted for a winner and a loser. But how different was the election of 1761. Woodbridge was now the most popular candidate and Carter was in trouble. The combination of two winners, Woodbridge and Carter, received only ninety votes, while 111 voted for a winner and a loser. Thirty men, representing all different kinds of property interests, voted for Carter only, and well they might, for if eleven of them had voted for the combination of Carter and Smith, Smith would have defeated Carter. As we have already seen, Carter was eventually defeated because, as he said, he did not pay enough attention to the voters, and his retirement from political life was by no means voluntary.

Since Landon Carter was an outstanding example of an "aristocratic" son of an "aristocratic" father, we have analyzed the vote for and against him in three elections when his popularity went from high to low. If the "aristocracy" controlled elections in Virginia, such control is not evident from Table 24. Of the 361 men who voted in all three elections, only fifty-two voted consistently for Carter and only seventy-three voted consistently for Woodbridge. Of special significance are the ninety-two who first voted for Carter, then changed and voted against him; the sixty-six who voted against him when they voted; and the sixty-four who voted for him and then failed to vote later. A few of these latter died, but the quitrent rolls show that most of them held property in 1751 and 1765; they were thus qualified to vote in all three elections.

Above all, these three Richmond elections demonstrate the political independence of the middle-lower classes, for this group was more prone to vote against Carter, to change its vote, or to stay at home than were the upper classes. Line 5 is especially revealing: the lower orders voted for Carter in 1755 when he was popular and voted against him later. Identifiable tenants were fully as independent as other voters. Ten of the twelve tenants who voted in 1755 supported Carter, but in 1758 only five of the ten voting tenants were for him, and in 1761 the twenty

TABLE 24.   ANALYSIS, RICHMOND COUNTY ELECTIONS, 1755, 1758, 1761 (CARTER)[21]

| Vote for and against Landon Carter in Richmond County Elections of 1755, 1758, and 1761 | Not on Rent Rolls | Voters on Rent Rolls & Acreages | | | | | | Total |
|---|---|---|---|---|---|---|---|---|
| | | 25-99 | 100-200 | 201-300 | 301-400 | 401-500 | 501 & over | |
| 1 For Carter, 1755, 1758, 1761 | 8 | 4 | 21 | 4 | 5 | 1 | 9 | 52 |
| 2 For Carter, 1755, 1758, did not vote 1761 | 5 | 1 | 8 | 3 | 1 | 1 | 6 | 25 |
| 3 For Carter, 1755, did not vote 1758 and 1761 | 8 | 2 | 9 | 4 | 1 | — | 3 | 27 |
| 4 For Carter, 1755 and 1758, against Carter 1761 | 1 | 4 | 7 | 1 | 1 | 1 | — | 15 |
| 5 For Carter, 1755, against Carter 1758 and 1761 | 3 | 8 | 21 | 4 | 1 | 1 | 2 | 40 |
| 6 For Carter, 1755, against Carter 1758, no vote 1761 | 1 | — | 7 | 2 | — | — | 2 | 12 |
| 7 For Carter, 1755, no vote 1758, against Carter 1761 | 1 | — | 2 | 2 | 1 | — | — | 6 |
| 8 For Carter, 1755, against Carter 1758, for Carter 1761 | — | 1 | 7 | 3 | 1 | — | 2 | 14 |
| 9 For Carter, 1755, no vote 1758, for Carter 1761 | 1 | 3 | 2 | — | 1 | — | 1 | 8 |
| 10 No vote 1755, for Carter 1758 and 1761 | 1 | 4 | 4 | 2 | — | 2 | 2 | 15 |
| 11 No vote 1755, against Carter 1758 and 1761 | 8 | 3 | 4 | 3 | — | — | — | 18 |
| 12 No vote 1755, for Carter 1758, no vote 1761 | 8 | 1 | 1 | — | — | — | 2 | 12 |
| 13 No vote 1755, for Carter 1758, against Carter 1761 | 3 | 2 | — | — | — | — | — | 5 |
| 14 No vote 1755, against Carter 1758, for Carter 1761 | 6 | 1 | — | — | — | — | — | 7 |
| 15 No vote 1755, against Carter 1758, no vote 1761 | 15 | — | — | — | — | — | — | 15 |
| 16 No vote 1755 and 1758, for Carter 1761 | 9 | 4 | 14 | 4 | 2 | — | 1 | 34 |
| 17 No vote 1755 and 1758, against Carter 1761 | 3 | 1 | 10 | 5 | 3 | 3 | 4 | 29 |
| 18 Against Carter, 1755, 1758, 1761 | — | 1 | 3 | 1 | 1 | 1 | 2 | 9 |
| 19 Against Carter 1755 and 1758, for Carter 1761 | — | 1 | 1 | — | 1 | 1 | — | 4 |
| 20 Against Carter 1755 and 1758, no vote 1761 | — | — | 2 | — | — | — | — | 2 |
| 21 Against Carter 1755, for Carter 1758 and 1761 | — | — | 1 | — | — | — | — | 1 |
| 22 Against Carter 1755, no vote 1758 and 1761 | 2 | 1 | 1 | — | — | — | 2 | 6 |
| 23 Against Carter 1755, for Carter 1758, no vote 1761 | 1 | — | — | — | — | — | — | 1 |
| 24 Against Carter 1755, no vote 1758, for Carter 1761 | 2 | — | — | — | — | — | — | 2 |
| 25 Against Carter 1755, no vote 1758, against Carter 1761 | — | — | 2 | — | — | — | — | 2 |
| TOTALS | 86 | 42 | 127 | 38 | 19 | 11 | 38 | 361 |

tenants voted eleven to nine against him. Eight tenants voted in all three elections, but only three voted consistently for Carter, and five tenants who voted against him in 1761 had previously voted for him.[22] Certainly the vote of the lower classes in tidewater Richmond County was not dictated by an "aristocracy."

Artisans in these three Richmond County elections were particularly independent in their voting. In the election of 1755, when there was little contest, the known artisan vote was sixteen to two in favor of Carter.[23] But the story was quite different in 1758 and 1761. In 1758, known artisans voted fourteen to four against Carter, and in 1761 the artisan vote was ten to six against him.[24] In the three elections, six artisans voted for Carter when they voted, eight voted both for and against him and seven always voted against him when they voted. This is just another striking example of the fact that an "aristocrat" could not control the vote of the common people.

The close elections of 1758 and 1761 were obviously factional fights between Carter and Tarpley in 1758 and Carter and Smith in 1761, for all the leading candidates were men of some property. We do not know exactly what Carter's holdings were, as he probably paid his quitrents in Williamsburg, but his diary indicates large holdings. Richmond rent rolls show that Tarpley had 680 acres in 1746 and 1,000 acres in 1765, Woodbridge had 1,160 acres in 1746 and 1,877 acres in 1765, and Smith was listed for 1,200 acres in 1746 and 1,244 acres in 1765.[25] These were sizeable holdings but at least twenty-three different men in the county held 1,000 acres or more on the rent rolls of 1746 and 1751, and fifteen men had this amount of land on the 1765 rental.

Most historians agree that there were more small farmers and fewer "aristocrats" in the piedmont and frontier counties than in the tidewater, so middle-lower-class domination should have been even more accentuated in the back counties than in the lowlands. Unfortunately the election polls are not as complete for these counties as for the tidewater, but the ones we have substantiate this generalization. Single election polls for Amelia in 1768, Spotsylvania in 1771, Halifax in 1765, and Prince William in 1741 merely confirm Governor Gooch's statement that the upper class seldom carried an election in the colony. Their choice might agree with that of the middle-lower class, but where there was a difference it was the latter which prevailed.[26]

The Prince William poll of 1741 (Table 25) does provide an opportunity to test the idea that tenants might have voted as their landlords did. The answer, of course, as one might expect from previous evidence, is that they did not. Forty-two tenants, who leased land from twenty-five different landlords, voted in the election, but only eleven of the twenty-five landlords voted; some landlords had died and were represented as estates and others lived out of the county. Of the eleven landlords who voted, six voted for the winning combination of Fairfax and Harrison; but of forty-two voting tenants, only eight supported both winners. Voting for

both winners were eighty-five voters including eight tenants and six landlords, but voting for a winner and a loser or two losers were 289 voters
including thirty-four tenants and only five landlords. The independence

TABLE 25.   TENANT-LANDLORD VOTING,
PRINCE WILLIAM, 1741[27]

| Candidates | Total Vote | Tenant Vote | Landlord Vote |
|---|---|---|---|
| Fairfax, William* | 249 | 27 | 8 |
| Harrison, Thomas* | 234 | 22 | 9 |
| Colville, Thomas | 175 | 21 | 3 |
| Peyton, Valentine | 141 | 11 | 2 |
| Blackburn, Richard | 29 | 3 | 0 |
| *Vote by Pairs of Candidates:* | | | |
| Fairfax* and Harrison* | 85 | 8 | 6 |
| Fairfax* and Colville | 89 | 12 | 1 |
| Fairfax* and Peyton | 49 | 4 | 1 |
| Fairfax* and Blackburn | 15 | 3 | 0 |
| Harrison* and Colville | 59 | 8 | 2 |
| Harrison* and Peyton | 72 | 6 | 1 |
| Harrison* and Blackburn | 5 | 0 | 0 |
| Colville and Peyton | 13 | 1 | 0 |
| Colville and Blackburn | 1 | 0 | 0 |
| Peyton and Blackburn | 8 | 0 | 0 |

*Winning Candidates

of tenants in this election was too great to indicate much coercion. Similar studies of tenant-landlord voting in Richmond County, 1755, and
Spotsylvania, 1771, yield the same patterns of tenant voting.[28]

A closer look at the voting of tenants and landlords in the Prince
William election of 1741 underscores the degree of independence among
the tenants. Only two tenants voted for both candidates favored by their
respective landlords: tenant Leonard Barker and landlord John Gregg
voted for both winners, while landlord William Bland and tenant James
Key voted for a winner and a loser. Twelve tenants voted for one candidate supported by their landlords, but three tenants showed complete
independence. Landlord George Brent voted for Fairfax and Colville; his
tenants Peter Glascock and John Hendron for Harrison and Peyton;
Landlord Thomas Pearson voted for Harrison and Colville; his tenant
Bond Veale voted for Fairfax and Peyton. In fact, Pearson had three
tenants, all of whom voted differently from Pearson and from each other.
If there was pressure by landlords on tenants, it does not appear in this
particular election.

In this same Prince William election, George Mason's tenants voted
in almost exact proportion to the total vote for the candidates. Only
fifteen of the thirty-seven voted, and they scattered their votes among four
candidates. Three tenants, John Mercer, Valentine Peyton, and John

Gregg, appear in the records as "gentlemen." Mercer and Gregg voted for both winners, Fairfax and Harrison, but Peyton voted for Fairfax and another minor candidate. Only four of the fifteen tenants, including the two gentlemen, voted for both winners. The other eleven all voted for a combination of a winner and a loser, a typical pattern in Virginia elections. And all three gentlemen-tenants voted late in the last half of the poll.[29]

In counties where slaveowners were a majority, they naturally had the greatest influence on the outcome of elections even though they always spread their votes among several candidates. The same was true in a county such as Halifax where the non-slaveowners were in the ascendancy (Table 26). The vote on the four major candidates indicates that

TABLE 26.  COMPARISON OF SLAVEHOLDER AND NON-SLAVEHOLDER VOTES IN A SECTION OF HALIFAX COUNTY IN THE ELECTIONS OF 1765, 1768, AND 1769[30]

*1765 ELECTION*

| No. of Voters* | No. of Slaves | W. Coles (313) | Booker (260) | Donilson (230) | Wade (214) | Others |
|---|---|---|---|---|---|---|
| 28 | 0 | 15 | 9 | 4 | 13 | 12 |
| 14 | 1-3 | 5 | 2 | 2 | 7 | 8 |
| 3 | 4-6 | 2 | — | 1 | 2 | 1 |
| 1 | 10-12 | — | — | — | — | 1 |

*1768 ELECTION*

| | | Terry (251) | Lewis (232) | W. Coles (212) | Wooding (195) |
|---|---|---|---|---|---|
| 30 | 0 | 25 | 23 | 3 | 4 |
| 17 | 1-3 | 13 | 15 | 1 | 2 |
| 6 | 4-6 | 3 | 3 | 3 | 3 |
| 2 | 10-12 | 2 | 2 | — | — |

*1769 ELECTION*

| | | Terry (194) | W. Coles (190) | I. Coles (135) | Lewis (134) |
|---|---|---|---|---|---|
| 21 | 0 | 14 | 5 | 5 | 16 |
| 15 | 1-3 | 13 | 3 | 2 | 12 |
| 5 | 4-6 | 2 | 2 | 3 | 3 |
| 0 | 10-12 | — | — | — | — |

* *Some voters cast only one vote.*

the non-slaveowners in this section of the county comprised the majority of voters in two out of three elections and undoubtedly could have dominated the third one had they voted. In these three bitterly fought elections, both slaveowning and non-slaveowning voters favored the same candidates, divided their votes widely in two elections for a winner and a loser (1765, 1769), and agreed on the winners in only one election

(1768). The independence of voters is reflected in the fluctuating fortunes of the candidates, for Walter Coles could drop from the most popular candidate in 1765 to third in 1768 and back to second in 1769; Lewis could be second in 1768 and last in 1769; Wade could not get elected even though he was the son of a former burgess; and two brothers, Walter and Isaac Coles, could not attract the same supporters.

If the voters on one tithable list in Amelia County, 1768, were typical (Table 27), and this is not an unreasonable surmise, voters often favored men whom they knew personally, especially men who lived in the same section of the county as the voters. Counties were always divided into tax districts with several collectors, each being responsible for a district. There is extant an election poll for Amelia in 1768 and also the tax list of Thomas Tabb. Tabb was the richest man in the county, and both he and John Scott, another candidate, lived in this same district.

Table 27 leaves little doubt that personal knowledge of and proximity to the candidate had a great influence on voters. Although Thomas Tabb and Robert Munford were the eventual winners, Tabb and John Scott received a very high percentage of the votes in their section of the county from all classes of men. Not a single large landowner nor a single large slaveowner voted for the winning combination of Tabb and Munford. Because of local support, Tabb and Scott were the second most popular combination (114 votes) but this did not prevent Scott from being last in the entire poll. Munford, who received only eleven votes in this part of the county, was the author of the quotation appearing at the head of this chapter and knew from experience how candidates won elections.

Obvious, also, is the fact that these Amelia voters did not vote along class lines. Nearly eighty-five per cent owned 400 acres of land or less and 76.4 per cent owned fewer than five tithable slaves, so the middle and lower classes were dominant. One might explain the vote for Thomas Tabb on the ground that he was the largest landowner (11,028 acres) and slaveowner (112 slaves) in the county. But John Scott, who received much support, was a lawyer with only two overseers or apprentices, eight slaves, and 1,400 acres of land. There were a number of men in this section of the county who had more land and slaves than did Scott.

Debtor-creditor voting, like that of the population in general, shows no clear-cut class patterns and no discernible influence of creditors on debtors. There might have been individual pressure on debtors by creditors, but if so it does not appear in the debtor-creditor vote. We have included only six of the fourteen Lancaster elections from 1741 to 1774, since these were the only close elections and the ones where creditors would be most apt to have tried to influence the votes of their debtors (Table 28). In 1741, debtors and creditors both favored the leading candidate, Conway, neither favored the second winner, and neither a debtor nor a creditor voted for both winners. In 1748, the creditors favored both winners, the debtors shunned the leading candidate, and while six creditors

## TABLE 27. VOTER PREFERENCE IN PART OF AMELIA COUNTY, 1768[81]

Candidates and Their Votes: Thomas Tabb—389, Robert Munford—296, John Winn—218, John Scott—159.

| Candidates | Voters by Landholding | | | | | | | Voters by Slaveholding | | | Totals for Tabb's List | Totals for County | Individual Totals for This District |
|---|---|---|---|---|---|---|---|---|---|---|---|---|---|
| | No Land | 25-99 Acres | 100-200 Acres | 201-300 Acres | 301-400 Acres | 401 Acres and Up | Acreage Unknown | No Slaves | 1-4 Slaves | 5 Slaves or More | | | |
| Tabb & Scott | 7 | 3 | 21 | 9 | 9 | 12 | 1 | 15 | 30 | 17 | 62 | 114 | Thomas Tabb—86 |
| Tabb & Winn | 4 | 1 | 8 | 3 | 1 | 1 | 0 | 13 | 1 | 4 | 18 | 95 | John Scott—70 |
| Scott & Winn | 2 | 0 | 3 | 0 | 0 | 0 | 0 | 3 | 1 | 1 | 5 | 11 | John Winn—29 |
| Munford & Winn | 2 | 0 | 2 | 0 | 0 | 1 | 0 | 1 | 3 | 1 | 5 | 79 | Robert Munford—11 |
| Tabb & Munford | 2 | 1 | 1 | 0 | 0 | 0 | 0 | 4 | 0 | 0 | 4 | 153 | |
| Scott & Munford | 0 | 0 | 0 | 0 | 0 | 0 | 0 | 0 | 0 | 0 | 0 | 19 | |
| Scott only | 1 | 0 | 2 | 0 | 0 | 0 | 0 | 1 | 1 | 1 | 3 | 15 | |
| Tabb only | 1 | 0 | 1 | 0 | 0 | 0 | 0 | 0 | 1 | 0 | 2 | 27 | |
| Munford only | 2 | 0 | 0 | 0 | 0 | 0 | 0 | 2 | 0 | 0 | 2 | 45 | |
| Winn only | 0 | 0 | 0 | 0 | 0 | 1 | 0 | 0 | 1 | 0 | 1 | 33 | |
| Totals | 21 | 5 | 38 | 12 | 10 | 15 | 1 | 39 | 38 | 25 | 102 | | |
| % of District Vote | 20.5 | 4.9 | 37.2 | 11.7 | 9.8 | 14.7 | 0.98 | 38.2 | 37.2 | 24.5 | | | |

TABLE 28.  VOTING OF DEBTORS AND CREDITORS, LANCASTER COUNTY[32]

| | Debtors | Creditors | Individual Vote | Debtors | Creditors | Total Vote |
|---|---|---|---|---|---|---|
| *1741 Candidates:* | | | | | | |
| Conway* & Stepto | 3 | 0 | Conway* | 5 | 4 | 116 |
| Conway* & Tayloe | 1 | 0 | Mitchell* | 2 | 2 | 79 |
| Conway* & Maj. Ball | 1 | 2 | Stepto | 4 | 0 | 56 |
| Conway* & Wm. Ball | 0 | 1 | Tayloe | 1 | 0 | 46 |
| Mitchell* & Jos. Ball | 2 | 2 | J. Ball | 4 | 3 | 40 |
| Jos. Ball & Maj. Ball | 0 | 1 | Maj. Ball | 1 | 3 | 32 |
| Jos. Ball & Wm. Ball | 1 | 0 | Wm. Ball | 1 | 1 | 31 |
| Jos. Ball & Stepto | 1 | 0 | | | | |
| *1748 Candidates:* | | | | | | |
| Chinn* & Conway* | 0 | 6 | Chinn* | 1 | 9 | 115 |
| Chinn* & Mitchell | 1 | 3 | Conway* | 8 | 9 | 106 |
| Conway* Pinckard | 2 | 1 | Pinckard | 2 | 1 | 73 |
| Conway* & Stepto | 4 | 2 | Mitchell | 1 | 3 | 70 |
| Conway* only | 2 | 0 | Stepto | 4 | 2 | 30 |
| *1752 Candidates:* | | | | | | |
| Conway* & Chinn* | 2 | 3 | Conway* | 10 | 8 | 101 |
| Conway* & Tayloe | 7 | 4 | Chinn* | 4 | 6 | 98 |
| Conway* & Ball | 1 | 1 | Tayloe | 7 | 4 | 82 |
| Chinn* & Ball | 2 | 3 | James Ball | 3 | 4 | 80 |
| *Dec. 1755 Candidates:* | | | | | | |
| Ball* & Selden* | 5 | 2 | Wm. Ball | 6 | 3 | 123 |
| Ball* & Heale | 1 | 1 | Selden* | 5 | 4 | 95 |
| Selden* & Heale | 0 | 2 | Heale | 1 | 5 | 63 |
| Heale only | 0 | 2 | | | | |
| *1761 Candidates:* | | | | | | |
| Carter* & Mitchell* | 3 | 1 | Carter* | 8 | 4 | 163 |
| Carter* & Heale | 5 | 3 | Mitchell* | 5 | 2 | 124 |
| Mitchell* & Heale | 2 | 1 | Heale | 7 | 4 | 108 |
| *1774 Candidates:* | | | | | | |
| Selden* & Carter* | 3 | 2 | Selden* | 5 | 3 | 151 |
| Selden* & Ball | 2 | 1 | Carter* | 8 | 8 | 139 |
| Carter* & Ball | 3 | 6 | Burgess Ball | 5 | 7 | 115 |
| Carter* only | 2 | 0 | | | | |

*Winning Candidates

voted for the two winners, no debtor did. In 1752, the debtors favored loser Tayloe over winner Chinn for second place and only two of them voted for the winning combination; in 1755 the debtors picked winners in the order of majority choice, but the creditors put the second choice first; in 1761, neither debtors nor creditors picked both winners; and in 1774, the leading candidate was not the first choice of either debtors or creditors.

As Table 29 illustrates, several debtors and creditors voted in each

TABLE 29. VOTING OF LANCASTER DEBTORS AND CREDITORS IN SAME ELECTIONS

| Date of election | 1741 | 1748 | 1752 | 1755 | 1761 | 1774 |
|---|---|---|---|---|---|---|
| No. of debtors voting | 9 | 9 | 12 | 6 | 10 | 10 |
| No. of creditors voting | 6 | 12 | 11 | 7 | 5 | 9 |
| Debtors & their creditors voting in same election | 2 | 3 | 4 | 2 | 2 | 1 |
| Agreed on two candidates | 0 | 2 | 3 | 1 | 0 | 0 |
| Differed on one candidate | 0 | 1 | 1 | 1 | 2 | 1 |
| Differed on both candidates | 2 | 0 | 0 | 0 | 0 | 0 |

election, but there were few instances in which the debtor and his creditor both voted in the same election; when they did, eight of the fourteen debtors differed with their creditors on one or both candidates. There could still have been influence by creditors in the six cases where debtors and their creditors agreed, but there is no evidence of this, and this influence, had it existed, would have been cancelled by the fact that the creditors themselves did not vote for the same men.

Voting by debtors and creditors in two Norfolk elections (Table 30) also precludes any doctrinaire conclusions about class patterns of behavior by these two groups. In 1768, more debtors than creditors favored the winning combination, Wilson and Newton, as many creditors (six) favored the two losers as the two winners, and a large number of both voted for a winner and a loser. In 1769, both debtors and creditors supported both winners, but a sizeable number of creditors split their votes and it is obvious that their debtors did not vote as they did. In both elections many in both groups did not vote at all.

Very often when there were several creditors for the same debtor, the creditors themselves disagreed completely on their choice of candidates. In Norfolk in 1768 there were thirteen mortgages involving more than one creditor or security, and the creditors in eleven of the thirteen mortgages disagreed on at least one candidate. In one mortgage involving three creditors, the debtor was dead but one creditor voted for Newton and Veale, a second for Wilson and Brickall, and a third for Wilson and Newton.

Similar patterns of debtor-creditor voting prevailed for Essex and Spotsylvania counties. In Essex (Table 31) a much higher percentage of

TABLE 30.   VOTING OF DEBTORS AND CREDITORS OF
NORFOLK ON COMBINED AND WINNING CANDIDATES[33]
(Winners in Italics)

| 1768 Election | Debtors | Creditors | Securities |
|---|---|---|---|
| *Wilson* & *Newton* | 12 | 6 | 3 |
| *Wilson* & Brickall | 5 | 7 | 2 |
| *Wilson* & Veale | — | 1 | 1 |
| *Newton* & Veale | 12 | 11 | 1 |
| Brickall & Veale | 3 | 6 | — |
| Veale & Lockhart | 1 | 1 | — |
| Brickall & Calvert | 1 | 1 | — |
| Brickall & Lockhart | — | 1 | — |
| *Newton* & Lockhart | 1 | — | — |
| *Wilson* only | 1 | — | — |
| *Newton* only | 2 | — | — |
| Total number voting | 38 | 34 | 7 |
| Did not vote | 50 | 30 | 5 |
| Total number | 88 | 64 | 12 |
| Votes for leading candidates: | | | |
| *Wilson* | 18 | 14 | 6 |
| *Newton* | 27 | 17 | 4 |
| Brickall | 9 | 15 | 2 |
| Veale | 16 | 19 | 2 |
| *1769 Election* | | | |
| *Wilson* & *Newton* | 28 | 20 | 3 |
| *Wilson* & Brickall | 5 | 13 | 2 |
| *Newton* & Brickall | 1 | 3 | — |
| *Newton* & Veale | 1 | — | — |
| Brickall & Lockhart | 1 | — | — |
| Total number voting | 36 | 36 | 5 |
| Did not vote | 52 | 29 | 7 |
| Total number | 88 | 65 | 12 |
| Votes for leading candidates: | | | |
| *Wilson* | 33 | 33 | 5 |
| *Newton* | 30 | 23 | 3 |
| Brickall | 7 | 16 | 2 |

debtors than creditors voted for a winner and a loser or two losers, and
when a creditor and his debtor voted in the same election, nearly twice
as many debtors differed with their creditors as agreed with them. In
Spotsylvania there were eighty-five debtors and 114 creditors, but in the
two elections of 1765 and 1771, there were 124 instances in which neither
creditor nor debtor voted, sixty-five in which the debtor but not the
creditor voted, and twenty-seven in which the creditor but not the debtor
voted. Of the eighteen creditors and their debtors who both voted, there
were ten agreements and eight disagreements. At least eight men were
both debtors and creditors. Partners in mercantile firms, such as Cun-
ningham and Stewart in 1765 and Hunter and Glassell in 1771, did not

vote the same way. Benjamin Waller and Joseph Brock, joint creditors
of John Waller, did not vote alike in 1771, and William Fitzhugh,

TABLE 31.  COMPARISON OF THE VOTING OF ESSEX
COUNTY DEBTORS AND CREDITORS[34]

| Elections of | 1748 | 1752 | 1755 | 1758 | 1761 | Total |
|---|---|---|---|---|---|---|
| Debtors voting for: | | | | | | |
| Winners only | 8 | 6 | 7 | 6 | 4 | 31 |
| 1 winner & 1 loser | 13 | 9 | 8 | 10 | 14 | 54 |
| Losers only | 3 | 5 | 5 | 1 | — | 14 |
| Creditors voting for: | | | | | | |
| Winners only | 10 | 11 | 6 | 1 | 6 | 34 |
| 1 winner & 1 loser | 9 | 4 | 6 | 13 | 11 | 43 |
| Losers only | 1 | 2 | 3 | 1 | — | 7 |
| When creditors and their debtors voted in same election: | | | | | | |
| Agreed on 2 candidates | 5 | 6 | 3 | — | 5 | 19 |
| Differed on one candidate | 13 | 4 | 3 | 8 | 5 | 33 |
| Voted entirely differently | 1 | 1 | — | 1 | — | 3 |

Esquire, of Stafford voted for his debtor, Benjamin Grymes, Esquire.[35]

In Halifax, a frontier county at the time, there were few creditors and
debtors compared with the number of voters, but these few do not reflect
significant creditor influence. Of thirty mortgages recorded between 1765
and 1770, only twenty-seven debtors and fourteen creditors lived in the
county. Twenty-two debtors voted in one or more of the four elections
from 1764 to 1769, and one of the five non-voters was Nathaniel Terry,
county burgess and also a creditor. Ten of fourteen creditors voted,
Terry being among the four who abstained. Of the thirty-one instances
in which creditors and their debtors voted in the same elections, they
agreed on two candidates eight times, agreed seven times on one winning
candidate (in the by-election of 1764), agreed on only one of two candidates seven times, and disagreed completely nine times. In fact, debtors
favored winning candidates more than did creditors—eight to one in
1764, two to one in 1765, four to two in 1768, and three to one in 1769.
Creditor John Legrand and debtor James Legrand, the largest debtor in
Halifax, did not agree on candidates in 1768.[36] Evidently the winning
candidates were more popular with debtors than with creditors.

Not only were debtors voters but, as previously mentioned, a man
could be an "insolvent debtor" and still be a voter. John Sehon, former
Lancaster servant later described as "planter," was declared an insolvent
debtor in 1761 when he had no property and only £7.11.2 due to him.
Sehon voted in 1755 and 1758, apparently sold five slaves in 1758, and
voted in 1765 and 1768. There is no record that he acquired land before
1769, but by 1773 he was listed on the rent rolls for fifty acres of rented
land plus fifty acres of his own. In the six elections in which he voted, he
picked only winning candidates.[37]

Debtor independence is well expressed by the action of one Hicks of

Hanover County. In the disputed Hanover election of 1752, Hicks planned to vote for Henry Robinson, apparently county clerk, for Hicks owed Robinson 200 pounds of tobacco for clerk's fees. When Robinson refused to postpone his demands for payment, Hicks voted against him.[38]

The evidence, then, would seem to verify the statements by Spotswood, Gooch, Fauquier, and Munford that the middle-lower classes controlled politics, that the better sort seldom carried a Virginia election, and that to win an election a candidate must "cajole, fawn, and wheedle" and "be nought but what each voter pleases." There is certainly no evidence, either in the opinions of contemporaries or in the election statistics, that the "slaveowning barons" cowed the voters and put their men in office. A "ruling aristocracy" could gain and retain office only by pleasing a sufficient number of the voters, a fact which is itself a contradiction of the word aristocracy. So if by democracy we mean a system in which the voters could elect or defeat candidates at will, Virginia was what we would call a representative democracy.

## NOTES

1. Robert Munford, *The Candidates; or the Humours of a Virginia Election,* ed. by Jay B. Hubbell and Douglass Adair (Williamsburg, 1948), p. 17. This play was written about 1770.

2. Beard, *The Rise of American Civilization,* I, 127.

3. This note contains the citations for the fourteen tables on Lancaster County. The many thousands of individual abstracts could not be cited here. Lancaster Deed and Will Books 13 through 20. Book 13 contains Order Book 8, Book 17 contains Order Book 12, and Book 18 contains Orders for 1767-68. Election polls are in Lancaster County Deed Book 13, pp. 249-50 (1741); Book 14, pp 400-01 (1748); Lancaster County Will Book 15, p. 167 (1754), p. 231 (Nov. 10, 1755), pp. 232-33 (Dec. 23, 1755); Lancaster County Deed Book 16, pp. 27-28 (July 18, 1758); p. 49 (Nov. 30, 1758); pp. 222-23 (1761); Book 18, pp. 42-43 (1765); pp. 133-34 (1768); p. 154 (1769); Book 19, pp. 58-59 (1771); pp. 112-13 (1774); see Lancaster County Loose Papers for election polls of 1752, 1754, Nov. 30, 1758, 1765, 1768, and a partial list of 1777; Lancaster County Tithable Lists for 1745, 1746, 1775, 1776, 1777, 1779, 1781 (most of these are not complete); Quitrent Roll for Christ Church Parish, 1748, in Lancaster County Rentals, 1748; Quitrent Roll for Christ Church and White Chapel parishes, 1750, in Lancaster County Rentals, 1750; "A Rental for Lancaster County for the Year 1773," VSL (includes both upper and lower precincts); Lancaster Soldiers in Washington Papers, X, 33 (1758); Lancaster County Oath of Allegiance list, 1777-78, in Lancaster County Deed Book 19, pp. 187-89. The wartime lists were not copied onto individual name cards as were the previous lists.

4. *Ibid.,* Book 14, p. 286; Lancaster County Will Book 15, p. 163; election of Jan. 28, 1752, Lancaster County Loose Papers, VSL.

5. Lancaster County Rentals 1748 and 1750; 1748 election poll in Lancaster County Deed Book 14, pp. 200-01. Whenever differences appeared in the 1748 and 1750 rentals for acreage of one individual, the 1748 was preferred.

6. Lancaster Rental of 1750, VSL, and election poll, 1752, in Lancaster County Deed Book 13, pp. 249-50.

7. *Ibid.,* Book 19, pp. 58-59, 112-13; Lancaster County Rental, Upper and Lower Precincts, 1773, VSL.

8. Survey of Essex County Deed Books 23 through 31, *passim,* for social designations of voters. For polls see Book 24, pp. 275-80; Book 25, pp. 301-07; Book 27, pp. 248-52; Book 28, pp. 95-99; Book 29, pp. 1-7; Book 30, pp. 235-42, 243-48, 318-24, 385, 496-502; Book 31, pp. 398-402, 405-06. For a differing view of the power of the "ruling class" in Virginia, see Bridenbaugh, *Seat of Empire,* Chp. 2.

9. Norfolk County Deed Book 24, pp. 112-15; for social status see Norfolk County Deed and Will Books, *passim.* Included in the upper class are all men with any distinguishing title, even schoolteachers and mariners.

10. Norfolk County Deed Book 24, pp. 211-15.

11. *Ibid.,* pp. 112-15, 211-15; Norfolk County and Borough Tithable lists, 1771.

12. Norfolk County Deed Book 25, pp. 97, 117, 154; Norfolk County and Borough Tithable lists, 1771.

13. *Ibid.* List of losses in Norfolk in *House Journals, Oct. 1778,* pp. 57-60; Norfolk County Deed Books 17-26, *passim.*

14. *Ibid.,* Book 20, p. 74; Book 25, p. 64; Norfolk County Tithables, 1771.

15. Norfolk County Deed Book 20, p. 239; Book 21, pp. 156, 219; Book 25, p. 107; Norfolk County Will Book 1, p. 77; Norfolk County and Borough Tithables, 1771; *House Journals, 1752-58, 1758-61, 1761-65.*

16. Norfolk County Deed Book 24, pp. 40, 246, 273; Book 25, pp. 4, 22, 23; Norfolk County Will Book 1, p. 194; Norfolk County Tithables, 1771.

17. For social data see Accomack County Deed Books 1737-46, 1746-57, 1757-70, *passim;* for election polls 1738, 1740, 1742, 1744, Book 1737-46 at end of book; 1748 poll in Book 1746-57, pp. 130-43; poll for 1758 in Book 1757-70, Pt. 1, pp. 52-56. Artisans and tenants were included in the lowest group because historians tend to place them a step below planters who owned property. As we have seen in previous chapters, however, artisans frequently owned considerable property and even tenants were on a par with most planters.

18. Richmond County Election poll, 1735; Richmond County Rentals, 1744 and before 1744.

19. Election poll in Richmond County Deed Book 13, pp. 338-40; Richmond County Rent Rolls, 1746, 1751, and 1765.

20. Election poll for 1761 in Richmond County Order Book 14, pp. 381-85; Richmond County Rent Rolls, 1746, 1751, 1765. For similar results, compare Prince William County Rental, 1760, with election poll, 1761, in Prince William County Deed Book P, pp. 68-73.

21. Richmond County election polls, 1755, 1758, 1761, in Richmond County Order Book 13, pp. 338-40; Book 14, pp. 264-68, 381-85; Richmond County Rentals.

22. Tenants from Richmond County Deed Books 10-13, *passim;* election polls in Richmond County Order Book 13, pp. 338-40; Book 14, pp. 264-68, 381-85; similar independence on the part of tenants is found in the 1769 election—see election polls 1769 and 1771 in Richmond County Order Book 16, pp. 491-97; Book 17, pp. 249-56; tenants from Richmond County Deed Books 12 and 13, *passim.*

23. Election poll in Richmond County Order Book 13, pp. 338-40; social designations in Richmond County Deeds, *passim.*

24. Election polls in Richmond County Order Book 14, pp. 264-68, 381-85.

25. Richmond County Rent Rolls, 1746 and 1765.

26. Amelia County Deed Books 3, 5, 7, and F; Amelia County Tithables, undated, 1742-43, 1749, 1762, 1768, 1771, 1778, VSL; election poll for 1768 in *Tyler's Quarterly,* XXXIII, 54-69; social designation from Spotsylvania County Deed Books E, F, G, H, *passim;* election poll for 1771, Spotsylvania County Will Book D, pp. 528-33; Halifax County Deed Books 1-7, *passim;*

election poll in Book 3, pp. 392-401; Prince William County Deed Books A, B, D, E; election poll in Book E, p. 524.

27. *Ibid.,* Books A, B, D, E; election poll in Book E, p. 524.

28. Election polls of 1755, 1758, 1761 in Richmond County Order Book 13, pp. 338-40; Book 14, pp. 264-68, 381-85; Richmond County Deed Book 10, p. 358; Richmond Rentals, 1751 and 1765; for additional information on tenant Thomas Connolly see Richmond County Deed Book 12, p. 74; election poll in Spotsylvania County Will Book D, pp. 528-33; tenants from Spotsylvania County Deed Books E, F, G, H, *passim.*

29. Prince William County Deed Book C, pp. 371, 379; Book E, p. 524.

30. List of James Turner, Jr., Halifax County Tithables; election polls in Halifax County Deed Book 3, pp. 389-411.

31. Thomas Tabb's tithable list, 1768, Amelia County Tithables; Amelia election poll, 1768, in *Tyler's Quarterly,* XXXIII, 54-69.

32. For references to mortgages see note 11 in Chp. V. For election polls see note 3 above.

33. Election polls are in Norfolk County Deed Book 24, pp. 112-15, 211-15; for names of debtors and creditors see mortgage references in note 10 of Chp. V. Only male residents were included in the debtor-creditor figures; non-voters such as women, orphans, non-residents and those known dead were not tabulated. Although a debtor or creditor may have held several debts or mortgages his vote is counted here only once.

34. For mortgages see reference note 14 in Chp. V. Polls are found in Essex County Deed Book 24, pp. 275-80 (1748); Book 25, pp. 301-07 (1752); Book 27, pp. 248-52 (1755); Book 28, pp. 95-99 (1758); Book 29, pp. 1-7 (1761).

35. Spotsylvania County Deed Books E, F, and G; Book F, pp. 739-41; Spotsylvania County Will Book D, pp. 528-33.

36. Halifax County Deed Book 3, pp. 389-92 (1764), 392-401 (1765), 401-07 (1768), 407-11 (1769). For Terry, see Book 1, pp. 88, 122, 155, 165, 215, 217, 417; Book 2, pp. 14, 116, 245, 300, 302, 358, 361; Book 3, pp. 6, 92, 113, 240; Book 4, p. 62; Book 5, pp. 223, 277, 285, 337, 339, 351, 353, 355, 476, 534; Book 6, pp. 155, 192, 273, 287, 288, 329, 331, 334, 441, 444, 449, 518, 526.

37. Lancaster County Deed Book 14, p. 12; Book 16, pp. 19, 149; Book 18, p. 135; Book 19, pp. 5, 192; Lancaster County Tithable List, 1745 [Sehon]; Lancaster Rental for 1773. For elections see Lancaster County Will Book 15, p. 231 (1755); Lancaster County Deed Book 16, pp. 27-28 (1758); Lancaster County Loose Papers (1765 and 1768); Lancaster County Deed Book 18, p. 154 (1769); Book 19, pp. 58-59 (1771); for a similar example see case of John Webb in Essex County Deed Book 28, pp. 48-50, 95-99.

38. *House Journals, 1752-58,* pp. 61-62.

# CHAPTER X

# *Representation: "The Echo of the People"*

GIVEN THE FACT that the common man voted and exercised his vote with a great deal of independence in Virginia, the question still remains as to whether the men he elected really represented him.[1] Did the people elect their own kind, or did they elect members of the upper classes? And once elected, did representatives, if upper-class, vote for class interests or did the wishes of the common man carry any weight in legislative halls? Was representation equitably apportioned, or did it favor an aristocratic tidewater over a democratic backcountry? In attempting to answer these questions, distinction must be made in a colony governed under British imperialism between those areas dominated by the British and those in which the people had a voice.

At the level of the province, democracy could function only in the election of the House of Burgesses. The other branches of the General Assembly, the Governor and the Council, as well as officials such as attorney-general, secretary, deputy auditor-general, and deputy receiver-general, were appointed from England. The Council served in three capacities—adviser to the Governor, upper house of the legislature, and with the Governor, supreme court or General Court of the colony.[2] How predominant British influence in colonial government was can be seen from the following account of Richard Henry Lee:

"With us the legislative power is lodged in a Governor, Council, and House of Burgesses. The two first appointed by the Crown, and their places held by the precarious tenure [?] of pleasure only. That security therefore which the constitution derives in Britain from the House of Lords, is here entirely wanting, and the just equilibrium totally destroyed by two parts out of three of the Legislature being in the same hands. It happens also unfortunately that the same persons who compose our Council during pleasure, with the Governor at their head, are the Judges of our General Courts (and only so long as they continue of the Council) where all causes ecclesiastical and civil, both common law and Chancery busi[ness are] determined. By this injudicious combination, all the executive, two thirds of the legislative, and the whole judiciary powers are in the same body of Magistracy. . . . But how must your surprise increase, when you are informed that even the third or democratic part of our legislature i[s] totally in the power of the Crown! Tis by usage only that elections are directed and Assembly's called; in our code of [laws] not

215

one is to be found that directs the calling of new Assembly[s] or that appoints any time for the meeting of the representa[tive] body when chosen."[3]

Although the people of Virginia had little direct voice in the selection of most of their officials, they did have some indirect influence. A Governor who desired a tranquil administration, as did William Gooch, might well oppose the appointment of Thomas Corbin to the Council because Corbin was "a person of no interest [influence] among the people" while other men had "great interest."[4] On another occasion Gooch recommended Col. Thomas Lee to the Council because Lee had good interest and esteem in his neighborhood. This was an important consideration in a remote part of the colony where he said the common people were generally more turbulent and unruly than elsewhere and were likely to continue this way because most of the convict transports were sold there.[5]

Like England, Virginia used the county system of local government, and again there was little democracy in the structure. Officials, including county justices, sheriffs, and coroners were appointed by the Governor, although county justices nominated the candidates for the county courts. Parish vestries, which exercised a good deal of power, were originally elected, but from then on, unless the vestry was dissolved and a new election was held, vacancies were filled by co-optation. Jurors were selected by the sheriff instead of being elected as they were in some colonies.

The people were not, however, completely at the mercy of these appointed local officials. The elected House of Burgesses exercised a great deal of power over sheriffs, justices, and vestries, recommending that certain men be denied appointment for conduct inimical to the interests of the people and dissolving vestries on petitions from the people and ordering new ones. Although the judges, justices, and sheriffs were appointed, an accused person, except a slave, could always demand a jury trial even before the highest court, and could challenge any jurors.[6]

However aristocratic the court system might appear in theory, in practice it seemed to favor the lower and middle classes rather than the upper classes. Jury qualifications, property worth £50 sterling for a county court and £100 sterling for the General Court, were lowered in 1748 to £50 and £100 current money.[7] But jurors, like voters, were usually from the middle and lower classes. Of the nineteen men on a grand jury in Richmond County, fifteen, or seventy-nine per cent, had 300 acres or less and the largest landowner among them had only 429 acres.[8] The Reverend James Maury in the Two-Penny Act trial complained that the sheriff, instead of selecting "gentlemen," picked a jury from "among the vulgar herd."[9] In 1756, Archibald Cary, gentleman and burgess from Chesterfield County, faced a suit for assault and battery by Henry Wetherburne, ordinary keeper of Williamsburg. Cary feared that he would not have a fair trial because of Wetherburne's friendship with or influence over the people who would probably comprise the jury.[10]

In practice, also, regardless of theory, the undemocratic method of appointing county justices did not meet with popular opposition. The *Virginia Gazette* carried proposals to reform county courts by speeding up justice and getting better judges, but there was no objection to the method of appointing justices. In fact, a writer suggested that the county lieutenant should be chosen by a majority vote of the other county officers, just as magistrates and vestrymen were chosen by a majority of their respective groups.[11] There might be complaints against individual justices and suggestions that justices should be well trained in the law, but there was little objection to the method of their appointment.[12]

Perhaps one reason for a lack of opposition toward undemocratic appointment of officials was the fact that these appointive positions were not as desirable as one might think. Governor Spotswood, who found it "very difficult to get persons to execute the office of sheriff," had to get a law passed forcing men to accept commissions.[13] Gooch had the same trouble, primarily because the office returned little profit in some counties and sheriffs were always subject to law suits.[14] Not everyone could be sheriff, for the Governor had to select from a list of three county justices selected each year by the county court. A sheriff could not hold office for more than two years in succession, and because of the large amounts of money that he handled he had to be bonded for £1,000 sterling.[15] Even the office of deputy auditor-general was no financial windfall. When Richard Corbin accepted the appointment in 1762, income from the office was only £650 a year. Of this, £500 went to a sinecurist in England, a clerk received £50, and Governor Fauquier insisted on a cut of two-thirds of the remainder. Corbin expected to get only £30 to £40, although he actually realized £156 in 1764.[16]

Sons sometimes followed fathers in public office, but the only office that smacked of heredity was that of county clerk, and then only in some counties. Although clerks were appointed by the Secretary of the colony, Governor Fauquier said that sons usually succeeded their fathers. The reason was that sons often worked in the clerk's office without reward in the expectation that they would in time become clerks, and in time they came to feel that they had the right of succession. This was true in the settled counties, but not in the distant ones.[17] In Lancaster County, one family held the clerkship from 1736 to 1770,[18] but there was little or no protest against such a practice.

It is clear that any discussion of democracy in colonial Virginia must be concerned largely with the House of Burgesses. This was the only important elective body in the colony, and while we might consider Virginia as aristocratic because of its many appointive offices, such aristocracy would be the result of imperialism rather than internal class structure. Our problem, then, is one of discovering whether the House was aristocratic or democratic—what laws governed the election of members, whether representation was equitable, what kind of men were elected, whether sectionalism was significant, and to what extent the burgesses reflected the views of their constituents.

If democracy means representation according to population, the Virginia House of Burgesses, like the United States Senate, was not strictly a democratic body. In March, 1660/1, the General Assembly restricted representation to no more than two burgesses from each county, allowed one representative for Jamestown (James City), and also one for any town of 100 acres inhabited by 100 tithable persons. In 1669, two burgesses from each county became mandatory.[19] These provisions were continued in the consolidated laws of 1705, with the addition that William and Mary College and any incorporated town received a burgess. A candidate had to be twenty-one years of age and a freeholder, amount not specified, but he did not have to be a resident of the county or town that elected him.[20]

On occasion the House followed practices or enacted laws that made its processes more democratic. Since there were no fixed legal times for meetings of the legislature, the House adopted the practice of short-term appropriations to make frequent meetings necessary.[21] Over protests of the Governor and Council, the House insisted that burgesses must serve for pay, thus eliminating the possibility that only the very wealthy could afford to serve.[22] After 1736, tobacco inspectors, who were in a position to influence voters, could not sit as burgesses, and an unsuccessful effort was made to require that a burgess be a resident as well as a freeholder of the county he represented.[23] Williamsburg and Norfolk, incorporated as boroughs by the King, received a representative each.[24] Sheriffs and coroners could not be burgesses, and if burgesses accepted any appointments that were remunerative they had to stand for re-election.[25] A man could run for a seat in the House from any county where he was a freeholder, but he could serve from one county only.[26]

As a rejected law of 1762 demonstrates, it was Britain rather than a ruling aristocracy in the House that prevented democratization of colonial politics. The General Assembly tried to correct some faults in the election machinery, especially the fact that Britain could control the convening of the House of Burgesses and the calling of elections. A new law required that a General Assembly had to be held at least once every three years and that a new House of Burgesses had to be elected at least once every seven years. These were the rules governing Parliament, but in Virginia the Governor decided both questions. Sheriffs, under-sheriffs, and tobacco inspectors could not run for the House until two years after they left office. Pay for burgesses was fixed at fifteen shillings a day plus travel expenses, both to be paid out of the treasury rather than by the counties. But this law, considered in England as an infringement on the King's prerogative, was disallowed.[27] The provision for paying burgessess is particularly interesting, for one would not expect an "aristocratic" tidewater to aid poor and distant counties in paying the expenses of their burgesses.

In addition to a theoretically undemocratic apportionment of two burgesses for each county regardless of size, there is the further problem of whether an aristocratic tidewater rigged representation in such a way that the backcountry was denied an equitable voice in government. After 1705, new counties were formed mainly on the frontier to the southwest, west, and northwest of the old counties, the new county usually being merely the western or upper part of an old county.

On its face, an act of 1705 establishing rules for the division of counties as people moved westward appears to discriminate against the westernmost counties. Because of increased expense due to Indian troubles, the law provided that counties in the west would be larger to increase the size of their militia and to render expense and duty less burdensome to each individual. No county was to be divided unless the "upper" or new part contained 800 tithables; and before the division, the whole county was to build a decent church, courthouse, and prison for the new county. If the "upper" inhabitants sought the division of the county, however, they would have to provide their own church, courthouse, and prison.[28] Larger size for each county meant cheaper county government, but at the same time the upper inhabitants, if they demanded a new county, incurred all the expense of establishing it. This was not a tidewater-piedmont conflict, however, for most of the new counties were in the piedmont and on the frontier, and if the people there desired increased representation for their section, they had the machinery for getting it.

Far from desiring to prevent the establishment of new counties, however, the tidewater-controlled House of Burgesses on occasion actually encouraged westward expansion, even though the motives were doubtless selfish ones. Because of a threat from the French and Indians in 1720, the General Assembly established the western counties of Brunswick and Spotsylvania and appropriated £500 for building a church, courthouse, prison, pillory, and stocks in each county. The Assembly also provided funds to supply arms and ammunition for anyone who would go to these counties. As a further inducement, inhabitants were exempt from all public taxes for ten years, and if they were foreign Protestants with their own minister, they and their tithables were to be exempt from church tithes for ten years. By 1738, Frederick and Augusta counties had been established west of the Blue Ridge Mountains.[29]

That the tidewater was not averse to establishing new counties in the piedmont is amply demonstrated by the division of what was Prince George County in 1714. In that year, the county had 1,040 tithables. By 1770, the same area contained 26,412 tithables and eleven counties— Amelia, Bedford, Brunswick, Charlotte, Dinwiddie, Halifax, Lunenburg, Mecklenburg, Prince Edward, Pittsylvania, and Prince George. Not only did the population double more than four and a half times in fifty-six years, or about once every twelve years, but all ten of the new counties were in the piedmont.[30]

The establishment of a new county did not give rise to a sectional conflict between tidewater and piedmont. The issue was not that the people of the county wanted a division and the General Assembly opposed it, but that the people of the county were themselves often at odds over the division. For example, the House in 1755 accepted as reasonable a petition from Amelia which opposed another petition advocating division of the county.[31] In 1764, a petition to divide Frederick County was rejected and at the same time the House accepted several petitions opposing the division. The people of Accomack sent petitions both for and against division of that tidewater county in 1770, but no action was taken.[32] And there was active opposition in Fincastle to a petition from the Holston River settlers for a new county. [33] Before interpreting rejected petitions for division of western counties as acts of the tidewater aristocracy, the historian must first determine whether opposition came from within or without the county.

In addition, not all counties wanted to be small in order to have more representation per capita than their neighbors. In 1718, the House rejected a petition from tidewater Charles City County asking that it be enlarged. Probably the inhabitants desired a larger population over which to spread expenses. On the same day, the House rejected a petition from Richmond County for a division there. In 1759, some of the people of Prince William County petitioned that 2,000 tithables be left in the old county if it were divided.[34] This would mean that the old county would remain large rather than small, and indicated perhaps that the people were more interested in having additional taxpayers to help defray the expense of government than they were in getting increased representation per capita.

Sometimes private interests and customs entered into the question of dividing counties. Governor Spotswood wanted to fix new boundaries for the counties between the York and James Rivers so that they would have a somewhat equal number of tithables. Two items prevented this. One was the private interests of the representatives, particularly one man, who would stand to lose the vote of many friends. In addition to private interests, the Governor said, the Assemblies were "so fond of their old customs and constitutions that they are afraid to make any alterations, tho' apparently for the better." And finally, the first settlers, who lived near the courthouses, would always be able to join with those who were indifferent to prevent change.[35] But of course these first settlers who lived near the courthouse were not necessarily "aristocrats." They would be motivated by personal rather than class interests.

Sometimes the General Assembly would cut off a part of a county and add it to another county to make the courthouse more accessible to the people. In 1753, petitions from Hanover and New Kent urged that part of Hanover be added to New Kent and part of New Kent be added to Hanover. There were also petitions against this accommodation, but they were ineffective in preventing the desired action. Part of King and Queen County was added to Caroline in 1762 because it was more convenient for the inhabitants in the upper end of the county to attend court and musters in Caroline.[36] James City and New Kent also exchanged parts of their respective counties to accommodate their inhabitants at the courthouses. And when division of Amelia was proposed because of inaccessibility of the courthouse, the House recommended that the courthouse be moved to a more convenient location.[37]

Some of the difficulties in making generalizations about restriction of representation can be seen in the division of Surry County. Landon Carter said that he went to hear the debates in the Committee on Propositions for and against division. These, he declared, were, "so confus'd that I could not form any opinion." He decided to await the debates on the floor of the House, as the Committee acted favorably on the petition. Here Carter observed "the most uncommon assertions & contradictions of each other imaginable which being of a piece with what passed in committee I gave my opinion for the division wch was carried by a great majority." In the Council, however, an argument developed over naming the new county, and the bill was thrown out when the House refused to accept the Council's amendments.[38]

A year later, 1753, Surry was divided, but not without considerable internal opposition. Three petitions from the county asking that there be no division were sent to the Committee of Propositions and Grievances. Then followed several petitions favoring a division. The Committee and the House rejected proposals that money belonging to the county be divided according to the number of tithables in each division, and also rejected petitions in opposition to dividing the county. After the bill passed the second reading, however, it was referred to a committee of five, amended, passed, sent to the Council, amended there, and finally passed by the House. The new county was Sussex.[39]

An effort to divide Prince William County in 1755 reveals some of the complexities inherent in the question of representation. The Committee on Propositions and Grievances rejected a petition asking division of the county, but the House reversed the Committee decision and ordered in a bill which it passed and sent to the Council. Landon Carter explained in his diary what occurred. Although there were many valid arguments against a new county—the poverty of the people, the lack of qualified justices of the peace, the way the division was to be made contrary to the petition, and the belief that the only purpose was the increase of burgesses—to Carter's "great astonishment," the bill passed the House by an overwhelming majority. Carter said that he appeared against the bill in the Council, and that the Council killed it.[40] We might argue that "aristocratic" influence defeated a bill which would have increased representation, but the influence had to be exerted in the appointed Council, not in the elected House, for obviously many tidewater members of the House had favored it or it would never have passed.

The move for dividing Prince William did not die in 1755, however, despite Landon Carter's influence with the Council. In 1757, the House again agreed to divide the county, decided that each part was to have an equal number of tithables, and rejected a petition opposing the division.

The bill was defeated on second reading, however, but another petition in 1758 finally received favorable treatment in 1759. It was not uncommon for a first petition to divide a county to be turned down, only to be granted on a subsequent try a short time later.[41]

Sometimes the House would reject one proposition for dividing a county but would accept another one at the same time. This happened in 1752 with the division of Prince George County. Probably the reason for accepting some petitions and rejecting others was the way the division was to be made. Also in 1753, the House accepted one proposition for the division of Amelia County but rejected two other petitions, presumably because they would have divided the county differently.[42]

Often the House would agree to divide some counties and refuse to divide others, indicating that the issue was not just the increase of western burgesses. In 1757, for example, the House approved the division of Fairfax County but turned down a similar proposal for Lunenburg, yet both were relatively frontier counties. At the same time that the House rejected an act to divide Prince William, it agreed to divide Albemarle.[43]

Petitions for division of counties appear to have had the best chance for success if the petitions came from the "upper" or "back" inhabitants, or those who wanted to be separated from the old county. This was natural, for the inhabitants in the old county would not be obligated to help build a courthouse, church, and prison in the new county. Many of the petitions stated that the upper inhabitants desired the division because of the distance from the courthouse, mustering place, and church. That petitions from the upper or back inhabitants had a better chance of success than those from the old county is attested to by the division of Fairfax in 1757. The House rejected one petition for dividing the county, but immediately accepted one from the back inhabitants and proceeded with the division exactly as they desired.[44]

Although petitions for division of counties often came from the upper inhabitants, sometimes even these people opposed a division. Three petitions from the upper end of Cumberland County, or what is now Buckingham County, were sent to Williamsburg in opposition to a petition supposedly presented to take parts of Cumberland and Albemarle and make a new county.[45]

Occasionally the issue of dividing a county got involved with a disputed election and was temporarily sidetracked. This happened in Lunenburg in 1758. Matthew Marrable, who won a burgess seat, was accused of cultivating the votes of the upper inhabitants by agreeing to forfeit £500 if he did not use his utmost efforts to get the county divided. For this, he was thrown out of the House, but in a new election was reelected. When Marrable's petition to divide the county came to Williamsburg, it received favorable action by the Committee on Propositions and Grievances, but the House ordered the committee report re-committed and then rejected it.[46] Eventually a new county was set off in 1764.

Dissenters from the Church of England sometimes opposed the division of a county even though the result would be twice as much representation for the area. The reason was that division would necessitate the support of twice as many Anglican churches and ministers, and dissenters already had their own ministers to care for. This came out in a disputed Hanover election in 1752 when dissenters prevailed on the winning candidates, John Chiswell and John Syme, to sign statements or execute bonds that they would oppose any division of the county.[47] This was the election in which Landon Carter insisted that the voters had a perfect right to demand bonds from candidates to carry out their election promises.

There was bitter internal conflict in Augusta from 1767 to 1770 over division of that county, but again this was on sectional and personal lines *within* the county rather than on class lines or between tidewater and backcountry. The men involved were John Madison and Israel Christian, both former burgesses. Christian wanted a division of the county, Madison opposed, and Madison was willing to use petitions or even an Indian war to prevent the division. This was in 1767; in 1770 the feud was still in progress, as men tried to prevent the election of other men who would divide the county. The accusation was that the outgroup wanted the division so they could be judges, county lieutenants, and burgesses in the new area.[48]

Far from opposing the establishment of western counties, the House acted on the principle that new counties should be established when they were needed. For example, Frederick County petitioned in 1772 to be divided into two or three counties. The House could have rejected the petition or divided the county into two, but instead it rejected a petition to set up two counties and ruled that three counties were reasonable. The Council agreed.[49] This certainly does not indicate a reluctance to establish western counties.

The bill to create Botetourt County contains provisions which indicate that the House considered new western counties as an inevitable necessity and acted on principle rather than mere interest. The House stated that the people in the southern part of Botetourt would be very remote from the courthouse and must necessarily become a separate county as soon as numbers were sufficient. As this would probably happen in a short time, the people in this area were to be exempt from levies in Botetourt to build a courthouse and prison. This was 1769, and by 1772 both the House and Council agreed to divide Botetourt, but the conflict with Britain seems to have prevented the division.[50]

From these examples, then, it is easy to see that the extension of representation through the establishment of new counties was an extremely complicated question that permits no easy answer. There was no simple pattern by which a dominant tidewater attempted to curtail the legislative power of a small-farmer backcountry, since, as we have seen, the colony did not divide along these lines. While there might have been some tidewater "aristocrats" who opposed extension of representation, obviously others were in favor of it. More often than not the opposition to division of counties came from within the counties themselves for various reasons. Doubtless some men acted from individual interests, but these interests are not easily placed in doctrinaire categories.

Although later writers might make much of the fact that some counties were smaller than others and that the large counties, particularly those of the west, were under-represented, the problem does not appear to have been considered important by contemporaries. As Table I in Chapter III indicates, a tidewater county such as Warwick might have few white tithables, but there were other tidewater counties that had more white tithables than many in the piedmont or frontier. To contemporaries, however, there were also other considerations. A county with few whites might have many slaves, and since taxes during most of this period were poll taxes, the counties with large slave populations paid a large share of the taxes. Then, too, people within some of these large western counties, as we have seen, strenuously opposed division of the county because such an action would mean an additional church and minister, a duplication of all county officials to be paid, and the building of a courthouse and jail. These were important considerations at the time, and while today we might deplore inequitable representation in colonial Virginia, we must do so with the full realization that this was not an important problem to the people then.

To the extent that there was any attempt to restrict representation in Virginia, that attempt, as in other colonies, came from the British rather than from an aristocratic colonial government. In 1771, instructions to a new governor, the Earl of Dunmore, prohibited the Governor from assenting to any acts by which the number of the Assembly might be enlarged or diminished, or any regulations made in respect to the Assembly inconsistent with the King's rights. An Order in Council was issued to this effect on February 6, 1771.[51]

As happened elsewhere in the colonies, the British failed in this attempt to restrict representation in Virginia. It was easier for the Privy Council in London to issue an Order than it was for the Governor in Virginia to carry it out. In March, 1773, the Lords of Trade reprimanded Dunmore for consenting to two bills for establishing new counties—one strategically named Dunmore—and thus increasing the size of the House. Dunmore could not be ignorant, said the Lords, that the practice in the colonies of increasing the number of representatives and making other regulations in that respect without the consent of the Crown had been the subject of very serious deliberation in England and had induced the instructions to prevent such acts.[52]

Colonial reactions to British restrictions of representation do not support a tidewater-backcountry interpretation of this issue. William Preston, prominent in the far-western counties, was against the division of Fincastle, which logically is entirely out of character. When he corresponded with Edmund Pendleton about this, Pendleton wrote that there would probably not be any division of counties since the Governor had instructions not to divide a county unless the people would forego the right of representation. Pendleton believed that the people would refuse; and if not, he thought that the Assembly would never consent to having a number of the people separated from the others in so essential a right as that of being represented in the legislature. Two years later, in 1776, a petition from Fincastle professed support for the cause of American freedom and declared that the county desired to be considered part of Virginia despite the base proceedings of a corrupt and wicked ministry to prevent the formation of new counties unless the inhabitants would be so pusillanimous as to give up their right of representation.[53] There was no mention of a corrupt and wicked tidewater aristocracy, and certainly Pendleton's statement does not indicate opposition in the tidewater to increased western representation.

Jefferson, presumably a liberal, manifested about the same reaction to British restriction of representation as that expressed by Edmund Pendleton, presumably a conservative. He condemned the instructions to Dunmore to restrict representation. The colony had no western boundary, Jefferson said, so western counties were of indefinite extent, some many hundred miles from their eastern limits. How could people in these counties attend county court for redress? Did the King believe that the colonists should give up the glorious right of representation and become absolute slaves to the King's sovereign will? Or was the purpose to confine the legislature to its present number so it could be bought off more easily. [54] Again it does not appear that representation was a sectional issue.

About the only evidence of sectional conflict over representation came from Landon Carter, and that came after the Revolution began. The issue was a new tobacco inspection law in 1776 which Carter believed to be the work of upcountry men for placing tobacco warehouses to benefit the upcountry. Carter did not think that this situation could last long, for, said he: "The low-land men can fight against laws that oblige them to be starved as well as upland men can fight for them because they are made to please them. I foretold this effect from the constant dividing back counties long ago." [55] Evidently others in the tidewater had not felt as Carter did, for the back counties had been divided.

In addition to apportionment, a second major problem concerning representation is the social status of the men who were candidates for election as burgesses. It is important to know about the men who ran for office as well as those who were elected, for only then can we ascertain what choice the people had. Unfortunately, many of the election polls have been destroyed or were not recorded, so the historian must content himself with representative examples. We have used Lancaster in the tidewater and Amelia in the piedmont, for samplings in other counties indicate that what was true in these counties was true in others as well.

In general, candidates for election came from the upper half of the property holders, as one would expect in a society in which most men owned property. The candidate might be the wealthiest man in the county, or he might be a man of relatively modest means. Often he was a self-made man who started life in very moderate circumstances and accumulated property with time. It is easy for historians to emphasize candidates from well-known Virginia families; it is much more difficult to identify the numerous men who ran for office but who were not born under affluent circumstances, yet this latter must be done if one would place Virginia politics in proper focus.

Amelia County exhibits all of these various characteristics among its numerous candidates. Thomas Tabb was eventually the wealthiest man in the county with 112 slaves and 11,028 acres of land in 1768. But Tabb, according to the tax records, had held only six tithable slaves in 1742, a number which he increased to thirty by 1749 and 112 by 1768. But the men who ran and won with Tabb were men of much less wealth. Captain Wood Jones, elected in 1752, paid only four tithes in 1742 and forty years later had only nine tithable slaves. Edmund Booker (1758) owned three tithable slaves in 1742 and by 1768 had an overseer, thirteen tithable slaves, and 568 acres of land. David Greenhill (1761) first appeared on the extant tax lists for eight tithables, a number which he increased to nineteen slaves by 1762.[56]

The example of John Scott of Amelia is especially revealing if we would understand colonial politics. Scott, who ran fourth in the election of 1768, was a lawyer who first appeared on the tithable lists as paying one tithe only. By 1768, he had a son, two servants or overseers, eight slaves, and 1,400 acres of land. The 1768 list included only perhaps a fifth of the county, yet in this small area there were thirty-six people who had eight or more slaves and eight who had more than 1,400 acres of land, most of whom never ran for office. As we have shown elsewhere, Scott could command a large number of votes among all classes in this small section of the county, but he was not sufficiently well-known in the county as a whole to win an election. Nevertheless, the poorer people throughout the county could have voted for him had they so desired.

Lancaster County was similar to Amelia: candidates for the House of Burgesses were somewhat above the common run in wealth, but often they were not wealthy men. In 1741, for example, the winners Conway and Mitchell had fourteen and six tithable slaves respectively. The other candidates in the order of their popularity had eight, eleven, sixteen, fifteen, and twenty-six slaves. Mitchell, son of a former burgess who had six slaves, owned nineteen tithable slaves in 1775, but he was more popular with the voters than was Charles Carter who owned over a hundred. In spite of the fact that John Tayloe was a member of the Council for many years, the name Tayloe carried no political magic whatever in Lancaster, for Colonel William Tayloe could never win an election even though he tried for at least twenty years.[57]

These examples of Amelia and Lancaster merely demonstrate that while the voters might elect the wealthiest men in the county, such as Thomas Tabb and Charles Carter, they also elected men of modest fortunes and often selected such men over others who were wealthier. In addition, many men who had more worldly goods than the candidates never ran for office. So the voters had a wide choice, for as we have seen there were usually several candidates from which to choose, sometimes as many as ten in one election.

Governor Spotswood and Edmund Randolph both described Virginia burgesses, but from the available evidence neither appears to have been very accurate. Spotswood characterized the burgesses as "persons of narrow fortunes and mean understandings," while Randolph saw both sectional and class differences—aristocrats from the lower counties selected for fortune, rank, and fashion, and men of humble means from the upper counties.[58] Actually, Thomas Tabb of Amelia; William Cabell, Jr., of Amherst who had 100 slaves by 1780; Washington and George William Fairfax from Frederick; William Preston of Augusta, who paid taxes on 6,485 acres and fourteen tithables in 1769; Walter Coles of Halifax, with thirty tithable slaves and much real estate; and Nathaniel Terry of Halifax who sold more than 15,000 acres of land—these were not much different from tidewater burgesses.[59]

The general impression that one gets by studying the records over the eighteenth century is that, with almost no exceptions, the people chose men above the average in economic and social status for their representatives.[60] Perhaps in a country where economic opportunity was so prevalent and where poor men could acquire land and slaves, the successful men inspired more confidence in politics than did the unsuccessful. Nowhere in the records could we find evidence that artisans desired to elect an ordinary artisan or that overseers wanted an overseer to represent them. Most artisans, many overseers, and most small planters had ample qualifications for the office and could have stood for election had they so desired. But the fact remains they did not do so and there is no evidence of popular demand that they should.

A third important question about representation is the number of men who served in the House of Burgesses during the years prior to the Revolution and their length of service. Did they hold office by "hereditary" right over long periods of years and then pass their offices on to their sons, so that only a few families dominated the House? Or did representatives serve for short terms and reflect the political influence of a large number of families?

Table I is a summary of a more extensive chart on which were plotted the terms of office of all burgesses who were elected in the eighteen general elections and many by-elections to fill vacancies during the twenty-nine years from 1752 to 1781. Certain difficulties are obvious— the confusion caused by the number of men with the same family names, such as Jones, Smith, and Taylor, and the use of *Jr.* and *Sr.* in cases of

TABLE I.   ANALYSIS OF VIRGINIA REPRESENTATIVES, 1752–1781[61]

| County | No. of Elections | No. of Individuals | No. of Families | Number of Terms Served by Individual Burgesses | | | | | | | | | | | | | | | | | No. Not Serving Consecutive Terms | No. Elected Both Before and After March 1775 |
|---|---|---|---|---|---|---|---|---|---|---|---|---|---|---|---|---|---|---|---|---|---|---|
| | | | | 1 | 2 | 3 | 4 | 5 | .6 | 7 | 8 | .9 | 10 | 11 | 12 | 13 | 14 | 15 | 16 | 17 | | |
| **TIDEWATER** | | | | | | | | | | | | | | | | | | | | | | |
| Accomack | 16 | 11 | 11 | 4 | 2 | 2 | 1 | 1 | — | — | 1 | — | — | — | — | — | — | — | — | — | 3 | 3 |
| Caroline | 18 | 11 | 9 | 4 | 3 | 2 | — | — | — | 1 | — | — | — | — | — | — | 1 | — | 1 | — | 3 | 2 |
| Charles City | 18 | 7 | 5 | 2 | 2 | 1 | 1 | — | — | 1 | — | — | — | 1 | — | — | — | — | — | — | 1 | 2 |
| Elizabeth City | 18 | 12 | 10 | 3 | 5 | — | 1 | 1 | 1 | — | — | — | — | — | 1 | — | — | — | — | — | 4 | 4 |
| Essex | 18 | 12 | 8 | 3 | 4 | 1 | 1 | — | — | 2 | 1 | — | — | — | — | — | — | — | — | — | 2 | 3 |
| Fairfax | 18 | 11 | 8 | 4 | 2 | 1 | 1 | 1 | 1 | — | — | — | — | — | — | — | 1 | — | — | — | 2 | 3 |
| Gloucester | 18 | 9 | 6 | 4 | 1 | 3 | — | — | — | — | 1 | — | — | — | — | — | — | — | — | — | 2 | 2 |
| Isle of Wight | 18 | 12 | 10 | 3 | 3 | 3 | 1 | 1 | 1 | 1 | — | — | 1 | — | — | — | — | — | — | — | — | 1 |
| James City | 18 | 9 | 7 | 4 | 3 | 1 | — | — | — | — | 1 | — | — | — | — | — | — | — | — | — | — | 1 |
| Jamestown | 13 | 4 | 2 | 2 | — | — | 2 | 1 | — | — | — | — | — | — | — | — | — | 1 | — | — | — | — |
| King & Queen | 18 | 13 | 12 | 4 | 4 | 1 | 2 | 1 | 1 | 2 | 1 | — | 1 | — | — | — | — | — | — | — | 3 | 1 |
| King George | 18 | 12 | 10 | 6 | 2 | — | 1 | — | 1 | 1 | — | 1 | — | — | — | — | — | — | — | — | 2 | 3 |
| King William | 18 | 14 | 11 | 5 | 6 | — | 2 | 2 | — | — | 1 | — | — | 1 | — | — | — | — | — | — | 3 | 2 |
| Lancaster | 18 | 16 | 10 | 9 | 2 | 1 | 2 | 1 | 1 | — | — | — | 1 | — | — | — | — | — | — | — | 3 | 2 |
| Middlesex | 18 | 12 | 12 | 4 | 3 | 2 | — | 1 | — | — | — | 1 | — | — | 1 | — | — | — | — | — | 3 | 3 |
| Nansemond | 18 | 11 | 8 | 5 | 2 | 1 | — | — | 1 | 1 | 1 | — | — | 1 | — | — | — | — | — | — | 3 | 3 |
| Norfolk | 18 | 14 | 12 | 4 | 3 | 2 | 1 | 2 | — | 1 | — | — | 1 | — | — | — | — | — | — | — | 2 | 2 |
| Norfolk Borough | 18 | 5 | 4 | 1 | — | — | 2 | — | — | — | — | — | — | — | — | — | — | — | — | — | — | 3 |
| Northampton | 17 | 16 | 14 | 7 | 2 | 5 | 2 | 1 | 2 | 1 | 1 | — | — | 1 | — | — | — | — | — | — | 1 | 2 |
| New Kent | 18 | 12 | 11 | 4 | 2 | 1 | — | — | 1 | 1 | 1 | — | — | — | — | — | — | — | — | — | 5 | 1 |
| Northumberland | 18 | 16 | 11 | 9 | 3 | 3 | 2 | — | — | — | — | 1 | — | — | — | — | — | — | — | — | — | 4 |
| Prince George | 18 | 9 | 8 | 3 | 1 | 2 | — | 2 | 1 | — | 1 | — | — | — | 1 | — | — | — | — | — | 1 | 2 |
| Prince William | 18 | 13 | 12 | 5 | 3 | 1 | 2 | — | 1 | 1 | — | — | 1 | — | — | 1 | — | — | — | — | — | 2 |
| Princess Anne | 18 | 10 | 9 | 3 | 2 | 1 | 1 | — | 2 | 1 | — | — | — | — | — | — | — | — | — | — | 4 | 2 |
| Richmond | 18 | 11 | 10 | 2 | 4 | — | — | 2 | 2 | 1 | 1 | — | — | — | — | — | — | — | — | — | 3 | 2 |
| Stafford | 18 | 10 | 10 | 3 | 1 | 2 | 2 | 1 | — | — | — | 1 | — | 1 | 1 | — | — | — | — | — | 5 | 2 |
| Surry | 18 | 15 | 11 | 9 | 1 | — | — | 1 | — | — | — | 1 | — | — | — | — | — | — | — | — | 1 | 4 |
| Warwick | 18 | 9 | 6 | 3 | 1 | — | 1 | — | — | — | — | 1 | — | — | — | — | 2 | — | — | — | 1 | 2 |
| Westmoreland | 18 | 8 | 5 | 4 | — | 2 | 1 | — | 1 | — | — | — | 1 | — | — | — | — | — | — | — | 2 | 2 |
| William & Mary | 10 | 6 | 4 | 2 | 3 | — | 1 | 1 | — | — | — | 1 | — | — | — | — | — | — | 1 | 1 | — | 1 |
| Williamsburg | 18 | 7 | 7 | 4 | 4 | — | — | 1 | — | — | — | 1 | — | — | — | — | — | — | — | — | 1 | 1 |
| York | 18 | 10 | 7 | 4 | 4 | — | — | — | — | — | — | — | — | — | — | 2 | 2 | — | — | — | — | 2 |
| **TOTAL** | | 136 | | 136 | 74 | 34 | 27 | 15 | 14 | 14 | 8 | 5 | 6 | 3 | 4 | 3 | 2 | 1 | 1 | 1 | 67 | 73 |

| | C1 | C2 | C3 | C4 | C5 | C6 | C7 | C8 | C9 | C10 | C11 | C12 | C13 | C14 | C15 | C16 | C17 | C18 | | |
|---|---|---|---|---|---|---|---|---|---|---|---|---|---|---|---|---|---|---|---|---|
| **PIEDMONT** | | | | | | | | | | | | | | | | | | | | |
| Albemarle | 18 | 16 | 11 | 8 | 3 | 2 | 1 | — | 1 | — | — | — | — | — | — | — | — | — | 3 | 3 |
| Amelia | 18 | 12 | 8 | 5 | 2 | 1 | 1 | 1 | — | — | — | — | — | — | — | — | — | — | 2 | 2 |
| Amherst | 15 | 7 | 4 | 1 | 2 | 2 | — | — | 1 | — | — | — | — | — | — | — | — | — | 2 | 2 |
| Bedford | 18 | 9 | 8 | 5 | — | 2 | — | — | — | — | — | 1 | — | — | — | — | — | — | 2 | 2 |
| Brunswick | 18 | 14 | 13 | 7 | 2 | 1 | 1 | 1 | — | — | — | — | — | — | — | — | — | — | 1 | 1 |
| Buckingham | 15 | 14 | 12 | 7 | 1 | 1 | 1 | — | 1 | — | — | — | — | — | — | — | — | — | 3 | 3 |
| Charlotte | 14 | 12 | 8 | 6 | 3 | — | — | — | — | — | — | — | — | — | — | — | — | — | 2 | 2 |
| Chesterfield | 18 | 12 | 12 | 5 | 4 | — | — | — | — | — | — | — | — | — | — | — | — | — | 5 | 3 |
| Culpeper | 18 | 13 | 10 | 5 | 4 | 2 | 1 | — | 2 | 1 | — | — | 1 | — | — | — | — | — | 4 | 3 |
| Cumberland | 18 | 10 | 7 | 2 | 2 | 1 | 1 | — | 1 | — | — | — | — | — | — | — | — | — | 5 | 3 |
| Dinwiddie | 18 | 10 | 8 | 2 | 2 | — | — | — | 1 | — | — | — | — | — | — | — | — | — | 5 | 2 |
| Fauquier | 15 | 6 | 6 | 4 | 2 | — | 1 | — | — | — | — | — | — | — | — | — | — | — | — | 3 |
| Goochland | 18 | 11 | 10 | 6 | 4 | 1 | 1 | 1 | 1 | — | — | — | 1 | — | 1 | — | — | — | 3 | 3 |
| Halifax | 18 | 13 | 11 | 7 | 4 | — | 1 | — | — | — | — | — | — | — | — | — | — | — | 3 | 3 |
| Hanover | 18 | 14 | 13 | 3 | 1 | 1 | — | 2 | — | 2 | — | — | — | — | — | — | — | — | 5 | 3 |
| Henrico | 18 | 10 | 8 | 1 | 1 | 1 | — | — | — | — | — | — | — | — | — | — | — | — | 2 | 2 |
| Loudoun | 16 | 6 | 6 | 5 | 1 | — | 1 | 1 | 1 | 1 | — | 2 | — | 1 | 1 | — | — | — | 2 | 3 |
| Louisa | 18 | 12 | 10 | 6 | 2 | 2 | 1 | 1 | 1 | — | — | — | — | — | — | — | — | — | 3 | 3 |
| Lunenburg | 18 | 17 | 16 | 1 | 5 | 1 | 1 | 1 | 1 | — | — | — | — | — | — | — | — | — | 7 | 1 |
| Mecklenburg | 14 | 8 | 7 | 2 | 3 | — | 1 | 1 | — | — | — | — | — | — | — | — | — | — | 3 | 4 |
| Orange | 18 | 11 | 10 | 1 | 4 | — | 1 | 1 | 1 | — | — | — | — | — | — | — | — | — | 3 | 2 |
| Pittsylvania | 12 | 8 | 8 | 8 | 2 | 3 | — | — | 1 | — | — | — | 1 | — | — | — | — | — | 2 | 2 |
| Prince Edward | 18 | 14 | 13 | 4 | 3 | 1 | — | — | — | — | — | — | — | — | — | — | — | — | 5 | 2 |
| Southampton | 18 | 10 | 6 | 3 | 3 | 1 | — | — | 1 | — | — | 1 | — | — | 1 | — | — | — | 3 | 2 |
| Spotsylvania | 18 | 13 | 11 | 5 | 1 | 4 | 1 | — | 1 | — | — | — | — | 1 | — | — | — | — | 2 | 2 |
| Sussex | 18 | 9 | 9 | 3 | 2 | — | 1 | — | 1 | — | — | 1 | — | — | — | 1 | — | — | 1 | 1 |
| **TOTAL** | 105 | 55 | 47 | 23 | 12 | 10 | 12 | 5 | 3 | 9 | 4 | 3 | 2 | — | 1 | — | — | — | 73 | 65 |
| **FRONTIER** | | | | | | | | | | | | | | | | | | | | |
| Augusta | 18 | 16 | 15 | 6 | 3 | 3 | 1 | — | 1 | 1 | 1 | 1 | — | — | — | — | — | — | 2 | 1 |
| Berkeley | 11 | 8 | 7 | 2 | 3 | 1 | — | 1 | 1 | — | — | — | — | — | — | — | — | — | 2 | 2 |
| Botetourt | 12 | 8 | 8 | 4 | 1 | — | 1 | — | — | — | 1 | — | — | — | — | — | — | — | 1 | 2 |
| Dunmore | 8 | 6 | 6 | 1 | — | 2 | 1 | 2 | — | — | — | — | — | — | — | — | — | — | 2 | 1 |
| Fincastle | 6 | 5 | 5 | 1 | 3 | 2 | 1 | 1 | 1 | — | — | — | — | — | — | — | — | — | — | 2 |
| Frederick | 18 | 14 | 14 | 8 | 1 | — | 1 | 1 | 1 | 1 | 1 | 1 | — | — | — | 1 | — | — | 2 | 2 |
| Hampshire | 18 | 12 | 11 | 6 | 3 | 2 | — | — | 1 | — | — | — | — | — | — | — | — | — | 2 | 3 |
| **TOTAL** | 28 | 16 | 8 | 4 | 2 | 2 | 2 | — | 1 | — | — | — | — | — | — | — | — | — | 12 | 13 |
| **GRAND TOTAL** | 707* | 592 | 269 | 145 | 89 | 54 | 31 | 26 | 28 | 15 | 9 | 16 | 8 | 7 | 5 | 2 | 1 | 1 | 152 | 151 |

\* This number includes the second election of 32 men (that is, those elected first in one county and later in another) and the triple county service of two more. Thus the actual number of individuals serving in all the counties would be 671 men.

doubtful reference—but these are minor difficulties and do not greatly affect the validity of the table.

Although a few men were able to hold office over long periods of time, as is still true today, long tenure in office was not typical. This twenty-seven-year period witnessed 671 different burgesses representing 592 different family names, the average service was 3.14 terms, and the average length of each term was 1.6 years. Of these men, 637 represented one county only, thirty-two were elected from two different counties or towns, and two served three different counties. Over half the burgesses (58.8 per cent) were elected only once, while 71.7 per cent were chosen for three terms or less. In addition, 152 of the men who were re-elected did not serve consecutive terms, a reflection in part of the heated political contests that occurred. And a large number of men, 151, were in office both before and after the Revolution started, an indication that internal revolution was not very significant in the Old Dominion.

It was the usual pattern in all sections that one or two burgesses in the county held office for longer terms, while others were unable to win sufficient popular support to stay in the House. For example, Thomas Jefferson was elected ten times in Albemarle County, but the majority of men there were chosen for only one or two terms. During the ten periods in which Jefferson served, his running mates included five different men. This pattern seems to have prevailed in most of the counties.

Among the small minority who were elected for ten terms or more, some had lengthy records of public service. Richard Lee of Westmoreland had the longest stay in the House during this period—seventeen consecutive terms—and in fact he continued to serve every year until 1790. Benjamin Harrison of Charles City was a close second with sixteen, although these were broken by his attendance in the Continental Congress in 1775 and after 1781 by his election as Governor. In the western county of Bedford, John Talbot served fifteen consecutive terms. And two men served fourteen times—Richard Bland of Prince George, who was in the House consecutively until his death late in 1776, and ex-apprentice Edmund Pendleton of Caroline, whose steady record was broken by other public duties.

Among those burgesses who went on to the Senate were a few with even longer terms of service. The record seems to be held by Burwell Bassett of New Kent County, who completed eight terms in the House between 1761 and 1775 and went on to serve in the Senate continuously from 1777 to 1805. Archibald Cary of Chesterfield County and Henry Lee of Prince William County were in either the House or Senate from 1756 to 1787. Others who served long periods in the House and Senate were Robert Rutherford of Berkeley (1772 to 1791), William Cabell of Albemarle and Amherst (1756 to 1781), and Richard Adams of New Kent and Henrico (1752 to 1778).

If the burgesses who were elected for long terms of office exerted more political power than did others who were in the House for brief periods only—and some of them undoubtedly did exert such power—it should not be forgotten that these men held their positions because they were elected by the people, not because they had "hereditary" rights to office, and could have been retired to private life at any time by the voters. Neither long tenure in office nor the power exerted by a man once elected is any measure of "aristocracy." The only issue at stake is how a man was elected and retained in office, and in Virginia this was done by democratic processes.

A fourth factor in representation is the importance of family relationships in Virginia politics—a factor emphasized in the past but difficult to assess.[62] That some family influence existed there can be little doubt, but how to determine the extent and direction is another matter. When we take each county or borough as a separate unit and calculate the number of different family names in each, then add them all together, there were 592 different family names in the House during those twenty-nine years. Figured on the basis of the colony as a whole, not county by county, men with 379 different family names were burgesses. Having said this, however, one faces the impossible task of determining whether men with the same name were related, and if related, whether they had the same political philosophies.

There are also other obstacles to asserting the importance of family relationships in politics. A counting of heads does not account for marriage ties and whether those with such ties thought alike. Then there is the question of whether family importance can be measured by numbers. Among the burgesses were five Robinsons, one Wythe, five Pendletons, five Washingtons, one Fairfax, one Spotswood, six Claibornes, three Henrys, one Byrd, four Cabells, five Harrisons, nine Carters, three Madisons, two Jeffersons, six Balls, eight Lees, ten Jones, ten Taylors, and eleven Smiths. Were the ten Jones or ten Taylors twice as important as the five Robinsons or five Washingtons, and were the eleven Smiths eleven times as influential as the one Wythe, Byrd, or Fairfax? And were all the Jones equal to each other?

Two examples among the many available must suffice to illustrate the danger of assuming unity of purpose among men with the same family name. In the Lancaster election of 1741, three Balls—Joseph Ball, Esquire, Major Ball, and Colonel William Ball—were all burgess candidates. Had they agreed on one Ball as candidate, and had they been able to influence their supporters to vote for him, they could have elected him. As it was, the three Balls ran fifth, sixth, and seventh on the poll. Only eight voters cast both their votes for two Balls, and the only two Balls who voted supported Major Ball and Edwin Conway.[63] In 1758, Alexander White of King William expressed fear over the concentration of power in the hands of John Robinson, who was both speaker and treasurer. As a safeguard for the independence of the legislature and the liberty of the subject, he believed that a county should change representatives occasionally, so he was pleased that King William was sending Peter Robinson and Harry Gaines in place of incumbents Bernard Moore and Francis West.[64] White obviously felt that the way to guard against the excessive influence of John Robinson was to elect another Robinson, Peter.

From the above evidence, it is clear that the historian who insists on family influence in Virginia politics should document that influence very carefully. It is not enough merely to assert or to assume that men with the same names or from the same families acted in concert in politics.

A fifth element for an understanding of representation is the fact that men of the upper classes were by no means unified on policy. When Landon Carter entered the House of Burgesses in 1752 after sixteen years of effort to get elected, he found Carter Burwell the most influential man in the House. Landon Carter, also of the upper class, deplored this situation and hinted at the development of another influence to offset Burwell.[65] In Halifax County, Nathaniel Terry defeated incumbent Walter Coles, who then accused Terry, a former sheriff, of making false entries in the under-sheriff's books and of stealing a horse. In a new election, both rivals were elected, a not unusual event in Virginia politics, and carried their fight into the House.[66] In that body, some members disciplined others for disobeying House rules, even to the extent of expelling them and forever barring them from the House. This happened, for example, to William Clinch of Surry County in 1756 when Clinch forced his creditors, John Ruffin and son, to cancel a debt at gunpoint, and it happened also to William Ball of Lancaster for knowingly passing counterfeit money.[67] Almost every election, in fact, revealed serious rifts among men of the upper classes, and judging by the measures adopted, these rifts were much deeper than mere passing differences.

The most important question concerning representation, however, is whether burgesses, whatever their wealth or social position, represented the people in general or were merely spokesmen for the upper classes. Was the House of Burgesses an exclusive club for the aristocracy, or did the people have it in their power to make their wishes felt?

One of the most democratic features of Virginia government, and one that insured a hearing for the people before the legislature, was the use of petitions. Of the six large standing House committees—Elections, Propositions and Grievances, Public Claims, Courts of Justice, Trade, and Religion—the Propositions and Grievances Committee was undoubtedly the most important from the standpoint of democracy, although the Committee on Elections was also significant. This committee heard grievances against old laws and proposals for new ones, and the system was regularized by 1705 so that *all* petitions got to the legislature and had to be heard and acted upon. County courts certified petitions to the General Assembly; and when they reached the House, that body voted on whether to reject the petitions or send them to the committee. On receiving a petition, the committee then made a decision, but that decision again had to be referred to the House for final action.[68]

Nothing in our legislative system today approximates the direct influence which the people of colonial Virginia could exert on their legislature. As the House said, its bills were "chiefly founded upon the Grievances and Propositions of the people" whom they represented. No man or group of men could stifle these petitions in committee, as often happens today, and the frequency with which the House reversed decisions of its standing committees indicates that men could not determine legislation by holding important positions on committees. Petitions also provided a means by which the House could get public reaction on a proposed controversial measure. A controversial bill, printed and distributed for an expression of public opinion, was sure to elicit many responses. For example, a bill to establish circuit courts was favored by county petitions, the petitions were rejected by the Committee on Propositions and Grievances, but the House reversed the committee.[69]

The House of Burgesses went to great lengths to safeguard the democratic right to petition. When justices in New Kent County refused to certify petitions, the House ordered them to appear for an apology and reprimand. Some did so and paid fines, but others refused and were voted as guilty of high misdemeanor and contempt. Governor Spotswood, engaged at the time in a bitter controversy with the House, refused to arrest the offending justices, but the House could always bar such men from its membership. The Governor, acting because he believed that the House was attempting to dominate appointed officials, claimed that petitions from the people reached the House even though justices refused to certify them. He said that the House held the doctrine that no courts could question the truth or reasonableness of these petitions and that justices were bound to certify them to the Assembly.[70]

The petition controversy between the House and Governor also resulted in a great deal of evidence to the effect that the burgesses represented the will of the people, not that of an upper class. Spotswood accused the burgesses of demonstrating their contempt for the King by refusing adequate support for his government, persecuting the King's justices of the peace, ordering the attorney-general to prosecute, censuring a proclamation by the Governor and Council, defrauding the King of his quitrents, imposing rules on the King for calling Assemblies, excluding from the Assembly those who were devoted to the King's service, and expelling the only burgess who held a seat by virtue of a charter from the King. Having assured the Governor of their desire to cooperate with him, they had done everything in their power to thwart him. Why? Said the Governor: "The true interest of your country, is not what you have troubled your heads about; all your proceedings have been calculated to answer the notions of the ignorant populace; And if you can excuse your selves to them, you matter not how you stand before God, your Prince, and all judicious men, or before any others to whom, you think, you owe not your elections." The Governor admitted that the House was almost unanimous in carrying out the wishes of the people, as only five or six gentlemen had objected to its proceedings.[71]

To Spotswood there was simply no question but that the burgesses represented their constituents, and these constituents were the people, not the rich. The bulk of the electors were "the meaner sort of people" who elected "men of their own stamp." These latter, in turn, would use any means to get elected, while "gentlemen of better understanding and more plentiful estates . . . despis'd making their court to the populace by such vile practices," and except in one or two counties were defeated as a result. The "mobish candidates" always outbid the gentlemen of sense and principles, Spotswood continued, and some of them had so little shame as to declare publicly "that if, in Assembly, any thing should be propos'd w'ch they judg'd might be disagreeable to their constituents, they would oppose it, tho' they knew in their consciences y't it would be for ye good of the country."[72]

Justices seldom had the temerity to block a petition, but on the few occasions when they did they found themselves at odds with the House and with no Spotswood to defend them. For example, Richard Blackburn presented a petition for a town at Occoquan Ferry in Prince William County, and another petition was presented for a town at Quantico Creek. The county justices, including Valentine Peyton, a county burgess, refused to receive and certify these petitions and gave no reason for their actions. The Committee resolved that the justices had acted illegally, arbitrarily, and contrary to the rights of the people. Burgess Peyton had to apologize to the House, and the other justices had to come all the way from Prince William to do likewise. A similar situation occurred in Northumberland County in 1745. Again the House branded the action of the justices as illegal, arbitrary, and contrary to the rights of the people, and then ordered the justices to appear before the House to apologize.[73]

Ordinarily the House acted favorably on petitions for the general good. We might suspect otherwise, however, if we took only a Spotsylvania petition of 1770 as evidence. The people complained that the courthouse was in one corner of the county some thirty-six miles away from many inhabitants, and they asked that it be changed to a central location. Their petition was thrown out, but it was thrown out because the law required that petitions be signed and this one was not. Two years later there were signed petitions both for and against moving the courthouse, but this time the House accepted the petition to move it. Then the House sent a message to the Governor, since only the Governor could change the location of the courthouse, urging that as the courthouse was built at the expense of all the people, it should be convenient to all the people for musters and for the administration of justice. Poor people could then go to the court and return home the same day, whereas now they had to be at the expense of remaining overnight.[74]

A survey of the petitions presented to the House fails to reveal any class or sectional favoritism. The House accepted propositions for quarterly instead of monthly courts from Brunswick, Lunenburg, Frederick, Albemarle, and Augusta counties, but rejected similar petitions from

Surry, Accomack, and Goochland. It allowed some petitions for establishing ferries but refused others, even from gentlemen William Taliaferro, Thomas Mann Randolph, and Benjamin Grymes, the last a burgess. William Byrd and Philip Ludwell Lee, Esquires and members of the Council, did not have sufficient influence to get tobacco warehouses built on their lands, and the House also turned down proposals for higher salaries for sheriffs and ministers.[75]

In addition to honoring petitions from the people, the House also attempted to carry out the will of the people on the issue of moving the capital from Williamsburg to a more convenient location, even though the tidewater counties outnumbered those of the piedmont at the time. When the capital buildings in Williamsburg burned in 1747, a "great majority" in the House and two-thirds of the "common planters" favored moving the capital to a more convenient location. A bill to effect the move passed the House but failed by a tie vote in the Council, a fact which greatly irritated the House. A second bill passed the House 44-34 in 1752, but again the Council killed it. Edwin Conway, burgess from tidewater Lancaster, complained that moving the capital westward fifty miles to aid western inhabitants would impose hardships on eastern men, but a majority of the House did not agree, and many who voted for the move had to be from the tidewater.[76]

Despite two previous failures, the House made a third attempt to move the capital in 1761—an attempt, according to Governor Fauquier, designed to win popularity just before an election. A large majority of the House favored the change but could not agree on a new location. It did not matter, however, for as Fauquier said, the Council, whose members lived near Williamsburg, could always be depended on to block the move.[77] In all probability, failure to change the location of the capital to aid western representatives was a factor in the passage of the representation law of 1762. This law provided that salaries and travel expenses of burgesses would be paid by the colonial treasury rather than the individual counties. This bill was disallowed, and the capital was not moved to Richmond until the Revolution ended the influence of an appointed Governor and Council.

Contemporaries provide additional evidence that elected representatives were in fact carrying out the collective will of their constituents. Governor Gooch once asserted that "the sentiments of the people are best known from their representatives."[78] Richard Henry Lee, who desired an appointment to the Council, noted that he had many reasons against "continuing a *popular* Candidate any longer."[79] In Accomack County the people, alarmed over the appointment of three county justices, petitioned the Governor and Council for redress. Their burgess, Southy Simpson, one of the committee to present the petition, was accused of prejudicing the people against the three justices to get himself elected. Simpson replied that if the road to popularity was to act against the wishes of the people, it was a road he would never travel.[80] Simpson had served since 1761 and continued to win elections until 1777. Landon Carter once accused a burgess of opposing a bill only to please the humors of the plebeians. On another occasion he said that burgesses who favored a certain bill were "bent upon pleasing their constituents." When out of the House, some of them talked against the bill, but they voted for it on every motion in the House.[81]

That the people were considered fundamental in Virginia politics is attested by a debate which took place in the House in 1754. The question was "whether a representative was obliged to follow the directions of his constituents against his own reason & conscience or to be governed by his conscience." Those who argued that a representative was bound to follow the directions of his constituents maintained that representative institutions were designed to avoid the confusion of the multitude. The representative was to collect the sentiments of his constituents and do whatever the majority decided. "Thus argued the favourers of popularity who were all headed by the speaker [John Robinson]," said Landon Carter, "for these were very nearly his own words." Opponents argued that when the issue concerned only the representative's constituents he was bound to vote as they dictated, but when the whole community was concerned the representative must use his own judgment in consulting the welfare of all. He should assume that his constituents would be sufficiently intelligent to be influenced by arguments that benefited everyone, not just the few.[82]

The debate was apparently never resolved except as each burgess applied the arguments to his own political fortunes, but Carter's report does raise an interesting question about Speaker John Robinson and his attitude toward democracy. Robinson, one of the wealthiest men in the colony, has been depicted as the very essence of aristocracy, yet here we have him catalogued as one of the favorers of popularity and advocating that burgesses must vote the will of their constituents. Perhaps the contradiction lies in our own failure to assess correctly Robinson's position in Virginia society. Whether in spite of his wealth or because of it, Governor Francis Fauquier characterized Robinson in 1758 as "the most popular man in the country; beloved by the gentlemen, and the idol of the people." On another occasion the Governor called Robinson "the darling of the country, as he well deserves to be for his great integrity, assiduity, and ability in business." [83] If Robinson believed as Carter said, it is little wonder that he was the idol of the people and the darling of the country, even though it might seem strange that he was beloved by the gentlemen.

The influence of the people and the extent to which the "aristocracy" had to consider the will of the people is evident in a satirical play on Virginia politics. *The Candidates*, written about 1770 by Robert Munford, a burgess from Mecklenburg County, depicts the campaigning before an election. The old burgesses were Worthy and Wou'dbe, but Worthy's decision not to run again brought out candidates Sir John Toddy, Mr. Strutabout, and Mr. Smallhopes, none of them considered an adequate running mate by Wou'dbe. In the end, Worthy decided to come out of retirement and he and Wou'dbe were elected. This is the play that has been considered by some historians as the epitome of the expression of aristocratic control in Virginia—as showing that "in every county the wealth and social position held by one or two families gave the *Worthys* such an overwhelming 'interest' at the polls that their political power was, in effect, hereditary and was accepted by all classes of Virginians as partaking of something akin to divine right."[84]

Actually, the play shows how dependent the candidate was on the people. For example, note the following statement by Wou'dbe which we have quoted previously: "Must I again be subject to the humours of a fickle croud? Must I again resign my reason, and be nought but what each voter pleases? Must I cajole, fawn, and wheedle, for a place that brings so little profit?" The freeholders then proceeded to grill Wou'dbe about the issues of the day—high taxes, lower price of rum, lower ferry rates for people across the river to attend church, and the tobacco law. Wou'dbe must commit himself on these issues so the people knew exactly where he stood. By refusing to support the candidacy of Sir John Toddy, Wou'dbe felt that he had lost the support of Toddy and his friend Guzzle. But he consoled himself with the thought that these two did not have enough interest among the people to make their loss a serious one. In fact, Wou'dbe believed that friendship with Toddy and Guzzle would discredit him with the people, for "the people of Virginia," he said, "have too much sense not to perceive how weak the head must be that is always filled with liquor." As he prepared to meet the freeholders at a barbecue, Wou'dbe soliloquized: "I find, in order to secure a seat in our august senate, 'tis necessary a man should either be a slave or a fool; a slave to the people, for the privilege of serving them, and a fool himself, for thus begging a troublesome and expensive employment."[85] Nowhere in the play is there evidence of an hereditary "aristocracy" that virtually held office by divine right.

That the candidates felt decided dependence upon the people is also clearly spelled out in a ballad published in the *Virginia Gazette* in 1768:[86]

> Hail glorious time
> Fit subject for rhyme,
> That every distinction can level.
> When the Gentleman greets
> Each blackguard he meets
> And pride must descend to be civil.
>
> The elegant Peer
> Must guzzle strong beer
> With freemen to gain their protection.
> And all who aspire
> To be Knights of the Shire
> Get drunk to secure their election.

How fervent the zeal
That candidates feel!
The friendship they vow how sincere!
But 'tis easy to guess,
When such zeal they profess,
That the time of election draws near.

By flattering and treating,
At every meeting,
With the voters they try to prevail;
No words can describe
How they promise and bribe,
Such eloquence never can fail.

As the Revolution neared, observers acknowledged that in order to win elections the candidate must have the same view on the British question as the people. Bryan Fairfax had been proposed as a candidate for burgess to serve with George Washington in 1774. Fairfax declined, however, first on the ground that his views on petitioning rather than threatening Britain were not generally popular and secondly because it would be too expensive from a personal standpoint for him at that time.[87] Attorney-General John Randolph, brother of House speaker Peyton Randolph and pro-British critic of his fellow Virginians, deplored the state of affairs just before the Revolution. Those who ran the race of popularity, he said, while they were the greatest sticklers for the liberty of others, were themselves the most abject slaves of politics. They had no opinion of their own, but were "the echo of the people." The people, he believed, could raise or pull down a man at will.[88] Landon Carter, as we have seen elsewhere, could confirm this only too well through his own political experience.

It is in the light of Randolph's statement that we must evaluate the unanimous and near-unanimous elections of many "aristocrats" as the opposition to British measures increased in intensity. Far from desiring to rid themselves of their "aristocratic overlords," the people elected them to office with greater enthusiasm than ever as long as these men did what the people wanted. At the same time that John Randolph was bitterly denouncing fickle popularity at the polls and was preparing to go into exile as a loyalist, his brother Peyton was winning unanimous elections as representative of Williamsburg. In 1774, the town expressed its appreciation to Randolph for his great attention to the people's interests. Condemning the old practice of treating the voters and desiring to abolish every appearance of venality, "that only poison which can infect our happy constitution," the town decided that it would reverse the usual procedure and treat the candidate as full proof that Randolph's merit alone had secured the unbought suffrages of a free people.[89]

Other "aristocrats" also found the road to political success equally easy as far as the votes of the people were concerned. Washington's election expenses dropped from nearly £40 in 1758 to £3.14.9 in 1774.[90] In

Amherst, the old burgesses, William Cabell and Cornelius Thomas, were chosen in 1769 "by the view & consent of the people without polling there being no opposition," and in 1774, William and Joseph Cabell were also elected without opposition.[91] Hampshire unanimously selected James Mercer and Abraham Hite in 1769 on the assumption that their future actions would conform with their past ones. Prince George sent Richard Bland and Peter Poythress, New Kent elected its old representatives Burwell Bassett and Bartholomew Dandridge, James City County sent treasurer Robert Carter Nicholas, and so it went. As the editor of the *Gazette* said, there was so much other important news to print that he could not include all the numerous examples of representatives who were elected by the unanimous approval of their constituents, and that statement will have to suffice for us, too.[92]

Finally, there is the long statement by Richard Henry Lee, quoted in the early pages of this chapter, in which Lee condemned the extent to which the British controlled the government of Virginia but spoke of the House of Burgesses as "the democratic part of our legislature."[93] Lee, often included among the "radicals" by historians of the Revolution, did not give any indication whatever of internal complaint about the way in which members of the House were chosen, about their social status, or about their apportionment among the counties: to him, the House was "democratic."

Representation, then, was either not a grievance or such a minor one that it cannot be considered as a major area for internal conflict. It is true that some counties had larger populations than others, which made for inequitable representation just as it does today in the United States Senate and in most states where representation is not equally proportioned. But apparently the people in general did not consider themselves discriminated against. Except for Landon Carter, there was no evidence to indicate a fear on the part of the tidewater of creating new counties and thus being outvoted by the backcountry. Nor can we conclude that the people were not adequately represented. They had the choice. They could elect one of their own status if they so desired, but they almost invariably preferred a man from the middle or upper social and economic strata. The evidence also shows that the representatives came from many families, and generally served only one or two terms. They were not a close-knit group representing only a few "aristocratic" families which "ruled" by heredity or something akin to divine right. The people chose them, they could readily get rid of them at the next election, and the representatives were well aware of this. And because of the system of petitions, popular views did reach the legislature and all evidence points to the conclusion that the representatives were, in fact, "the echo of the people."

## NOTES

1. For recent research on the colonial franchise, see Chilton Williamson, *American Suffrage from Property to Democracy, 1760-1860* (Princeton, N. J.,

1960); David S. Lovejoy, *Rhode Island Politics and the American Revolution, 1760-1776* (Providence, R. I., 1958); Milton M. Klein, "Democracy and Politics in Colonial New York," in *New York History*, XL, No. 3, pp. 221-45, July 1959; Theodore Thayer, *Pennsylvania Politics and the Growth of Democracy, 1740-1776* (Harrisburg, Pa., 1953); Richard P. McCormick, *The History of Voting in New Jersey* (New Brunswick, N. J., 1953); Charles S. Grant, *Democracy in the Connecticut Frontier Town of Kent* (New York, 1961); Robert E. Brown, *Middle-Class Democracy and the Revolution in Massachusetts, 1691-1780* (Ithaca, N. Y., 1955). For a summary of current views, see Edmund S. Morgan, *The American Revolution*.

2. Beverley, *History*, pp. 237-43.

3. Richard Henry Lee to Arthur Lee, Dec. 20, 1766, Lee Papers.

4. Gooch to Lords of Trade, Jan. 9, 1730, Gooch Papers, I, 148.

5. To Lords of Trade, Oct. 5, 1752, *ibid.*, II, 313; PRO, CO 1323/5, p. 127.

6. Dinwiddie to Lords of Trade, Jan. 1755, Dinwiddie Papers, I, 383-84; Burnaby, Travels, pp. 46-48; Hening, *Statutes*, III, 277-78; V, 489, 541-57; VI, 201, 325-50; Beverley, *History*, pp. 257-59.

7. Hening, *Statutes*, III, 367-71; V, 523-26.

8. Richmond County Order Book 14, p. 376; Richmond County Rentals, 1746, 1751, 1765.

9. Maury to Reverend John Camm, Dec. 12, 1763, *House Journals, 1761-65*, pp. li-lii.

10. Petition of Archibald Cary to the General Court, June 9, 1756, Archibald Cary Papers, 1756-85, VHS.

11. *Virginia Gazette* (R), May 19 and July 28, 1774.

12. *Ibid.*, Oct. 10, 1745; *ibid.* (P & D), Feb. 13, April 15, and May 13, 1773; Feb. 3, 1774; *House Journals, 1770-72*, pp. 38-39.

13. Spotswood to Lords of Trade, March 6, 1711, Spotswood, *Letters*, I, 56: *House Journals, 1702-12*, p. 277; Hening, *Statutes*, III, 498-501.

14. Gooch to Lords of Trade, Dec. 5, 1736, Gooch Papers, II, 445.

15. Hening, *Statutes*, III, 246-50. For a bond, see Bond of Moulson, Feb. 4, 1745/6, Berkeley Papers, Alderman Library, Univ. of Va.

16. Corbin to Roberts, July 29, 1762; to Hanbury, Dec. 14, 1762; to Dinwiddie, Dec. 14, 1762; to Roberts, May 10, 1763, and Dec. 17, 1764, Richard Corbin Letterbook.

17. *House Journals, 1712-26*, pp. 187, 189; Fauquier to Amherst, Feb. 25, 1763, Amherst Papers, Vol. 37, Pt. II, pp. 335, 338.

18. Lancaster County Deed Books 13-18, *passim*.

19. Hening, *Statutes*, II, 20, 272-73; Julian A. C. Chandler, *Representation in Virginia* (Baltimore, 1896), p. 17.

20. Hening, *Statutes*, III, 236-45, 414.

21. Beverley, *History*, pp. 241-42; see also the negative action of the House in 1705 on Lancaster County's proposal that the custom of annual assemblies be discontinued, *House Journals, 1702-12*, p. 165.

22. *Ibid., 1712-16*, pp. 125, 128, 141, 152, 159, 165.

23. *Ibid., 1727-40*, p. 279; Hening, *Statutes*, IV, 481-82; Draft of election law of 1736, Lee-Ludwell Papers.

24. Hening, *Statutes*, IV, 542.

25. *House Journals, 1758-61*, p. viii, n.

26. *Ibid.*, p. 12; *ibid., 1702-12*, p. 6.

27. Hening, *Statutes*, VII, 517-30; Fauquier to Lords of Trade, March 12, 1763, PRO, CO5, v. 1330, pp. 299-302, 305.

28. Hening, *Statutes*, III, 284; *House Journals, 1702-12*, p. 24. In 1710 Governor Spotswood made an unsuccessful attempt to take the right to divide counties away from the House. See *ibid.*, pp. 281, 339-40, 344.

29. Hening, *Statutes*, IV, 77-78; V, 78-80; Gooch to Lords of Trade, Feb. 22, 1738/9, Gooch Papers, II, 529.

30. *Virginia Gazette Supplement* (P & D), June 14, 1770.

31. *House Journals, 1752-58*, p. 240. For a similar view, see Freeman H. Hart, *The Valley of Virginia in the American Revolution, 1763-1789* (Chapel Hill, 1942), p. 64.

32. *House Journals, 1761-65*, p. 233; *ibid., 1770-72*, pp. 20, 37.

33. William Preston to William Byrd, May 14, 1774, Draper MSS, 3QQ24 (Preston Papers, III).

34. *House Journals, 1712-26*, pp. 182-83; *ibid., 1758-61*, p. 82.

35. To Lords of Trade, Dec. 15, 1710, Spotswood, *Letters*, I, 36-39.

36. *House Journals, 1752-58*, pp. 146, 152; Hening, *Statutes*, VII, 620.

37. *Ibid.*, VIII, 208-10; *House Journals, 1766-69*, pp. 59, 62, 81, 83, 85.

38. Landon Carter Diary, March 13, 1752; *House Journals, 1752-58*, pp. 32, 60-64.

39. *Ibid.*, pp. 114, 117, 120, 125, 130, 140, 142; Hening, *Statutes*, VI, 384-85.

40. *House Journals, 1752-58*, pp. 246, 263; Landon Carter Diary, May 14, 1755.

41. *House Journals, 1752-58*, pp. 430, 444; *ibid., 1758-61*, pp. 22, 82, 98, 119, 128; for other examples see cases of Richmond and Frederick counties in *ibid., 1712-26*, p. 182; *ibid., 1752-58*, pp. 18, 130, 160, 170; Hening, *Statutes*, IV, 95.

42. *House Journals, 1752-58*, pp. 14, 109.

43. *Ibid.*, pp. 432, 439, 444-45.

44. Hening, *Statutes*, IV, 303, 450-51, 467-68; V, 208, 266; *House Journals, 1752-58*, p. 432.

45. *Ibid.*, p. 424.

46. *Ibid., 1758-61*, pp. vii, 8, 83, 85, 92.

47. *Ibid., 1752-58*, pp. 61-62; Landon Carter Diary, March 31, 1752.

48. Madison to [William Preston?], March 1, 1767, and ? to ?, April 4, 1770, Preston Papers.

49. *House Journals, 1770-72*, pp. 187, 197, 268.

50. Hening, *Statutes*, VIII, 395-98; *House Journals, 1770-72*, pp. 271, 306.

51. Lords of Trade to King, Jan. 30, 1771, PRO, CO5, v. 1369, p. 40; Order in Council, *ibid.*, v. 1334, p. 31; Royal Instructions to Lord Dunmore, Feb. 7, 1771, Aspinwall Papers, Mass. Hist. Soc. *Collections*, 4 ser., X, 635-36.

52. Lords of Trade to Dunmore, March 2, 1773, PRO, CO5, v. 1369, p. 61.

53. Pendleton to Preston, June 4, 1774, Draper MSS, 3QQ36 (Preston Papers, III); Fincastle Petitions, Oct. 8, 1776, VSL.

54. Summary View of the Rights of British America, July, 1774, Jefferson Papers, I, 130.

55. Carter to Washington, Oct. 31, 1776, Force, *American Archives*, 5 ser., II, 1306.

56. Amelia County Tithables, 1742, 1749, undated list, 1762, 1768, 1782.

57. See note 3, Chp. IX; Lancaster County Deed Book 18, p. 118 for Ewell.

58. To Lords of Trade, Dec. 28, 1711, Spotswood, *Letters*, I, 136; Randolph, History, pp. 104-05.

59. Amelia County Tithable List, 1768; William Cabell Diary, Sept. 25, 1780; *Letters to Washington*, II, 401-09; taxes paid Nov. 10, 1770, by William Preston, Preston Papers, VHS; Halifax County Tithable List, 1770; Halifax County Deed Book 4, pp. 43-44; Book 5, p. 447; and Books 1-6, *passim*.

60. For similar conclusions see Jack P. Greene; "Foundations of Political Power in the Virginia House of Burgesses, 1720-1776," in *The William and Mary Quarterly*, 3rd ser., XVI, No. 4, pp. 485-506, Oct. 1959.

61. Data compiled from *House Journals,* Convention *Proceedings* and from "A Register of the General Assembly of Virginia" by Earl G. Swem and John W. Williams, published in the *Fourteenth Annual Report of the Library Board of the Virginia State Library, 1916-1917* . . . (Richmond, 1917), pp. 1-12.

62. Sydnor, *Gentlemen Freeholders,* pp. 64, 78, 79; Bridenbaugh, *Seat of Empire,* pp. 8-17; introduction by Hubbell and Adair in Robert Munford, *The Candidates.*

63. Lancaster County Deed Book 13, pp. 249-50. The candidates were Col. Edwin Conway (116), Mr. Mitchell (79), Capt. Wm. Stepto (56), Capt. Wm. Tayloe (46), Joseph Ball, Esquire (40), Major Ball (32), and Col. Wm. Ball (31).

64. Alex. White to [Richard Henry Lee, 1758], Lee Papers.

65. Landon Carter Diary, March 13, 1752.

66. *House Journals, 1766-69,* pp. 181-82, 206, 209, 212-13, 221-22.

67. *Ibid., 1752-58,* pp. 155-56, 162, 177, 180, 346-47, 351, 353, 436-37; *ibid., 1758-61,* pp. 5, 50.

68. Hening, *Statutes,* III, 245-46; VII, 305-17; *House Journals, passim.*

69. May 28, 1718, *ibid., 1712-26,* p. 213; *ibid., 1761-65,* pp. 250, 256.

70. *Ibid., 1712-26,* pp. 124, 130-31, 135, 139-49, 152-53, 164-70. Offending justices were George Keeling, Richard Littlepage, Thomas Butts, and Alexander Walker.

71. *Ibid.,* pp. 166-70.

72. Spotswood to Lords of Trade, Oct. 24, 1715, Spotswood, *Letters,* II, 133-35.

73. *House Journals, 1727-40,* p. 414; *ibid., 1742-49,* p. 180.

74. *Ibid., 1770-72,* pp. 38-39, 257, 276.

75. *Ibid., 1752-58,* pp. 47-59, 156, 254, 257, 453; *ibid., 1758-61,* pp. 105, 213.

76. Gooch to Lords of Trade, June 10, 1747, Gooch Papers, III, 910; petition of Beverley Randolph, Oct. 26, 1747, PRO, CO5, v. 1326, pp. 341-46; *House Journals, 1752-58,* pp. 76, 80, 81; *Virginia Gazette,* April 17, 1752.

77. To Lords of Trade, May 12, 1761, *House Journals, 1758-61,* p. 294.

78. Gooch to Lords of Trade, May 27, 1732, Gooch Papers, II, 284.

79. Richard Henry Lee to William Lee, July 7 and 9, 1770, Lee-Ludwell Papers. Italics added.

80. *Virginia Gazette* (R), March 12, 1772.

81. Landon Carter Diary, April 15, 1752; May 6, 1755.

82. *Ibid.,* Oct. 17, 1754.

83. Fauquier to Lords of Trade, June 28, 1758, PRO, CO5, v. 1329, p. 137; May 12, 1761, *ibid.,* v. 1330, p. 89; *ibid.,* v. 1331, p. 147.

84. See Hubbell and Adair introduction in Robert Munford, *The Candidates.*

85. Munford, *The Candidates,* pp. 17, 18, 24, 29-31.

86. *Virginia Gazette* (P & D), Aug. 4, 1768.

87. Bryan Fairfax to Washington, July 3, 1774, *Letters to Washington,* V, 20-22.

88. Attributed to John Randolph, attorney general and brother of Peyton Randolph, Speaker of the House of Burgesses, *Considerations on the Present State of Virginia* . . . [1774], edited by Earl G. Swem (New York, 1919), pp. 15-17, 36.

89. *Virginia Gazette* (P & D), Nov. 21, 1771; *ibid.* (R), July 7 and 14, 1774.

90. Washington, *Diaries,* I, 301 and n.; II, 156-57.

91. William Cabell Diary, Sept. 12, 1769 and July 15, 1774.

92. *Virginia Gazette* (R), Oct. 5, 1769; July 7 and 14, 1774.

93. See note 3 above.

CHAPTER XI

# Religious Practices and Conflicts

As IN ITS ECONOMIC and political aspects, a society can also be democratic or aristocratic in its religious doctrine and church organization. The purpose of this chapter is to examine the religious life of the Old Dominion to determine what sort of organization the church had, the prevalence of religious toleration, the extent to which the people or the upper classes dominated religion, and the presence or absence of religious controversy.

Religious organization in Virginia was patterned after that of the mother country: the Church of England was the "established" or government-supported church, but other religions were tolerated as long as their adherents also paid tithes to the established church. Among the laws passed by the first representative assembly in 1619 was one declaring that all ministers were to read divine service and exercise their ministerial functions according to the ecclesiastical laws and orders of the Church of England.[1] By 1703, there were forty-nine parishes, thirty-four with ministers and fifteen vacant, and only five small "Conventicles" or meetings of dissenters, two Presbyterian and three Quaker. Each parish was governed by a vestry of twelve men chosen originally by the parishioners with vacancies filled later by the vote of the remaining vestrymen.[2] Vestrymen had many duties—levying and collecting tithes, care of the poor, processioning of land, choosing church wardens, and, in theory, selection of the minister.[3]

On its face, filling vacancies on the vestry by co-optation would appear to be extremely undemocratic, but two factors tended to modify this effect. One was that there was no great demand before 1770 to change the method of vestry selection. In 1712 one county petitioned for a law empowering freeholders to elect vestrymen every seven years, but this and a similar petition from Accomack County three years later were both rejected by the House.[4] A second factor was that the House granted petitions for new vestry elections whenever popular demand seemed to require. In dissolving the vestry of Elizabeth City and calling a new election because of the general complaint of the inhabitants, Governor Gooch informed the Lords of Trade that it was sometimes necessary to yield to popular humors when the public received no prejudice by it, rather than increase discontents for the sake of private interest.[5]

Throughout the century there were many petitions for new elections of specific vestries; while these reflected numerous grievances, class differences do not appear to have been among them. A common complaint was that actions of individual vestries were illegal, arbitrary, and oppressive. There were accusations that vestry elections were illegal, that vestrymen served without being legally elected, that vestrymen were too old and infirm to perform their duties, that they refused to serve once elected, and that they could not read or write. If the House refused to grant petitions for new elections, it was usually because there were more petitions urging the opposite.[6] Had the House failed to grant the many petitions against vestries there doubtless would have been a much stronger feeling in the colony to change the laws regarding vestry elections.

In one respect the Virginia church was more democratic than it is today—both whites and Negroes attended the same church although the Negroes appear to have been segregated from whites within the church itself. Jonathan Boucher baptized over 100 Negro children and some thirty to forty adults during his first six months as minister in King George County, and on one Easter Monday he baptized 313 adult Negroes and lectured to more than a thousand.[7] Negroes probably sat apart in the church balcony, if it had one, a conclusion suggested by an account of the collapse of the Negro section of a church in Richmond County.[8] There was some opposition to the baptism of Negroes, sometimes on the ground that this made them "proud, and not so good servants," but the practice continued nevertheless.[9]

The laws of 1705 spelled out in great detail the moral and religious code by which the church expected its members to conduct their lives. Church attendance once a month was compulsory, the fine for failure to attend was five shillings or fifty pounds of tobacco, and for failure to pay, the offender was to receive "on his or her bare back, ten lashes, well laid on." Similar fines were prescribed for swearing, cursing, or drunkenness; and on Sunday certain activities, such as attending disorderly meetings, gaming, tippling, traveling except to and from church, adultery, and fornication were prohibited. Presumably some of these were permissible during the week. In addition, any person brought up in the Christian religion was to be punished if he denied the being of God or the Holy Trinity, asserted that there were more gods than one, or denied the truth of the Christian religion and the divine authority of the Old and New Testaments. Punishments were severe, although absolution could be gained by public confession within six months of conviction.[10]

Despite the fact that the Church of England was the legally established church with all the privileges accompanying establishment and a strict code to guide the conduct of the people, the position of the church gradually declined throughout the eighteenth century. This decline was caused in part by democratic inroads into church government and in part by the physical nature of the country and the character of the ministers. But especially important was the rising influence of dissenters, both those already outside the church and those who defected from within. Even before the Revolution came, the church had its back to the wall, and of all possible internal conflicts, that over religion was by far the greatest; in fact, it was the only one of any importance.

During the first half of the eighteenth century, one of the chief religious problems, and one that weakened the church, involved a tug of war between the Governor and the people over which had the power of appointing ministers. An act of 1662 provided that ministers must produce certificates of ordination from a bishop in England and must be conformable to the orders and constitutions of the Church of England, but the act did not state how appointment of ministers was to be made. The King instructed the Governor to collate any person to any church or chapel, but this instruction was never consistently carried out and by 1700 ministers definitely looked to the local vestries instead of the Governor for their appointments.[11]

Despite continual urging of the Bishop of London, the royal Governors were never able to take the power of choosing the ministers away from the vestries. Governor Spotswood told the Bishop of London that yearly agreements between the people and their ministers were the custom and that the people were very touchy about any interference with their right. The people retained this attitude for many years in spite of the efforts of Governors Spotswood and Gooch to change their minds. The Governors could recommend a minister for a particular parish, but the vestry did not always honor their recommendations.[12] Whether the vestry or the Governor had the right to select the ministers became a chief issue in a convention of the clergy in 1719, with the clergy divided on the subject and those siding with the people finally maintaining the majority. The subject was also the basic contention in a suit in court brought by Bruton Parish, a suit financially supported by the House of Burgesses, indicating House support for the people in the cause.[13]

Historian Jones also maintained that it was the "people" who elected the minister, much to the detriment of the church's power and future development, and he claimed that there were not more than three or four rectors collated or instituted and inducted by the Governor in the entire colony. Jones feared the power of the vestry "who erroneously think themselves the masters of their parson, and aver, that since they compacted but from year to year with him as some have done, they may turn off this their servant when they will; be without one as long as they please, and choose another, whom and when they shall think most proper and convenient; which liberty being granted them (I believe) some few would be content rather never to appoint a minister, than ever to pay his salary." Jones also maintained that the people were suspicious and fearful of the power of the church. Neither conventions nor the commissary exerted much authority, he complained, and visitations had been attempted in vain "for the corrupt abuses and vigour of ecclesiastical courts have so terrified the people, that they hate almost the very name, and seem more inclinable to be ruled by any other method, rather than the spiritual courts." Little wonder that the people wanted to elect their own ministers.[14]

The next decade saw no change in the controversy: the vestry and the people still insisted on the final say in appointing their ministers. One James Blumfield explained to the Bishop of London in 1737 that he did not like the "footing the Clergy are on" in Virginia and though he did not choose to ramble, he felt compelled to go to Jamaica. The Virginia Governor had sent him to a parish, he explained, but the vestry there refused to receive him. "While this Affair of Presentation remains undetermined: & the People are Suffer'd to treat the Clergy in the Manner they now & heretofore have Done: I cannot But think it a Cruel & unfair proceeding to Send to your Lordship for Ministers to Supply the Church here: Since the people Cannot be Satisfyed with your Choice & will not Acquiesce in yr. Lordships Appointment."[15]

The long controversy was finally settled in 1748 with a victory for the vestry and the people. A law passed in October, 1748, gave the vestries the "sole right" of presentation of the ministers for and during twelve months following the vacancy. After that time the vacancy could be filled by the governor. The Bishop of London later cited the law, which continued in force until the Revolution, as the beginning of the downfall of the clergy in Virginia because it put the clergy "under the Power of the Vestry" and made them subject "to the Humours of the People."[16]

Although the law gave the power of election of ministers to the vestry, a self-perpetuating body, there was little doubt in the minds of contemporaries that the vestries spoke for the people and that in the final analysis the people had the ultimate power. Governor Dinwiddie believed that the people were so fond of the law that it would be impossible to alter it without a royal mandate.[17] When the Reverend Mr. Yancey of Louisa County considered offering himself to another parish in 1772, he was hindered by the good understanding subsisting "between me & my parishioners—The obligation I was laid under to them for choosing me for their minister when several more promising chances offered. . . ."[18]

According to the Reverend Mr. Jonathan Boucher, the clergy were dependent on "the People, and on them alone. In Virginia, they were elected to their benefices by the People: and though, as those acts appear on paper, the Clergy, after their election, might have been thought to have been placed beyond the reach of popular control, yet every man who had a practical acquaintance with that country before the revolution must know this was not the case."[19] And finally a dispute between the vestry and parishioners of St. James Parish in Mecklenburg County on the eve of the Revolution leaves no doubt that the people believed they, not the vestry, had the final power in choosing their parson. The St. James vestry, having agreed to receive a certain minister into the parish—one already approved by the parishioners—suddenly received another one who was a stranger to the people and of whom they did not approve. The parishioners petitioned the House to dissolve the vestry, and the language of their petition left no doubt that they, not the vestry, should have final choice of their minister.[20]

The substantial power that the people had in church affairs helped to generate the spirit which eventually promoted separation from Great Britain, according to one contemporary observer. Jonathan Boucher, a critic of this power, said it was "surprising what improper and indecent contentions" the elections of clergy occasioned. "I have oftener than once known half-a-dozen candidates all trying for a vacant parish, and preaching alternately, to give their electors an opportunity of determining which they liked best. *Voice and action,* as is remarked in a very humorous pamphlet respecting London lectureships, almost constantly carried it. These frequent appeals and applications to the people, in this way, as well as from the merchants who meanly solicited and *begged,* as it was called, consignments of tobacco, gave them an opinion of their importance and a consequence, unknown to people in other countries." What influence this had on future commotions between the colony and Great Britain could only be ascertained by those observers on the spot, Boucher said, but the ministers so elected remained in some degree subservient to the people and continued to cultivate those arts by which they first gained favor— "their sermons were light, flippant, and ordinary; but their manner of preaching was pleasing and popular." And, on writing of the American Revolution after the war, Boucher maintained that the established church in Virginia was more popular in discipline and church government than the Presbyterian Church under the establishment in Scotland. Since Boucher presided over two different parishes during his stay in Virginia, he had first-hand acquaintance with the church development in that colony.[21]

In addition to the appointment of clergymen by the people, other influences also tended to weaken the position of the church. Although they were all presumably members of the same upper class, the clergy and their vestries were not always on the best of terms. One minister, sympathizing with the complaints of a neighboring cleric, declared that the latter's was "a common case" as every clergyman in the colony was affected by the arbitrary and illegal proceedings of the vestries.[22] In addition, large parishes resulting from conditions in a frontier community made frequent contact between minister and parishioner difficult. Some ministers complained that their parishes were at least thirty or forty miles in length, while some were sixty, seventy, and even one hundred miles. Frederick Parish had seven churches or chapels, but it was impossible for the minister to perform his duties properly or for the people to attend divine service frequently.[23]

In general, also, the people of Virginia did not take their religion as seriously as did men, for example, in the northern colonies. Philip Fithian noted the difference between southern and northern practices of observing the Sabbath. By Saturday afternoon, he said, every face, and especially those of the Negroes, looked festive and cheerful. All the lower class, the servants, and the slaves considered Sunday as a day of pleasure and amusement, spending it in such diversions as they chose. Gentlemen went to church, but it was a matter of convenience, for they used the church as "a useful weekly resort to do Business." Later he divided attendance at service into three segments. Time before service was spent in giving and receiving letters of business, reading advertisements, consulting about commodity prices, and settling the lineage, age, or qualities of favorite horses. At service, the prayers were read over in haste and the sermon, "seldom under & never over twenty minutes," was of sound morality and deep, studied metaphysics. After the service, one spent three-quarters of an hour strolling among the crowd and receiving several invitations to dinner. This differed decidedly from the custom in Fithian's original home in New Jersey. On Sunday up north there were no rings of beaux chatting before and after the sermon on gallantry, no assembling in crowds after service to dine and bargain, "no cool, spiritless harangue" from the pulpit. In Virginia, unlike New Jersey, Fithian declared, neither the minister nor the people seemed to reverence the Sabbath.[24]

Landon Carter and William Byrd both provide evidence that religion was not a serious matter with some Virginians. Carter, a church warden, went to a special service on sacrament day which, according to the minister's notice, was to have begun at eleven o'clock. "The Parson came there about 10 recd prayers & was gone before any body but a few was there & said it was 11 mints [minutes] after 11 o'clock by his W[atch] I got there 25 m'ts after 10 with my family and got back 25 before 11. Col'o Lee came to church after me and was at my house before 11. I am contented the Gen'tn entertains me when he pleases to go into his Pulpit, and I said nothing. God knows I went to Commemorate the love and Passion of my devoted redeemers & if [his] servant was otherwise dispos'd I hope it is to be imputed to some other cause than my neglect."[25] Byrd frequently stayed at home on Sunday, especially when the weather was wet, or sometimes sent the children only. And in his view the worth of the sermons varied greatly. One time he heard a "poor sermon," another Sunday one that "nobody understood," and on still another a "good sermon." Prayer at home was a common habit of Byrd's and, on occasion, a useful tool for placating his conscience, as the following excerpt from his diary illustrates: "I rose about 6 and played the fool with Sarah, God forgive me. However, I prayed and had coffee."[26]

Still another factor in the declining influence of the church in the Old Dominion was the character of some of the ministers. There were, of course, many good clergymen who won and kept the respect of their congregations, but there were others who left much to be desired.[27] James Maury was much beloved by his parishioners and had "a pretty income," while Jonathan Boucher retained his popularity either in spite of or because he was "always of a social temper" and had numerous acquaintances, which, combined with the fact that it was fashionable "to drink freely," led him "to hard drinking," though never, he thanked God, "to intemperance."[28]

The career of Isaac Giberne, minister of King George and Richmond counties, might well explain why some men who took religion seriously decided not to take it within colonial Virginia's Church of England. Jonathan Boucher, also a minister, claimed that Giberne "was the most admired and popular preacher in Virginia," having preached to the House of Burgesses and received their thanks for his effort.[29] Giberne married a rich widow and moved to Richmond County, but his popularity did not prevail long with his new wife, for she soon eloped and kept company "Every *Night* with some *strolling Players!*"[30] The minister, an inveterate gambler, came to Landon Carter's one Thursday and except while sleeping and eating, played cards constantly for several days with Carter's son Robert Wormeley and his overseer Billy Beale—hardly an aristocratic thing to do.[31] And on another occasion Philip Fithian reported that Giberne had been ill as the result of three successive nights of drinking and playing cards—"A rare tale this to relate of a Man of God."[32]

But by far the greatest reason for the decline in the position of the Church of England in Virginia was the rising tide of dissenter strength both without and within the church itself. This force, from small beginnings at the opening of the century, gained strength with the law of 1748 placing the appointment of ministers in the hands of the vestry instead of the Governor, and swelled to flood stage just as the Revolution erupted. That event was to administer the coup de grâce to an institution that had deviated increasingly from the mother church in England and that had long been subjected to serious assault from dissident groups within the colony.

One of the basic elements in the decline of the church was that it had no such governing hierarchy as did the church in England. Here there was no archbishop or bishop to give personal direction to ecclesiastical affairs. The diocesan was the Bishop of London who appointed a commissary to preside over religious affairs in the colony, but the commissary did not possess powers comparable to those of the bishop. He could not ordain ministers and he could not appoint them to posts in the colony; all he could do was to call them into convention and censure or suspend them on moral or neglect charges. His salary of £100 did not compare with that of a bishop, and while he received additional remuneration when he was also on the Council and was president of William and Mary College—as he customarily was—he had neither the position nor the power of the head of the church in England.

Another element in the decline was a gradual breakdown of uniform practices beginning early in the eighteenth century, which resulted in considerable local control and contributed to the later increase of dissenters. Hugh Jones wrote in 1724 that the clergy in several respects were "obliged to omit or alter some minute parts of the liturgy, and deviate from the strict discipline and ceremonies of the Church," either through custom, to avoid giving offense, or to prevent absurdities and inconsistencies. Surplices, long out of use, were being brought back into vogue only with difficulty. In some parishes the people received the

communion in their seats, a custom introduced to influence those inclined toward Presbyterianism, and it was not easy "to bring them to
the Lord's Table decently upon their knees." Prayers were altered to
conform with actions of the colonial assembly instead of Parliament
because ministers could not know when Parliament was sitting. In fact,
ministers were independent in their own parish in respect to some little
particular circumstances and customs to which they were often occasionally obliged, Jones warned, and this liberty without restraint might
"prove of bad consequence hereafter; when the bad tenets and discipline
of any heterodox, libertine, or fantastical persons may plead prescription
for their establishment, and be difficult to be eradicated"[33]—a warning
that proved only too true.

As a matter of fact, dissenters had been encouraged to come to the
colony and had been given many privileges as a part of colonial defense
against the Indians on the frontier. An act of 1705 created a separate
parish for French Protestants above the falls of the James River, exempted them from parish and public levies until 1708, and allowed them
liberty to have and to pay their own minister. In Brunswick and Spotsylvania counties, foreign Protestants had their own ministers and were
freed from tithes for ten years after May, 1721. Germans in Stafford
were exempted from parish levies in 1730, and William Byrd prevailed on
the assembly in 1739 to free all foreign Protestants from payment of taxes
for ten years when he wanted Swiss and German Protestants to settle
his lands.[34]

Such policies by the government inevitably exposed the people to new
ideas and brought conflicts between dissenters and the church. Governor
Gooch lamented in 1735: "Tis a melancholly truth, the Church and
Clergy have many Enemies in this Country, ffree [sic] thinkers multiply
very fast having an eminent *Layman* for their Leader, and the Current
runs in some places almost with out opposition."[35] The eminent layman
was probably the attorney general, Sir John Randolph, whose will revealed that he had been reproached by the clergy for his religious beliefs
and had been called a deist, heretic, and schismatic. Randolph, who
believed that a supreme being would judge people eventually for their
immorality, religious disputes, and hatred toward one another, declared
that his religion came from the gospel and that he had no need for
learned doctors who made religion a science of difficulty and mystery.[36]

The Indians also hindered the expansion of the Church of England on
the frontier. James Maury spoke of a vacancy that had no offers, so he
invited someone from Gloucester, but believed that the candidate would
"think his Scalp in such Danger, that he'll deem it more eligible to run
the Risque of starving there, than of being scalped here."[37]

While Protestants were not only tolerated but encouraged to migrate
to Virginia, Catholicism was still not popular in the Old Dominion. An
article in the *Virginia Gazette,* commenting on the marriage of the Prince
of Wales to a Protestant princess, linked "our Religion" with "our Liber-

ties." Marriage to a Papist would forfeit the succession and discharge subjects from their allegiance even to the ruling prince.[38] Virginians appeared to be solidly behind the King when the son of James II attempted to regain the throne. Dissenters as well as churchmen expressed horror at the thought of an arbitrary Popish government—"that shocking Medley of civil and religious tyranny."[39]

In time, itinerant dissenting ministers began to cause concern in the colony. In directing a grand jury against itinerants, Governor Gooch explained how the laws regulating dissenters worked in practice. Itinerants should be suppressed, he declared, but Presbyterian missionaries who had proper testimonials, who complied with the laws, and who performed divine service in certain places designated for that purpose, without disturbing the quiet and unity of the sacred and civil establishments, would be protected.[40] The influence of George Whitefield and other itinerants finally brought a proclamation by Governor Gooch and the Council strictly requiring all magistrates and officers to discourage the teaching and preaching of all itinerant preachers, whether New Lights, Moravians, or Methodists.[41]

Churchmen became increasingly concerned about the incursions of these dissenters, even the Presbyterian missionaries who obeyed the letter of the law. Presbyterian Samuel Davies had obtained orders from the General Court allowing him to preach in seven different meeting houses in five different counties—Hanover, Henrico, Louisa, Goochland, and Caroline. Commissary William Dawson and Acting Governor Thomas Lee both expressed the opinion that allowance of such liberty to Davies was probably more than was intended by the Act of Toleration. Dawson expressed concern over the schism spreading through the colony and the fact that Davies held forth on working days to great numbers of poor people.[42]

English officials failed to see the threat to the church, however, for the Lords of Trade clearly indicated that religious toleration was a needed accessory to mercantilism. The Lords said that a free exercise of religion was a valuable branch of true liberty and so essential to the improving and enriching of a trading nation that it should ever be held sacred in the colonies. They earnestly urged that nothing be done to affect that great point, but at the same time they suggested admonishing Mr. Davies to make proper use of the indulgence the laws so wisely granted to those differing from the established church, and to be cautious not to afford just complaint to the clergy of the church nor to the people in general. The Lords' opinion stopped action against Davies in the colony.[43]

The growing strength of the dissenting elements in the colony elicited numerous arguments for and against the encouragement of such people. Fear that the Indians would go over to the French, as well as the threat of the French and Indians, caused some to urge more freedom for dissenters. This freedom had filled Pennsylvania with people and Virginia would have to follow a similar policy to attract settlers to her frontiers.[44]

Dinwiddie and Fauquier also insisted that the church establishment discouraged settlers and should be modified to meet circumstances.[45] Writers in the *Virginia Gazette* argued at great lengths the merits of religious freedom for frontier settlers, pointing out sometimes that such settlers strengthened the colony by bringing needed manufacturing skills. Others, however, linked slavery and sectaries as two great dangers should favorable occasions present themselves.[46]

As time went on, an increasing number of church members were lured into the ranks of the dissenters. In 1752 Commissary William Dawson expressed great concern over the increase and power of dissenters in the colony. He reported to the Bishop of London that lately one Mr. Todd, a dissenting minister qualified according to law, had been appointed an assistant to the Presbyterian minister Mr. Davies in the seven licensed meeting houses. Prior to the arrival of these teachers from the north, the dissenters were "but an inconsiderable Number" and, having no meeting houses, "they quietly conformed to the Doctrine and Discipline of our Church, constantly frequented the Public Worship of God, and the Christian Sacrifice." But since the arrival of Mr. Davies, there had been a great defection from the Church of England assemblies, the greatest part of his following being "born and bred in our Communion." In spite of an indulgence greater than either the King's instruction or the Act of Toleration intended, continued Dawson, the dissenters were not satisfied; they now wanted more licensed meeting houses and even exemption from payment of parochial levies. "I think it is high Time," warned the Commissary, "for the Government to interpose, to give their Immodesty a Check, and to restrain their Teachers within the Bounds of a Parish, lest their Insolence sh'd grow to a *dangerous* Height."[47]

Even within the established church itself, there appeared continued evidence of nonconformity in rituals. In discussing the election of William Stith as president of William and Mary College, John Blair said Stith was charged with being "an Anti-Trinitarian." To confirm this, it was said he had long disused St. Athanasius's creed in his church. Stith confessed his long disuse of that creed but "pretended to excuse it by his Congregation's aversion & refusing the responses." He said he had acquainted both the late Governor and the Commissary of this, but Blair was puzzled about this explanation, since both Governor and Commissary were dead and were, when alive, "very Orthodox in that point, & strict adherers to the Canons."[48]

The growing strength of dissenters can be seen in the fact that they began to feel free to preach where they were not licensed and also in the many requests from various counties for unorthodox ministers. James Maury complained that Presbyterian ministers were preaching sermons in his parish without either license or place to preach. Maury, expressing doubt that the Act of Toleration really extended to the colonies, insisted that he believed in toleration but he wanted the positions of churchmen and dissenters precisely defined.[49] Requests for Presbyterian ministers came to the Hanover Presbytery from the western counties of Albemarle, Halifax, and Augusta, from piedmont Amelia, Lunenberg, Prince Edward, Louisa, Orange, and Cumberland, from tidewater Lancaster, Northumberland, Westmoreland, and Richmond, and from the town of Petersburg, an indication that non-conformity was not confined to the frontier.[50]

Other evidence of the increasing number of dissenters in this period can be found in the deed and will books of the various counties. In tidewater Lancaster County, two Presbyterians notified the court that they planned to establish a place of public worship on a certain piece of land. The county court forbade the building because an act of Assembly "now in force" prohibited preaching by anyone who had not been ordained by the Bishop in England. The Presbyterians appealed to the General Court and won a license for the building.[51] In 1758, forty-one Essex County men signed a statement addressed to the county court that they planned to use a piece of one Thomas Miller's land as a place of public worship for Protestants of the "Prespiterian Denomination," and in Amelia and Augusta counties the Presbyterians also bought land for churches.[52]

A detailed study of dissenters in tidewater Lancaster County showed that far from being lower-class, the leaders of the movement against the church were some of the outstanding men in the county. The men involved in procuring the land and building for the Presbyterians in Lancaster, for example, included William Tayloe, who was a sheriff, a colonel, a justice of the peace, a frequent candidate for burgess, a "gentleman," and was listed as one of the trustees of the Presbyterian Church of Lancaster and Northumberland counties. James Gordon, another Presbyterian trustee, was a leading figure in the county and a very wealthy merchant and gentleman. The inventory of his estate showed that he owned 58 slaves, a sloop, and £5,049 in goods in several stores, and he willed large estates in land and money to all his children plus giving the Presbyterian minister £100 sterling. Richard Selden, also a Presbyterian trustee, was the county sheriff the year the meeting house was bought; he had been elected burgess in December, 1755, and was consistently called a "gentleman" in the records.[53] With these three leading gentlemen of Lancaster among the trustees of the newly-formed Presbyterian church, one cannot class the growth of dissenters there as a lower-class movement.

Even the Board of Visitors of the College of William and Mary were de-emphasizing religion at the college. The express purpose of the school was to train boys for the Church of England, declared William Robinson, but when Camm was displaced as professor of divinity one of the Visitors said there was no need for a professor of this subject, and this opinion prevailed. Furthermore, the Visitors desired that all other professors should be laymen and were even choosing laymen as Visitors to replace the churchmen who died. Robinson did not agree with all this but said he did not have any influence at the meetings of the Visitors, even being refused the liberty of entering his dissenting opinions.[54] Apparently the power of the Commissary, never very great at best, was decreasing as dissenters increased.

From 1750 on, dissenting views became increasingly prevalent. One evidence of this is to be found in the numerous instances in which men who were elected to the vestries of the Church of England later appeared as dissenters. So serious did this problem become that the Assembly passed a law in 1759 stipulating that all vestrymen take oaths to support the monarchy, take and subscribe the test, and be conformable to the doctrine and discipline of the church. The law explained that many vestrymen, subsequent to their elections to the vestries, had left the Church of England and joined dissenting congregations. Previously a man could not resign his duty on the vestry, but a man who had become a dissenter after being placed on the vestry must now resign, although he could be elected again if he rejoined the church. The law obviously did not eliminate dissenters on vestries, for there was a new election in Augusta in 1769 because a majority of the vestry were dissenters.[55]

Even among the orthodox the ways of the church in Virginia were not those of the English church. Landon Carter not only differed with his minister, Isaac Giberne, over drinking and gambling but over religious doctrine as well. At one point Giberne expressed the view that Carter's religion was "so very different from what I am ordained to teach." Carter's reply was that religion should be based on common sense, and he took the humanistic view that God should be thanked or appealed to on such occasions as birthdays, losses, afflictions, and droughts.[56]

In part, also, the decline of the church was reflected in a loss of respect on the part of the people for ministers. Had devotion to the church been very strong, the following episode related in the *Virginia Almanack* for 1764 would have had little point. An "honest bluff Country Farmer" met a parson in a by-lane, and when the farmer did not step aside as readily as the parson expected, "the Parson, with an erected Crest, told him, He was better *fed* than *taught*. *Very true, indeed, Sir,* replied the Farmer, for you *teach* me, and I *feed* myself." Where clerks instead of ministers frequently read the sermons and prayers, said Hugh Jones, the people had "no right notions of the office, respect, and dignity of a clergyman."[57]

Ministers, themselves, were suspected of being unorthodox, a fact which certainly would not strengthen the church. Hugh Jones wrote that in addition to ministers whose learning, actions, and manners had not been as good as might be wished, there were some whose outward behavior caused them to be suspected of being either Jacobites or Presbyterians at heart.[58] In 1752, following the death of Commissary Dawson, Governor Dinwiddie favored the appointment of Dawson's brother Thomas to fill the position. But William Stith, who had defeated Dawson by a close vote for the presidency of William and Mary College, was also attempting to get the appointment. Dinwiddie refused to vote for Stith in part because one of the college trustees, or Visitors, said "that Mr.

Stith was not an Orthodox Clergyman, & of a Turbulent Spirit." In terms of aristocracy and class conflict, it is also of interest to note Dinwiddie's accusation that Stith had "been endeavouring to make a Party of the lower Class of People" the Governor's enemies.⁵⁹

In the House of Burgesses there was also an increasing antagonism toward ministers which did little to strengthen the position of the church. In 1755, the clergy petitioned for higher salaries on the ground that low salaries discouraged migration of ministers from English universities and allowed so many, who were "a disgrace to the ministry," to fill parishes. Higher salaries would also entice sons of gentlemen, few of whom thought it worthwhile to bring up sons in the study of divinity. Burgesses who professed strict attachment to the church opposed the salary petition, however, and some did so because the petition itself was a confession of the dissolute behavior of many clergymen. When the petition was rejected "by almost ye whole house," according to Landon Carter, the clergy tried unsuccessfully to get the petition stricken from the records lest it remain as evidence of the poor quality of clergymen.⁶⁰

With the reputation of the clergy at a low ebb and their relations with the House of Burgesses not the best, their actions in what was known as the Two-Penny Act did little to improve their position either in the House or in the colony at large. This act rested on a precedent by which the colony, in times of tobacco crop failures, allowed people to pay in money those debts which were payable in tobacco. As early as 1711 Governor Spotswood had attempted unsuccessfully to get such a law.⁶¹ In 1752, the House passed a bill allowing Albemarle County to pay certain officials in money instead of tobacco but a power struggle between House and Council prevented passage.⁶² Some counties apparently had long permitted payment of some officials in money, and in 1753 the Assembly allowed several counties to pay ministers £100 in currency instead of tobacco. Then in May, 1755, the Assembly allowed justices of Norfolk and Princess Anne to fix tobacco prices each fall and permitted people to pay in money instead of tobacco.⁶³

This was the background when in 1755 the legislature, confronted with severe crop failures and high taxes to support what came to be the French and Indian War, passed the famous Two-Penny Act. James Maury, who later gained fame in opposition to the act, pointed out the justification for it at the time. Vast numbers of livestock perished and little tobacco was grown, he said, and the main sufferers were the poorer people. The legislature had been so sensible of conditions that it passed the Two-Penny Act allowing the people to pay their public dues to the Secretary, county clerks, clergy, and other public creditors in money at the rate of 2d. per pound of tobacco. Maury philosophized that this would cost him money, but that "each Individual must expect to share in the Misfortunes of the Community to which he belongs."⁶⁴

The Two-Penny Act was in fact a temporary aid to all debtors, but at the expense of their creditors. The act made it lawful for persons to pay all levies, judgments, bonds, rents, and contracts either in tobacco or in money "at the rate of sixteen shillings and eight pence, for every hundred pounds of nett tobacco. . . ." The law was passed without a suspending clause and was to be in force for ten months only. It would seem that the Assembly, knowing the current price was far out of bounds because of the drought, had attempted to bring it into temporary balance for relief of debtors until the next tobacco crop was harvested. The law did not extend to any county where the inhabitants were entitled by law to discharge their payments in money. Although the fixed rate of 16s. 8d. was higher than the previous rate of 12s. 6d., it was not as high as the market price of 26 shillings. As James Maury said, the law saved a considerable amount for those who had tobacco to sell "while it deducts the same from the annual Salaries & Revenues of the Creditors, which, in my own Case, who am entitled to upwards of 17,000 lb of Tobacco per annum, amounts to no inconsiderable Sum."[65]

The unanimity and speed with which the House and Council considered and passed the Two-Penny Act not only indicates feeling toward the clergy but also complicates any interpretation of debtors and creditors along aristocratic-democratic lines. On October 28, 1755, the House ordered the bill brought in, a committee of the whole House considered it, and on Friday, October 31st, the House passed the measure and sent it to the Council. The following Monday, November 3rd, the Council agreed to the bill without amendment.[66]

Not all clergymen were as philosophical about the Two-Penny Act as was James Maury, for in 1756 ten of them sent an address of protest to the Bishop of London. They called the law "a breaking in upon our establishment, an insult to the Royal Prerogative & contrary to the liberty of the subject, as well as to natural Justice & Equity." They complained about the low fixed value of tobacco and the fact that ministers had to accept tobacco when tobacco prices were low but were not permitted to do so when the price was high. Although the law presumably discriminated against all creditors, the ministers insisted that it was aimed primarily at the clergy and especially that it took their salaries and divided them among the rich who benefited most by the law. The law, they said, will "keep us in debt & so in a dependent State, a thing much aimed at by the great men of this Country." Both clergy and church were on a very precarious footing in Virginia, they had never been totally deserted by every branch of the legislature until now, and, said the ministers, the act would aid dissenters who were rapidly gaining ground in Virginia.[67]

Although the Two-Penny Act expired after ten months, recriminations between House and clergy over its passage continued. Jacob Rowe, professor of philosophy at William and Mary and a minister, made public remarks asking how many members of the House were to be hanged, and declared that any who voted for payment of ministers' salaries in money were scoundrels and that he would refuse to administer the sacrament to any of them. The House resolved that these words were "scandalous and malicious, highly reflecting on the Honor and Dignity" of the House, and that Rowe was "guilty of an open Violation and Breach of the privileges" of the House. Rowe had to appear before the House, apologize, and pay costs. Another man, who defended Rowe and condemned burgess William Kennon, also had to apologize and pay costs.[68]

In spite of opposition by the clergy, and at the behest of a Prince George petition, the Assembly in 1758 passed another Two-Penny Act, a fact which demonstrated not only anti-clerical feeling but also response of the legislature to popular demands and the general welfare. To the Lords of Trade, Governor Fauquier explained why he had signed the law although it did not contain a suspending clause. The clergy had urged him to oppose the act but had not done so themselves when it was being passed. So he signed the bill because it was a temporary law to ease the people of a burden which the country thought too great for them to bear. The people were very intent on it and the House and Council were almost unanimous in their vote. Had he vetoed it, he said, he would never have gained any influence in either body.[69]

Rebuffed in the colony, the clergy next appealed to England where they received a more sympathetic hearing. They sent John Camm, minister and former professor at the college, who had been dismissed from his professorship and was at odds with Governor Fauquier.[70] The Bishop of London considered the Two-Penny Act as a step toward colonial independence and as the work of men who intended to abridge the maintenance of the clergy while studiously avoiding direct reference to them. Since ministers' salaries had been settled by an act approved by the Crown, the Two-Penny Act was in effect treason because it assumed a power to bind the King's hands. Until lately, the Bishop said, Virginia was submissive to the Crown and all were Church of England men, "but these days are over. . . ." To him, the law of 1748 giving the vestry power to appoint the clergy was the beginning of the trouble. The Bishop could not understand why the Governor and Council seemed "to act in Concert with the People, to lend their authority to support their unreasonable demands," and he warned that it was time to consider the various steps taken by Virginians to diminish the royal influence and prerogative.[71]

Success attended the efforts of the clergy, but their appeal to England over the Assembly left deep and lasting resentment in Virginia. The King disallowed all acts permitting the people to pay their tobacco debts in money.[72] But in Virginia, the clergy were condemned for failing to apply to the Assembly before turning to England, and according to Andrew Burnaby, their action "greatly exasperated" the people and resulted in animosity that would "not easily subside, or be forgotten." Burnaby implied that the Assembly would have been reasonable had the clergy applied there first. He also declared that the Governor had had to sign

the Two-Penny Act or "he would never have been able to have got sup-
plies during the course of the war. . . ."[73]

At stake in the Two-Penny Act controversy was more than the mere
salaries of ministers. To the clergy, church and state stood or fell together
as equals, and whatever harmed one harmed both. James Maury believed
that the many public measures in Virginia had only one end—to reduce
the church from its position of equality and alliance with the state to
one of "abject Vassalage & Servile Dependance on it."[74] The colonial view
was expressed by William Robinson, however, when he said it was "to
be reckon'd dangerous to the State here for the clergy to apply to
Authority in England on any occasion whatever. . . ."[75] At stake also was
the Governor's position, for the British, instead of notifying him directly
and privately, allowed the news of their decision to reach the Governor
indirectly through John Camm's friends and then directly through Camm
himself when the latter returned and delivered the King's royal orders
and instructions, both open, dirty, and worn. According to report, Fauquier flew into a rage, abused Camm in violent terms, and ordered that
he should not be allowed to enter the Governor's mansion again.[76]

John Camm himself later related the role of democracy in this dispute.
He claimed that the clergy appealed to England only after failing to get a
hearing before the Assembly prior to passage of the Two-Penny Act. Not
succeeding in the Assembly, the clergy then urged the Governor to veto
the act for otherwise he would violate his instructions. Said Camm: "He
told us this was not the point to be considered. We represented to him
the injustice of the Bill. He answer'd, just or unjust is not the point to be
consider'd. I then had the Unhappiness to ask him what was the point to
be considered? To which he replied, what will please the People." Shocked
by the Governor's response, the clergy lingered only "a few, silent &
distressful minutes" to recover their astonishment and then departed.[77]
But antagonism between the Governor and the clergy continued for
years after the Two-Penny Act controversy.[78]

The sequel to disallowance of the Two-Penny Acts was several trials,
one in particular now known as the "Parson's Cause," which further
alienated church and clergy from the people and also generated a spark
of rebellion. Some of the clergy sued for back salaries; the most famous
case was that of the Reverend Mr. James Maury of Louisa County, the
same James Maury who had seen the justice of the Two-Penny Act in
1755. At the trial on November 5, 1763, the court declared the Two-
Penny Act null and void and a later trial was set to fix damages. The
defendants then secured the services of a rising young lawyer named
Patrick Henry; and, according to Maury, the sheriff, after two feeble
attempts to get "gentlemen" as jurors, went "among the vulgar Herd" to
fill the jury, including on the list several known dissenters.[79]

In his defense, Patrick Henry attacked the very foundations of both
the English state and the Church of England in the colony. The Two-
Penny Act, he argued, was a good law which could not, under the com-

pact, be annulled, and a king who did so degenerated into a tyrant and forfeited all rights to his subjects' obedience. The only use for an established church or clergy was to enforce obedience to civil sanction. When the clergy ceased to answer these ends, society had no further need for them and could justly strip them of their appointments. By refusing to acquiesce in the law in question, he continued, the clergy had notoriously repudiated the great reasons for their being and should be declared enemies of the community. Unless the jury "were disposed to rivet the chains of bondage on their own necks," they should make an example of Maury as a warning to other ministers not to dispute the laws in the future—laws authenticated by the only authority, in his conception, which could give force to laws for governing the colony, the authority of legal representatives, the Council, and a kind, benevolent, and patriotic Governor.[80]

Throughout the trial it seems apparent that to Henry, as to Governor Fauquier, the main issue was to please the people. Henry's reference to the King brought statements from some men that he "had spoken treason," but the justices on the bench heard Henry "without Emotion, or any mark of Dissatisfaction." One member of the jury was so highly pleased with Henry's doctrines that he "now and then gave the traitorous declaimer a nod of Approbation." After the trial, in which the jury found damages of one penny, Maury declared that Henry apologized for what he said, alleging that his sole aim in engaging in the cause and saying what he did was "to make himself popular." "You see, then, it is so clear a Point in this Person's Opinion," Maury declared, "that the ready road to Popularity here, is, to Trample under Foot the Interests of Religion, the Rights of the Church, & the Prerogative of the Crown." Henry was asserting a supremacy in provincial legislatures that was inconsistent with the dignity of the Church of England and tended to draw the people of the plantations away from their allegiance to the King.[81] If Maury was correct, not only the church but the British government in Virginia stood on precarious footing.

Among those who benefited most by the Two-Penny Act controversy and the Parson's Cause, the latter presumably designed to strengthen the church, were the dissenters. Jonathan Boucher noted that after the episode the clergy experienced "every kind of discourtesy and discouragement." The church was in great want and was threatened with being reduced "to an humble dependence on popular authority and popular caprice." One consequence of this change in public opinion and conduct toward the established clergy, explained Boucher, was that "although thirty years ago there was not in the whole colony a single dissenting congregation, there are now, according to the best information I can obtain, not less than eleven dissenting ministers regularly settled, who have each from two to four congregations under their care." As to the many sectaries and itinerant priests, and in particular "those swarms of separatists who have sprung up among us within the last seven years, under the name of anabaptists and new-lights," Boucher continued, "I might almost as well pretend to count the gnats that buzz around us in a summer's evening."[82]

The decade after the fall of Quebec and Montreal witnessed an acceleration in the activities of dissenters and the receptiveness on the part of churchmen to unorthodox views. Jonathan Boucher claimed that it was characteristic at this time to read "chiefly such publications as are filled with sneers at orthodoxy, cavils against the national church, and (above all) with incessant lavish encomiums on all uncontrolled freedom of enquiry." Boucher did not disparage freedom of inquiry, but he believed that the vogue of these principles lessened men's reverence for government and encouraged sects and parties.[83] Menonists, who came to the colony "in Hopes of enjoying the free Exercise of their Religion," were able to get their principles against bearing arms incorporated into the militia act, and Lutherans in Augusta bought land for a church.[84]

Dissenting ministers became more aggressive, challenging orthodox ministers to open debate or entering parishes uninvited to spread their doctrines. The *Virginia Gazette,* for example, carried a debate between Presbyterian James Waddell and a Richmond County rector over whether Waddell had been invited to preach or merely stole into the pulpit under a pretended invitation.[85] Jonathan Boucher boasted of having no dissenters in his parish although they had taken over two adjoining parishes, one without a minister and the other with a weak one. He attributed success to avoidance of all disputes with dissenting ministers, and when challenged to public debate, he sent a carpenter with a "good tongue" to defeat his opponents.[86]

Some of the opposition to toleration of dissenters came from slaveowners who felt that these unorthodox sects had a wicked influence on their slaves. One master, William Lee, wrote to the steward of one of his plantations that he was told the wandering New Light preachers from the north had put most of the Negroes "crazy" with their New Light and and their New Jerusalem. These vagabond preachers, said Lee, instigated more wickedness than any other kind of men, and the Negroes should be discouraged from going to hear them. He advised his steward to encourage the Negroes to go to their parish church by giving those who attended most regularly a larger allowance of food or an additional shirt. The steward should make it of interest for the slaves to do their duty.[87]

So intense had become the public foment over religion by 1769 that the House appointed a new standing committee—a Committee on Religion. Created by an act of May 8, 1769, the Committee on Religion was to deal with "all Matters and Things relating to Religion and Morality." It was to have the same subpoena power as other major House committees, power to send for persons, papers, and records for its information. Three days after creating the Committee on Religion, the House ordered it to prepare a bill exempting Protestant dissenters from the penalties of certain laws. Just what this law would have involved is not known, for before the bill matured the Assembly was abruptly dissolved for its resolves against British actions. In November of the same year, the House ordered a bill prepared "for granting Toleration to his Majesty's Subjects, being Protestant Dissenters," but again nothing came of this bill during the fall session.[88]

In February, 1772, the House, prompted by an Anabaptist petition asking for the same privileges granted to other dissenters, brought in another toleration act by general agreement of all members. This act noted that since some dissenters could not subscribe to the British Toleration Act because they would not subscribe to the Articles of the Church of England as required, toleration in Virginia must be more extensive than in England and dissenters should not be required to subscribe to articles of the established church. The only tests required in this new bill were swearing or affirming an oath to the King and his government, subscribing the test, and declaring assent to the truth of the sacred Scriptures. There were also clauses in the bill to guard against corruption of slaves, to prescribe a method for establishing meeting houses, and to confine teachers to certain places and times of worship. To get the general reaction of the people, the House had this proposed toleration act printed and distributed.[89]

The growing strength of dissenters, aided, no doubt, by difficulties between Britain and the colonies, is attested by the fact that instead of welcoming a liberalized toleration act, some of them demanded even greater freedom. The Hanover Presbytery, speaking for numerous Presbyterian congregations, objected to limitations on preaching in stated places and on restrictions against night meetings and meetings with closed doors. What they wanted was not just toleration to worship as they pleased but all the rights enjoyed by the Church of England, such as speaking out and writing on religious subjects and the right for churches and schools to hold property.[90]

Dissenters had ample reason to be optimistic about their progress in the colony. Several new Presbyterian churches were established in Augusta County alone between 1771 and 1773.[91] One witness said in 1772 that all the ladies, and almost every order of people in Norfolk, were becoming proselytes to Methodism. The church was quite deserted, but nearly three thousand people heard the Methodist minister, Mr. Pilmore, in the fields on Sunday. They flocked to him from all quarters, invited him to preach in every neighborhood, and the women called him "the dear divine man."[92]

What was even more important, support for the dissenters was coming increasingly from the upper classes. Fithian was informed that Anabaptists grew in both numbers and affluence in Loudoun County and were numerous in many other counties, in spite of the fact that they were "destroying pleasure in the Country" by advocating ardent prayer, strong and constant faith, and an end to all gambling, dancing, and Sunday diversions. In Richmond County, Parson Giberne found it necessary to preach several sermons against dissenters as he labored to convince his own congregation that dissenting doctrines were "only whimsical Fancies or at most Religion grown to Wildness and Enthusiasm!" There was also the Presbyterian minister Mr. Woddell [Waddell] who preached to people under trees in summer and in private homes in winter. Ordinary people did not esteem him more than the Anabaptist ministers, "but the People of Fashion in general countenance, & commend him." Fithian had heard "Mr and Mrs *Carter* speak well of him, Mr and Mrs Fantleroy also, & all who I have ever heard mention his Name."[93] If the Carters and Fantleroys were favorably inclined toward any dissenters, the latter were doing very well, indeed.

Imprisonment of dissenting ministers for preaching in violation of the law, while indicating that complete religious freedom had not yet been achieved, seemed to help rather than retard the movement toward religious liberty for all. On the one hand, a writer in the *Gazette* sanctioned imprisonment on the ground of common law and the original compact, claiming that while he favored religious toleration, this must be accomplished under the law, and those imprisoned had violated it.[94] But another writer insisted that Governor Dunmore could increase his reputation by freeing those people who had been imprisoned for religious preaching.[95]

Of special importance in the imprisonment controversy are the views of James Madison, who probably did more for religious freedom in Virginia than any other man, not excluding Thomas Jefferson. Writing to a friend in Pennsylvania about his concern for the "state and liberty" in Virginia, Madison said he hoped to visit the friend and "breathe your free air." Noting the pride, ignorance, and knavery among the priesthood and the vice and wickedness among the laity, Madison wrote: "That diabolical, hell-conceived principle of persecution rages among some; and to their eternal infamy, the clergy can furnish their quota of imps for such business. This vexes me the worst of anything whatever. There are at this time in the adjacent county not less than five or six well-meaning men in close jail for publishing their religious sentiments, which in the main are very orthodox. I have neither patience to hear, talk or think of anything relative to this matter; for I have squabbled and scolded, abused and ridiculed, so long about it to little purpose, that I am without common patience. So I must beg of you to pity me," he concluded, "and pray for liberty of conscience to all."[96]

While Virginia continued to grant some toleration, supposedly under the British Toleration Act, and while the General Court continued to rule on the licensing of dissenting ministers and meeting houses, there was still doubt in some minds about the legal basis of toleration in the colony in 1773. The problem was spelled out clearly by a "friend to the rights of mankind." He asked whether the act of toleration was in force in Virginia, and if so whether the General Court had any authority under the act to license meeting houses or refuse to register them when applied to for that purpose. If the act was not in force in Virginia, did the General Court derive its power from any other law and did the General Court have a right on principles of common law to debar any person from worshipping God according to the dictates of his own conscience?[97]

Dissenters benefited immeasurably, and the church suffered corresponding reverse, as the result of an internecine battle that raged within both the colony and the church in 1771-72. At issue was the question of establishing an American Episcopate to regulate the conduct of Church of England ministers and to strengthen the position of the church in the colonies. Long advocated but never adopted, the proposal reached a boiling point in 1771 when the Commissary, apparently at the urging of church clergymen in the northern colonies, called a meeting of the Virginia clergy to formulate a policy. At the meeting, attended by only twelve out of more than one hundred ministers in the colony, the vote was eight to four to petition for an American bishop. The four who opposed, however, wrote protests in the newspapers and were supported by a unanimous vote in the House of Burgesses. The people of the colony were fearful of church courts, which would violate their constitution as it had developed, and many clergymen apparently did not want the strong restraining hand of a bishop to interfere with their way of life. Richard Bland, pointing out the threat to civil government, declared that a colonial bishop would "produce greater convulsions than any thing that has ever as yet happened in this part of the globe."[98]

That dissenters were the main beneficiaries of the controversy seemed only too apparent to contemporaries. In fact, one writer in the *Gazette* openly accused one of the protesters, the Reverend Mr. Samuel Henley, of being an avowed dissenter in principle who stayed in the church only because of the salary. Dr. Samuel Auchmuty, rector of Trinity Church in New York, accused the protesters of betraying the cause of the Church. Had the wretches lost all shame, he asked? Were their characters so bad that they could not endure the inspection of a superior? Were they not Presbyterians at heart and ready to accept lay ordination? Such rotten sheep—wolves, he meant—ought to be universally despised. One or two of these conceited cockscombs, he heard, were professors at the college —a blessed church college indeed that harbored such reptiles. And wrote Jonathan Boucher: "Heretofore, the objectors to episcopacy were found only among avowed dissenters. *Their* dislike to it is consistent. . . . But, it is our singular fate to have lived to see a most extraordinary event in church history: professed churchmen fighting the battles of dissenters, and our *worst enemies* now literally *those of our own houshold.*" Where opposition to an American episcopate had once been confined chiefly to New England demagogues and independents, it was "now espoused with much warmth by the people of Virginia."[99]

Although dissenters gained by the unsuccessful attempt to bring a bishop to the colonies, their battle for more religious freedom was far from over. The last effort toward religious toleration under the British, an effort snuffed out when Lord Dunmore dissolved the Assembly, resulted in divided opinions over how successful the effort would be. James Madison was pessimistic, for "incredible and extravagant stories" had been related when toleration was considered the previous year and the bill had lost support. There were still men too much devoted to the established church to tolerate dissenters or examine their principles. Madison believed that the sentiments of people of fortune and fashion were on the wrong side; and while there were some men in the legislature "of generous principles both in Religion and Politics," numbers, not merit, were necessary to carry points. With the clergy a numerous, powerful body of great influence in England, the coming trial on the issue would show how far Virginians would go toward liberty of conscience.[100] William Christian, on the other hand, was quite optimistic about the chances for a toleration bill. A Toleration Act and Fee Bill were to be considered, and while the fee bill would be committed for amendments, he believed "that we shall succeed as we wish about Toleration, though there will be some opposition."[101] And as historian-politician Edmund Randolph said, this effort for complete toleration was the most promising to date, but was cut off by dissolution of the Assembly.[102]

Whatever might have been the outcome of a vote on toleration in 1774, and historians can regret that the vote was never taken, it is certain that the climate of opinion by that date was definitely oriented toward greater religious freedom. Even as staunch a churchman as colonial treasurer Robert Carter Nicholas believed in limited toleration for some dissenters.[103] Madison expressed his views by saying that "Religious bondage schackles and debilitates the mind, and unfits it for every noble enterprise, every expanded prospect."[104] Washington, little given to philosophical discourse, promised that Palatines who avoided Virginia because of their fear of religious persecution would not be restrained in any way in their civil and religious principles, a fact, he said, that immigrants were anxious to know.[105] According to Edmund Randolph, Patrick Henry favored complete toleration and his predilection in the cause of liberty was nourished by his partiality toward dissenters. Henry saw a close relation between civil liberty and the principles inherent in the religious doctrines of dissenters.[106] And Thomas Jefferson had early proposed an act exempting dissenters from contributions to the established church.[107]

As the war clouds gathered in the colonies, dissenters used the crisis to increase demands for complete religious freedom. Shortly before independence, Baptists in Prince William County petitioned the Williamsburg Convention for greater privileges. Now, they wrote, when fighting for civil rights of mankind, they thought it right to petition for the religious privileges they had not yet been indulged with in Virginia. They asked that "they be allowed to worship God in their own way; that they be permitted to maintain their own ministers, and none others; that they may be married, buried, and the like, without paying the clergy of other denominations. . . ." If these things were granted, they said, they would gladly unite with all others in promoting the common cause.[108]

The wish of Baptists for complete freedom was given theoretical sanction by the Williamsburg Convention when it adopted the Virginia Declaration of Rights in June of 1776. Religion, said the Declaration in the last article, can be directed "only by reason and conviction, not by force and violence; and therefore, all men are equally entitled to the free exercise of religion, according to the dictates of conscience." And the Declaration added, almost with a sense of prophecy, that it was the mutual duty of all to practice Christian forbearance, love, and charity towards each other.[109] This last caution was not always heeded in the coming decade, but the philosophical statement of religious freedom was to become a reality in many ways before long.

Although there were some minor indications of religious divisions along class lines, on the whole class conflict appears to have been little if at all involved. If Presbyterians were more acceptable to the upper classes than to the common people, who approved of Baptists and others, it is also true that both Church of England and dissenting churches embraced all classes, including Negroes. Neither was the conflict sectional, for while dissenters were stronger in the west than in the tidewater at an early date, they were everywhere, and especially in Norfolk, by 1774. In structure, the unorthodox churches were more democratic than the orthodox, but contemporaries believed that the people made the ultimate decisions even in the strongholds of orthodoxy. In doctrine, however, the advocacy of complete religious equality, with church and state separated, placed the dissenters on the side of democracy.[110]

With the evolution of religious toleration in the advanced stage that it had reached by 1774, it seems almost inevitable that the trend would have continued even had there been no Revolution. In effect, the power of the Church of England was on the verge of being broken by that date. In the score of years before the Declaration of Independence, it had lost much of its influence from a combination of several factors—a gradual breakdown of uniformity in ritual, the low caliber of some of its ministers, the imperial need to settle the frontier, the growth of dissenters, and the general antagonism against the mother country. During this period, dissenters had increased vastly in both numbers and strength. Presbyterians and Baptists led the way, with Quakers, Methodists, Menonists, Moravians, New Lights, Deists, and Lutherans all being represented. It would take another ten years, and a plethora of words, before the evolutionary process was completed, but by 1776 the foundation for complete religious freedom had been well laid in the Old Dominion.

## NOTES

1. *House Journals, 1619-1658/9*, p. 13.
2. Beverley, *History*, pp. 261-63.
3. Hening, *Statutes*, IV, 210, 211; V, 426-27; VI, 90, 447; VII, 132. In the

land laws of 1705 and 1710, the vestry and church wardens played an important part in enforcing the law and registering land ownership, *ibid.,* III, 325-26, 530-33. For vestry duties, see "At a Vestry held for Christ Church Parish. . . ," Berkeley Papers.

4. *House Journals, 1712-26,* pp. 11, 138.

5. Gov. Gooch to Board of Trade, c. Oct. 8, 1728, Gooch Papers, I, 57 in PRO, CO5, v. 1321/5, p. 79.

6. Hening, *Statutes,* V, 274-75; VI, 258-60, 501-03, 516, 518; VII, 144-45, 616; VIII, 432-33; *House Journals, 1702/3-1712,* pp. 275, 322; *ibid., 1752-58,* pp. 194, 220, 236, 246, 264, 275, 277, 419; *ibid., 1758-61,* pp. 7, 164; *ibid., 1761-65,* p. 12; *ibid., 1770-72,* pp. 10, 39.

7. Boucher to Reverend Jno. Waring, Dec. 31, 1762, MSS of Dr. Bray's Associates, American Correspondence, Film No. 175-77; Boucher, *Reminiscences,* pp. 57-59.

8. *Virginia Gazette* (P & D), Sept. 16, 1773.

9. Boucher, *Reminiscences,* pp. 57-59; Jones, *Present State of Virginia,* p. 99; Fithian, *Journal,* pp. 252-53.

10. Hening, *Statutes,* III, 358-62; V, 226.

11. Copy of an Act of March 23, 1662, PRO, CO5, v. 1318, p. 327, c. Aug. 14, 1718. For a detailed analysis of this controversy up to 1722 see George M. Brydon, *Virginia's Mother Church,* 2 vols. (Richmond, Va., 1947, 1952), I, 344-53; Beverley, *History,* p. 264; Richard L. Morton, *Colonial Virginia,* II, 465-71.

12. Spotswood, *Letters,* I, 2, 4-5, 16, 27, 66-67; II, 137; Gov. Gooch to Bishop of London, Oct. 18, 1727, Gooch Papers, I, 10, in Fulham MSS—Virginia.

13. William Stevens Perry, ed., *Historical Collections Relating to the American Colonial Church,* 5 vols. ([Hartford], 1870-78), I, 199-247; Letter of May 30, 1719, Fulham MSS, Va., Box 2, No. 233; Note on Bruton Parish controversy, Lee-Ludwell Papers; *Legislative Journals of the Council of Colonial Virginia, 1680-1776,* ed. by H. R. McIlwaine, 3 vols. (Richmond, Va., 1918, 1919), II, 655; *House Journals, 1712-26,* p. 301.

14. Jones, *The Present State of Virginia,* pp. 95-96, 123-24; see also editor's note p. 225 for slightly different definition of collation.

15. Joseph Blumfield to [Bishop of London], Sept. 3, 1737, Fulham MSS, Virginia, Box 2, No. 124; see also Reverend Robert Rose Diary, Aug. 1, 1748; announcement of unanimous election of John Fox as minister in Gloucester County, *Virginia Gazette,* Jan. 21, 1736.

16. Hening, *Statutes,* VI, 88-90, Oct., 1748; for an example of the practice under this law, see Dinwiddie, *Papers,* I, 14-15 and Francis Fauquier, Commission of induction of John Brandon, March 12, 1761, VHS; Bishop of London to Lords of Trade, June 14, 1759, *House Journals, 1761-65,* pp. xlviii-1.

17. Dinwiddie to Bishop of London, Aug. 11, 1755, Fulham MSS, Virginia, Box 3, No. 66; see also Dinwiddie to Lords of Trade, June 5, 1752, PRO, CO5, v. 1327, pp. 353-57.

18. Reverend Yancey to vestry of the Parish, June 23, 1772, The Papers of James Madison, 1723-1845, 90 vols. Library of Congress. Hereafter these papers will be referred to as Madison Papers.

19. Boucher, *American Revolution,* pp. xlix-1.

20. *House Journals, 1770-72,* pp. 257-58.

21. Boucher, *American Revolution,* pp. xlix-1; *Reminiscences,* pp. 30, 40-41, 102-03.

22. Charles Rose to ?, March 29, 1748, Fulham MSS—Virginia, Box 2, No. 230.

23. *House Journals, 1761-65,* pp. 50-51, 233; *ibid., 1770-72,* pp. 36-37.

24. Fithian, *Journal,* pp. 180-81, 220-21.

25. Landon Carter Diary, Oct. 25, 1772.

26. William Byrd, *Another Secret Diary*, pp. 25, 30, 40, 47, 69, 102, 137.

27. Jones, *Present State of Virginia*, pp. 118-19.

28. Boucher, *Reminiscences*, pp. 42, 59. For a more recent sympathetic view of the clergy, see Morton, *Colonial Virginia*, II, 753, and Eckenrode, *Separation of Church and State in Virginia*, p. 35.

29. Boucher, *Reminiscences*, pp. 30-38; *Virginia Gazette* (P & D), Sept. 16, 1773.

30. Giberne to Landon Carter, July 8, 1768, Sabine Hall Papers.

31. Landon Carter Diary, March 13, 1770; June 17 and Aug. 14, 1774.

32. Fithian, *Journal*, p. 262.

33. Jones, *Present State of Virginia*, pp. 96-98.

34. Hening, *Statutes*, III, 478-79; IV, 77-79, 306; William Byrd to John Bartram, March 23, 1738/9, Other Byrd Papers, VHS.

35. Gooch to [Bishop of London], July 8, 1735, Fulham MSS—Virginia, Box 1, No. 68; Gooch Papers, II, 392.

36. *Virginia Gazette*, May 6, 1737.

37. Rev. James Maury to Rev. William Douglas, May 31, 1758, Maury Papers.

38. *Virginia Gazette*, Sept. 24, Oct. 1, 1736.

39. *Ibid.*, Jan. 16, 1745/6; Hanover Presbytery Minutes, July 12, 1758, in *Virginia Magazine of History and Biography*, LXIII, 62.

40. *Virginia Gazette*, Nov. 21, 1745.

41. *Ibid.*, Oct. 31, 1745; Gov. Gooch's Proclamation, April 3, 1747, PRO, CO5, v. 1326, p. 321; also in Gooch Papers, III, 843.

42. Fulham MSS—Virginia, Box 2, No. 128; William Dawson to [Bishop of London], July 27, 1750, *ibid.*, Box 1, No. 184; Thomas Lee to Lords of Trade, May 11, 1750, Gooch Papers, III, 1021; also in PRO, CO5, v. 1327, p. 179.

43. Lords of Trade to Thomas Lee, Sept. 1, 1750, Gooch Papers, III, 1051; also in PRO, CO5, v. 1366, p. 457; William Dawson to [Bishop of London], Aug. 6, 1751, Fulham MSS—Virginia, Box 1, No. 113; Lord Halifax *et al.* to Dinwiddie, Nov. 29, 1752, PRO, CO5, v. 1366, pp. 278-80.

44. Thomas Lee to Lords of Trade, Nov. 6, 1750, Gooch Papers, III, 1046.

45. Dinwiddie to Lords of Trade, Aug. 1751, PRO, CO5, v. 1327, pp. 309-10; Fauquier to Lords of Trade, Dec. 1, 1759, *ibid.*, v. 1330, p. 37; also in *House Journals, 1758-61*, p. 282.

46. *Virginia Gazette*, March 5, March 20, April 3, and April 10, 1752.

47. William Dawson to [Bishop of London], June 17, 1752, Fulham MSS—Virginia, Box 1, No. 11.

48. John Blair to Bishop of London, Aug. 15, 1752, *ibid.*, No. 183.

49. James Maury to Thomas Dawson, Oct. 6, 1755, The Dawson Papers, 1728-1775, British Transcripts, Fulham Palace Manuscripts, Virginia, Library of Congress (on film at Colonial Williamsburg).

50. Hanover Presbytery Book, *Virginia Magazine of History and Biography*, XLIII, 54-75.

51. Lancaster County Will Book 15, pp. 290, 321; Lancaster County Deed Book 16, p. 51.

52. Essex County Deed Book 28, p. 94; Augusta County Deed Book 8, p. 212; Amelia County Deed Book 7, p. 336.

53. Tayloe in Lancaster County Deed Book 13, pp. 6, 174, 249; Book 16, p. 51; Book 17, p. 6; Lancaster County Will Book 15, p. 155; Lancaster County Loose Papers, Jan. 28, 1752, and March 23, 1754, VSL. Gordon in Lancaster County Deed Book 13, pp. 312, 329; Book 14, pp. 1, 118, 156, 215, 216, 243, 264, 295; Book 16, pp. 51, 121; Book 17, p. 6; Book 18, pp. 4, 105, 108-09; Lancaster County Will Book 15, pp. 155, 192, 282, 283, 295. Selden in Lancaster County Deed Book 14, p. 203; Book 16, pp. 38, 51, 156, 220; Book 17,

pp. 6, 28; Book 18, pp. 73, 78; Book 19, p. 268; Lancaster County Will Book 20, pp. 8-9.

54. William Robinson to [Bishop of London?], c. 1761, Fulham MSS—Virginia, Box 1, No. 117.

55. Hening, *Statutes,* VII, 301; VIII, pp. 432-33.

56. Landon Carter Diary, July 15 and Aug. 19, 1771; Giberne to Carter and Carter's comments, May 13, 1771, Sabine Hall Papers.

57. Jones, *Present State of Virginia,* pp. 96-97.

58. *Ibid.,* pp. 118-19.

59. Dinwiddie to [Bishop of London], Aug. 15, 1752, Fulham MSS—Virginia, Box 1, No. 130. See also John Blair to Bishop of London, Aug. 15, 1752, *ibid.,* No. 183, for Stith's election and lack of orthodoxy.

60. *House Journals, 1752-58,* pp. 8, 257; Landon Carter Diary, May session, 1755.

61. Spotswood to Bishop of London, Nov. 11, 1711, Spotswood, *Letters,* I, 128-29.

62. *House Journals, 1752-58,* p. 92; *ibid., 1758-61,* pp. 189-90.

63. Hening, *Statutes,* VI, 369-70, 372, 502; *House Journals, 1752-58,* pp. 246, 260, 274, 276, 286. The counties involved included Frederick, Augusta, Hampshire, Halifax, Bedford, Princess Anne, and Norfolk.

64. James Maury to John Fontaine, Jan. 15, 1756, Maury Papers.

65. Hening, *Statutes,* VI, 568-70; James Maury to John Fontaine, Jan. 15, 1756, Maury Papers.

66. *House Journals, 1752-58,* pp. 321, 324, 326.

67. *Ibid., 1761-65,* pp. xlii-xlvi. The names of the ten signers were John Brunskill, Henry Dunbar, Patrick Henry, Alex. White, John Robertson, Alex. Finnie, Thomas Wilkinson, Peter David, John Barclay, William Willie.

68. *Ibid., 1758-61,* pp. 16-17, 34-36.

69. *Ibid.,* pp. 5-6, 21, 32, 45, Sept. 15, 1758; Hening, *Statutes,* VII, 240-51; Fauquier to Lords of Trade, Jan. 5, 1759, PRO, CO5, v. 1329, pp. 166-68. A letter of Rev. James Maury to Rev. John Camm said the price of tobacco in May and June, 1759, was fifty shillings per hundred; see *House Journals, 1761-65,* p. lii.

70. *House Journals, 1758-61,* pp. 285-86n.; Fauquier to Lords of Trade, Jan. 5, 1759, PRO, CO5, v. 1329, pp. 166-68.

71. Bishop of London to Lords of Trade, June 14, 1759, *House Journals, 1761-65,* pp. xlviii-1.

72. Petition of Virginia clergy to Lords of Trade, May 23, 1759, PRO, CO5, v. 1329, pp. 195-202; see also Fulham MSS—Virginia, Box 2, No. 92 (on film at Colonial Williamsburg); *House Journals, 1758-61,* p. 298; *Acts of the Privy Council,* IV, 420-21; copy of disallowance of religious laws, Aug. 10, 1759, in Letter Book, 1763, Maury Papers; PRO, CO5, v. 1329, p. 229, Aug. 3, 1759; Fauquier to Lords of Trade, July 14, 1759, *ibid.,* p. 245.

73. Burnaby, *Travels,* pp. 49-52.

74. Rev. James Maury to Rev. William Douglas, Oct. 25 and Nov. 20, 1759, Maury Papers.

75. William Robinson to [Bishop of London?], undated but contents indicate c. April, 1761, Fulham MSS—Virginia, Box 1, No. 117.

76. Fauquier to Lords of Trade, June 30, 1760, *House Journals, 1758-61,* pp. 285-86; Perry, *Historical Collections,* p. 463.

77. John Camm to [Bishop of London?], Sept. 8, 1768, Fulham MSS—Virginia, Box 1, No. 188.

78. John Camm to ?, Oct. 23, 1761, *ibid.,* No. 17; Letter of William Robinson, Nov. 3, 1761, *ibid.,* No. 31; John Camm to Bishop of Bangor in London, Jan. 1, 1762, *ibid.,* No. 104.

79. William Robinson to [Bishop of London?], undated but contents in-

dicate c. 1761, *ibid.,* No. 117; James Maury to John Camm, Dec. 12, 1763, Maury Papers.

80. *Ibid.*

81. *Ibid.*

82. Boucher, *American Revolution,* pp. 99-100.

83. *Ibid.,* p. 58n.

84. *House Journals, 1766-69,* p. 256; Augusta County Deed Book 16, p. 477.

85. *Virginia Gazette* (R), July 21, 1768; *Virginia Gazette Supplement,* Aug. 18, 1768.

86. Boucher, *Reminiscences,* p. 48.

87. Lee to Cary Wilkinson, May 22, 1771, in William Lee Letter Book, 1769-1772, Lee-Ludwell Papers.

88. *House Journals, 1766-69,* pp. 190, 205, 252.

89. Robert Carter Nicholas' reply to "Hoadleianus," *Virginia Gazette* (R), June 10, 1773.

90. Petition of Hanover Presbytery, 1774-75, Brydon, *Virginia's Mother Church,* II, 553-57.

91. Augusta County Deed Book 18, p. 253; Book 19, pp. 84, 220, 268.

92. *Virginia Gazette* (P & D), July 30, 1772.

93. Fithian, *Journal,* pp. 96-97.

94. *Virginia Gazette* (P & D), Feb. 20, 1772.

95. *Ibid.,* May 21, 1772.

96. James Madison, *The Writings of James Madison . . . ,* ed. by Gaillard Hunt, 9 vols. (New York, 1900-10), I, 20-21; for evidence that the clergy promoted the persecution see *Virginia Gazette* (P & D), Sept. 16, 1773, concerning an address by the Reverend Mr. Giberne; Rev. Isaac W. Giberne to Landon Carter, June 4, 1772, Sabine Hall Papers; Boucher, *Reminiscences,* p. 100.

97. *Virginia Gazette* (R), Dec. 2, 1773. In England at this time, the problem of dissenters did not create much concern in Parliament; see *ibid.* (P & D), July 1, 1773.

98. Fulham MSS—Virginia, Box 1, No. 94; Box 2, No. 195; Box 3, Nos. 44, 45, 69; Hugh Jones, *Present State of Virginia,* pp. 118-19, 127; Chalmers Collection, p. 107; *Acts of the Privy Council,* IV, 100; *Virginia Gazette* (P & D), Sept. 8 and Oct. 27, 1768; July 6, 1769; May 9, May 23, May 30, June 6, June 13, June 20, Oct. 10, 1771; Boucher, *American Revolution,* pp. 92-96, 101-04; William Nelson to Edward Hunt, May 16, 1771, Nelson Letter Book; William Nelson to Lord Hillsborough, May 27, 1771, PRO, CO5, v. 1349, p. 135; Lee, *Letters of Richard Henry Lee,* I, 59; Richard Bland to Thomas Adams, Aug. 1, 1771, Adams Papers; *House Journals, 1770-72,* p. 122.

99. *Virginia Gazette* (P & D), Nov. 21, 1771; Auchmuty to St. George Tucker, Feb. 15, 1772, Tucker Papers; Boucher, *American Revolution,* pp. 92-96, 101-04.

100. James Madison to William Bradford, Jr., April 1, 1774, Madison, *Writings,* I, 22-24.

101. William Christian to William Preston, May 11, 1774, Preston Papers.

102. Randolph, History, pt. 2, p. 24.

103. *Virginia Gazette Supplement* (P & D), May 20, 1773.

104. James Madison to William Bradford, Jr., Jan. 24 and April 1, 1774, Madison, *Writings,* I, 19, 22-24.

105. Robert Adams to Washington, Feb. 14, 1774, *Letters to Washington,* IV, 325-27; Washington, *Writings,* III, 187, 90.

106. Randolph, History, pt. 2, p. 3.

107. Considerations on the Present State of Virginia, preface, Jefferson, *Writings,* I, 53.

108. Williamsburg Convention *Proceedings,* May 1776, p. 58.

109. *Ibid.,* pp. 42-43.
110. Brydon, *Virginia's Mother Church,* II, 551; *House Journals, May 17, 1774,* p. 103; for a discussion of the forms of church government in dissenting groups in Virginia, see Wesley M. Gewehr, *The Great Awakening in Virginia, 1740-1790,* pp. 194-200. Gewehr's account must be read with caution as he overemphasizes the class struggle and internal revolution in the colony.

CHAPTER XII

# Education in Colonial Virginia

SINCE THE ARISTOCRATIC or democratic tendencies of any society may
be judged to some extent by its philosophy of learning and the facilities
which it offers for education, we cannot fully assess the nature of Virginia
society without some evaluation of its educational system. This would
include the public attitude toward education and especially the extent to
which education was necessary and available for the lower classes.

During the time of William Berkeley there was apparently little by way
of public education in Virginia—a fact very much approved by the
Governor. In a letter to England, Berkeley wrote in 1671: "But I thank
God, *there are no free schools* nor *printing,* and I hope we shall not have
these hundred years; for *learning* has brought disobedience, and heresy,
and sects into the world, and printing has divulged them, and libels against
the best government. God keep us from both!"[1] The Governor would
undoubtedly have vetoed any laws to establish public-supported schools,
even had such laws been passed.

Governor Berkeley, however, was not able to prevent the ultimate
development of either free schools or printing in the colony. Of free
schools, Robert Beverley wrote in 1705: "There are large tracts of land,
houses, and other things granted to free-schools, for the education of
children, in many parts of the country; and some of these are so large,
that of themselves they are a handsome maintenance to a master: But the
additional allowance, which gentlemen give with their sons, render them
a comfortable subsistence. These schools have been founded by the
legacies of well inclin'd gentlemen, and the management of them, hath
commonly been left to the direction of the county-court, or to the vestry
of the respective parishes, and I have never heard, that any of these pious
uses have been mis-apply'd. In all other places, where such indowments
have not been already made, the people joyn, and build schools for their
children, where they may learn upon very easie terms."[2] If Beverley was
correct, thirty-four years had made a great difference in educational opportunity in Virginia.

There is some indication, however, that the educational facilities were
not as adequate as Beverley indicated. Hugh Jones reported that there
were schools in most parishes, with little school houses built on purpose
for the teaching of English and writing. But to prevent the sowing of
seeds of dissension and faction, he wished that the appointment of masters

271

and mistresses was under proper supervision. The editor of Jones' book, Morton, says that public schools admitted any child able to pay tuition, while private schools were restricted. In 1724, he said, twenty-eight ministers reported to the Bishop of London as follows: three stated that there were no schools in their parishes, ten that there were no public schools, ten others that there were no public schools but several private schools; one (Newport) reported four public schools, and four reported endowed public schools. Some twenty ministers did not report.[3]

Although only three of the twenty-eight parishes that reported had no schools in 1724, this fact alone does not tell us how many of the other twenty-five provided education for poor students. We can assume that wealthy people could educate their children under almost any circumstance, so our main concern is with education for the poor. And, of course what was true of 1724 was not necessarily true fifty years later.

Free or cheap education was naturally of fundamental importance in the education of poor students, and while the evidence does not enable us to say with certainty how many free schools existed, it does indicate that there were some. In 1752 Benjamin Welden announced that he planned to open a school for the three r's at the Free School near Williamsburg, and in the same year Syme's Free School in Elizabeth City County advertised for a tutor, the pay to be £31 from rent of the school lands plus perquisites. In 1770, Patrick Thomas Duke advertised that he would teach English, writing, and accounts at the Free School, that he would attend gentlemen's children in their own homes, and that his wife would take in needle-work and teach children.[4] Landon Carter, who paid £30 for his grandsons' tutor, also hired one for his free school at £20.[5]

To provide education for the poor, men sometimes willed property for free schools, or counties provided charity schools. Henry Peasley of Gloucester, for example, willed 600 acres with stock and slaves for a free school in each of two parishes. Arthur Smith of Isle of Wight County gave his 2,275-acre estate for a free school in Newport Parish if none of his children survived. And Syme's Free School in Elizabeth City County was made possible by the will of Benjamin Syme, who gave 200 acres to support a teacher "to keep a free public school."[6] This same county, which had at least two free public schools, also had a school for the poor called Eaton's Charity School. There was some trouble at this school when trustees admitted children whose parents were "well able to pay for their education."[7] In Princess Anne County, James Jouslin left 100 acres for the maintenance and education of orphans in the parish.[8]

In addition to his own free school, Landon Carter proposed to set up a school in Richmond County to provide for a limited number of poor boys. There would be forty students—twenty under the English master and twenty under the language master—but six boys under each master would "be of the poorer sort whose parents are not able to bear the expense of such an education." An additional encouragement to the poorer scholars was a provision that if a vacancy occurred in the position of English master, one of the poor boys would be promoted to fill the position, if he were capable of doing so, and he would receive the same salary as the master.[9]

How much the tutors of the wealthier planters' children engaged in teaching poorer children will probably never be known, but the following account indicates that the practice existed. John Harrower, tutor for the Daingerfields near Fredericksburg, had ten scholars including three Daingerfield children. In addition, Harrower taught writing and arithmetic to one Thomas Brooks, a carpenter for Spotswood, at night and on Sunday when Brooks did not go to church. Brooks earned £30 a year and keep, and of this he paid Harrower 40s. a year for the evening classes. Unfortunately for both tutor and pupil, after six months Brooks moved some forty miles away and had to stop his work with Harrower.[10]

If there were no free schools, charity schools, or planters' tutors available, it was possible to educate children at public schools where students paid tuition. Apparently it was common practice for men who had some education to open such schools in the colony. William Proctor, tutor for William Byrd at Westover, for example, suggested that a Mr. Laing, who had not received an expected commission, could open a public school at 16s. sterling a year for each student (20s. current money).[11] Since 20s. current money would be about five days' wages for a skilled artisan, schooling would not be beyond the reach of artisans' children, and even the overseer Brooks could have afforded to educate his children. Thomas Brewer of Nansemond County advertised for a sober, diligent person to keep a county school. Brewer would guarantee at least twenty-four scholars, an indication that they paid tuition so the prospective tutor would know what he would receive as compensation. And John Walker and wife of Williamsburg combined teaching of both boys and girls with storekeeping and needle-work.[12]

Support for education varied from locality to locality. One H. John Burges announced in December, 1770, that he would open a grammar school in Isle of Wight County, but in October, 1771, he claimed that it had not been successful and that continuation would depend upon the support that he received. At about the same time, however, other localities were advertising for teachers. In Norfolk, John Bruce did so well that he wanted to add an assistant, preferably one who could teach Greek, Latin, English, mathematics, and writing.[13]

The fact that many of the lower classes—illiterates, small farmers and artisans—were interested in educating their children implies that educational facilities were available and also tells something about the poorer people. A carpenter willed that his gun, sword, clothes, and carpenter tools should be sold to educate his son as far as the money would go. A blacksmith desired that the money due to him should be used to educate his daughter, and a cabinetmaker left half of the income from his swamp land for the same purpose. A man might even provide for the education of his illegitimate children, as did mariner George Carlton for his natural son William Rhonalds. The will of an illiterate in 1780 provided eighteen months of schooling for children Joshua, Elizabeth, and Nancy, three years for John and Tamer, and four years for Shadrick. Eldest son Spivy had apparently received his share earlier.[14] Such examples are common in the wills and deeds.[15]

Although much of the impetus for education came from wealthier men, even some tenants were interested in the education of their children. Daniel Lightfoot of Richmond County leased a plantation for himself and also owned or leased a second plantation which he rented to William Tarpley. The difference in the two rents was 300 pounds of tobacco a year in Lightfoot's favor, and this tobacco was to be used to educate Lightfoot's children. Daniel's son William was apprenticed to a carpenter in 1761, and since the indenture did not stipulate an education for the apprentice, it is probable that William Lightfoot had already received some formal education.[16] In Loudoun County, tanner Samuel Mead donated an acre of land to specified neighbors to show "the esteem he bears for a school." Among the ten neighbors listed were Jacob Janny, blacksmith, and Solomon Hoge and Samuel Combs, tenants.[17]

We do not know how extensive the opportunity for education was on the frontier, but we do know that the frontier had schools. The Reverend John Brown from Augusta wrote that their school flourished, having twenty-three boys "pulling away ambitiously." Norborne Parish in Frederick County also advertised in 1771 for a schoolteacher to teach writing and arithmetic. If he could teach Latin the salary would be larger, and he would not be expected to teach more than fifteen or twenty scholars. The advertisement added that a dancing master would meet encouragement in the county.[18]

Advertisements and requests for tutors and teachers would seem to indicate that there was either a considerable number of schools or a shortage of qualified teachers. Requests in the *Gazette* for teachers show that anyone with any claim to an education could always get a position in the colony.[19]

Another indication of either a growing demand for teachers or a shortage of supply was the fact that salaries increased as the Revolution approached. In 1745, Theophilus Field of Prince George advertised for someone to teach reading, writing, and ciphering at £20 a year. In 1752, John Edlet of Charles City offered £25 a year and board for a teacher of the three r's.[20] Washington hired a tutor, Walter Magowan, at £16 sterling in 1761, but by 1766 he was paying Magowan £55.8.4.[21] Captain John Lee of Essex County wanted a tutor from Scotland at £30 in 1770, but the next year David Greenhill of Amelia was offering £50 and living expenses.[22] Landon Carter was willing to pay £50 "besides boarding as a companion at all leisure hours," while another Carter offered £65 plus accommodations, a private room for a study, the use of an "elegant" library, a horse to ride, and a servant.[23] The fact that an increase in salaries came during a not-too-prosperous time would suggest an increase in demand for teachers.

There is also some indirect evidence that schools were more numerous than we might suspect. Occasionally a deed or will designated land location by using the "schoolhouse" as one of the boundary markers, or indicated the construction of a schoolhouse.[24] As we have already noted, the deeds also contain purchases or sales of land by "schoolteachers" in counties where we have no other information about schools. The same was true of election polls, where a voter was sometimes designated as schoolteacher or schoolmaster.

Apprenticeships, as has already been noted, provided a means of education, especially for poorer children and orphans. Designed primarily as a method by which a child learned to earn a living, the apprenticeship also usually included some provision for education other than mere use of the hands. Typical of apprentice indentures was the one made by Thomas Nelson of Fauquier County who took a fourteen-year-old boy as an apprentice blacksmith with the provision that the boy was to receive eighteen months of schooling. In 1769 the law required that illegitimate children were to be taught reading and writing in addition to a trade or profession.[25] Even boys who were not of the lower classes were often bound as apprentices to learn a trade after they had finished their formal education at age fifteen or sixteen.[26]

There was, of course, considerable illiteracy among the poorer people of Virginia—and some that were not so poor—but this seems to have been more prevalent among immigrants than among the native-born, and appears to have been declining as the Revolution approached. Militia lists, for example, show a much higher percentage of illiteracy among men who came to Virginia than among those who were born there.[27] The deeds, wills, election polls, and petitions also demonstrate a declining rate of illiteracy as the century advanced, especially on the frontier where illiteracy would be expected. In 1777, a Washington County petition to change the county line contained 331 names, but only seven signed with a mark. In Hanover, only one out of 405 was illiterate, and in Yogohanie, all 134 petitioners signed their names. Even in Prince William, where there were many tenants and convict servants, only twenty-nine out of 188 petitioners signed with a mark. A 10,000-name petition against the established church in 1776 contained only twenty-three signatures by marks, and the differences in signatures indicate that individuals signed their own names.[28]

How much of a role the newspapers and almanacs played in the education of the people is impossible to say. We do know that the *Gazette* was read on the frontier, for on June 13, 1766, Alexander Boyd of Augusta County paid £3.15.0 in subscription fees for the *Gazette* until June 13, 1772, and William Cabell of Amherst paid subscriptions for numerous persons in his county when he attended the legislature in Williamsburg.[29]

In a society largely agricultural, where the great bulk of men were either farmers or artisans, the three r's probably sufficed for most people. We cannot judge the educational system of the eighteenth century by using as a yardstick the educational needs of a complex industrial society. Perhaps the soldier who was recommended to Washington for a commission in 1757 was somewhat typical: it was said that his education "seems to have been a good country education[.] He writes a good hand & is acquainted with figures."[30]

When the education offered was for girls, it usually combined the three r's with both practical learning and training in the social graces. E. Armston in Norfolk Borough taught fancy work, decoration, reading, writing, arithmetic, music, and dancing. Miss Wright's school in Fredericksburg taught reading, writing, arithmetic, dresden, tentwork, shellwork, and needlework. The cost, including board and washing, was £12 a year Virginia money plus a guinea and a half entrance fee. Some women in Norfolk advertised for a well-bred woman of character to teach young ladies needlework, reading, writing, and other subjects. Tutors sometimes taught the girls in the family and also taught neighboring girls.[31]

There were even several attempts to establish schools for both free and enslaved Negroes, but for obvious reasons these were never too successful. A proposal to set up a free Negro school in Norfolk encountered the objections that it would be difficult to get a woman at the salary offered or one who could control as many as thirty students, that ladies and gentlemen would send their slave children to fill the school and not give the poor free Negroes and mulattoes a chance, and that the Commissary rather than the local minister should be in charge if ill will were to be avoided.[32]

Difficulties attending efforts to educate Negroes, as well as rifts in the upper classes, are apparent from the report of the Reverend Alexander Rhonnald of Norfolk. He tried to discourage the establishment of a school for free Negroes unless the Commissary and the Society in England would back him fully. He said he would not even be a trustee "lest I might find it worse than it was, when I had a Charity School in a neighbouring County where the Gentlemen's Children were many Years educated, & the objects of Charity disdained, till I was oblig'd to leave the School, & lodge a Complaint in the Assembly, which has prevented the Grandees to reign longer, but from that time, they use me with the most invidious terms of Ill nature for my pains, & because I baptise more Negroes than other Brethren here & instruct them from the Pulpit . . . & encourage the good among them to come to the Communion after a due Sense of the matter, I am vilified & branded by such as a Negro Parson."[33] Obviously the gentlemen were divided over education of the poor and the Negro, for Landon Carter had promoted a charity school and Robert Carter Nicholas favored education of Negroes.

There was also an effort to educate some Negroes in Williamsburg and Fredericksburg, but these efforts met strong opposition from some slaveowners. Robert Carter Nicholas, later the colonial treasurer, seems to have been the leading spirit in Virginia behind the Williamsburg school, which was fostered by the Church of England. In 1762, eighteen masters sent a total of thirty Negro pupils to the school. Nicholas explained that as slaves were the chief instrument of labor, many owners treated them as so many beasts of burden who were not entitled to any of the privileges of human beings. Others used their slaves well, but did not concern themselves with their morals or religion. In addition, slaves were corrupted by the examples of whites, so that it was almost impossible to reform slaves without first reforming the whites. Many owners wanted the services of their slaves as soon as they were old enough to do anything: others feared that education for slaves might cause them to become impatient with their condition and rebel. Nicholas admitted that the smartest slaves were the most troublesome. In Fredericksburg, the school was not successful; there were only nine students in it in 1768.[34]

Reverend Jonathan Boucher went so far as to broach the idea of a Negro school to his parishioners, but the parishioners made great objections to it and in addition Boucher felt that there were even more important objects to accomplish in his parish than that of the Negro school. "I am griev'd to be oblig'd to make such Reports to you," Boucher explained, "but it is a melancholy Truth that several Whites, of respectable Characters, think Themselves at Liberty to live totally negligent of either of ye sacraments. I have had several white adults to baptize—alas! Some of Them seem to think it rather a Matter of Form than of Important Consequence." But Boucher promised to try to civilize the unhappy servants.[35]

Within a few years, however, Boucher must have overcome some of these objections against educating Negroes, for he succeeded in setting up several Sunday schools for them. Years later Boucher related how he "set up two or three serious and sensible black men as schoolmasters to teach the children around them merely to read at their leisure hours, and chiefly on Sunday afternoons, something as Sunday schools now are here in England. I had in consequence almost every Sunday twenty or thirty who could use their prayerbooks, and make the responses: and I had towards the last of my ministry there thirteen black communicants. I continued this attention to, and care of the blacks of my parish, who amounted to upwards of a thousand taxables, all the time I remained in Saint Mary's."[36]

Whatever the educational method used, the general practice seems to have made for a practical rather than a liberal education. The Reverend James Maury doubted the wisdom of Greek and Latin for Virginia youths who aspired to positions above manual labor and servile employment. Maury could not name a son of parents of large fortune who had been educated for the learned professions. Most Virginians, he said, could not tell a quack from the real thing. The question, then, was what kind of education was best for people who would be masters of competent fortunes which they would be expected to improve by farming, merchandizing, or some other method besides the learned professions. These were the ones who classed themselves with the gentry. Few of them studied beyond their twentieth year, they commonly married young, and were soon encumbered with families. A Virginia gentleman needed some history, a smattering of geography and chronology, and a general knowledge of the laws, constitution, interests, and religion of his country. There were very few fortunes in Virginia that could be considered affluent, so most men must do something to help in the support of themselves and their families. Since youths would generally be men of business, they should study the things that would aid them. But above all, Virginians differed in so many ways from Europeans that a plan of education for Europeans would no more fit Virginians than an almanac calculated for London would fit Williamsburg.[37]

The tradition of a practical rather than a theoretical or liberal education can be traced back a good many years before the Revolution. Hugh Jones, writing in 1724, declared that the climate tended to make Virginians bright and sharp in trade, but they were more apt to read men through business and conversation than by diving into books. For the most part, they desired to learn only what was "absolutely necessary, in the shortest and best method." Some Virginians went to England for schooling, he continued, but they neither acquired as much learning nor admired it as did people in England. And Richard Ambler, in 1749, cautioned his sons in England not to neglect practical studies as one or both of them would likely be engaged in trade and commerce.[38]

Someone must have understood the desire in Virginia for an easy and practical education, for by 1751 a do-it-yourself book appeared in the colony. Notice of the sale of *The American Instructor: or Young Man's Best Companion* promised that the book contained spelling, reading, writing, and arithmetic in an easier way than any yet published. This book would qualify a person for business without the help of a master, for it had instructions on writing letters, indentures, bonds, bills of sale, receipts, wills, leases, and releases. It also taught accounting, bookkeeping, carpenter's rules, and all kinds of practical work.[39]

As the Revolution approached, there seems to have been a lessening of demand for classical and an increase in concern for English and practical education. Several men in Sussex advertised for two teachers to teach English reading and writing, arithmetic, and common mathematics. In the same year, Samuel Duval offered £30 a year for a schoolmaster able to teach English and arithmetic. Many advertisements for schoolmasters or tutors gave the subjects desired as English, writing, arithmetic, and grammar. Even Washington suggested that his stepson Jack Custis might better study more useful subjects than Greek, such as French, arithmetic, mathematics, and moral and natural philosophy.[40]

The trend away from classical and toward practical education is evident in the formation in 1772 of the Virginia Society for the Promotion of Useful Knowledge. The group, to meet at appointed times in Williamsburg, would discuss geography, natural history, natural philosophy, agriculture, practical mathematics, commerce, physic (medicine), and American history. New members were to be admitted by a majority vote of the old members, and the charter members were Theodoric Bland, Dabney Carr, John Page, Mann Page, Jr., George Muter, and John Walker.[41]

Virginia provided an opportunity for higher education at William and Mary College, chartered by the King in 1691, and even here some provision was made for poor students. In 1718, the House of Burgesses voted £1,000 to be used either for the education of poor children or for setting up scholarships, a move approved by both the Council and the Governor. Furthermore, professors at the college had to take a certain number of poor students, for which they were not compensated. The two masters of the grammar school were to accept twenty poor students each without payment of fees, the two masters of the philosophy school were to accept ten free students each, and the professor of divinity did not receive fees from any students.[42]

That poor boys did receive an education at William and Mary is attested by at least three pieces of evidence. John Tennent petitioned the House of Burgesses as follows: "That the petitioner's said father left his family in very indigent circumstances, and the petitioner having obtained his education at the College on a public foundation, and since applied himself to the study of physick [medicine] to complete which he hath been advised to go to England." There was also the example of one Pasteur of Williamsburg, the son of a tradesman "in low circumstances," who attended William and Mary, was an usher there, was characterized as a young man of learning, ingenuity, modesty, and sobriety, and was recommended to the Bishop of London for holy orders by Governor William Gooch. In 1770 an usher received £75 plus perquisites and board. We also know that Granville Smith was a £30 scholarship student at the college who quit to take a £40 tutorship in the Mann Page family when the scholarship was not paid. Smith, though a scholarship student, expected to be treated as one of the Page family.[43] Since the time was 1776, the failure of the scholarship was probably due to trouble with England.

In fact, according to a memorial from the officials of William and Mary College during the early part of the Revolution, the educational philosophy of the college was democratic rather than aristocratic. From the foundation of the college, said the officials, "science hath been attainable at the easiest price. That the expenses of education have never injured the most scanty fortune," and education would still be open "to every class of men" but for the effects of the war. The trouble was financial, and the officials did not want to cure this malady by raising tuition because "it would eventually preclude all such as are not born to wealthy inheritances." This would thwart the design of the founders who wanted "to open the door of knowledge to all persons willing to enter."[44] Such an educational philosophy has the familiar ring of that espoused today by land-grant universities.

Like the institutions of lower education, William and Mary College was increasingly concerned with practical and worldly affairs. Laymen replaced clergymen as professors and Visitors, and in 1763 the House of Burgesses voted £450 sterling for the purchase of "apparatus for the instruction of students . . . in natural and experimental philosophy."[45] Part of the education at William and Mary, however, was more worldly than "enlightened." One Mr. LeFevre, a professor sent over by the Bishop of London, had to be discharged after part of a year because of negligence and irregularities—irregularities, according to Governor Spotswood, "owing to an idle hussy he brought over with him." After she departed for England, LeFevre stopped drinking, became a different man, and secured a position as tutor in a private family. Robert Carter would not send his sons to William and Mary because he said he had known professors to play cards all night in public houses in Williamsburg and had often seen them drunk in the streets.[46]

Whether or not it was due to the troubles with England we cannot say, but by 1770 the education of Americans in England was being subjected to some criticism in Virginia. Landon Carter said he believed everybody was beginning to laugh at English education. Those who were educated in England returned with a stiff priggishness and as little good manners as possible, especially when the cut of the waistcoat, the trim of the hat, or the cap of a buckle did not attract great admiration. In short, students who went to England learned little more than foppishness. In 1770, also, Arthur Lee in England wrote to his brother Richard Henry as follows: "I have seen so much mischief & so little good arise from sending children over here for education, that I cannot recommend it for yours." A writer who signed himself *A County Justice* advocated the establishment of professorships of law and medicine at William and Mary to end the need for an English education. This writer favored the enlargement of the college to handle more than the eighty students then attending. He believed that students should attend law lectures and the General Court for two years before being allowed to practice.[47]

Another development as the Revolution approached was a change in the character of tutors in Virginia. Philip Fithian wrote in 1773 that hitherto Virginians had hired all of their tutors and schoolmasters from Scotland, but now they began to be willing to employ their own countrymen. Fithian was educated at Nassau Hall (Princeton) and was tutor in the Robert Carter home. Another Nassau Hall graduate advertised for a position as tutor in Virginia in 1773. When Fithian left Robert Carter, Carter wanted Fithian to get him another tutor from Princeton.[48]

The conflict with Great Britain also seems to have stimulated a greater interest in education in Virginia. In 1770, the *Gazette* carried a proposal for an academy in New Kent County, probably by the Presbyterian minister Charles Jeffery Smith at Providence. He pointed out that literature, of great importance to both church and state, had been supported by every wise nation. Lack of schools had long been lamented in Virginia, even though education had flourished more lately than formerly. So he proposed to establish an academy in New Kent with two separate departments. One would provide a practical education—reading, writing, arithmetic, bookkeeping, navigation, surveying, geography, and other learning useful in common life. The other would provide education in the languages, arts, and sciences—Latin, Greek, logic, rhetoric, natural and moral philosophy, astronomy, speaking, writing, theology, law, medicine, politics, and history. In short, here was the division between vocational and liberal education. The academy would have a library of perhaps a thousand volumes. At the end of his article, the writer said that the purpose of his school would be to impart loyalty to the King and to kindle and fan the sacred flame of genuine liberty which was so characteristic of true Americans and so essential to their existence.[49]

Interest in education continued in spite of the trouble with England. In 1774, a *Gazette* writer advocated a greatly improved educational system for the colony. He said that no inconvenience was so universally complained of as lack of proper education for youth, which was important to everyone and should be fostered by all. Everyone conceded that the colony had neither a sufficient number nor the proper kind of schools. There were no public schools nor anything like a seminary except William and Mary, which was so established that it did not serve its purpose. This writer wanted William and Mary converted into a university like Oxford and Cambridge, with fellowships, professorships, and scholarships so that scholars would have comfortable retreats where they could pursue their studies with ease and independence. He also proposed a grammar school at Fredericksburg like Eton or Westminster, and a fund of £5,000 a year to educate poor but promising students. Another writer in the same paper urged the necessity of a medical school.[50]

The newly-stimulated interest in education led to the establishment of one other institution of higher education before the war was far advanced—Hampden-Sydney Academy in Prince Edward County in 1776. The sponsors hoped that the need for a school in that area, as well as its importance to the country, would recommend it to the legislature for support. In addition, the urgent need for educated men was evident in a new country just breaking away from England, especially in a republic extensive, young, and unexperienced, which might otherwise be guided by the councils and defended by the arms of unskilful and unlettered men. The sponsors believed that knowledge should be diffused "as equally and as extensively as possible among the people," and they aimed "to banish those invidious distinctions, which, however little they may have been felt under a monarchial government, are improper and injurious in a republic state." If the school had the accommodations, the sponsors said, it might double the hundred students who had already applied. To help get it started, William Cabell of Amherst pledged £12 toward the establishment of the academy.[51]

Although Virginia did not provide as much educational opportunity for the people as did a colony such as Massachusetts, there were educational facilities available even for the poor. The Old Dominion had no system of compulsory, tax-supported schools, but free schools, charity schools, private tuition schools, and tutors made possible the acquisition of some formal learning. Education was considered important enough so that by law orphans, apprentices, and illegitimate children were required to have some schooling. At the level of higher education, William and Mary College provided the cheapest and most easily accessible, if not the best, training. The college also made possible the education of poor boys, and if we are to judge by its products, perhaps it did as good a job at that time as did other schools. Certain it is that some important Virginians were numbered among its students. And in spite of the claim of the writer in the *Gazette* that no inconvenience was so universally complained of as the lack of proper education for youth, petitions to the legislature did not indicate a great demand for publicly-supported schools. If the poorer sort did not approve of their educational opportunities, they were strangely quiet about them at a time when they were not quiet about religion and many other matters.

## NOTES

1. Berkeley to Lords in England, 1671, Hening, *Statutes,* II, 517.
2. Beverley, *History,* pp. 275-76.
3. Hugh Jones, *Present State of Virginia,* pp. 98, 229n.
4. *Virginia Gazette,* Jan. 2 and March 5, 1752; Nov. 29, 1770 (R).
5. Landon Carter Diary, March 12, 1771 and May 6, 1772.
6. Hening, *Statutes,* VI, 41-43, 309, 389-92; *House Journals, 1752-58,* pp. 119, 139, 163-64, 350.
7. *Ibid., 1758-61,* p. 18; Hening, *Statutes,* VII, 317-20.
8. *House Journals, 1752-58,* p. 345.
9. Undated, Sabine Hall Papers.
10. John Harrower Diary, Aug. 17 and Dec. 6, 1774; Jan. 10, 1775.
11. William Proctor to his brother, Nov. 9, 1742, Amelia County Deed Book 8, p. 162.
12. *Virginia Gazette,* Feb. 9, 1738/9; Nov. 17, 1752.
13. *Ibid.* (P & D), Dec. 13, 1770; July 18, Oct. 17, and Nov. 21, 1771; Jan. 2 and Dec. 25, 1772.
14. Norfolk County Will Book 1, pp. 17, 39, 81; Book 2, pp. 47, 180.
15. Lancaster County Deed Book 13, p. 26; Book 14, p. 128; Norfolk County Will Book 1, pp. 18, 43, 66, 73, 118, 134.
16. Oct. 6, 1755, Richmond County Will Book 6, pp. 80-81; Dec. 7, 1761, Richmond County Deed Book 12, p. 332.
17. Loudoun County Deed Book D, p. 95.
18. Brown to his brother, Feb. 18, 1774, Preston Papers, Draper MSS, 3QQ8; *Virginia Gazette* (P & D), April 11, 1771.
19. For examples, see *ibid.,* Dec. 5, 1745; March 5 and Dec. 22, 1752; Nov. 29, 1770 (R); July 18, 1771 (P & D); March 12, 1772.
20. *Ibid.,* Dec. 5, 1745; Dec. 22, 1752.

21. Washington, *Writings,* II, 368, 387, 419, 434.

22. Richard Henry Lee to Arthur Lee, April 5, 1770, Lee Papers; *Virginia Gazette* (P & D), July 18, 1771.

23. *Ibid.* (R), March 12, 1772; Fithian, *Journal,* pp. 7-8.

24. Norfolk County Will Book 1, p. 153; Prince William County Deed Book P, p. 74.

25. Beverley, *History,* p. 260; Essex County Deed Book 26, p. 110; Fauquier Petitions, Nov. 12, 1777, VSL; Hening, *Statutes,* VIII, 374-77.

26. See, for example, Lancaster County Deed Book 14, p. 128.

27. Washington Papers, V, 563. On one list, forty-one of fifty-seven, and on another, twenty-four of thirty-seven, signed with a mark.

28. Washington County Petitions, Nov. 6, 1777; Hanover Petitions, Oct. 23, 1778; Yogohanie Petitions, Oct. 27, 1778; Prince William Petitions, May 16, 1780; Religious Petitions, Oct. 16, 1776, VSL.

29. Preston Papers, VHS; William Cabell Diary, May 31, 1770.

30. Officers to Washington, Oct. 10, 1757, *Letters to Washington,* II, 209-10.

31. *Virginia Gazette* (P & D), Feb. 20, April 23 (R), and Nov. 26, 1772 (P & D); John Harrower Diary, June 6 to 8, 1776.

32. Letter to Alexander Rhonnald, Sept. 27, 1762, MSS of Dr. Bray's Associates, American Correspondence, 1742-68, Society for the Propagation of the Gospel, Library of Congress.

33. *Ibid.*

34. Nicholas to Rev. John Waring, June 23, 1762, and Fielding Lewis to Nicholas, Oct. 31, 1768, MSS of Dr. Bray's Associates, on film at Colonial Williamsburg.

35. Rev. Jonathan Boucher to Rev. Jno. Waring, Dec. 31, 1762, *ibid.*

36. Boucher, *Reminiscences,* pp. 58-59.

37. Maury to Robert Jackson, July, 1762, Maury Papers.

38. Jones, *Present State of Virginia,* pp. 81-82; Richard Ambler to his sons, May 20, 1749, Elizabeth Barbour Ambler Collection, Alderman Library, U. of Va.

39. *Virginia Gazette,* Sept. 19, 1751.

40. *Ibid.* (P & D), June 21, 1770 and (R) Nov. 29, 1770; Jan. 2 and March 12, 1772; to Jonathan Boucher, June 2, 1771, Washington, *Writings,* III, 36-37.

41. Nov. 20, 1772, Tucker Papers.

42. *House Journals, 1712-26,* pp. 199, 201, 202, 210, 212, 214, 217; Fulham MSS—Virginia, Box 1, No. 48.

43. *House Journals, 1758-61,* p. 160; Gooch to Bishop of London, Sept. 20, 1735, Gooch Papers, II, 408; *Virginia Gazette* (R), Sept. 27, 1770; Smith to William Preston, Jan. 17, 1776, Preston Papers.

44. *House Journals, May, 1777,* pp. 34-35.

45. William Robinson to [Bishop of London?], Fulham MSS—Virginia, Box 1, No. 117; *House Journals, 1761-65,* p. 151.

46. Spotswood to the Bishop of London, May 8, 1712, Spotswood, *Letters,* II, 156-57; Fithian, *Journal,* pp. 86-87.

47. Landon Carter Diary, March 23, 1770; Sept. 10, 1770, Lee Papers; *Virginia Gazette* (R), Dec. 30, 1773.

48. Fithian, *Journal,* pp. 39, 125; *Virginia Gazette* (R), Nov. 18, 1773.

49. *Ibid.,* March 1, 1770.

50. *Ibid.* (P & D), May 12, 1774.

51. *House Journals, Nov., 1776,* pp. 58-59; William Cabell Diary, Oct. 27, 1775.

# CHAPTER XIII

# The Revolution as a Social Movement

SINCE REVOLUTIONS often either result from internal conflict and demands for internal change or present excellent opportunities for achieving
internal reform, a look at the American Revolution as it affected Virginia
should tell us a great deal about the structure of society in the Old
Dominion and the nature of the Revolution there. The extent to which
Virginia's institutions and practices suffered alterations as the result of
upheaval should throw much light on whether the colony had been aristocratic or democratic. Because historians have placed considerable emphasis
on internal social changes brought about by the American Revolution,
this aspect of the problem as it related to Virginia should be of vital
importance.[1]

If economic opportunity was as prevalent as contemporaries and other
supporting evidence indicate, one would expect the Revolution to bring
little change in this aspect of Virginia society. The coming of the war
did interrupt a projected increase in land prices and quitrents, but this
increase was a British policy, not that of a local aristocracy.[2] There were
still vast amounts of unoccupied land in the state: Dunmore estimated
Virginia's area at 50,000,000 acres in 1774 with only 10,000,000 taken
up and only 1,000,000 under cultivation.[3] Land speculators were offering
500 acres for £5, including all fees, in 1776; the Virginia government
granted pre-emption rights up to 400 acres per family for squatters, voided
several large grants made by the British where terms of the grant had not
been fulfilled, and passed a new land law in 1779 creating a land office
for granting lands. Purchasers could buy unlimited amounts of land at
£40 in inflated money per 100 acres, which amounted to £2 hard money
when the act was passed and rapidly decreased because of inflation.[4] In
1781, people in the western counties of Lincoln, Fayette, and Jefferson
could buy up to 400 acres at twenty shillings specie per hundred, so poor
people could still get land at reasonable prices.[5]

Slavery as an institution underwent very little alteration as a result
of the war. Jefferson's statement in 1774 that "the abolition of domestic
slavery is the great object of desire in those colonies where it was un-
happily introduced in their infant state" might have represented his own
views but not those of Virginians as a whole.[6] In fact, the section of the
Declaration of Independence in which Jefferson condemned the King
for fostering slavery was deleted in the final copy.[7] What Virginia did

about slavery was very mild, indeed. Although there had been efforts to exclude slave imports before the war, the state did not prohibit this practice until 1778.[8] As a war measure, however, the House resolved in May, 1778, that all free Negroes or mulattoes who enlisted or served in the army should have all the rights and privileges of other subjects, but this had nothing to do with slaves.[9]

Before the war, no slave could be freed except by the Governor and Council and then only for meritorious service to the colony, and in spite of numerous attempts, it was not until 1782 that manumission was permitted.[10] One effort at limited manumission died as a result of a conflict between House and Senate; James Madison's proposal to free slaves and enlist them as soldiers failed in spite of his arguments that such an act not only would be consonant with principles of liberty in a war being fought for liberty, but also that freedmen soon lost all sympathy for former fellow slaves. Quakers, much opposed to slavery, failed to get a manumission law in 1781, but in 1782 the legislature enacted a law permitting a man to free his slaves by will or affidavit witnessed by two persons and proved in a county court, provided slaves under age or infirm were supported by the owner or his estate.[11]

Even this minimum manumission law did not go unchallenged, and while the legislature did enact some Negro legislation, it neither extended emancipation nor repealed limited manumission. Petitions from Accomack demanded repeal of the manumission law on the ground that while universal liberty was desirable, freed slaves would shelter other slaves who had joined the British, manumission would depreciate slave property, and meritorious service to the public was not involved. The legislature did free any slave who served as an army substitute for free persons, and in 1784 it modified the slave code somewhat. White women who had colored children had to leave the state within a year; Negroes or mulattoes brought into the state were to be free, but they also had to leave the state—as did any slaves who were emancipated. Negroes could testify only in cases involving other Negroes, and only free white persons could be citizens.[12]

Something of a showdown over manumission came in 1785, two years after the war was over, nine years after it started, and eleven years after Jefferson indicated a desire on the part of the colonies to end slavery. A petition, probably instigated by Quakers, asked that all slaves be freed because slavery violated the fundamental principles of both the Christian religion and the state's government.[13] Countering petitions from piedmont counties such as Amelia, Mecklenburg, Lunenburg, Brunswick, Pittsylvania, Halifax, and others not only objected to total emancipation but even demanded repeal of the manumission law on the ground that the Revolution had been fought to preserve liberty and property, that the state had adopted a constitution to protect both, that slave property was now being threatened, and that the Bible sanctioned slavery.[14] In the House of Delegates, the vote against total emancipation was unanimous, even though "sundry respectable members" favored the principle. Then the House voted 51-50 to bring in a bill to repeal manumission, defeated the bill 52-35 when it came to a vote, and defeated another bill to amend the existing law.[15] So Virginia, contrary to Jefferson's statement, decided to keep slavery with limited manumission.

It was also Jefferson, writing many years after the event, who gave us an erroneous view of the abolition of entail. He said that entail had allowed some of the early settlers to obtain large grants of land and to perpetuate family dominance of a "Patrician order" through entail. Jefferson said he desired to eliminate this privileged aristocracy of wealth for one of virtue and talent, the latter scattered equally among all ranks of people.[16] Actually, entail had been greatly weakened and circumvented in colonial times, and when Jefferson introduced a bill to abolish the practice just five days after the first Assembly met under the Virginia Constitution of 1776, this relic of feudalism died with barely a struggle. The preamble of the act itself contains several valid and more realistic reasons than the one given by Jefferson:

> Whereas the perpetuation of property in certain families, by means of gifts made to them in fee taille, is contrary to good policy, tends to deceive fair traders, who give a credit on the visible possession of such estates, discourages the holder thereof from taking care and improving the same, and sometimes does injury to the morals of youth, by rendering them independent of and disobedient to their parents; and whereas the former method of docking such estates taille by special act of assembly, formed for each particular case, employed very much time of the legislature, and the same, as well as the method of defeating such estates, when of small value, was burthensome to the public, and also to individuals. . . .[17]

All available evidence points to the fact that entail had few champions, even among the "aristocracy" it was supposed to perpetuate. The House that passed the bill contained representatives of only twenty-eight counties west of the fall line out of a total of sixty-two, there was not a single petition either for or against it in a state where the people were accustomed to petitions on everything, there was no discussion in the *Virginia Gazette,* and no vote on the bill was recorded. In his "Notes on Virginia" written a few years after passage of the entail bill, Jefferson had only this to say: "Slaves, as well as lands, were entailed during the monarchy; but, by an act of the first republican assembly, all donees in tail, present and future, were vested with the absolute dominion of the entailed subject."[18]

One can only conclude that the end of entail was approved by most men of the time, and was not simply a move aimed at the destruction of aristocracy. Two men opposed Jefferson's bill on entails, one from an old family and one not. Landon Carter called proponents of the bill "monsters" of an "agrarian cast," claimed that Virginians were "overturning the very principles of justice on which they built their very claim to freedom" by loading future generations with debts while robbing them of the estates to pay these debts. This, said Carter, was sowing seeds of contention that must spring up sooner or later "from the poisoned soil of popularity," and he placed much of the blame on the "famous" Thomas Jefferson. The other opponent, ex-orphan-apprentice Edmund Pendleton, was zealously attached to "ancient establishments," according to Jefferson, and when he could not preserve the old law as it had been, he attempted in vain to substitute voluntary instead of compulsory breaking of entail. Pendleton received some support, but his proposal was eventually defeated.[19]

Unlike entatil, primogeniture remained in effect in Virginia until the revision of the laws in 1785, and then its elimination was accomplished almost without protest. Edmund Pendleton objected, as he had against the ending of entail, and attempted to get a double portion for the eldest son, but Jefferson, author of the bill to end primogeniture, countered that this would be just only if the eldest son ate or worked twice as much as the other children. Jefferson's view prevailed and primogeniture came to an end in 1785, but at the time Jefferson did not indicate that the law was of special significance and Madison did not include primogeniture among those parts of the revised code over which there was some disagreement.[20]

In view of these mild reactions by Jefferson and Madison, as well as the failure of the primogeniture law to prevent the amassing of large estates, it is difficult to understand Jefferson's later emphasis on the law. Writing in 1821, he declared that "the abolition of primogeniture and equal partition of inheritances removed the feudal and unnatural distinction which made one member of every family rich, and all the rest poor, substituting equal partition, the best of all Agrarian laws." Jefferson certainly knew that the general practice, regardless of entail and primogeniture, had been the division of property among all the children. Furthermore, Keim has shown that equal division of property among all children after 1776 and 1785 did not result in a general levelling of property holding. Both before and after 1776, some estates were disintegrating as others were building, but in the years after 1776 there were more large estates in most counties surveyed than there had been before that date.[21] If entail and primogeniture had really been important in colonial days, their abolition should have had the effect of reducing the number of large estates.

In the realm of politics, independence also brought little that could be classified as internal social revolution. The famous Virginia Bill of Rights declared that the suffrage should be free—the right of all men with "sufficient evidence of permanent common interest with, and attachment to, the community." The Constitution itself provided that the right of suffrage would "remain as exercised at present," a natural provision in view of the absence of any previous objections to voting qualifications. Even the right of plural voting was retained for men with sufficient property in more than one county. There was a proposal that a man should be a voter if he had a seven-year lease on land, or if he was a housekeeper who had resided one year in the county and had fathered three children, but this proposal received little support. As Edmund Randolph put it: "That the qualification of electors to the general assembly should be restricted to freeholders was the natural effect of Virginia having been habituated to it for many years, more than a century. The members of the convention were themselves freeholders, and from this circumstance felt a proud attachment to the country, in which the ownership of the soil was a certain source of comfort. It is not recollected that a hint was uttered in contravention of this principle. There can be no doubt that if it had been, it would have soon perished under a discussion."[22]

A petition from frontier Washington county in 1777 makes it appear that the frontiersmen were not anxious to abolish voting qualifications. This petition complained that the Constitution did not provide for the nomination of land surveyors. Surveyors should be nominated either by the county courts or by the people at large, and only properly qualified persons should have the right to vote.[23] The petitioners obviously did not object too much to the old practice of nomination of officers by the county courts and selection by the Governor, but if the people did the electing they were to be properly qualified.

When the state finally altered the franchise requirements in 1785, it adopted those provisions that the colony had unsuccessfully attempted to establish in 1762 and 1770—which hardly makes the 1785 law "revolutionary." As proposed in these previous bills, the freehold requirement was still twenty-five acres if improved, but the 100 acres of unimproved land were reduced to fifty acres. Town voters as formerly needed a house and part of a lot. The only real changes were that the requirement for unimproved land was cut in half and that houses on improved land or on lots in town had to be twelve feet square. In Norfolk or Williamsburg, men were also voters if they had a visible estate of £50 or had served a five-year apprenticeship.[24] Had the British not nullified the law, the franchise provisions of 1785 would have been enacted in 1762.

What happened to the voting franchise, however, could scarcely under any circumstance be classed as a part of the internal social revolution. If aristocrats controlled the House before the Revolution, why did they want to reduce the freehold requirement from 100 acres to fifty acres? And if the lower classes were in command after the Revolution, why did they want to preserve the voting qualifications that an aristocratic legislature had tried to adopt twenty-three years earlier? Since the franchise remained unchanged after the Revolution began, there could have been little alteration in the electorate except for those few who would have qualified after 1785 under the reduction from 100 to fifty acres of unimproved land. If most men could vote before the Revolution, as our evidence indicates, then most adult men were still voters after 1776.

The assertion that most men were voters, however, confronts us with another statement by Jefferson that is often cited and appears difficult to reconcile with our generalizations. In the "Notes on Virginia," Jefferson wrote as follows:

> The majority of the men in the state, who pay and fight for its support, are unrepresented in the legislature, the roll of freeholders entitled to vote, not including generally the half of those on the roll of the militia, or of the tax-gatherers.[25]

At first glance, Jefferson might mistakenly be interpreted as saying that half or more of the adult men could not vote. But this is not what he said. He included the freeholders only, which seems to mean that he did not count tenants and non-freeholders who could vote by some other qualification. But even more important, the militia rolls and tax rolls would include many young men from sixteen to twenty-one years of age who were not old enough to vote. Whether Jefferson, a liberal, was under-estimating the qualified voters just as he over-estimated the desire of colonists to end slavery and the importance of the abolition of entail and primogeniture is not certain. But it would appear that others who described a very wide electorate were more accurate than was Jefferson.[26]

Far from stirring up a political revolution in voting participation, the coming of the war brought increased political apathy, according to both statistics and contemporary opinion. Essex County, where we have a fairly complete set of election polls, furnishes the statistics.

## NUMBER OF VOTERS IN ESSEX COUNTY ELECTIONS, 1748-1789[27]

| Year | Voters | Year | Voters | Year | Voters | |
|------|--------|------|--------|------|--------|---|
| 1748 | 377 | 1768 | 352 | 1786 | 255 | |
| 1752 | 318 | 1769 | 329 | 1787 | 387 | |
| 1755 | 356 | 1771 | 245 | 1788 | 351 | |
| 1758 | 356 | 1777 | 239 | 1789 | 315 | (Va. H. of Del.) |
| 1761 | 374 | 1778 | 112 | 1789 | 108 | (H. of Rep.) |
| 1765 | 376 | 1785 | 288 | 1789 | 217 | (President) |

Voter participation dropped steadily from 376 in 1765 to 112 in 1778, although we might expect the opposite to happen. At the same time the number of tithables in the county increased from 2,620 in 1750 to 2,850 in 1773. Lowering the franchise from 100 to fifty acres did not bring a startling upsurge in numbers, although the adoption of the Federal Constitution did stir up some interest in 1787 and 1788—about as much interest as there had been in 1748 and 1755. And in 1789 there was much more concern with the election of the local legislature than there was in the election of the United States Representative or the President. As John Page said in 1778, the freeholders were in a "torpid state, for so few of them attend at elections now that any man may get into either house."[28]

If the Revolution had been primarily or even incidentally a conflict for internal democracy instead of merely a War for Independence, there should have been an increase rather than a decrease in voter interest. We know, for example, that 421 different men voted in the Essex elections that were held within a short time of each other in 1768 and 1769. Since there was no change in voting requirements, at least that many could doubtless vote at a later date. Some men were probably in the army, but not that many. So the only logical conclusion is that there was little if any internal revolution and that the people became increasingly satisfied with the position of their representatives as the war approached and got under way.

In the area of representation there was also no sharp break with the past. The Constitution of 1776 provided that each county should elect two delegates, regardless of size or population, and that Williamsburg, Norfolk, and other cities and boroughs created by the legislature were to have one each. One minor change was the elimination of representation for William and Mary College and Jamestown, both in the tidewater. This latter provision brought a vigorous protest from William Lee, an ardent supporter of the Revolution, whose wife had inherited considerable property near Jamestown—evidence that not all "revolutionaries" were adamant for equitable representation where their own interests were concerned. The only significant change in representation was that candidates for the legislature had to be residents and freeholders "or duly qualified according to law" in the county or borough where they were elected. Candidates could not run from any county, or from more than one county, as they had in the past.[29]

Virginia also kept its upper house of the legislature—the old Council—and an executive council to advise the Governor, but it separated the two functions, and naturally members were not appointed by the King. There were twenty-four senators elected from geographic districts. Senators had to be at least twenty-five years of age and qualified by residence and property as were the representatives, and they were elected for four-year terms with one-fourth of the members to be elected each year, not a particularly democratic procedure. The Governor's council of eight was chosen by joint ballot of the House and Senate, and councillors could not sit in either house.[30]

In terms of internal revolution, it is significant to note that the proposal to liberalize the franchise in 1776 also contained a plan to increase greatly the requirements for membership in the House or Senate. Members of the House were to possess an estate in land of at least £1,000; senators were to be elected by electors chosen by qualified voters, but the electors were to have an estate of at least £500 within the electoral district, and the men they elected as senators were to possess at least a £2,000 estate.[31] Neither the more liberal voting franchise nor the more conservative requirements for the legislature were incorporated in the Constitution.

The pattern of representation remained much the same after as before the Revolution. While many representatives won easily in 1776, there were "warm contests" in some counties just as there had been before the Revolution. George Mason in Fairfax and Henry Lee of Prince William were "much push'd" to win; the other Prince William incumbent, Thomas Blackburn, was replaced by Cuthbert Bullett; William Brent defeated Charles Carter from Stafford, and Martin Prichet displaced Thomas Marshall in Fauquier.[32] Furthermore, the men who replaced the defeated candidates were usually of the same general social position, as had been the case before 1776.

As we have already noted in Table I, Chapter X, many men who had served in the House before the dissolution of the last official legislature in 1774 continued to serve in the revolutionary conventions and in the legislatures after 1776. Every county (last column, Table I, Ch. X) had at least one such, five counties had as many as four, and the total was 151. This did not mean that they had served consecutive terms throughout the entire period, but that they had been in the House at one time or another both before and after hostilities started. In short, there was little if any "revolution" in representation.

The Essex County election polls previously alluded to give us an excellent picture of the continuity of election practices after the Declaration of Independence. Many of the same men and the same families ran for office both before and after the war. Sometimes they won; sometimes they lost. There were always several candidates, ten in 1752 and 1778, nine in 1755 and 1787, so the voters had ample choice. William Beverley won in 1748, but no Beverley was ever successful in the county thereafter, although Robert ran in 1765, 1771, 1787, and 1788. Over a period of forty years, 1748-1788, the county was represented by fourteen different men—William Beverley, William Daingerfield, Thomas Waring, Francis Smith, John Upshaw, Francis Waring, John Lee, William Roane, James Edmondson, Meriwether Smith, William Smith, John Edmondson, William Gatewood, and James Upshaw. Robert Beverley, Robert Waring, George W. Smith, Thomas Roane, Spencer Roane, Thomas Edmondson, Jr., William Edmondson and nineteen other candidates ran for the office but never succeeded.

The problem of representation also raises a question about Jefferson's interpretation. In his "Notes on Virginia," Jefferson made a great issue of the fact that the tidewater after the Revolution was heavily overrepresented in comparison with the piedmont and frontier. With only 11,205 square miles of land out of 121,525 and 19,012 fighting men out of 49,971, the tidewater had seventy-one representatives out of 149 and twelve senators out of twenty-four. Jefferson said that Warwick county, with only 100 fighting men, had the same representation as Loudoun with 1,746.[33] Certainly, if Jefferson was correct, there was no internal revolution as far as representation was concerned, for if the tidewater was overrepresented before the Revolution, it was still over-represented after the Constitution of 1776.

Jefferson's statement, however, merely begs the question of whether his views were held by the people in general, and the answer seems to be no. Randolph was probably more nearly correct when he declared that in spite of objections against inequality of representation in the British House of Commons, "it was submitted to in Virginia without a murmur, and even without a proposition to the contrary."[34] There is little if any evidence before the Revolution that Virginians considered unequal representation as a grievance, probably because the interests of the large and small counties were fundamentally the same. If the people considered their representation adequate, we would not expect much change even if Warwick was greatly over-represented in comparison with other counties.

Jefferson also miscalculated the problem for another reason—the influence of property rights as well as human rights in the distribution of eighteenth-century representation. Virginians thought in terms of tithables, not fighting men, and some of the smaller counties or counties with relatively few white fighting men had a considerable number of black tithables for payment of taxes. We have also suggested earlier that some of the people preferred lower taxes to additional representation and often petitioned against the division of counties. Jefferson was perfectly right in saying that some counties had greater per capita representation, but this does not appear to have been an issue among the people.

The creation of an executive and the powers allotted to him were more the reflection of colonial experience with a strong British-appointed Governor than of an internal social revolution. The Governor was chosen annually by joint ballot of both houses, not elected by the people as one would expect if internal revolution had been involved. He could not hold office for more than three years in succession and then was not eligible for re-election for four years. He could not veto bills, prorogue or dissolve the legislature, or prevent a meeting of the legislature, as former Governors could do, for the Constitution provided at least one meeting each year.

In many respects the Constitution of 1776 continued old practices that had been operative before the Revolution. In addition to the franchise and representation, the President of the Council succeeded as Governor when necessary; the Governor, on recommendation of the county courts, appointed militia officers, justices of the county courts, sheriffs, and coroners; and clerks of the county courts, as in former times, held office during good behavior. Joint election by both houses replaced the appointive power in some instances, such as judges of the Supreme Court, General Court, Chancery, and Admiralty, and the Secretary and Attorney-General, but they were all to hold office during good behavior.[35]

There was no question of "radicals" riding roughshod over aristocratic opposition to put over an ultra-democratic constitution. Richard Henry Lee, now often referred to as a "radical," urged the establishment of a government in Virginia in April, 1776, to prevent "popular commotions" and anarchy. Lee proposed a plan of government, written by a "sensible gentleman" in Philadelphia, which, with some variation, "would in fact, be nearly the form we have been used to." Lee wanted a government of checks and balances, a blending of the three forms of government to prevent the inordinate views of one group from unduly affecting the others. He also favored Thomas Nelson, former president of the Council, as Governor.[36] In fact, the leading candidates for Governor were Patrick Henry, Thomas Nelson, and John Page. Nelson had been Secretary and Acting Governor before the war, and John Page had been a member of the Council.[37]

Jefferson, himself, was no "radical" in many of his views on government. In speaking of the government under the Constitution of 1776, he said that the Senate was "too homogeneous with the house of delegates." Both Senate and House were "chosen by the same electors, at the same time, and out of the same subjects," so naturally the men selected were of the same description. Virginia did not benefit from the plan of having two houses, since the purpose of such was "to introduce the influence of different interests or different principles," such as protection of persons in the House and property in the Senate. The concentration of all legislative, executive, and judiciary powers in the House, Jefferson declared, was "precisely the definition of despotic government." Jefferson also wanted a fixed constitution that could not be altered at the whim of the legislature. If checks and balances and protection of property are considered conservative, as they seem to be, Jefferson must be labelled a conservative on these points.[38]

The truth seems to be that instead of an internal revolution in which "radicals" displaced "conservatives," Virginia experienced a situation in which what we now call "liberals" and "conservatives" joined hands against Britain, but disagreed among themselves as to the nature of man and society. Since the term "radical" now has a Marxian flavor, there were probably few men whom we would call radicals, even though that term has been widely and loosely used to describe some of the revolutionary generation. For example, Robert Carter Nicholas, colonial treasurer and a strong advocate of opposition to Great Britain, was equally forceful in opposition to the first article of the Virginia Bill of Rights, which declared that all men were "by nature equally free and independent." [39] It would be very difficult to call Nicholas a "radical" in the sense in which we now use the term, even though he advocated revolution.

If one can relate "aristocracy" to "conservatism" and "democracy" to "liberalism"—and that does not appear wholly unreasonable—the conflict between the two after the Revolution began makes any doctrinaire interpretation difficult indeed. Edmund Randolph called the effort to elect Thomas Nelson as Governor instead of Patrick Henry the "last expiring act of aristocracy." But John Page, the other candidate, was not exactly proletarian, and to confuse the issue further, "radical" Richard Henry Lee supported Nelson. Randolph also injected the aristocratic-democratic dichotomy by characterizing articles twelve (freedom of the press) and thirteen (militia rather than standing army) of the Bill of Rights as "the fruits of genuine democracy and historical experience." Then to confuse the issue still further, he said that Patrick Henry denied that his espousal of article sixteen on unfettered religion was a prelude to an attack on the established church and that Henry also defeated an article prohibiting bills of attainder. Thomas Ludwell Lee, former member of the Council and presumably an "aristocrat," spoke of "a certain set of Aristocrats" who tried to block the Bill of Rights because their system could not be built on such a foundation. Lee apparently excluded himself from this "set of Aristocrats." [40]

Like many modern historians, John Adams apparently failed to realize the extent of popular government in Virginia before the Revolution, for he, too, overestimated the amount of internal change. He said that "the colonies to the south are pursuing the same maxims which have hitherto governed those to the north. In constituting their new governments, their plans are remarkably popular, more so than I could ever have imagined; even more popular than the 'Thoughts on Government'; and in the choice of their rulers, capacity, spirit, and zeal in the cause, supply the place of fortune, family, and every other consideration which used to have weight with mankind." But having said this, Adams added that "although the colonies have differed in religion, laws, customs, and manners, yet in the great essentials of society and government, they are all alike." [41] Perhaps Adams was confusing elected and appointed officials, or it might have been that he did not know how democratic the elected branch of the government in Virginia was before the Revolution, for the men who took over after the departure of the British were mostly men who had held either elective or appointive office before 1776.

Although contemporaries, including John Adams, characterized the Virginia constitution as "very much of the democratic kind," it does not in fact appear to have been very radically democratic except for the elimination of the British. It is true that the House and Governor were elected annually and the Governor had no veto power, but Senators had four-year terms, the House and Senate, not the people, selected judges and other high officials, and many of these appointed officials held office during good behavior. In addition, there was no change in the franchise and, except for the elimination of Jamestown and the college, no alteration in the mode of representation, in spite of the fact that twenty-one of the thirty-three members of the committee to write the constitution were from the piedmont and frontier.[42]

Undoubtedly the elimination of the British was responsible for most of the internal changes that took place. With no alteration in the franchise and representation, the people could elect exactly the same type of men that they had always elected. Men who had depended upon family and wealth for appointments by the British could no longer reach high office by this method. But we must remember that Thomas Nelson and John

Page, both of whom had held high office under the British, were considered as two leading candidates for the governorship. Page, certainly not lower-class, called the Virginia constitution "the most perfect in the World." [43] Edmund Pendleton, generally considered a conservative, was president of the convention which drafted the Constitution of 1776, and when the first legislature met, Pendleton was elected speaker of the House.[44] Naturally there were changes to fill the vacuum left by the British, and many of these changes reflected experiences under the British, but these matters did not signify great internal upheaval.

If the Revolution brought little that was new in political and economic life, the same cannot be said for religion. By all odds the greatest internal controversy in the Old Dominion was in the area of religion, not of the franchise, or representation, or entail, or primogeniture. This comes as no great surprise, for religious differences appeared to be building up to a climax before the outbreak of the Revolution. Since the controversy involved the Church of England and dissenters, the removal of British church-state restraints made religious conflict almost inevitable.

Almost before the ink on the Declaration of Independence had dried, dissenters and churchmen were at each other over the status of religion in the new state. Instructions from Augusta County to the county's representative demanded that "all religious denominations" be given "equal liberty" and that there should be no established religious sect. There was also a not-too-well-veiled threat that failure to grant religious equality might have some bearing on the fighting of the Revolution. Published in the *Virginia Gazette,* the Augusta instructions quickly elicited a response from a churchman in defense of the established church. It had served a good purpose for nearly two hundred years, he said; its clergy and laity had been more forward "in the present glorious contest" than any other religious sect. Dissenters were tolerated and should not threaten unanimity by raising religious questions, he declared, and there was a need to support clergymen so that they would not be forced to become "popular disclaimers" or starve.[45]

Thus were the issues drawn between defenders of the old order and advocates of the new. It was not enough that the Virginia Convention ordered a revision of the Book of Common Prayer to remove all vestiges of the royal family from its pages. Neither did it suffice that article sixteen of the constitution, drawn up by the same convention, declared that religion could be directed only by reason and conviction, not by force or violence, and that therefore all men were "equally entitled to the free exercise of religion." This merely signified religious toleration, not religious equality, and toleration was not enough.[46]

When the first legislature met under the new constitution in the fall of 1776, there was a deluge of petitions both for and against the established church. Those against demanded relief from "a long night of ecclesiastical bondage," and while they considered the Bill of Rights as "the rising star of religious liberty," they nevertheless expected the legislature to complete what was so nobly begun. They wanted all church establishments pulled down, the abolition of all taxes upon conscience, and a clear distinction between civil and ecclesiastical authority. One petition, an estimated 180 to 200 feet in length, contained nearly 10,000 signatures.[47] Those for the church claimed that dissenters were causing irreparable breaches between husbands and wives, masters and slaves, and urged that final action on religion be delayed until the collective opinion of the people could be known, as they believed that a majority favored the church.[48] The force of the arguments on both sides gave every indication that the revolution in religion was going to be neither quick nor easy.

What happened to religion in Virginia during the ten years following the Declaration of Independence—a slow, step-by-step process until the achievement of complete religious freedom in 1786—was anything but revolutionary, and the reason was that the legislature could never move decisively because it was never sure of the collective sentiments of the people. The prediction that general opinion would cause abolition of the church establishment during the first session of the legislature never materialized. The legislature granted dissenters complete religious tolera- tion and suspended tax-supported salaries for ministers on a year-to-year basis before making the suspension permanent in 1779, thus continuing a trend that was apparent before the war began.[49] Still uncertain about its actions, the Assembly in 1779 published a bill on religious freedom to get public reaction, but postponed until 1780 any action on the by- then-burning issue of who was to get the church property that had been paid for by taxes on all the people.[50]

By 1780, several clearly-defined and closely-associated issues had emerged to complicate the whole religious question. Was there to be complete or only partial religious freedom? Augusta and Amherst counties highly approved of the proposed bill of 1779, but petitioners from Culpeper, Essex, Lunenburg, and Amherst were opposed, the latter professing a willingness to tolerate even Catholics but hoping that no Catholic, Jew, Turk, or infidel would be allowed to hold civil or military office. Should there be no established church, one established church, or should all churches be established? Culpeper, Essex, Lunenburg, and Amherst favored a general assessment for all religions, thus making them all established.[51] What should be done about vestries: should the old ones continue, with replacements provided in the usual way, or should there be new elections for all vestries? Amherst wanted completely new elec- tions, but the legislature only ventured to dissolve the vestries and divest them of their powers over the poor in seven western counties.[52] Should dissenting ministers have the same rights over marriage as did church clergymen? The Assembly in 1780 passed a law removing all doubts about the legality of marriages by dissenting ministers, but did not finally settle the matter until 1784.[53]

When the war ended in 1783, three of these major religious questions still remained to be settled. By this time there was no chance that the Protestant Episcopal Church could continue its monopoly. There was still a burning controversy, however, over whether there should be no established church or whether all churches should be established, over what disposition was to be made of church property, paid for by churchmen and dissenters alike, and over what was to be done with church vestries.

These three problems were further complicated by a law to incorporate the Protestant Episcopal Church. The church petitioned for repeal of some religious laws, then asked that all property belonging to the church be secured to that body forever by law and that the legislature incorporate the church so that it could regulate spiritual matters, alter its form of worship, and create its own rules of government.[54] One item that caused dissension was a request by the Episcopal clergy that they, and not the members of the church, be incorporated and given power to regulate church affairs. John B. Smith, Presbyterian minister from Hampden-Sydney College, branded the clergy's request to exclude the people as revolting and "very insulting," and he claimed that this was an attempt to draw the legislature into an alliance with that church alone.[55] James Madison called the proposal by the clergy "a notable project for re-establishing their independence of the laity," and claimed that it was "preserved from a dishonorable death by the talents of Mr. Henry."[56]

As finally passed, the incorporating act gave the clergy but not church members what they wanted. Adopted by a vote of 47-37, the bill did provide for three-year elections of twelve-man vestries, but it did not make church members parties to the incorporation. Ministers and vestries were to be bodies corporate with power to hold all church property and to make all decisions by a majority vote. The act also created an Episcopal Convention with more powers than some people intended, for it did not include the provision that the convention was to be composed of two laymen for every clergyman, and vestries discovered that they did not have the uncontrolled right of electing their clergymen unless the convention permitted this.[57] The fact that it took eight years after the Revolution to get elected vestries does indicate, however, that this was not a pressing issue.

The same session that passed the incorporating act also resolved that all people should pay a moderate tax for the support of the Christian religion. The vote was 47-32, with Patrick Henry voting for it, and a bill was ordered to be brought in. This resulted in a spate of petitions both for and against tax-supported churches, some believing that civil power should be divorced from religion, others favoring a union of the two. Presbyterian clergymen desired a general assessment for all churches, but they were alienated from the Episcopal Church by the incorporation act and legislative interference in religion. How they expected to have a general assessment without legislative interference is not clear.[58]

General assessment resulted in a strange alignment of friends and foes on the question of religious freedom. In addition to Patrick Henry, "radical" Richard Henry Lee also believed that religion was the guardian of morals and that religious toleration did not mean that the people should not be compelled to contribute to the support of religion in general. The Episcopalian-Presbyterian coalition that favored general assessment was broken by the fact that Presbyterians disliked the incorporation act and wanted to include all religions, not just Christian ones. James Madison strongly opposed assessment on the ground that establishment was not essential to religion and that religion was not within the jurisdiction of civil authority. He also believed that the incorporation act had done much to weaken assessment. A bill was brought in and ordered to be engrossed by a close vote of 44-42, but whether because of the closeness or the divided views as represented in petitions, the House voted 45-38 to postpone a third reading and to have the bill printed for consideration by the people.[59]

As it was sent out for public consideration, the assessment bill would have provided tax money to support teachers of the Christian religion only. The bill stated that religion was a moral force for the good of the state and that therefore taxes were to be collected to support religion. All distinctions of pre-eminence among the different Christian religions would be abolished, persons were to designate the church of their choice, and undesignated taxes would be used by the legislature to encourage seminaries of learning. The people were requested to signify their opinion on the bill.[60]

The vote to postpone action on the assessment bill raises some interesting questions about sectionalism in religion.

TABLE 1. VOTE ON POSTPONEMENT OF ASSESSMENT BILL, 1784[61]

|  | Tidewater | Piedmont | Frontier | Total |
|---|---|---|---|---|
| For Postponement | 8 | 21 | 16 | 45 |
| Against Postponement | 26 | 11 | 1 | 38 |
| Not Voting | 24 | 30 | 15 | 69 |

Since postponement of the vote on the bill undoubtedly weakened its prospects of passage, we can assume that those who voted to postpone were against assessment. On this assumption, the tidewater, where the Church of England had been strongest, was heavily in favor of tax-supported religion, the piedmont was about two to one against, and on the frontier, where the church had always been weakest, sentiment was almost unanimous against assessment. But equally significant is the number of men who did not vote either way. Had all the delegates from the tidewater supported the bill, it could have passed easily—assuming, of course, that all non-voters from the piedmont and frontier still abstained.

By spring of 1785, much public debate on the proposed assessment bill resulted in a fairly clear separation of views. According to Madison, this bill, which was the only one passed in the last Assembly to make "a noise" through the country, was generally favored by the Episcopalians, "tho' I think," he added, "the zeal of some of them has cooled." The laity of other sects were equally unanimous on the other side, continued Madison, and so were all the clergy except the Presbyterians "who seem as ready to set up an establishm't which is to take them in as they were to pull down that which shut them out." A few weeks later Madison wrote that the bill had produced "some fermentation below the Mountains & a violent one beyond them. The contest at the next Session on this question will be a warm & precarious one." [62]

The decision to submit the question of assessment to the people resulted in an excellent demonstration of the workings of democracy. Madison led the opposition with a well-reasoned remonstrance which was circulated in many counties. He reported that the printed bill had "excited great discussion" which would redound to the benefit of religious freedom; that he had heard "of several Counties where the late representatives have been laid aside for voting for the Bill, and not a single one where the reverse has happened." Presbyterian clergy, once friendly, were now on the other side, and in the middle and back counties the people threatened not to enforce the law even if it passed.[63]

By the fall of 1785, intense feeling on the assessment bill generated an unprecedented shower of petitions to the legislature, the overwhelming majority of which opposed the bill. Never had a public question concerning Virginia's internal affairs aroused so many people. Petitions against passage of the bill came from all sections—from five counties in the far west, from twenty-eight counties in the piedmont (five of which sent two petitions), from thirteen counties in the tidewater (two of which sent two petitions) and from a general group of "citizens" of the Commonwealth, from Presbyterian ministers and laymen, from Frederick County Presbyterians, from sundry members of several Presbyterian societies, from the Baptist Association, from Baptists in Orange County, and from several groups of Quakers. Most of these petitions were signed by more than 100 people, and the Presbyterian petition had 1,019 signatures. Petitions favoring passage of the bill were fewer in number and had fewer signatures. No petition from the far west supported the bill. But from five counties in the piedmont and another five in the tidewater came petitions in favor of the act. However, eight of these ten counties (four from each section) also sent in petitions opposing passage of the bill, thus indicating divided sentiment in the majority of counties showing any support for the general assessment.[64]

Democracy in the form of petitions won the day, for the assessment bill was never brought to a vote in the House; in its place came a bill to establish religious freedom. The petitions themselves contained every imaginable reason for avoiding establishment of any and all religions, but also pointed out how reluctant the legislature had been to remove distinctions based on religious opinions. The defeat of men who had voted for assessment was perhaps the most persuasive argument, as it usually is in a democracy.[65] Before the legislature finally passed the bill on religious freedom, however, it took another step in separating ecclesiastical and civil functions by placing the care of the poor in secular hands instead of the hands of church vestries.[66]

The bill of religious freedom was the same bill that had been introduced in 1779, and whether or not it was drafted by Jefferson, as has been believed, it was certainly to his liking. Presented for consideration on December 14, 1785, the bill, after a few minor amendments, a change in the wording of the preamble, and some "warm opposition," was signed into law a little more than a month later.[67]

The act for establishing religious freedom finally completed the long, slow process of separating church and state in Virginia. It effectively made a legal reality of the philosophy expounded in the Virginia Declaration of Rights in 1776. The preamble of the act provided the philosophical basis for religious freedom, declaring that it was presumptuous for legislators and rulers, civil or ecclesiastical, to assume dominion over the faith of others, that it was sinful and tyrannical to force a man to support a religion he did not believe, that civil rights had no dependence on religious opinions, and that truth was great and would prevail if left to itself. The act then declared that no man should be compelled to attend or support any religious worship, place, or minority whatsoever. All men were to be free to profess, and by argument to maintain, their opinions in matters of religion, and this should in no way affect their political capacities. The act then ended with the declaration that although this legislature could not restrain future legislatures, any future act to repeal this present act or to narrow its operation would be an infringement on natural rights.[68]

The act to establish religious freedom did not end all religious controversy in Virginia, however, and another year was required to accomplish this purpose. Feeling against the act incorporating the Protestant Episcopal Church mounted as another wave of petitions rolled in on the legislature. Nineteen piedmont and twelve tidewater counties sent demands for repeal, while six piedmont and five tidewater counties supported incorporation. Even Episcopalians objected because the act gave too little power to laymen, while others contended that property controlled by the corporation belonged in part to other denominations.[69] In the end the legislature compromised by allowing all churches to hold the property they then possessed but repealing the law of incorporation. So, except for an occasional petition about church property, the religious conflict in Virginia came to an end in 1787.[70]

Although religion undoubtedly furnished the greatest arena for internal conflict in the colony and state both before and after the Revolution, what happened in religion after the war broke out can hardly be characterized as revolutionary. The elimination of the British naturally enabled the people to end the established church, something that could not have been done had the British remained. But this was a gain due to the elimination of imperialism, not aristocracy, and the gradual evolutionary process by which it was accomplished marked a continuation of a trend that was evident in the years long before the war began.

In education, the Revolution also brought little change in the old order. The Virginia Bill of Rights did not mention education unless one reads into the first article (Section 1) that education is essential to "the enjoyment of life and liberty" or a necessary "means of acquiring or possessing property, or pursuing and obtaining happiness and safety." [71] There had been some talk during the Revolution of establishing a system of education, but it did not materialize. Richard Henry Lee expressed the hope to Jefferson that the Assembly would "not neglect that noble and best foundation for public liberty, general diffusion of knowledge, for which you left the House so excellent a system." But a bill "for the more general diffusion of knowledge" in June, 1780, was postponed and apparently fell victim of the pressing events of war.[72]

Even Jefferson's "excellent" plan, had it been adopted, would not have measured up to what now passes as "liberal" educational philosophy, even though it would have been a tremendous gain for Virginia at the time. Today "liberal" educators assume that all children have the right to a high school education and many believe that the right extends to college as well. But Jefferson included only the first three years of elementary school as the right of all. After the first three years, those who could pay could go on as could also twenty of the best students from among those who could not pay, and these would be educated for six years at higher grammar schools, the poor students at public expense. At the end of six years, ten of the twenty poor students would be sent to William and Mary College. Speaking of the first elimination, Jefferson said that "by this means twenty of the best geniuses will be raked from the rubbish annually," a statement that does not express great confidence in the common people as a whole. But on the other hand, he believed that nature had sown talents "as liberally among the poor as the rich," and that the state should seek out and cultivate these talents.[73] But whether one considers Jefferson's plan as "liberal" or "conservative," it was to be a long time before Virginia would have a public-supported educational system.

Judging by the results, the Revolution in Virginia, as in Massachusetts, was designed primarily to preserve a social order rather than to change it. In this respect, it was one of the unique revolutions in history. Revolutions usually occur because people are dissatisfied with the status quo, but except for areas where Britain had prevented normal evolution, Virginians appear to have been satisfied with their social order.

In summary, then, we can say that the Revolution as a social movement in Virginia was not very revolutionary. The suffrage requirements, the general form of government, representation, and even the type of representative remained basically the same. Only British controls and appointments were eliminated. The great bulk of the first laws sanctioned by the new government merely restated the old order except for British restraints. The few changes that were made immediately had been desired by many people for some time and had been retained for the most part only because of British pressure. Entail, which had long been circumvented and had become a legislative nuisance, was repealed, and support for the clergy of the established church was cut off. But this too, as we have seen, had long been in the making. A "radical" such as Jefferson might favor complete disestablishment of the church, but other "radicals" such as Richard Henry Lee and Patrick Henry were not ardent leaders in the cause of complete religious freedom and separation of church and state. Looking back at the Revolution in Virginia as a whole, we find that the greatest changes came in those areas where the British government had prevented normal evolution. In a society in which the middle class comprised such a large segment and economic opportunity was readily available, there was, as one might expect, very little, if any, internal revolution.

## NOTES

1. John Franklin Jameson, *The American Revolution Considered as a Social Movement* (Princeton, 1925); John C. Miller, *Origins of the American Revolution* (Boston, 1943, 1959).

2. Additional Royal Instructions to Lord Dunmore, Feb. 3, 1774, Chalmers Collection; Dunmore to Dartmouth, April 2 and May 16, 1774, PRO, CO5, v. 1352, pp. 70-71, 99; St. George L. Sioussat, "The Breakdown of the Royal Management of Lands in the Southern Provinces, 1773-1775," *Agricultural History*, III, 67-98 (1929); Jefferson, *Papers*, I, 133; Address to the Inhabitants of Albemarle, c. 1775, Dr. George Gilmer, Diary and Revolutionary Memoranda, VHS; Richmond Convention *Proceedings*, March, 1775, p. 8.

3. Answers to queries, March 18, 1774, PRO, CO5, v. 1352, p. 6.

4. Williamsburg Convention *Proceedings*, May, 1776, p. 52; *House Journals, Oct., 1777*, p. 142; *ibid., Oct., 1778*, pp. 28, 31, 36, 42, 47, 53-54, 64, 66, 68, 70, 79, 87-88, 91, 92, 96, 100, 105, 108, 111; George Mason to Richard Henry Lee, June 19, 1779, Lee Papers; Hening, *Statutes*, X, 50-65. In Jan., 1779, money was 8 to 1, in May it was 20 to 1, and in Dec. it was 40 to 1. By Dec., 1780, it was 75 to 1, and by Dec., 1781, it was 1,000 to 1 (Jones Family Papers No. 4859).

5. *House Journals, May, 1781*, pp. 28, 41-42, 45.

6. "Summary View," Jefferson, *Papers*, I, 130.

7. Jefferson's Draft of the Declaration of Independence, Lee-Ludwell Papers, VHS.

8. *House Journals, May, 1777*, pp. 73, 79; *ibid., Oct., 1777*, pp. 17, 75, 84, 88, 93, 97, 102, 106; *ibid., Oct., 1778*, pp. 13-29; Hening, *Statutes*, IX, 471.

9. *House Journals, May, 1778*, p. 12.

10. Hening, *Statutes*, IV, 132.

11. *House Journals, Oct., 1778*, pp. 56, 64, 65, 67, 98, 100, 105, 113, 116, 119; Madison to Joseph Jones, Nov. 28, 1780, Madison, *Writings*, I, 106-07; Robert Pleasant to his brother, Feb. 15, 1781, Robert Pleasant Letter Book, 1771-1780, on photostat at William and Mary Library; Hening, *Statutes*, XI, 39-40.

12. Accomack Petitions, June 3, 1782; Henrico Petitions, Nov. 16, 1784; Hanover Petitions, Nov. 16, 1784; *House Journals, Oct., 1783*, p. 13; *ibid., Oct., 1784*, p. 25; *Report of the Committee of Revisors Appointed by the Gen-*

*eral Assembly of Virginia in 1776* (Richmond, Va., Nov., 1784), on film at Colonial Williamsburg, pp. 40, 41.

13. Yearly Meeting of Friends, Sept. 26, 1785, Friends Records: Letters and Miscellaneous Papers, 1749-1827, VSL; James Hunter to his wife, 1785, Hunter Collection; *House Journals, Oct., 1785*, p. 27. The petition apparently came from Amelia County, Carter Papers, Day Book XVI, Nov. 8, 1785.

14. Mecklenburg Petitions, Nov. 8, 1785; Pittsylvania Petitions, Nov. 10, 1785, Amelia Petitions, Nov. 10, 1785, Halifax Petitions, Nov. 10, 1785, Brunswick Petitions, Nov. 10, 1785, Lunenburg Petitions, Nov. 29, 1785, *House Journals, Oct., 1785*, pp. 27, 30-31.

15. James Madison to Washington, Nov. 11, 1785, and to Ambrose Madison, Dec. 15, 1785, Madison, *Writings*, II, 192, 203; *House Journals, Oct., 1785*, pp. 31, 65, 91, 110, 145.

16. Jefferson, *Writings*, I, 49-50.

17. Hening, *Statutes*, IX, 226-27.

18. Jefferson, *Notes on the State of Virginia*, William Peden, ed., pp. 134-35; survey of *Virginia Gazette*, 1776.

19. Undated, Landon Carter Diary, 1770-77; Carter to Washington, Oct. 16, 1776, Force, *American Archives*, 5 Ser., II, 1307; Jefferson, *Writings*, I, 49-50.

20. *Ibid.*, pp. 56-60; Hening, *Statutes*, XII, 138, 146; Jefferson, *Notes on Virginia* (Peden), pp. 137-43; Madison, *Writings*, I, 199, 203, 207, 212; III, 532, 580, 583, 612.

21. Jefferson, *Writings*, I, 68-69; C. Ray Keim, "Influence of Primogeniture and Entail in the Development of Virginia," pp. 164-86.

22. Madison, *Writings*, I, 37; Benjamin Perley Poore, *The Federal and State Constitutions, Colonial Charters, and Other Organic Laws of the United States*, 2nd ed., 2 parts (Washington, D. C., 1878), II, 1909-10; Hening, *Statutes*, I, 52; "A Plan of Government," Madison, *Writings*, I, 44; Randolph, History, Pt. 2, p. 67.

23. Washington County Petitions, Nov. 6, 1777.

24. Hening, *Statutes*, XII, 120-29.

25. Jefferson, *Notes on Virginia* (Peden), p. 118.

26. Paul L. Ford exonerates Jefferson by saying that in drafting the Constitution of 1776, Jefferson acquiesced in limiting the franchise to freeholders because he knew that he could not gain any extension of the ballot from the aristocrats. He neutralized this acquiescence, however, by distributing public lands to create manhood suffrage. Jefferson, *Writings*, I, xxv.

27. Election polls in Essex County Deed Book 24, pp. 275-80; Book 25, pp. 301-07, Book 27, pp. 248-52; Book 28, pp 95-99; Book 29, pp. 1-7; Book 30, pp. 235-42, 243-48, 318-24, 496-502; Book 31, pp. 398-402, 405-06; Book 32, pp. 3-6, 405-10; Book 33, pp. 55-59, 120-25, 168-71, 171, 185-90, 326-29.

28. "A general list of tithables taken in 1750 . . . ," Chalmers Collection; *Virginia Magazine of History and Biography*, XXVIII, 81-82; Page to [R. H. Lee], May 6, 1778, Lee Papers.

29. Poore, *Constitutions and Charters*, II, 1910; William and Hannah Lee to R. C. Nicholas *et al.*, Oct. 15, 1778, Lee-Ludwell Papers.

30. Poore, *Constitutions and Charters*, II, 1910-11.

31. "A Plan of Government . . . ," Miscellaneous MSS—Virginia, Library of Congress; Madison Papers, I, 13-24; Film 964, Alderman Library, U. of Va.

32. Robert Brent to R. H. Lee, April 26, 1776, Lee Papers.

33. Jefferson, *Notes on Virginia* (Peden) pp. 118-19.

34. Randolph, History, Pt. 2, p. 67.

35. Poore, *Constitutions and Charters*, II, 1910-12.

36. Lee to Robert Carter Nicholas, April 30, 1776, *Letters of Richard*

# 304 VIRGINIA 1705–1786: DEMOCRACY OR ARISTOCRACY?

*Henry Lee*, I, 184; Lee to [Edmund Pendelton?], May 12, 1776, Lee Family Papers, Lee Transcripts, III, 187.

37. Randolph, History, Pt. 2, p. 70.

38. Jefferson, *Notes on Virginia* (Peden), pp. 119-21.

39. Randolph, History, Pt. 2, p. 65.

40. *Ibid.*, pp. 65, 70; T. L. Lee to R. H. Lee, June 1, 1776, Lee Papers, Alderman Library, U. of Va.

41. To Mrs. Adams, July 10, 1776, Force, *American Archives*, 5 Ser., I, 170.

42. Richard Henry Lee to Charles Lee, June 29, 1776, *Letters of Richard Henry Lee*, I, 203; Williamsburg Convention *Proceedings*, May, 1776. Tidewater members were: Meriwether Smith, Essex; Henry Lee, Prince William; Robert Carter Nicholas, James City; Bartholomew Dandridge, New Kent; Dudley Digges, York; Thomas Ludwell Lee, Stafford; Joseph Jones, King George; John Blair, William and Mary College; Edmund Randolph, Williamsburg; Richard Cary, Warwick; Cuthbert Bullett, Prince William; and David Mason, Sussex. Piedmont members were Archibald Cary and Benjamin Watkins, Chesterfield; Patrick Henry, Hanover; George Gilmer, Albemarle; Richard Bland, Prince George; Paul Carrington and Thomas Reade, Charlotte; William Cabell, Amherst; William Fleming, Cumberland; Henry Tazewell, Brunswick; William Watts, Prince Edward; John Bannister and Bolling Starke, Dinwiddie; Richard Adams, Henrico; James Madison, Orange; Micajah Watkins, Halifax; and John Cabell, Buckingham. The frontier was represented by James Mercer, Hampshire; Thomas Lewis, Augusta; and Robert Rutherford, Berkeley.

43. Page to St. George Tucker, Sept. 28, 1776, Tucker Papers.

44. Robert Honeyman, Diary of Robert Honeyman, M. D., Jan. 2, 1776 to March 11, 1782, on film at Colonial Williamsburg, Oct. 27, 1776, p. 78.

45. "The Sentiments of the Several Companies of Militia and Freeholders, in Augusta, in Virginia . . . ," Force, *American Archives*, 5 Ser., II, 815-17.

46. *Ibid.*, I, 8-9, July 5, 1776; Poore, *Constitutions and Charters*, II, 1909.

47. Religious Petitions, Oct. 16, 1776, VSL. Other petitions were from Prince Edward, Oct. 11, Berkeley, Oct. 16, Albemarle, Amherst, and Buckingham, Oct. 22; *House Journals, Oct., 1776*, pp. 7, 15, 21, 24, 25, 26, 35, 48; Brydon, *Virginia's Mother Church*, II, 562-63.

48. Force, *American Archives*, 5 Ser., III, 1092-93; *House Journals, 1776*, pp. 30, 47; Religious Petitions, Nov. 8, 1776, VSL; Williamsburg Petitions, General Convention of Methodists, Oct. 28, 1776, VSL.

49. Honeyman, Diary, pp. 78-79; Hening, *Statutes*, IX, 164-67; Brydon, *Virginia's Mother Church*, II, 571-72; Jefferson, *Papers*, I, 526-29n.; Roger Atkinson to "Dear Sammy," Nov. 20, 1776, Roger Atkinson Letterbook, 1769-1776, Alderman Library, U. of Va.; *House Journals, 1776*, pp. 27, 63, 76, 78-80, 82, 83, 89, 90; *ibid., May, 1777*, pp. 34-36, 51, 69; *ibid., Oct., 1777*, pp. 100-01, 107, 110, 114; *ibid., May, 1778*, pp. 18, 21, 23, 31; *ibid., Oct., 1778*, pp. 101, 105-06, 120, 122-23; *ibid., Oct., 1779*, pp. 13, 69, 76, 79, 106, 108, 112, 120 Hening, *Statutes*, IX, 164-67. Julian Boyd and his associates contend it was the adoption of the last clause of the Virginia Declaration of Rights which provided the impetus for disestablishment of the church and full equality of rights for dissenters. But the previous history of dissenters in Virginia would indicate this clause alone did not generate the move in itself. The clause was merely an expression of public temper of the times and it was this public mood which was to hasten the already obvious trend. See Julian Boyd, ed., *The Papers of Thomas Jefferson*, I, 526n.

50. *House Journals, May, 1779*, pp. 41, 50, 53; *ibid., Oct., 1779*, pp. 71, 89, 90, 106. See Boyd in Jefferson, *Papers*, II, 548n. for a discussion of publication.

51. Essex Petitions, Oct. 22, 1779; Lunenburg Petitions, Nov. 3, 1779; Amherst Petitions, Nov. 1 and 10, 1779, VSL; *House Journals, Oct., 1779*, pp. 22, 24, 25, 32, 39, 45, 62.

52. Hanover Petitions, Oct. 23, 1778; Caroline Petitions, May 25, 1779; Amelia Petitions, May 12, 1780, VSL; *House Journals, Oct., 1777*, p. 8; *ibid., Oct., 1778*, p. 9; *ibid., May, 1780*, pp. 8, 64, 66, 67, 69, 77, 78, 82, 86; Hening, *Statutes*, X, 288-90; XI, 62-63.

53. On the problem of marriages, see Royal Instructions to Lord Dunmore, No. 74, Feb. 7, 1771, Chalmers Collection; *House Journals, Oct., 1778*, pp. 64, 100-01; *ibid., Oct., 1779*, pp. 28, 56, 91; *ibid., May, 1780*, pp. 35, 40, 73-83; *ibid., Oct., 1780*, pp. 55, 56, 84, 87, 117, 119; *ibid., May, 1783*, pp. 76, 81, 83, 85, 90, 99; *ibid., Oct., 1783*, pp. 66, 68, 73; *ibid., May, 1784*, pp. 71, 76, 77, 79, 80, 81-82; *ibid., Oct., 1784*, pp. 18, 22, 65, 71, 83, 84, 92, 95, 99; Amelia Petitions, May 12 and 31, 1783; Baptist ministers' petition. Spotsylvania Petitions, June 5, 1780, and Powhatan Petitions, Nov. 6, 1783; Memorial of Committee of the Several Baptist Associations, Oct. 9, 1784, Religious Petitions, Nov. 11, 1784, VSL; Hening, *Statutes*, X, 361-63; XI, 281, 503-05.

54. Petition of the Clergy of the Protestant Episcopal Church, June 4, 1784, Religious Petitions, VSL; *House Journals*, May, 1784, p. 36.

55. Smith to James Madison, June 21, 1784, Madison, *Writings*, II, 213n.

56. Madison to Jefferson, July 3, 1784, *ibid.*, II, 58-59.

57. *House Journals, Oct., 1784*, pp. 27, 65, 75, 77-79, 83, 91. See also Irving Brandt, *James Madison*, 4 vols. (Indianapolis, 1941—), II, 345; Hening, *Statutes*, XI, 532; James Madison to Thomas Jefferson, Jan. 9, 1785, Madison, *Writings*, II, 112-14.

58. *House Journals, Oct., 1784*, pp. 11, 19, 21, 32; Madison, *Writings*, II, 90n.; Rockingham Petition, Nov. 18, 1784; Rockbridge Petition, Dec. 1, 1784; Surry Petition, Dec. 1, 1784, VSL; Address of the Presbyterian Clergy, Nov. 12, 1784, Religious Petitions, VSL.

59. Lee to James Madison, Nov. 26, 1784, Lee Papers; Madison to R. H. Lee, Nov. 14, 1784, Lee-Ludwell Papers, Miscellaneous; Madison, *Writings*, II, 88-89, 94, 112-14; *House Journals, Oct., 1784*, pp. 51, 52, 80-82. Madison gave the vote as 45-38.

60. Madison to Jefferson, Jan. 9, 1785, Madison, *Writings*, II, 112-14; Brandt, *Madison*, II, 343-55.

61. The vote was tabulated from Mecklenburg Petition, Dec. 24, 1784, and the *Fourteenth Annual Report of the Library Board of the Virginia State Library, 1916-17*, pp. 19-20.

62. Madison to James Monroe, April 12, and Madison to Jefferson, April 27, 1785, *Writings*, II, 131-32, 137.

63. G. Nicholas to Madison, April 22, 1785, Madison Papers; see also Madison, *Writings*, II, 183n.-184n.; "Memorial and Remonstrance Against Religious Assessments," *ibid.*, pp. 183-91; Madison to James Monroe, May 29 and June 21, 1785, *ibid.*, pp. 145, 146; Madison to Jefferson, Aug. 20, 1785, *ibid.*, pp. 163-64.

64. *House Journals, Oct., 1785*, pp. 6, 7, 9-11, 18, 19, 20-21, 24, 26, 29, 30, 34, 36, 38, 42, 43, 61, 63, 68, 85; Religious Petitions and Assessment Petitions, 1785, VSL; Powhatan Petitions, Nov. 3, 1785 and Pittsylvania Petitions, Nov. 7, 1785, VSL.

65. Memorial of the [Presbyterian] Convention of Ministers and Lay Representatives, Bethel, Augusta County, Aug. 10, 1785, Assessment Petitions, Nov. 2, 1785, VSL; Pittsylvania Petitions, Nov. 7, 1785; *House Journals, Oct., 1785*, pp. 6, 7, 9-10, 20-21, 36.

66. Hening, *Statutes*, XII, 27-30; *House Journals, Oct., 1785*, pp. 9, 22, 60, 74, 104, 105, 119, 148.

67. *House Journals, May, 1779*, pp. 41, 50, 53; *ibid., Oct., 1785*, pp. 92, 94, 95, 96, 115, 117, 135, 138, 139, 143, 148; Jefferson, *Papers*, II, 545-53; *Report of the Committee of Revisors*, p. 58, Ch. LXXXII; Madison, *Writings*, II 205, 216. See Boyd edition of Jefferson, *Papers*, II, 548-49, for discussion of passage of the act.

68. Hening, *Statutes*, XII, 84-86. Jan., 1786.

69. For the petitions concerning this issue both in 1785 and 1786 see Memorial of the [Presbyterian] Convention of Ministers and Lay Representatives, Bethel, Augusta, Aug. 10, 1785, Assessment Petitions, Nov. 2, 1785; Gloucester Petitions, Oct. 7, Oct. 31, Nov. 17, 1786; Louisa Petitions, Oct. 13, Nov. 17, 1786; Henrico Petitions, Oct. 31, 1786; Orange Petitions, Nov. 1, 1786; Halifax Petitions, Nov. 6, 1786; Cumberland Petitions, Nov. 9, 1786; Richmond County Petitions, Nov. 1, 1786; *House Journals, Oct., 1785*, pp. 34, 42, 81, 85, 118, 141, 143; *ibid., Oct., 1786*, pp. 13-14, 15, 19, 24-25, 32, 36, 41-42, 47, 62, 67, 72, 86, 88, 92, 94. Piedmont counties sending petitions for repeal were Louisa, Henrico, Brunswick, Mecklenburg, Dinwiddie, Orange, Goochland, Spotsylvania, Hanover, Halifax, Lunenburg, Cumberland, Buckingham, Albemarle, Powhatan, Chesterfield, Fauquier, Caroline, Culpeper; those against repeal were: Amelia, Cumberland, Hanover, Louisa, Culpeper, and Albemarle. Tidewater counties for repeal were New Kent, Gloucester, Lancaster, Nansemond, King and Queen, Essex, Westmoreland, Northampton, Southampton, King George, Surry, Elizabeth City; those against repeal were Westmoreland, Richmond, York, Stafford and King George. See also Richard Terrell to Col. Garrett Minor, Dec. 4, 1786, Watson Papers, Alderman Library, U. of Va.

70. Hening, *Statutes*, XII, 266; *House Journals, Oct., 1786*, pp. 88, 94, 142, 148, 149, 151; see also Madison to Jefferson, Feb. 15, 1787, Madison, *Writings*, II, 212-14, 310.

71. Poore, *Constitutions and Charters*, II, 1908.

72. Oct., 13, 1779, *Letters of Richard Henry Lee*, II, 157; also in Lee Papers; *House Journals, May, 1780*, p. 14.

73. Jefferson, *Writings*, III, 251-55.

# Conclusion

Was colonial virginia, then, aristocratic or democratic? Throughout this work, we have attempted to answer this question by a detailed examination of the various aspects of the society. Our conclusions have been that Virginia was far more democratic than we have been led to believe in the past, and that to the extent that there was aristocracy, it was an aristocracy with a basis far different from that usually attributed to it.

On the democratic side were many features formerly considered to be aristocratic. Economic opportunity provided by cheap land and a severe shortage of labor contributed to an open, mobile class structure; and while there were differences in class status, social mobility made easy advancement possible for men with ability and ambition. In politics, there were property qualifications for voting, but the almost universal acquisition of property gave the colony a very broad electorate, and economic independence appears to have made for political independence. Elected representatives, as is true today, generally came from the upper classes, but such men gained and held elective office only by satisfying the wishes of a sufficient number of the electorate. If the educational system was not all that could be desired, it did provide some measure of education for most Virginians and seems not to have been a source of internal conflict. And even the Church of England, aristocratic though it appeared in outward form, was in fact controlled by the democratic wishes of the congregations.

While one might call certain features of Virginia society aristocratic, these features were not aristocratic in the accepted sense of the term. Men did not gain and pass on political office because of family, wealth, and privilege except perhaps in some instances where such offices were at the disposal of the British government. But this was not a true aristocracy, for while family and wealth might have been an asset, these possessions were not decisive. A man's attitude toward British colonial policy mattered much more. In designating Virginia as aristocratic, historians must distinguish clearly between appointive and elective offices and then examine carefully whether appointive office rested on aristocracy or imperialism. Differences of wealth might be considered aristocratic, but these differences were very moderate compared with the Europe of that day or the America of today. And the fact that some men exerted more influence than others might be called aristocratic, but this is also true today in the United States.

Undoubtedly the most aristocratic feature of Virginia society, and the one that differentiated it from the societies of northern colonies, was slavery. Slavery resulted in the widely-held and non-Puritan belief that physical labor was degrading and should be done by slaves. The great ambition among all classes of whites, and an ambition that was fulfilled for a large number of men, was to own a slave. Slaveownership conferred status: it relieved the master of the necessity for doing some or all menial labor and it placed him in a definitely superior group which could pursue leisure of all types and cultivate the "genteel" life. But again one must remember that slavery was a matter of race, not class, and that most whites were united rather than divided over the desirability of slavery.

Except for slavery and British influence, what now passes in this country as middle-class, representative democracy was well-entrenched in the Old Dominion long before the American Revolution. Small wonder that the Revolution resulted in so little internal social change, and that much of the social change that did emerge either was clearly developing before the Revolution or had been thwarted by the British. Possessed of a relatively democratic society in colonial times, Virginians saw little need for drastic internal alterations when revolution occurred. Virginia democracy gained a great deal by the elimination of the British, a fact which should not be underestimated, but gains from the elimination of British imperialism and gains from the elimination of a local aristocratic, upper-class domination are two entirely different problems.

# Bibliography

## I. SOURCES

*Printed Sources.*

A. Legislative Records.

COUNCIL:

*Executive Journals of the Council of Colonial Virginia, 1680-1739.* Ed. by H. R. McIlwaine, 4 vols. Richmond, 1925-30.

*Executive Journals of the Council of Colonial Virginia, 1726-1753.* Photocopies from Public Records Office in *Virginia Magazine of History and Biography*, XXXII-XXXVII (1924-29), *passim.*

*Legislative Journals of the Council of Colonial Virginia, 1680-1776.* Ed. by H. R. McIlwaine. 3 vols. Richmond, 1918, 1919.

HOUSE JOURNALS:

*Journals of the House of Burgesses of Virginia, 1619-1777.* Ed. by H. R. McIlwaine and J. P. Kennedy. 13 vols. Richmond, 1905-15. These *Journals* do not have volume numbers but are titled and cited in this work according to date.

*Journal of the House of Delegates of Virginia, 1776.* Richmond: Printed by Samuel Shepherd and Co., 1828.

*Journal of the House of Delegates, 1777-1780.* This volume contains the *Journals* of the sessions dated May 5, 1777; Oct. 20, 1777; May 4, 1778; Oct. 5, 1778; May 3, 1779; Oct. 4, 1779; May 1, 1780; Oct. 16, 1780. There is no main title page for the volume—each session has its own and is paged individually. Richmond, 1827.

*Records of the States of the United States. A Microfilm Compilation Prepared by the Library of Congress in Association with the University of North Carolina.* Collected and edited under William Sumner Jenkins. Library of Congress, 1949. Includes the *Journals* of the House of Delegates through 1787.

*Journals of the House of Delegates, 1781-1786.* Richmond: Printed by Thomas W. White, 1828. This volume includes the *Journals* of the sessions of Oct. 1, 1781; Oct. 21, 1782; May 5, 1783; Oct. 20, 1783; May 3, 1784; Oct. 18, 1784; Oct. 17, 1785. Each session has separate title and paging.

CONVENTIONS, PROCEEDINGS, AND ORDINANCES (RICHMOND AND WILLIAMS-BURG):

*At a very full meeting of delegates from the different counties in the colony and dominion of Virginia, begun in Williamsburg the first day of August, in the year of Our Lord 1774. . . .* [Williamsburg, 1774]. Microfilm—Library of Congress, 1949.

*The Proceedings of the Convention of delegates for the counties and*

309

*corporations in the Colony of Virginia, held at Richmond Town, in the county of Henrico, on the 20th of March, 1775.* Reprinted by resolution of House of Delegates, Feb. 24, 1816. Richmond, 1816.

*The Proceedings of the Convention of delegates for the counties and corporations in the Colony of Virginia, held at Richmond Town, . . . on Monday the 17th of July 1775.* Also contains Ordinances (but without separate title page for them). Reprinted in Richmond, 1816.

*The proceedings of the Convention of delegates, held at the town of Richmond, . . . on Friday the 1st of December, 1775, and afterwards, by adjournment, in the city of Williamsburg.* Also contains ordinances passed at this session. Williamsburg: Printed by Alexander Purdie [1776]. Reprinted, Richmond, 1816.

*The proceedings of the Convention of delegates, held at the Capitol, in the city of Williamsburg . . . , on Monday the 6th of May, 1776.* Also contains ordinances and the new constitution. Williamsburg: Printed by Alexander Purdie [1776]. Reprinted in Richmond, 1816.

*Debates and Other Proceedings of the Convention of Virginia, Convened at Richmond, on Monday the 2nd Day of June, 1788, for the Purpose of Deliberating on the Constitution Recommended by the Grand Federal Convention.* 3 vols. Petersburg: Printed by Hunter and Prentis, 1788.

B. Virginia Laws.

*The Charters of the British Colonies in America.* London: Printed for J. Almon, [1774?].

*The Acts of the Assembly . . . 1662-1715.* London: Baskett, 1727.

*A collection of all the Acts of Assembly, now in Force. . . .* Williamsburg: Printed by William Parks, 1733.

*An Exact Abridgment of All the Public Acts of Assembly, of Virginia, In Force and Use.* By John Mercer, Gent. Williamsburg: Printed by William Parks, 1737.

*The Acts of Assembly, Now in Force, in the Colony of Virginia. . . .* Williamsburg: Printed by William Hunter, 1752.

*[An Exact] Abridgment of all the Public Acts of Assembly of Virginia In Force and Use. January 1, 1758.* By John Mercer, Gent. Glasgow: Printed by John Bryce and David Paterson, 1759.

*The Acts of Assembly, Now in Force, In the Colony of Virginia. . . .* Williamsburg: Printed by W. Rind, A. Purdie, and J. Dixon, 1769.

*A collection of all such public acts of the General assembly and Ordinances of Virginia, passed since the year 1768. . . .* Richmond: Published by Thomas Nicolson and William Prentis, 1785.

*A collection of all such acts of the General Assembly. . . .* Richmond: Davis, 1794.

*A plan of government Laide before the Committee of the House, which they have ordered to be printed for the perusal of the members.* [Williamsburg, 1776]. Microfilm—Library of Congress, 1949.

*Report of the Committee of Revisors Appointed by the General Assembly of Virginia in 1776.* Publ. by order of the General Assembly. Richmond: Dixon and Holt, Nov., 1784. Miscellaneous MSS, Va., Library of Congress. Microfilm—Colonial Williamsburg.

*The Federal and State Constitutions, Colonial Charters, and other Organic*

*Laws of the United States.* Compiled by Benj. Perley Poore. 2 parts, 2nd ed. Washington: Government Printing Office, 1878.

*The Statutes at Large; Being a Collection of all the Laws of Virginia, From the First Session . . . in the Year 1619.* Ed. by William Waller Hening. 13 vols. Richmond, 1809-23.

C. Other Printed Sources.

*Acts of the Privy Council of England.* Colonial series. Ed. by W. L. Grant and James Munro. 6 vols. Hereford and London, 1908-12.

*American Archives. . . .* Ed. by Peter Force. 9 vols. Washington: Prepared and published under authority of an Act of Congress, 1837-53.

Anburey, Thomas. *Travels Through the Interior Parts of America; in a Series of Letters. By an Officer.* New ed., 2 vols. London: Printed for William Lane, 1791.

Asbury, Francis. *The Journal of the Rev. Francis Asbury, Bishop of the Methodist Episcopal Church, from August 7, 1771, to December 7, 1815.* 3 vols. New York: Publ. by N. Bangs and T. Mason for Methodist Episcopal Church, 1821.

*Aspinwall Papers* in *Collections* of the Massachusetts Historical Society, 4 Ser., Vols. IX and X. Boston: Publ. by the Society, 1871.

Beverley, Robert. *The History and Present State of Virginia* [1705]. Ed. with introd. by Louis B. Wright. Chapel Hill: Univ. of North Carolina Press, 1947.

Bland, Richard. *A Letter to the Clergy of Virginia, in which, The Conduct of the General-Assembly is vindicated. . . .* Williamsburg: Printed by William Hunter, 1760.

————. *An Inquiry Into the Rights of the British Colonies.* Williamsburg: 1766. Ed. by Earl G. Swem. Richmond, Va.: Reprinted by The Appeals Press for the William Parks Club, 1922.

————. *A Fragment on the Pistole Fee, claimed by the Governor of Virginia, 1753.* Ed. by Worthington C. Ford. Brooklyn, N.Y.: Historical Printing Club, 1891. Microfilm—Colonial Williamsburg.

Bland, Theodorick. *The Bland Papers.* Ed. by Charles Campbell. 2 vols. in 1. Petersburg, Va.: E. and J. Ruffin, 1840-43.

Boucher, Jonathan. *Reminiscences of an American Loyalist, 1738-1789.* . . . Ed. by Jonathan Bouchier. New York: Houghton, Mifflin, 1925.

————. *A View of the Causes and Consequences of the American Revolution. . . .* London: Printed for G. G. and J. Robinson, 1797.

Brissot DeWarville, Jacques Pierre. *New Travels in the United States of America . . .* [1788]. London: (front page missing) [1794].

Burnaby, Andrew. *Travels Through the Middle Settlements in North-American in the years 1759 and 1760.* 2nd ed. London: Printed for T. Payne, 1775. Also used 3rd ed. of 1798 with introd. by Rufus R. Wilson. New York: A. Wessels Co., 1904.

Byrd, William. *The Secret Diary of William Byrd of Westover, 1709-1712.* Ed. by Louis B. Wright and Marion Tinling. Richmond, Va.: Dietz, 1941.

————. *Another Secret Diary of William Byrd of Westover, 1739-1741.* . . . Ed. by Maude H. Woodfin, trans. by Marion Tinling. Richmond, Va.: Dietz, 1942.

*Calendar of Virginia State Papers and Other Manuscripts, 1652-1781*

# 312 VIRGINIA 1705–1786: DEMOCRACY OR ARISTOCRACY?

*Preserved at the Capitol in Richmond.* Arranged and edited by W. P. Palmer. 11 vols. Richmond: R. F. Walker, Supt. of Public Printing, 1875-93.

Camm, John. *A Review of the Rector Detected: or the Colonel Reconnoitered.* Williamsburg: Printed by Joseph Royal, 1764.

Carter, Landon. *A Letter to the Right Reverend Father in God The Lord B[isho]p of L[ondo]n.* 1759. Virginia State Library.

————. *The Rector Detected: Being a Just Defence of the Two-penny Act.* . . . Williamsburg: Printed by Joseph Royle, 1764.

Carver, J[onathan]. *Travels through the Interior Parts of North-America, in the Years 1766, 1767, and 1768.* London: Printed for the author, 1778.

*The case of the tobacco planters in His Majesty's Colony of Virginia, as to the Bill now depending in the House of Lords, for the more easy recovery of debts in His Majesty's plantations.* . . . [London, 1732].

*The case of the planters of tobacco in Virginia, as represented by themselves.* . . . London: 1733.

Council addresses to governors. *The Humble Addresses of the Council in Assembly to the Honourable William Gooch.* . . . [Aug. 21, 1740— May 5, 1774]. Microfilm—Library of Congress.

Council address to the people, [May 1775]. *To all the Good People of Virginia.* Signed by Order of the Members of the Council, John Blair, C. C. Undated. Microfilm—Alderman Library, Univ. of Va.

Council negative on tobacco bill, Oct. 28, 1773. [A message from the Upper House of Assembly to the Lower House . . . on why they negatived the tobacco bill]. By the Upper House of Assembly, Oct. 28, 1773. Microfilm—Alderman Library, Univ. of Va.

Dinwiddie, Robert. *The Official Records of Robert Dinwiddie, Lieutenant-Governor of the Colony of Virginia, 1751-1758* . . . in *Collections* of the Virginia Historical Society. Intro. and notes by R. A. Brock. 2 vols. Richmond, Va.: Publ. by the Society, 1883.

Dunmore, Lt. Gov. *A Hue & Cry* [against Henry]. May 6, 1775. Microfilm—Alderman Library, Univ. of Va.

————. *A PROCLAMATION* By his Excellency the Right Honourable John Earl of Dunmore . . . Given . . . on Board the Ship William, off Norfolk, the 7th Day of November, in the 16th Year of his Majesty's Reign. Microfilm—Alderman Library, Univ. of Va.

————. *A PROCLAMATION* [forbidding the election of delegates to the next Congress]. March 28, 15 George III. Microfilm—Alderman Library, Univ. of Va.

Eddis, William. *Letters From America, Historical and Descriptive; Comprising Occurrences from 1769, to 1777, Inclusive.* London: Printed for the Author, 1792.

*The Fairfax Correspondence.* Ed. by George W. Johnson. London: R. Bentley, 1848.

Fithian, Philip Vickers. *Journal and Letters of Philip Vickers Fithian, 1773-1774: A Plantation Tutor of the Old Dominion.* Ed. by Hunter D. Farish. Williamsburg, Va.: Colonial Williamsburg, Inc., 1943.

Hanover Presbytery. "Early Minutes of Hanover Presbytery." Ed. by William M. E. Rachal. *Virginia Magazine of History and Biography,* Vol. 63, pp. 53-75 (Jan. 1955), and pp. 161-85 (April, 1955).

Hartwell, Henry, James Blair, and Edward Chilton. *The Present State of Virginia, and the College* [1697]. Ed. by Hunter D. Farish. Williamsburg: Colonial Williamsburg, Inc., 1940.

Henry, Patrick. [A printed note signed by Patrick Henry, dated: Head Quarters, Williamsburg, November 20, 1775]. Microfilm—Alderman Library, Univ. of Va.

*Historical Collections Relating to the American Colonial Church*. Ed. by William S. Perry. 5 vols. Hartford: Printed by the Subscribers, 1870-78.

Jarratt, Devereux. *The Life of the Reverend Devereux Jarratt, Rector of Bath Parish, Dinwiddie County, Virginia, Written by Himself*. . . . Baltimore: Printed by Warner and Hanna, 1806.

Jefferson, Thomas. *Notes on the State of Virginia*. Ed. by William Peden. Chapel Hill, N. C.: Publ. for the Institute of Early American History and Culture at Williamsburg, by the Univ. of North Carolina Press, 1955.

———. *Notes on the State of Virginia*. . . . Paris, 1785. Microcard—Michigan State University.

———. *The Papers of Thomas Jefferson*. Ed. by Julian Boyd, et. al. Vols. 1-16. Princeton, N. J.: Princeton University Press, 1950-61.

———. *The Writings of Thomas Jefferson*. Ed. by Paul L. Ford. 10 vols. New York: G. P. Putnam's Sons, 1892-99.

Jones, Hugh. *The Present State of Virginia*. . . . Ed. by Richard L. Morton. Chapel Hill, N. C.: Univ. of North Carolina Press, 1956.

"Journal of a French Traveller in the Colonies, 1765" in *American Historical Review*, XXVI (July, 1921), 726-47.

*Journal of the Commissioners for Trade and Plantations*. . . . Preserved in Public Record Office. 14 vols. London: His Majesty's Stationery Office, 1920-38.

*Journals of the Council of State of Virginia*. Ed. by H. R. McIlwaine. 2 vols. Richmond, Va.: Publ. by the Virginia State Library, 1931-32.

*Justices of the Peace in Colonial Virginia, 1757-1775*. Virginia State Library, Bulletin 14 (Richmond, 1922).

Lee, Richard Henry. *The Letters of Richard Henry Lee*. Ed. by James C. Ballagh. 2 vols. New York: Macmillan, 1911, 1914.

———. *Memoir of the Life of Richard Henry Lee, and his Correspondence*. . . . Ed. by his grandson Richard H. Lee. 2 vols. Philadelphia: H. C. Carey and I. Lea, 1825.

Lee, William. *Letters of William Lee . . . 1766-83*. Ed. by Worthington C. Ford. Brooklyn, N. Y.: Historical Printing Club, 1891.

*Letters to Washington and Accompanying Papers*. Ed. by Stanislaus M. Hamilton. 5 vols. Boston: Houghton, Mifflin, 1898-1902.

Madison, James. *Letters and Other Writings of James Madison*. Publ. by Order of Congress. 4 vols. Philadelphia: Lippincott, 1867.

———. *The Writings of James Madison*. . . . Ed. by Gaillard Hunt. 9 vols. New York: G. P. Putnam's Sons, 1900-10.

Maury, James. *To Christians of Every Denomination among us, especially those of the Established Church, An Address enforcing an Inquiry into the Grounds of the Pretensions of the Preachers, called Anabaptists*. . . . Annapolis: Printed by Anne Catherine Green, 1771.

Munford, Robert. *The Candidates; or the Humours of a Virginia Election*.

Written about 1770. First published 1789. Ed. with introd. by Jay B. Hubbell and Douglass Adair. Williamsburg, 1948.

*Narratives of Early Pennsylvania, West New Jersey and Delaware, 1630-1707.* Ed. by Albert C. Myers. New York: Scribner's, 1912.

*Official Letters of the Governors of the State of Virginia.* Publ. by the Virginia State Library. 3 vols. Richmond: Davis Bottom, Superintendent of Public Printing, 1926.

Randolph, John. *Considerations on the Present State of Virginia.* Attributed to John Randolph, Attorney-General. [Printed in the Year 1774]. And *Considerations on the Present State of Virginia Examined.* By Robert Carter Nicholas. Ed. by Earl G. Swem. New York: Sixty-three copies printed for Charles F. Heartman, 1919.

*Reports of Cases determined in the General Court of Virginia. From 1730, to 1740; and from 1768 to 1772.* Charlottesville: F. Carr, 1829.

Revel, James. *The Poor Unhappy Transported Felon's Sorrowful Account of His Fourteen Years Transportation at Virginia in America.* London: Printed and Sold in Stonecutter-Street, Fleet-Market. No date. Photostatic copy in William and Mary Library.

Smyth, John Ferdinand D., Esq. *A Tour in the United States of America.* . . . 2 vols. London: Printed for G. Robinson, J. Robson, and J. Sewell, 1784.

Spotswood, Alexander. *The Official Letters of Alexander Spotswood, Lieutenant-Governor of the colony of Virginia, 1710-1722* . . . in *Collections* of the Virginia Historical Society. 2 vols. New series. Richmond, Va., 1882, 1885.

Stith, William. *The History of the First Discovery and Settlement of Virginia.* . . . [Williamsburg, 1747]. New York: Reprinted for Joseph Sabine, 1865.

Tarleton, Banastre. *History of the Campaigns of 1780 and 1781 in the Southern Provinces of North America.* London, 1787.

Virginia Almanacs. The Virginia almanacs for the years 1749, 1752, 1755, 1758, 1762, 1764, 1765, 1768?, 1769, 1770, 1771, 1772, 1774, 1775, 1776, and 1778 are to be found at the Alderman Library at the University of Virginia, either in the original or on film from the Huntington Library.

*Virginia Colonial Decisions* . . . *the reports by Sir John Randolph* . . . *of decisions of the General Court of Virginia, 1728-1741.* Ed. by R. T. Barton. 2 vols. 2nd edition. Boston: Boston Book Co., 1909.

*The Virginia Gazette.* First printed by William Parks and William Hunter and later by others including Purdie and Dixon, 1736-1780. A second paper by the same name was printed by William Rind from 1766-1776. A third *Virginia Gazette* was printed by Alexander Purdie from 1775-1780.

Washington, George. *The Diaries of George Washington, 1748-1799.* Ed. by John C. Fitzpatrick, 4 vols. Boston: Houghton, Mifflin, 1925.

———. *The Writings of George Washington from the Original Manuscript Sources, 1745-1799.* Ed. by John C. Fitzpatrick. 39 vols. Washington: United States Govt. Printing Office, 1931-44.

———. *The Writings of George Washington.* Ed. by Worthington C. Ford. 14 vols. New York: Putnam, 1889-92.

————. *The Writings of George Washington*. Ed. by Jared Sparks. 12 vols. Boston: 1834-37.

Webb, George. *The Office and Authority of a Justice of Peace And Also the Duty of Sheriffs, Coroners, Churchwardens, Surveiors of Highways, Constables, and Officers of Militia*. Williamsburg: Printed by William Parks, 1736. Miscellaneous MSS—Va., Library of Congress. Microfilm—Alderman Library, Univ. of Va.

*Manuscripts.*

Accomack County—see County Records.

Adams Papers. Virginia Historical Society.

Albemarle County—see County Records.

Allason, William. Papers and Letter Book, Virginia State Library.

Ambler, Elizabeth B. Elizabeth Barbour Ambler Collection, Alderman Library, Univ. of Va.

Amelia County—see County Records.

Amherst County—see County Records.

Amherst Papers in British Transcripts, Public Record Office: War Office 34, Vol. 37—Correspondence between the governor of Virginia and the commander-in-chief, 1756-63.

Atkinson, Roger. Letter Book, 1769-1776. Alderman Library, Univ. of Va.

————. Roger Atkinson Account Book, 1762-89, Alderman Library, Univ. of Va.

Auditor's Papers. Virginia State Library.

Augusta County—see County Records.

Ball Family Papers. Virginia State Library.

Bancroft Transcripts: American Stamp Act, 1764-68. Library of Congress.

Banister, John. Letters, 1772, 1778-1783 to Theodorick Bland. Virginia Historical Society.

Bassett-Lewis Papers, 1693-1886. Virginia Historical Society.

Baylor, John. Letter Book, 1752-65. Original owned by Col. Bernard Baylor of Richmond, Va. Photostat, Virginia State Library.

Berkeley County—see County Records.

Berkeley Papers. Alderman Library, Univ. of Va.

Beverley MSS. Virginia Historical Society.

Beverley, Robert. Letter Book, 1761-1793. Library of Congress. Also on film Colonial Williamsburg.

Blair, John. Diary. Virginia Historical Society. Also in *William and Mary Quarterly*, 1 ser., Vol. VII, 133-54.

————. "List of Virginia Counties and Estimated Number of Freeholders, 1763" in British Museum, Add. MSS 38337, 321 verso. From John Hemphill II of Colonial Williamsburg.

Bland MSS. Charles Campbell Collection of Theodorick Bland Papers.

Bland, Dr. Theodorick. Letters and miscellaneous manuscripts, 1749-1783. Accession No. 1341. Library of Congress.

Bray, Dr. MSS of Dr. Bray's Associates: American Correspondence, 1742-1768. Society for the Propagation of the Gospel, Library of Congress.

————. MSS of Dr. Bray's Associates: Minute Book, 1735-1774. Microfilm—Colonial Williamsburg.

Breckinridge, James. Letters to James Breckinridge. Alderman Library, Univ. of Va.

British Museum: Additional MSS. 35909—40690. Microfilm—Alderman Library, Univ. of Va.

Brock Notebook. Virginia Historical Society. Microfilm—Colonial Williamsburg.

Browne, Mrs. Journal of a Voyage from London to Virginia, 1754. Virginia Historical Society.

Buckingham County—see County Records.

Brunswick County—see County Records.

Byrd Papers. Other Byrd Papers. Virginia Historical Society.

Cabell Family Papers. William and Mary College Library.

Cabell Papers. Alderman Library, Univ. of Va.

Cabell, William. Diaries, 1751-1825. Virginia State Library. Also on Microfilm—Alderman Library, Univ. of Va.

————. Diary, 1751-1795. Photostat. Virginia Historical Society.

————. Memorandum Book, 1787-1799. Photostat. Virginia Historical Society.

Campbell Papers. William and Mary College Library.

Campbell-Preston Papers. Library of Congress. Vols. I and II cover 1741-1794.

Carleton, Sir Guy. Papers, 1747 [1777]—1783 (British Headquarters). Photostats. Colonial Williamsburg.

Caroline County—see County Records.

Carrington, Paul. Paul Carrington Collection. Virginia Historical Society.

Carter, Keith. Papers. Virginia Historical Society.

Carter, Landon. Diary of Colonel Landon Carter in Sabine Hall Papers. Alderman Library, Univ. of Va.

————. "Diary of Col. Landon Carter (1710-75), for 1763, Nov. 15 & before, to 1764 Dec. 15." Written in the Virginia Almanack of 1764.

Carter Papers. Letter Books, 1772-1785. Duke Univ. Microfilm—Colonial Williamsburg.

————. Carter Papers, William and Mary College Library.

Carter, Robert. Letter Books. Virginia Historical Society.

————. Robert Carter Papers, 1705-1771. Virginia Historical Society.

————. Robert Carter's Day Book (1774-75). Library of Congress.

————. Robert Carter's Inventory, 1733. Virginia Historical Society.

Carter, Robert Wormeley. Diary. Colonial Williamsburg.

————. Robert Wormeley Carter Notes in *Virginia Almanacks* for 1764 and 1765. Clements Library, Univ. of Michigan. Microfilm—Colonial Williamsburg.

Carter's Grove Account Books, 1736-1786. Virginia Historical Society.

Cary, Archibald. Papers, 1756-1785. Photostatic copies. Virginia Historical Society.

Cary Papers. Virginia Historical Society.

Caswell, Richard. Papers. North Carolina Dept. of Archives and History. Microfilm—Colonial Williamsburg.

Chalmers Collection. New York Public Library. Microfilm—Colonial Williamsburg.

Chesterfield County—see County Records.

Chisolm Papers, 1749-1955. Virginia Historical Society.

Cholmondeley (Houghton) Papers. University Library, Cambridge, England. Microfilm—Colonial Williamsburg.

"Church of England in America. Thoughts upon the present state of the Church of England in America, 1764" (June). Clements Library, Univ. of Michigan. Microfilm—Colonial Williamsburg.

Clark, Jonathan. The Diary of General Jonathan Clark (1750-1811). Photostat. Virginia State Library.

Conventions, 1775-1776. Miscellaneous Material, Virginia State Library.

Corbin, Richard. Letterbook, 1758-1768. Colonial Williamsburg.

County Records. Unless otherwise listed, all county records and petitions cited in this volume can be found in the Virginia State Library either on film, on photostat, or in manuscript. This includes all deeds, wills, tithable lists, elections polls, petitions, quitrent rolls, and other tax lists. The great bulk of these records has been filmed by the Utah Genealogical Society.

Court Records. United States District Court for the Eastern District of Virginia. Virginia State Library.

Crèvecoeur Transcripts, 1783-1788 and undated. Library of Congress.

Culpeper County—see County Records.

Cumberland County—see County Records.

Cuninghame Letterbooks. William Cuninghame & Co. Letterbooks, 1767-1773. National Library of Scotland, Edinburgh. Microfilm—Colonial Williamsburg.

Custis Papers. Virginia Historical Society.

Dabney Papers, 1776-1782. Virginia Historical Society.

Dawson Papers, 1728-1775. British Transcripts, Fulham Palace Manuscripts—Virginia, Library of Congress. Microfilm—Colonial Williamsburg.

Dinwiddie County—see County Records.

Dunmore Letters. Virginia State Library.

Dunmore County. A Census List, taken in Dunmore County, 1775, in folder of Bird-Samuels Papers, Virginia Historical Society.

Dunscomb, Andrew. Letterbook, 1785-1787. Virginia State Library.

Edgehill, Randolph. Papers. Alderman Library, Univ. of Va.

Election polls—see County Records.

Elizabeth City County—see County Records.

Emmet Collection. New York Public Library. Microfilm—Colonial Williamsburg.

Essex County—see County Records.

Fairfax Correspondence. Correspondence of the Fairfax Family. British Museum: Additional MSS. 30306—Vol. II, 1701-1827. Photostats. Library of Congress.

Fairfax County—see County Records.

Fairfax Papers. Fairfax Family Northern Neck Proprietary Papers, 1688-1810. Virginia State Library.

————. Papers of Lord Fairfax, 1735-1739. Virginia Manuscripts, Vol. 32. Library of Congress.

Fauquier County—see County Records.

Fauquier, Francis. Letters of Francis Fauquier to Lords of Trade. Bancroft Transcripts. Library of Congress.

————. Commission of Induction of John Brandon, March 12, 1761. Virginia Historical Society.

Fitzgerald, John. Papers, mainly commercial and relating to Alexandria, Va., 1756-1797 and undated. Library of Congress.

Fitzhugh, William. William Fitzhugh of Chatham: Letters to his nephew Benjamin Grymes of Eagles Nest, 1776-1803. Alderman Library, Univ. of Va.

Frederick County—see County Records.

Friend's Records: Letters and Miscellaneous Papers, 1749-1827. Virginia State Library.

Fulham Palace Manuscripts: Virginia, 1695-1776 and Miscellaneous MSS. Library of Congress.

Gage Papers. Clements Library, Univ. of Michigan. Microfilm—Colonial Williamsburg.

George Family Papers, 1718-1936. Virginia Historical Society.

Germain Papers, 1768-1782. Clements Library, Univ. of Michigan. Microfilm—Colonial Williamsburg.

Gilmer, Dr. George. Diary and Revolutionary Memoranda. Virginia Historical Society.

Gloucester County—see County Records.

Gooch Papers. Transcripts. 3 vols. Virginia Historical Society.

Goochland County—see County Records.

Griffith, David. Papers, 1760-1789. Virginia Historical Society.

Grigsby, Hugh Blair. Papers. Virginia Historical Society.

————. The Virginia Convention of 1776. Manuscript in Virginia Historical Society.

Grinnan Papers. Alderman Library, Univ. of Va.

Grove, William Hugh. Diary, 1732, April 17 [August?]. Alderman Library, Univ. of Va. Photostat. Virginia Historical Society.

Halifax County—see County Records.

Hanover County—see County Records.

Harrower, John. Diary of John Harrower, 1773-1776. Colonial Williamsburg.

Henrico County—see County Records.

Henry, Patrick. Papers, 1762-1881 and undated. Acc. 1125, 2850, 4891, 6961. Library of Congress. Also on microfilm at Colonial Williamsburg.

————. Patrick Henry Letters, 1778-1799. Photostats. Virginia State Library.

Heth, William. Diaries, Feb. 1—June 1, 1776, June 2—July 3, 1776, and Feb. 15, 1788—March 30, 1789. 3 vols. Library of Congress.

————. Heth Papers. Alderman Library, Univ. of Va.

Honeyman, Robert. Diary of Robert Honeyman, M. D., Jan. 2, 1776—March 11, 1782. Library of Congress. Microfilm—Colonial Williamsburg.

Hook, John. Papers, 1771-1784. Duke University. Microfilm—Colonial Williamsburg.

————. John Hook Letter Book, 1772-1774; Letter Book, 1763-1772; Letter Book, 1774-1784; Letters and Papers, 1781-1829; and Letters and Miscellaneous MSS. Virginia State Library.

Hubbard, E. W. Papers. Univ. of North Carolina. Microfilm—Colonial Williamsburg.

Hunter, R. M. T. Collection. Alderman Library, Univ. of Va.

Jamieson, Neil. Papers. Library of Congress. Microfilm—Colonial Williamsburg.

Jefferson, Thomas. The Papers of Thomas Jefferson, Library of Congress. Microfilm—Colonial Williamsburg.

Jerdone, Francis. Memorandum Book, 1766-67. Virginia State Library.

Jerdone Papers. Including Francis Jerdone Account and Letter Book, 1736-37, 1738-44; Letter Book, 1756-1763 (Francis Jerdone); and (John Morton) Jerdone & Co., Letter Book, 1769-1776. William and Mary College Library.

Johnston, James Ambler. Papers, 1784-1902. Virginia Historical Society.

Johnston, Zachariah. Letters to Zachariah Johnston, 1781-1797. Photostats. Virginia State Library.

———. Zachariah Johnston Papers. Photostats. Virginia State Library.

Jones Family. Papers of the Jones Family of Northumberland County, Virginia, 1649-1889. Bound in 35 vols. Library of Congress. Also on film Colonial Williamsburg.

Journals of the House of Delegates, Richmond, Monday, May 6, 1776. MSS. Virginia State Library.

Joynes Papers. Virginia Historical Society.

Keith of Woodburne Papers, 1776-1865. Virginia Historical Society.

Keith, Thomas. Execution and Receipt Book, 1767 October—1794 February, kept in his capacity as deputy sheriff at Fauquier Co., Va. Virginia Historical Society.

King George County—see County Records.

King and Queen County—see County Records.

Knox, William. Papers. Clements Library, Univ. of Michigan. Microfilm—Colonial Williamsburg.

Lancaster County—see County Records.

Lee Family Papers, 1761-1882. 6 vols. Includes many transcripts from other repositories. Virginia Historical Society.

Lee-Ludwell Papers. Virginia Historical Society.

Lee Papers. Alderman Library, Univ. of Va.

———. Papers of the Lee Family of Virginia, 1753 to 1866 and undated. Library of Congress.

Lee, Richard Bland. Papers, 1700-1825. Library of Congress.

Lee, William. Letterbooks. Virginia Historical Society.

Leeds Manor Leases, 1786. Virginia State Library.

Leedstown Resolutions on the Stamp Act. Virginia Historical Society.

Loan Certificates. Virginia: Register of Loan Certificates. Virginia State Library.

Loudoun County—see County Records.

Louisa County—see County Records.

Lunenburg County—see County Records.

Madison, James. The Papers of James Madison, 1723-1845. 90 vols. Library of Congress.

———. Papers, May 21, 1723—April 16, 1781. Microfilm—Virginia State Library.

Manuscript Ordinances for Revision of Laws, with Autograph Index by Thomas Jefferson. Alderman Library, Univ. of Va.

Mason, George. The Papers of George Mason, 1763-1791. 1 vol. Library of Congress.

————. Various Accessions. Library of Congress.

————. George Mason Collection. Photostats of original at Gunston Hall, Va. Library of Congress.

Massie Papers. Correspondence of Thomas Massie. Virginia Historical Society.

Maury, James. Papers. Alderman Library. Univ. of Va.

Mazzei, Philip. Letter Book, 1780-83. Library of Congress.

————. Philip Mazzei Papers, 1773-1817. Library of Congress.

————. Philip Mazzei Letters and Papers, 1772-1780. Photostats. Virginia State Library.

Mecklenburg County—see County Records.

Mercer, James. Papers, 1760-1771. Virginia Historical Society.

Miscellaneous Manuscripts. Original at Clements Library, Univ. of Michigan. Microfilm—Colonial Williamsburg.

————. Original at Duke University. Microfilm—Colonial Williamsburg.

————. Original at Historical Society of Pennsylvania. Microfilm— Colonial Williamsburg.

————. Original at Massachusetts Historical Society. Microfilm—Colonial Williamsburg.

————. Original at New York Public Library. Microfilm—Colonial Williamsburg.

————. Original at Pierpont Morgan Library. Microfilm—Colonial Williamsburg.

Miscellaneous Petitions, 1782-1783. Virginia State Library.

Monroe Papers. William and Mary College Library.

Morris Papers. The Morris Family Papers. Alderman Library, Univ. of Va.

Nansemond County—see County Records.

Nelson Letter Book, 1766-1775. Microfilm—Colonial Williamsburg.

Nelson, Thomas. Letters. Virginia State Library.

New Kent County—see County Records.

Nicholas, Robert Carter. Account Books. Library of Congress. Microfilm—Colonial Williamsburg.

Nicholas, Wilson Cary. The Papers of Wilson Cary Nicholas, 1765-1831. Library of Congress. Microfilm—Colonial Williamsburg.

————. Wilson Cary Nicholas Papers. Alderman Library, Univ. of Va.

Norfolk County and Borough—see County Records.

Northampton County—see County Records.

Norton, John. Papers. Colonial Williamsburg.

Nourse Family Papers. Alderman Library, Univ. of Va.

Olden Manuscript. Virginia State Library.

Orange County—see County Records.

Page, John. Letters. Virginia State Library.

Parker Family Papers. Liverpool Record Office, England. Microfilm— Colonial Williamsburg.

Peckatone Papers, 1758-1898. Virginia Historical Society.

Pendleton, Edmund. Letters. Photostats. Virginia State Library.

————. Edmund Pendleton Papers. Univ. of North Carolina. Microfilm —Colonial Williamsburg.

Petitions. Unless otherwise listed, all petitions to the General Assembly—county, town, and miscellaneous—which have been cited in this volume are to be found in manuscript in the Virginia State Library, Richmond, Va.

Piper, Harry. Letterbook, 1767-1775. Alderman Library, Univ. of Va.

Pittsylvania County—see County Records.

Pleasant, Robert. Letter Book, 1771-1780. On photostat at William and Mary College Library.

Powhatan County—see County Records.

Preston Papers. Virginia Historical Society. Others found in the Draper Collection at the Univ. of Wisconsin, or at Duke University, Library of Congress, and Alderman Library, Univ. of Va.

Prince George County—see County Records.

Prince William County—see County Records.

Religious Petitions—see Petitions.

Richmond County—see County Records.

Rockbridge County—see County Records.

Rockingham County—see County Records.

Southampton County—see County Records.

Spotsylvania County—see County Records.

Stafford County—see County Records.

Stephen, Adam. Papers, 1750-1834 and undated. Library of Congress.

Strachey Papers. Clements Library, Univ. of Michigan. Microfilm—Colonial Williamsburg.

Stuart, Archibald. Papers. Virginia Historical Society.

Surry County—see County Records.

Taylor, Francis. Diaries. Virginia State Library.

————. Colonel Francis Taylor Diary 1786-1792, 1794-1799. Microfilm —Alderman Library, Univ. of Va.

Tithables. Unless otherwise listed, all tithable lists cited in this volume may be found in manuscript, on film, or on photostat at the Virginia State Library.

Tucker, St. George. Papers. William and Mary College Library.

Tucker-Coleman Papers, 1768-1860. Colonial Williamsburg.

Vestry Book. Wicomico Parish, Northumberland County, Vestry Book, 1703-1795. Photostat, Virginia State Library.

Virginia Convention, 1775. Committee Report, July 27, 1775. Miscellaneous MSS. Virginia State Library.

Virginia Miscellany 1773. Library of Congress. Microfilm—Colonial Williamsburg.

Wallace Papers. Alderman Library, Univ. of Va.

Washington, George. The Papers of George Washington. Library of Congress.

————. Mount Vernon Washington Manuscripts. Microfilm—Virginia State Library.

————. Ledgers A & B. Library of Congress. Microfilm—Colonial Williamsburg.

————. Washington Papers. Duke University Library. Microfilm—Colonial Williamsburg.

Washington, Mrs. Lund. Diary: Mrs. Lund Washington, 1779-1796. Library of Congress.

Washington, Lund. Letters to George Washington, 1767-1790. Photostats. Virginia State Library.

Watson Papers. Alderman Library, Univ. of Va.

Webb-Prentis Papers. Alderman Library, Univ. of Va.

Weedon, Gen. George. Letters. Photostats. Virginia State Library.

Westmoreland County. Minutes of the Freeholder's Meetings from Nov. 28, 1775 to Aug. 27, 1776. Fordham Univ., N. Y. Microfilm—Colonial Williamsburg. For other petitions and records, see County Records.

Williamsburg and James City County, Va., Sheriff's Tax Book, 1768-1771. Colonial Williamsburg.

Williamsburg Petitions—see Petitions.

Yohoganie County—see County Records.

York County. "Election Returns & Qualifications of Delegates to the General Assembly at Williamsburg in the years 1776 & 1777." Virginia State Library. For other records and petitions, see County Records.

## II. SELECTED SECONDARY WORKS

Abernethy, Thomas Perkins. *Western Lands and the American Revolution.* New York: Russell and Russell, 1959.

Alden, John Richard. *The South in the Revolution, 1763-1789.* Baton Rouge, La.: Louisiana State University Press, 1957.

———. *Rise of the American Republic.* New York: Harper and Row, 1963.

*American Jurisprudence. . . .* By the editorial staff of the publishers. 49 vols. Rochester, New York: The Lawyers Co-operative Publ. Co., 1936 to date.

Andrews, Charles M. *The Colonial Background of the American Revolution.* New Haven: Yale Univ. Press, 1924.

Andrews, Matthew Page. *Virginia, the Old Dominion.* Garden City, N. Y.: Doubleday, Doran, 1937.

Bailey, Thomas. *The American Pageant.* Boston: D. C. Heath, 1956.

Bailyn, Bernard. "Political Experience and Enlightenment Ideas in Eighteenth-Century America," *American Historical Review,* LXVII (Jan., 1962), pp. 339-51.

Baker-Crothers, Hayes. *Virginia and the French and Indian War.* Chicago, Ill.: Univ. of Chicago Press, 1928.

Ballentine, James. *Law Dictionary with Pronunciations.* 2nd ed. Rochester, N. Y.: The Lawyers Co-operative Publ. Co., 1948.

Bean, R. Bennett. *The Peopling of Virginia.* Boston: Chapman and Grimes, 1938.

Beard, Charles. *An Economic Interpretation of the Constitution of the United States.* New York: Macmillan, 1913.

——— and Mary Beard. *The Rise of American Civilization.* 2 vols. New York: Macmillan, 1936.

Becker, Carl Lotus. *The History of Political Parties in the Province of New York, 1763-1776.* Madison, Wis.: Univ. of Wis. *Bulletin,* No. 286, history series, 1909.

Blackstone, Sir William. *Commentaries on the Laws of England in Four Books.* 4th ed. With notes by Thomas M. Cooley. Chicago: Callaghan, 1899.

Brant, Irving. *James Madison.* 4 vols. Indianapolis: Bobbs-Merrill, 1941-53.

Bready, Marcia Brownell. "A Cavalier in Virginia—the Right Hon. Sir William Berkeley, His Majesty's Governor," in *William and Mary Quarterly,* 1 ser., XVIII, 115-29.

Bridenbaugh, Carl. *Seat of Empire: The Political Role of Eighteenth-Century Williamsburg.* Williamsburg, Va.: Colonial Williamsburg, 1950. New Edition 1958.

Brock, Leslie Van Horn. Currency of the American Colonies, 1700-1764: A Study of Colonial Finances and Imperial Relations. Ph.D. Thesis. Univ. of Michigan, 1941. Microfilm—Colonial Williamsburg.

Brock, Robert K. *Archibald Cary of Ampthill: Wheelhorse of the Revolution.* Richmond, Va.: Garrett and Massie, 1937.

Brooks, Jerome E. *Tobacco: Its History.* . . . 5 vols. New York: Rosenbach, 1937-52.

Brown, Robert E. *Middle-Class Democracy and the Revolution in Massachusetts, 1691-1780.* Ithaca, N. Y.: Cornell University Press, 1955.

Bruce, Philip Alexander. *The Colonial Period, 1607-1763.* Vol. I in *The History of Virginia.* 6 vols. Chicago: American Historical Society, 1924.

————. *The Virginia Plutarch.* 2 vols. Chapel Hill, N. C.: Univ. of North Carolina Press, 1929.

Brydon, George MacLaren. *Virginia's Mother Church and the Political Conditions Under Which It Grew: The Story of the Anglican Church and the Development of Religion in Virginia, 1727-1814.* 2 vols. Philadelphia: Church Historical Society, 1947, 1952.

Burk, John Daly. *The History of Virginia, from its first settlement to the present day.* 4 vols. Petersburg, Va.: Printed for the author, 1804-1816.

Chandler, Julian A. C. *The History of the Suffrage in Virginia.* Baltimore: Johns Hopkins Press, 1901.

————. *Representation in Virginia.* Baltimore: Johns Hopkins Press, 1896.

Chitwood, Oliver P. *Justice in Colonial Virginia.* Baltimore: Johns Hopkins Press, 1905.

Cooke, John E. *Virginia: A History of the People.* Boston: Houghton, Mifflin, 1883.

Coulter, Calvin B. The Virginia Merchant. Ph.D. Thesis, Princeton, 1944. Microfilm—Colonial Williamsburg.

Daggett, Leonard M. "Wills" in *Two Centuries' Growth of American Law, 1701-1901.* New York: Scribner's, 1902.

Decatur, Stephen. *Private Affairs of George Washington.* . . . Boston: Houghton, Mifflin, 1933.

Douglass, Elisha P. *Rebels and Democrats: The Struggle for Equal Political Rights and Majority Rule During the American Revolution.* Chapel Hill: Univ. of North Carolina Press, 1955.

Dowdey, Clifford. *The Great Plantation: A Profile of Berkeley Hundred and Plantation Virginia from Jamestown to Appomattox.* New York: Rinehart, 1957.

Eckenrode, Hamilton J. *The Randolphs*. . . . Indianapolis: Bobbs-Merrill, 1946.

——. *The Revolution in Virginia*. Boston: Houghton, Mifflin, 1916.

——. *Separation of Church and State in Virginia*. . . . Richmond, Va.: Davis Bottom, Supt. of Public Printing, 1910.

*The English and Empire Digest*. . . . 49 vols. London: Butterworth, 1919-30.

Evans, Emory G. "Planter Indebtedness and the Coming of the Revolution in Virginia," *William and Mary Quarterly*, 3rd Ser., XIX (Oct., 1962), pp. 511-33.

Fishwick, Marshall W. *Virginia: A New Look at the Old Dominion*. New York: Harper, 1959.

Fiske, John. *Old Virginia and Her Neighbours*. 2 vols. Boston: Houghton, Mifflin, 1897.

Flippin, Percy S. *The Royal Government of Virginia, 1624-1775*. New York: Columbia Univ. Press, 1919.

Freeman, Douglas S. *George Washington, A Biography*. 7 vols. New York: Scribner's, 1948-57.

George, John A. "Virginia Loyalists," in *Richmond College Historical Papers*, Vol. I, No. 2 (1916).

Gewehr, Wesley M. *The Great Awakening in Virginia, 1740-1790*. Durham, N. C.: Duke Univ. Press, 1930.

Grant, Charles S. *Democracy in the Connecticut Frontier Town of Kent*. New York: Columbia Univ. Press, 1961.

Greene, Jack P. "Foundations of Political Power in the Virginia House of Burgesses, 1720-1776" in *William and Mary Quarterly*, 3 ser., XVI (Oct., 1959), No. 4, pp. 485-506.

——. "Landon Carter and the Pistole Fee Dispute" in *ibid.*, 3 ser., XIV (Jan. 1957), pp. 66-69.

Harrell, Isaac S. *Loyalism in Virginia*. . . . Durham, N. C.: Duke Univ. Press, 1926.

Hart, Freeman H. *The Valley of Virginia in the American Revolution, 1763-1789*. Chapel Hill, N. C.: Univ. of North Carolina Press, 1942.

Hicks, John D. and George E. Mowry. *A Short History of American Democracy*. Boston: Houghton, Mifflin, 1956.

Hilldrup, Robert L. Virginia Convention of 1776: A Study in Revolutionary Politics. Ph.D. Thesis, Univ. of Va., 1935. Microfilm—Colonial Williamsburg.

Hubbard, William. *A General History of New England*. . . .Cambridge, Mass.: Massachusetts Historical Society, 1815.

Jameson, J. Franklin. *The American Revolution Considered as a Social Movement*. Princeton, N. J.: Princeton Univ. Press, 1925.

——. "Virginian Voting in the Colonial Period (1744-1774)" in *The Nation* (April 27, 1893), p. 56.

Jensen, Merrill M. *The Articles of Confederation*. Madison, Wis.: Univ. of Wis. Press, 1940.

——. *The New Nation*. New York: Knopf, 1950.

——. "Democracy and the American Revolution," in *Huntington Library Quarterly*, Aug., 1957, pp. 321-41.

Keim, Clarence Ray. Influence of Primogeniture and Entail in the Development of Virginia. Ph.D. thesis, Univ. of Chicago, 1926.

Kent, James. *Commentaries on American Law*. 4 vols. 14th ed. Ed. by John M. Gould. Boston: Little, Brown, 1896.

Klein, Milton M. "Democracy and Politics in Colonial New York" in *New York History*, Vol. XL, No. 3 (July 1959), pp. 221-246.

Knight, Edgar W. *A Documentary History of Education in the South before 1860*. 5 vols. Chapel Hill: Univ. of North Carolina Press, 1949-53.

Koch, Adrienne. *Jefferson and Madison; the Great Collaboration*. New York: Knopf, 1950.

———. *The Philosophy of Thomas Jefferson*. New York: Columbia Univ. Press, 1943.

Koontz, Louis K. *Robert Dinwiddie*. . . . Glendale, Calif.: Arthur H. Clark, 1941.

———. *The Virginia Frontier, 1754-1763*. Baltimore: Johns Hopkins Press, 1925.

Leake, James M. *The Virginia Committee System and the American Revolution*. Baltimore: Johns Hopkins Press, 1917.

Lee, C. F., Jr., and J. Packard, Jr. *A Record of the Descendants of Colonel Richard Lee of Virginia*. Boston: David Clapp, 1882.

Lingley, Charles R. *The Transition in Virginia from Colony to Commonwealth*. New York: Columbia Univ., 1910.

Lovejoy, David S. *Rhode Island Politics and the American Revolution, 1760-1776*. Providence, R. I.: Brown Univ. Press, 1958.

Main, Jackson Turner. "The Distribution of Property in Post-Revolutionary Virginia" in *Mississippi Valley Historical Review*, XLI (Sept. 1954), pp. 241-58.

———. "Sections and Politics in Virginia, 1781-1787" in *William and Mary Quarterly*, 3rd Ser., XII (1955), pp. 96-112.

Malone, Dumas. *Jefferson and His Time*. 2 vols. Boston: Little, Brown, 1948-51.

Mapp, Alf J., Jr. *The Virginia Experiment*. . . . Richmond, Va.: Dietz, 1957.

Mays, David J. *Edmund Pendleton, 1721-1803*. 2 vols. Cambridge, Mass.: Harvard Univ. Press, 1952.

Mazzei, Philip. *Memoirs of the Life and Peregrinations of the Florintine Philip Mazzei, 1730-1816*. Trans. by Howard R. Marraro. New York: Columbia Univ. Press, 1942.

McCormick, Richard P. *The History of Voting in New Jersey*. New Brunswick, N. J.: Rutgers Univ. Press, 1953.

McIlwaine, Henry R. *The Struggle of Protestant Dissenters for Religious Toleration in Virginia*. Baltimore: Johns Hopkins Press, 1894.

Middleton, Arthur P. Anglican Virginia. Unpublished MSS. Colonial Williamsburg.

Miller, Elmer Isaiah. *The Legislature of the Province of Virginia, its Internal Development*. New York: Columbia University Press, 1907.

Miller, John C. *Origins of the American Revolution*. Stanford, Calif.: Stanford Univ. Press, 1943, revised reprint, 1959.

Morgan, Edmund S. *The American Revolution: A Review of Changing Interpretations*. Washington, D. C.: American Historical Assoc., 1958.

———. *The Birth of the Republic*. Chicago, Univ. of Chicago Press, 1956.

————. *Virginians at Home.* Williamsburg, Va.: Colonial Williamsburg, 1952.

Morison, Samuel Eliot and Henry Steele Commager. *The Growth of the American Republic.* 2 vols. New York: Oxford Univ. Press, 1950.

Morris, Richard B. "Class Struggle and the American Revolution" in *William and Mary Quarterly,* 3rd Ser., XIX (Jan., 1962), pp. 3-29.

————. "Primogeniture and Entailed Estates in America" in *Columbia Law Review,* XXVII (1927), pp. 24-51.

Morton, Louis. *Robert Carter of Nomini Hall. . . .* Princeton, N. J.: Princeton Univ. Press on behalf of Colonial Williamsburg, 1941.

Morton, Richard L. *Colonial Virginia.* 2 vols. Chapel Hill, N. C.: Pub. for the Virginia Historical Society by the Univ. of North Carolina Press, 1960.

Nettels, Curtis P. "The Washington Theme in American History" in *Proceedings of the Massachusetts Historical Society,* Vol. LXVIII (Oct. 1944—May 1947), pp. 171-198. Boston: Published by the Society, 1952.

————. *George Washington and American Independence.* Boston: Little, Brown, 1951.

Norkus, Nellie. Francis Fauquier, Lieutenant-Governor of Virginia, 1758-1768: A Study in Colonial Problems. Ph.D. Thesis. Univ. of Pittsburgh, 1954. Microfilm—Colonial Williamsburg.

Owen, James K. The Virginia Vestry: A Study in the Decline of a Ruling Class. Ph.D. Thesis. Princeton University, 1947. Microfilm—Colonial Williamsburg.

Palmer, Robert R. *The Age of the Democratic Revolution: A Political History of Europe and America, 1760-1800.* Princeton, N. J.: Princeton Univ. Press, 1959.

Porter, Albert O. *County Government in Virginia, A Legislative History, 1607-1904.* New York: Columbia Univ. Press, 1947.

Prufer, Julius F. "The Franchise in Virginia from Jefferson Through the Convention of 1829" in *William and Mary Quarterly,* 2 ser., VII (Oct., 1927), pp. 255-70.

Sheick, Donald B. The Regulation of Commodity Currency in Colonial Virginia. Ph.D. Thesis. Indiana University, 1954.

Sioussat, St. George L. "The Breakdown of the Royal Management of Lands in the Southern Provinces, 1773-1775" in *Agricultural History,* III (1929), pp. 67-98.

Smith, Abbot E. *Colonists in Bondage. . . .* Chapel Hill: Univ. of North Carolina Press, 1947.

Smith, Glenn Curtis. "The Affair of the Pistole Fee, Virginia, 1752-55" in *Virginia Magazine of History and Biography,* XLVIII, No. 3 (July, 1940), pp. 209-21.

Smith, James Allen. *The Spirit of American Government.* New York: 1907.

Smith, Robert A. The Technologies and Working Conditions of Colonial Free Laborers. Ph.D. Thesis. Univ. of Illinois, 1950. Microfilm—Colonial Williamsburg.

Stanard, Mary N. *Colonial Virginia: its People and Customs.* Philadelphia: Lippincott, 1917.

Swem, Earl G. and John W. Williams. *A Register of the General As-*

*sembly of Virginia, 1776-1918, and of the Constitutional Conventions.* Richmond, Va.: Davis Bottom, Supt. of Public Printing, 1918, in *Fourteenth Annual Report of the Library Board of the Virginia State Library, 1916-1917.*

Sydnor, Charles S. *Gentlemen Freeholders. . . .* Chapel Hill, N. C.: Univ. of North Carolina Press, 1952.

————. *Political Leadership in Eighteenth-Century Virginia.* Oxford: Clarendon Press, 1951.

Tate, Thad W. "The Coming of the Revolution in Virginia: Britain's Challenge to Virginia's Ruling Class, 1763-1776" in *William and Mary Quarterly,* 3 Ser., XIX (July, 1962), pp. 323-43.

Thayer, Theodore. *Pennsylvania Politics and the Growth of Democracy, 1740-1776.* Harrisburg, Pa.: Pennsylvania Historical and Museum Commission, 1953.

Thom, William T. *The Struggle for Religious Freedom in Virginia: The Baptists.* Baltimore: Johns Hopkins Press, 1900.

Tucker, St. George. *Blackstone's Commentaries: with Notes of Reference, to the Constitution and Laws, of the Federal Government of the United States; and of the Commonwealth of Virginia. . . .* 5 vols. Philadelphia: Publ. by William Young Birch and Abraham Small, 1803.

Tyler, Lyon G. "Aristocracy in Massachusetts and Virginia" in *William and Mary Quarterly,* 1 Ser., XXVI (April, 1918), pp. 277-281.

————. *The Federal Period, 1763-1861,* Vol. II in *The History of Virginia,* 6 vols. Chicago: American Historical Society, 1924.

————. "The Leadership of Virginia in the War of the Revolution" in *William and Mary Quarterly,* 1 Ser., XVIII (Jan. 1910), pp. 145-64.

————. "Society in East Virginia" in *William and Mary Quarterly,* 1 Ser., XXII (April, 1914), pp. 221-28.

————. "Virginians Voting in the Colonial Period" in *William and Mary Quarterly,* 1 Ser., VI, 7-13.

Wertenbaker, Thomas Jefferson. *The Shaping of Colonial Virginia.* New York: Russell and Russell, 1958.

————. *Give Me Liberty; the Struggle for Self-Government in Virginia.* Philadelphia: American Philosophical Society, 1958.

Whitelaw, Ralph T. *Virginia's Eastern Shore, A History of Northampton and Accomack Counties.* 2 vols. Richmond, Va.: Virginia Historical Society, 1951.

Williams, Joshua. *Principles of the Law of Real Property.* 24th ed. Ed. by R. A. Eastwood. London: Sweet and Maxwell, 1926.

Williams, T. Harry, Richard N. Current, and Frank Freidel. *American History: A Survey.* New York: Knopf, 1961.

————. *A History of the United States.* 2 vols. New York: Knopf, 1959.

Williamson, Chilton. *American Suffrage from Property to Democracy, 1760-1860.* Princeton, N. J.: Princeton Univ. Press, 1960.

Wilson, Howard M. *The Tinkling Spring, Headwater of Freedom.* Richmond, Va.: Garrett and Massie, 1954.

Wineman, Walter Ray. Calendar of the Landon Carter papers in the Sabine Hall collection and a biographic sketch of Colonel Landon Carter. Microfilm copy of typescript. Ann Arbor, Mich.: University Microfilms, 1957.

Woodward, William E. *George Washington: The Image and The Man.*

Garden City, N. J.: Garden City Publishing Co., 1926 (1942 ed.)
*Words and Phrases: All Judicial Constructions and Definitions of Words and Phrases by the State and Federal Courts from the Earliest Times.* . . . 1658 to date. 45 vols. St. Paul, Minn.: West Publishing Co. [1940]

Wright, Louis B. *The First Gentlemen of Virginia: Intellectual Qualities of the Early Colonial Ruling Class.* San Marino, Calif.: Huntington Library, 1940.

# Index

Abernethy, Thomas P., 57
Accomack County, social status of voters in, 140-41; voters in, 145, 163; analysis of voting in, 197
Adams, John, 294
Albemarle County, land sales in, 19; and paper money, 116
Alden, John, 57, 92
Amelia County, land sales in, 19; slaveownership in, 75; apathy of voters in, 146; analysis of voting in, 206-07; status of representative, 226-27
Anabaptists, growth of, 261
Anburey, Thomas, 37, 38, 42, 46; defines classes in Virginia, 32-33
Apprentices, opportunities for, 24-25, 52-53; class status of, 51; training of, 51-52, 275; and the franchise, 139, 143-44; see also Servants
Aristocracy, versus democracy, 3, 4, 307-08; in colonial Virginia, 34, 307-08; and slavery 77, 307-08; and voting, 125, 127, 133, 136, 140, 146, 151, 153-58, 165, 169-212; and representation, 215-239; and Constitution of 1776, 292-295; see upper classes
Artisans, become planters, 8-9; wages of, 21-22; property of, 22-23; and social mobility, 39-40, 44-45; as middle class, 44; and voting, 138-39, 144, 203
Augusta County, landholding in, 14; debtors in, 102, 107, 108; election of 1755, 153-54; division of, 223

Bailyn, Bernard, 5
Baptists, 264, 265, 299
Beard, Charles A., 5, 146, 212; on Constitution, 3, 92
Becker, Carl L., 5; view of Revolution, 3
Berkeley, Governor William, 271
Beverley, Robert, 53, 97; on land, 10; on economic opportunity, 10-11; on social classes, 39; on slavery, 65; estate of, 91; on elections, 151; on schools, 271

Bishop, absence of, 249; controversy over, 263
Botetourt County, division of, 223
Botetourt, Governor, 19
Boucher, Jonathan, property of, 24; defines gentlemen, 35; on slavery, 63-64; on religion, 246, 247, 260, 263; on educating slaves, 277
Boyd, Julian, 304
Bridenbaugh, Carl, 5, 57, 92, 147, 213, 242
Burnaby, Andrew, on land, 10; on frontier, 20; on labor, 43-44; on slavery, 64, 72; on religion, 257-58
Byrd, William, 20, 92, 273; landholdings of, 16-17, 18; and religion, 248

"The Candidates," 212, 236-37
Carter, Charles, 18; estate of, 37; debts of, 97
Carter, Landon, 35, 39, 50-51, 53, 82-83, 88, 115, 163, 221, 225, 232, 236, 238; on women, 55; and slaves, 67, 69, 71; as politician, 157-58, 197-203; and religion, 248, 254; and schools, 272, 280
Carter, Robert, 66, 69, 71
Carter, Robert "King," property of, 36, 89
Carter, Robert Wormeley, 39, 157-58
Catholics, not excluded from franchise, 131; not popular, 250-51
Church of England, and franchise, 126; established, 243-44; causes of decline, 244-64; after Independence, 295-302; see also religion
Class conflict, 57; and slavery, 76-77; and paper money, 117, 118; and debtors, 118; not in religion, 265; lack of, 284-302
Classes, 32-61; debts of, 98, 99, 100-108; and religion, 265
Colonial society, interpretation of, 3; contemporary opinions on, 32-34; classes in, 32-61
"Conservatives," 293
Constitution of 1776, 290-95
Constitution, U. S., interpretation of, 3

# segment